KEEPING
SECRETS

KEEPING

SECRETS

Suzanne Somers

WARNER BOOKS

A Warner Communications Company

Grateful acknowledgment is given for permission to quote from the following:

"Dearie" by Bob Hilliard and Dave Mann. Copyright © 1950 by Music of the Times Pub.Co. Copyright renewed and assigned to Range Road Music Inc., Quartet Music Inc., and Better Half Music Co. International copyright secured. All rights reserved. Used by permission.

"My Fair Lady" by Alan Jay Lerner and Frederick Loewe. Copyright © 1956 by Alan Jay Lerner and Frederick Loewe. All rights administered by Chappell & Co., Inc. International copyright secured. All rights reserved. Used by permission.

"I'm the Greatest Star" by Jule Styne and Bob Merrill. Copyright © 1963 by Jule Styne and Bob Merrill. All rights administered by Chappell & Co., Inc. International copyright secured. All rights reserved. Used by permission.

"Some People" by Jule Styne and Stephen Sondheim. Copyright © 1959 by Norbeth Productions Inc., and Stephen Sondheim. All rights administered by Chappell & Co., Inc. International copyright secured. All rights reserved. Used by permission.

"Adelaide's Lament" and "Guys and Dolls" by Frank Loesser from *Guys and Dolls*. Copyright © 1950 by Frank Music Corp. Copyright © 1978 by Frank Music Corp. International copyright secured. All rights reserved. Used by permission.

"We've Only Just Begun." Lyrics by Paul Williams, music by Roger Nichols. Copyright © 1970 by Irving Music, Inc. (BMI). All rights reserved. International copyright secured. Used by permission.

"New Attitude." Words and music by Bunny Hull, John Gilutin, and Sharon T. Robinson. Copyright © 1984, 1985 by Texascity Music, Inc., Unicity Music, Inc., Brassheart Music, Rockomatic Music and Robinhill Music. Rights administered by Unicity Music, Inc., Los Angeles, California. All rights reserved. Used by permission.

"You've Got a Friend" by Carole King. Copyright © 1971 by COLGEMS-EMI Music Inc. All rights reserved. Used by permission.

The poems that appear on pages 230–231 and 262 are from *Touch Me: The Poems of Suzanne Somers* by Suzanne Somers (New York: Workman Publishing, Inc., 1980), © 1973, 1980 by Suzanne Somers.

 A Warner Communications Company

Printed in the United States of America
First Printing: January 1988
10 9 8 7 6 5 4 3 2 1

Library of Congress Cataloging-in-Publication Data
Somers, Suzanne, 1946–
Keeping secrets.
I. Title.
PS3569.0652K4 1988   792'.028'0924   [B]   87-40174
ISBN 0-446-51395-4

Designed by Giorgetta Bell McRee

*To my family for their trust and courage
in allowing me to tell this story,
especially my dad.
It takes a big man to be so brave.*

The unexamined life is not worth living.
    —Plato

Acknowledgments

I couldn't have finished this book without the help of the following people. It is with great pleasure I take this opportunity to thank them.

My husband and best friend, Alan Hamel, who believed in me and this project from the beginning. His complete support and love gave me the courage to continue.

My father, Frank Mahoney, my mother, Marion Mahoney, my sister, Maureen Gilmartin, my brothers, Dan Mahoney and Michael Mahoney. Each of them spent countless hours giving me their perspectives and feelings, allowing me to dig deep inside where the pain lives.

My son, Bruce Somers, for his goodness, his trust, and for understanding my need.

My stepchildren, Leslie Hamel and Stephen Hamel, for their love and enthusiasm.

Larry Kirschbaum, president of Warner Books, for his editorial assistance, enormous enthusiasm, and single-mindedness to pursue and direct this project and his pure boyish spirit.

My wonderful editor and publisher, Nansey Neiman, for helping me find a clear, cohesive route through this story and recognizing the difference between irrelevant and important material. Picking fresh, wild blueberries on her farm for homemade pie didn't hurt either.

Eric Lasher, my dear friend and tour guide through the treacherous jungles of the book world.

Maureen Lasher, my literary agent and close trusted friend, who has been saying for years I had a book inside me. While I can't exactly articulate what Maureen does, she does it better than anyone; asking appropriate questions, and forcing me to listen to my inner dialogue and feelings. Her contributions were invaluable.

Marsha Yanchuck, my secretary and friend, who did so much more than type this manuscript. She was my reader; her tears my barometer. I thank her for all the backaches about which she never complained.

Michael Levine, my publicist, who bombarded me with literature and research on alcoholism and children of alcoholics, knowing my schedule did not leave much time to do this myself.

Joyce Burland, my brilliant friend, who said exactly what I needed to hear at precisely the time I needed to hear it that night on her mountain in Vermont.

To Jack Hanson and Mrs. Kilgore, who were there for me when I needed them.

To Duffy for his time and information, and thanks to Betty Ford for opening the door.

I don't give a shit that everybody knows I was a drunk,
I just care what they think about you.

—My dad,
November 1986

Prologue

I am an adult child of an alcoholic. My childhood and that of my brothers and sister was robbed by a terrible and painful disease no one ever wanted to talk about, including me.

I've always been able to make jokes of the lighter side of living with a drunk, but I never went any deeper than that. I never allowed myself to wonder what my real past meant or how it had affected me. I had buried it. I didn't want to know. But recently on vacation in Santa Fe, New Mexico, I was forced to understand.

I woke up in the middle of the night and started to write; and as I wrote, I cried. My memories had been buried for a reason. Alcoholism did have a devastating effect on me and my entire family. And I began to relive the pain I had been avoiding. Five hours later, when my husband awakened and asked what I was doing, I realized I was exploring a part of me I had never entered before. I had been in therapy, but I had never gone this deep. I began to sob as I read to Alan. I couldn't stop. I had begun a personal journey into my past, and I had to continue this task. It was difficult to recall the pain and trauma of my childhood. It was hard to confront the person I became after I moved out of my parents' house. I used to laugh at that part of me. It was embarrassing, but now I couldn't laugh anymore. Now I was beginning to understand.

Everyone thought I emerged from the family intact and okay. Out of six of us, four were alcoholics. I was the only child who didn't drink; and like millions of others, I did not understand why my life had been messed up for so long. I always blamed myself. I never connected growing up with an addict to my behavior as an adult. I had been sick for a long time.

My childhood was *not* normal. I grew up watching my dad behave so horribly, I hoped he'd pass out, while my mother prayed and covered up for him, hoping one day it would all just go away.

I watched my parents argue and abuse one another. Eventually, all of us children joined in the violence. I listened to my parents yell and scream at each other long into the night. I never knew what would happen next. I didn't know what was real. The house was filled with violence, anger and fear; but we pretended to the outside world everything was okay.

I believed that once I left that environment, my troubles would disappear. Not so. The pain didn't go away; I just repressed it. Years and decades later I still carried the stigma. My childhood was my training ground for life. In order to get better, I needed to deal with the ordeal of my childhood. I had to relive it to get rid of it.

There are an estimated twenty-eight million children of alcoholics in the United States today. Research has shown that sons of alcoholic fathers have a four times greater risk of becoming alcoholics themselves. Daughters of alcoholic mothers have a three times greater risk than other women. Experts blame a genetic link coupled with growing up in an environment where children learn to drown their woes. But what about the children who don't drink? What happens to them?

Alcoholism affects the whole family. I never thought I was good enough to be happy. I knew that what was going on in our home wasn't normal. I longed to have a home life like my classmates. I didn't dare bring friends home because I was afraid I'd find my dad drunk or passed out on the floor.

Children of alcoholics never get to be children. The family's attention is focused on the parents' state of drunkenness, so the child's needs and feelings are ignored.

I hated what the disease did to my childhood and to my family. I never knew what to expect. We never confronted our reality. Once I left home, I retreated into a fantasy life. My new life was a lie. I was so ashamed of who I was, I tried to become someone I was not. My old life didn't exist. My fantasy became my reality. Being unrealistic threatened my mental health; it threatened my freedom. It was impossible to get close to any other human being. I became lonely. I lacked self-esteem. I lived in constant crisis. I was suicidal. But I didn't drink, so I thought I was "okay."

Thank God I was lucky enough to get help for myself and break the cycle of pain, humiliation and low self-worth. Alcoholism is a family disease, and it's contagious.

When you read this story, it's easy to dislike my dad. I always loved my dad with all my heart. I just never understood. None of us knew back then that this was a disease and could be treated.

No one knew anything about alcoholism, and it was not something you talked about. There were no self-help groups, no therapy. It was not discussed in the press or the media. All those with the "secret" kept it a secret, and that is what we did.

My dad was a good man with dreams and talent, who wanted to be the best. He never planned to be an alcoholic. He never said, "When I grow up, I'm going to drink a lot and abuse my wife and children." He wanted to be a good husband, a good father, a successful man. When he got the disease, he was unable to do or be any of these things. He tried to give us good times, but it always ended in disaster.

Mother was always in the middle, protecting us when Dad became violent and then protecting Dad from us when he went too far and we became violent ourselves.

My rage started at an early age. Too much missed sleep, too many violent nights, too much craziness.

My mother's personality had changed. She is a sweet, nonviolent woman with a pink face and soft white curly hair. It is not natural for her to yell and scream; yet during those years, she yelled and screamed a lot. During those years Mother became nervous, introverted and insecure. When you live with an alcoholic, his main thing is to beat you down. As long as you don't have confidence, you won't leave. I think of the frustration my mother must have felt. She wanted to do something, but she didn't know what to do. She was deeply religious, but her church didn't provide any answers. Mother didn't realize that as the wife of an alcoholic, she had become addicted to her husband's disease.

It was all so sad to feel the disintegration of our family. It was like being on a sinking ship and not knowing how to swim.

Alcoholics can't remember their past. In that sense the disease is merciful; but it leaves in its wake emotionally battered and bruised victims, usually the family. There is so much joy attached to the recovery of the addict that the victims are forced to push away all anger and resentment built up over the years as co-addicts. They say, "Let the past rest," but it can sit and smolder down at the bottom of the soul.

The truth brings freedom from pain, freedom from anger and finally forgiveness. Once the victims can truly forgive, they can truly forget.

This is a story about a family that made it. It is my story, from my point of view, as I remember it. This is the imprint it left on my memory. The language is rough, but that is the way it was.

It was very difficult to write this book. I cried a lot. I had no idea, when I started on this project, of the pain and anguish I would endure as I journeyed into that secret part of my soul.

But upon completion, I found resolution. I was no longer angry with my father. I loved him. I felt sorry for him to have been burdened with such a horrible disease for so long. I finally understood alcoholism as a disease, and I could forgive him.

I also felt relief at having a label—adult child of an alcoholic. I *had* been affected by the disease as had everyone in the family. The pieces of the puzzle were starting to fit. The relief was overwhelming.

At this point I could have put the book away. I had completed my personal task. But gnawing away at me were the millions of children who are hiding in their closets, afraid of the night and afraid of the day; the millions of children who suffer violence and emotional and physical abuse as part of their daily lives; the millions of children who feel ashamed and who don't learn what they are supposed to learn at school because they are exhausted physically and sapped emotionally; the millions of children who endure the humiliation and embarrassment of living with a drunk.

I thought of all the people, like myself, leading productive lives but not enjoying the relief that comes from understanding a troubled past. As difficult as I knew it would be, I wanted to share my story.

My family was outraged when I asked for their permission. They went through all the same emotions I experienced while writing it. They were angry, horrified, distraught and sad.

Everyone in my family is recovering from their disease. They are living happy, productive lives. On occasion they can make light of "the drinking years," but, like myself, it had never gone beyond that. The friends they have today don't know of the past (certainly not the ugly, dark side), and now I was asking them to share this story with the world. I wanted to let the secret out—the secret of my life and theirs. I didn't blame them for kicking and screaming.

It created a distance between my mother and myself at first. I felt anguished. My mother is my dearest friend.

After my sister read the book, she said, "I just thought you liked us better than that."

I can't put them through this, I thought. It's not worth the risk of hurting the people I love.

I realized they had a code of silence, a system of denial. They did not want to remember the past. It was buried, so let it rest. Denial gets passed on from generation to generation. It allows the disease to continue. I was asking a lot. Reading my book forced them to go back in their past, relive it and deal with it.

We talked a lot during this time. We argued and we cried. A new level of love, trust and communication passed through all of us and finally resolution and relief.

We all realized it was not important who we *were*, but who we *are* today; that we could celebrate the end of our long, painful journey.

One by one they gave me their blessing.

My brother Dan realized the benefit of the truth when after his daughter read the story, she wrote her own story for a class assignment about being a child of an alcoholic. She had been freed to express the pain and release it.

My brother Michael said that he was relieved to know after all this time it wasn't him.

My dad said, "I don't care that everyone knows I was a drunk, I just care what they think about you."

My sister Maureen said, "With your sense of excellence, I know you'll do this right."

My mother, after seeing Betty Ford on television, said, "If the President and his wife have the courage to tell their family secrets, then we can tell ours."

There are no words to describe my feelings of admiration for each member of my family. Their trust and courage in allowing me to tell this story is the greatest display of their love.

We are lucky. As a family we can look back and say, no it's not pretty. It's hard to tell and difficult to think about, but it happened. If the telling of this story can help others, then everything we went through has meaning and was worth it.

There is hope, and there is help at any age for anyone who has endured this kind of life. I made it out, and so can they. Those who have lived this way can learn to understand and finally to forgive. They can survive and be normal and happy. They no longer have to live their lives *Keeping Secrets*.

Part ONE

1

"**B**e quiet, for Godsakes," my mother pleaded.

"Oh, fuck you," Dad yelled drunkenly. "Your ol' man ain't nothin'! Goddamn leech! Gobbles everything in two minutes. I could beat the shit outa him. The pig! Two kind words—ass and hole. Zero! Big nothin'!"

"Shut up," my mother screamed.

"Tell your ol' man he's nothin," Dad slurred. "I could take him."

"Sure, you could beat up an old man. Would that make you feel good?" she asked angrily.

I was nine years old. I lay in my bed listening to the same old drunk talk night after night. Well, some nights Dad would pass out and sleep through; but on other nights, usually when he was drinking lots of whiskey, he might sleep for four hours or so; and then he'd wake up belligerent—ready to fight anyone. Somehow, someone would become the victim of his rage. Often it was my grandfather, whom we called Father. I guess that ticked him off. Sometimes his rage would be aimed at me because I made it very clear I liked my mother better. Some nights, for no reason in particular, it would be Danny, my thirteen-year-old brother, or Maureen, my sixteen-year-old sister, who set him off. Maybe Danny didn't mow the lawn just right or Maureen wore lipstick. You never knew. He'd just get full of "stinkin' thinkin' " and one little thing would set him off all night.

"Can I get into bed with you?" my mother asked me. "He's starting to shadow box in bed, and I don't want a black eye."

I loved my mother so much. It made me hate my father when he'd do this to her. It was four o'clock in the morning. Mom would have to go to work at 9 A.M. Maureen, Danny and I all had school at 8 A.M. None of us would have had any sleep. It had been one of the "terrible nights." Dad came home from work drunk. Sometimes he would start drinking after he got home, but the nights he came home from work already drunk were the worst—like tonight. He had stumbled in the front door earlier this evening and saw Father sitting in the living room reading the paper. That set him off. He was jealous of Father and resented his being "at home" in our house. I loved Father and felt very protective of him when Dad started in on him.

Mom had quickly called us all to dinner. She was nervous and figured if she got food into Dad, he might feel better, or best yet, fall asleep. Of course, we all "knew" he wouldn't eat food or fall asleep when he was like this. We sat down at our places at the table.

"Where'd you get this meat?" Dad yelled. "Your ol' man bring this shit?" Tension.

"Yes," said Father. "They were going to throw it out at the butcher shop, so I took it and told Marion [my mother, his daughter] to marinate it in a little vinegar for a while and it would be just fine."

"Why don'cha tell your ol' man we don't need his old meat around here!" he yelled drunkenly to my mother.

"Pass the potatoes, please," I said. I hated when dinners started like this. Maybe I could change the subject of meat. Actually, I hated the meat, too. It smelled, and I wished Father wouldn't bring it.

Father was a product of the Depression and couldn't waste anything. When they were cleaning up at the butcher shop at the end of the day, he would take the meat or fish that couldn't be sold anymore because of the smell and the color and he would bring it to my mother. It was hard to say anything to him about it because his intentions were so sweet. My mother didn't want to hurt his feelings.

Father was getting older now, about seventy-five, and needed to feel he was contributing. He ate dinner with us three times a week. The other four days he divided his time between my Aunt Helen's and Uncle Ralph's—my mother's sister and brother.

"Danny, don't eat all the potatoes. There are five of us, you know," I said. I loved potatoes. I practically lived on them because of the meat. I usually ate just potatoes and salad. "Pass the butter, please," I said. I also loved butter.

Dad watched the butter pass from Danny to Maureen to me. He watched my knife go into the butter. I knew he was going to make butter an issue this meal, so I deliberately took a teeny bit. Ha, ha. There's nothing he can say. Using too much butter could send him into a crazy rage.

"Danny, go in the garage and get me a beer," Dad said.

"Eat some dinner first," Mom said nervously.

"I don't want this shit! Old rancid meat! Your father thinks he's a big man bringing this shit! Know what I think about this SHIT? Huh? NOTHIN'!" He threw his chop at the kitchen door.

"Stop it," Mom shouted.

"Oh, why do you have to be this way?" Father asked painfully.

"You know why?" Dad screamed. "You wanna know why? Because I've got assholes like you leeching off me every night."

"I'm not here every night," Father said.

"My ass, you're not."

"You want me to leave?" Father asked.

"Yeah! Get the fuck outa here," Dad yelled.

"No, Father! Please don't go!" I cried.

Mom got up and ran from the table crying. Danny sat at the table seething. You could tell he wanted to kill Dad; Maureen's eyes filled with tears. I hated Daddy. He ruined everything. Father walked to the living room. I followed him.

"Please don't go, Father," I said. "We love you. We want you to come here. I wish you lived with us all the time. I wish he'd go away and you would be our father."

"I think if I leave now, he might calm down," Father said. He was shaking. "Your dad's in one of 'those moods' tonight, and I think looking at me is not going to make him any better."

I walked Father to the door. I felt so bad when Dad treated him like this. He lived alone, and I knew he went home only to sleep. He could probably go over to Auntie Helen's for coffee right now, I thought.

When I returned to the kitchen, Maureen and Danny were clearing the table of half-eaten food. Dad was still sitting at the table drinking his beer. He never left his beer. He also knew where my mother hid all his "bottles" (that meant whiskey). He had probably found the one in the laundry hamper because he was starting to get that real mean look in his eye. If we all get the dishes done perfectly, then he won't be able to get crazy mad at us, I thought nervously. Maureen washed, Danny dried and I put away. Usually, Danny would use the dish towel to whip me. He would twist up the wet towel and snap it at me. I would scream and cry and yell at anyone who would listen, "Danny's hurting me." It was a great way to get attention. But tonight we'd do none of this. We all knew. Do the dishes quietly and then sneak off to our rooms and hope he'd leave us alone.

Dad walked from the dinner table to the refrigerator. Oh no, he's really looking tonight, I thought.

"What's this?" he yelled. "Two peas in a dish!" He threw the dish across the kitchen. *Crash!* "Look at this. Some old salad." He threw it at the cabinet. The sound of breaking glass brought my mother running in.

"Oh, stop this," she screamed.

"I hate the way you keep the refrigerator," he yelled drunkenly. With that, he started throwing everything he saw in the refrigerator. Suddenly, milk was on the floor, smashed eggs, broken dishes with leftovers.

Danny couldn't stand it. He leaped on Dad punching him, trying to throw him on the floor. Dad was drunk so he went down easily.

"You cocksucker," Dad yelled.

"Stop it, Danny. You'll get hurt," Mom screamed.

"Stop it," I cried.

Maureen watched icily. I could tell she couldn't wait to move out of this house.

For the moment it was over.

"You better go stay at the Mullins' house tonight," Mom whispered to Danny. She knew that later Danny would be Dad's target.

I was trembling. I hated these evenings. It was always the same. I clung to my mother. She was shaking. We both started to clean up the mess of broken dishes and food.

Dad sat and watched us—looking mean. The night wasn't over. This was a whiskey night. Sometimes on whiskey nights he wouldn't fall asleep till the sun was rising.

Maureen must have called Bill, her boyfriend, because he came by and Maureen went out.

Mom and I finished cleaning up the mess. Mom cut her hand on one of the broken dishes. She ran cold water over it. I could see that her hands were trembling.

"Let's go to Shaw's and get an ice cream," Mom said. Her eyes looked tired.

I loved ice cream, but right now I would welcome any excuse to get out of this house. We left. We hoped that when we returned, Dad would be asleep.

Mom and I got our ice cream and then stopped by Auntie Helen's. We were killing time. Father was there having coffee. We didn't mention to him what had happened after he left. It would only upset him more. We told him Dad was asleep. He could relax now. Tomorrow would be a better day.

We got home around 9:30 P.M. Maureen was still out with Bill. Dad was asleep sitting up at the kitchen table. His legs were wrapped around each other. His cigarette in one hand had completely burned out; probably burned his finger, but he couldn't feel a thing. His other hand was wrapped around his beer. Maybe he'll just stay here all night, we hoped. Mother and I tiptoed past him and quietly got ourselves ready for bed. I got under the covers and prayed that when he awakened, he would quietly get into bed and sleep the rest of the night. Mother didn't kiss me good-night. She was lost in her own thoughts.

The sound of Dad's stumbling woke me up. Maybe he'll go right to bed, I prayed.

"Where's Danny?" I heard him yell. "Where the fuck is he?"

Suddenly, the overhead lights flipped on in our bedroom. Maureen and I sat bolt upright in our twin beds. My mother came running in.

"Get out of here. Let them sleep. Some people sleep, you know!" she shouted.

With that, he sat at the foot of my bed, slightly on the edge of my feet, pulling the covers so tight I couldn't move my feet.

"You like Mommy?" he said. "I like Mommy."

Oh, God, I thought. This again. He'd slip in and out of moods. From rage to sloppy, lovey-dovey. It made me so nervous. I never knew what to expect.

"Oh, would you come to bed?" my mother said angrily and pulled him off the end of my bed. She understood this mood. He wasn't violent now; just drunk, insensitive and obnoxious. She pushed and pulled him down the hall.

He kept saying "bullshit."

Six A.M. The alarm rang. I felt so worn out. My mother was already up. Oh, God, I wet the bed. I didn't know why I couldn't stop. If anyone at school knew, I'd die. Sandy knew (she was my best friend), although Sandy didn't know that I did it every night. I opened the window and pushed the mattress outside to dry. I put the wet sheets in the wash and wiped clean the rubber sheet. Dad came out of the bathroom. I waited in my room till I was sure he was in the kitchen. I didn't want to see him. He was always real edgy in the morning, and he was probably still a little drunk. I'm sure he didn't feel very good. All that whiskey and beer and no food.

My sister dashed past me and locked herself in the bathroom.

"Hurry in there," I said. "I'm all wet." My pajamas smelled and stuck to me. It was cold.

My dad walked by. "Wet the bed again, pisshead?" he said.

I hated him. I wished he would go away and never come back. "Maure-e-en! Hurry up. I have to go to school, too! Mom, tell Maureen to get out."

"Quit whining," Dad said. He smelled like stale beer. He went into the garage, and I heard the engine start. Thank God, he's gone.

I took a bath in two inches of water. It took too much time to fill the tub in the morning; and besides, five people had to share the hot water and one bathroom.

"Suzanne, come eat your oats!" Mom called from the kitchen.

I finished putting on my uniform and sat down at the breakfast table.

"It's Wednesday so I'll be going grocery shopping after work," my mother said. "Do you want to come?"

I loved to go grocery shopping with her on payday. That way I could get her to buy my favorites—mortadella and cheese, sourdough French bread and Hostess Twinkies. Lunches on Thursday were always great. By Friday all the food would be gone because Danny always made himself three or four sandwiches after dinner. "Yes! I want to go with you," I said. "I'll come home right after school." When the bell rang at three o'clock that afternoon I skipped home eagerly.

Mom and I returned from shopping around 5:30. No one was home. We never mentioned last night. We didn't want to acknowledge what had happened; maybe then it would go away. Above all, we knew never to let anyone outside our home know the truth. It was too shameful, too embarrassing, too crazy.

There was a note on the kitchen table from Father saying he wouldn't be able to stay for dinner tonight. He was a widower and his girlfriend had asked him out. (His girlfriend, Mrs. Miller, was sixty-five years old.)

Mom and I didn't say anything to each other, but I felt relieved that Father wouldn't be here. If Dad wasn't home by this time, it wasn't good news. He started out this morning still a little drunk (and *not* in a good mood), so he'd probably been drinking all day to take the edge off his hangover. Dad had the worst job in the world for someone who liked to drink a lot. He loaded cases of beer onto boxcars at Lucky Lager Brewery. For every few cases of beer he put onto the train, he took one beer for himself. After eight hours of this, he would get pretty "looped."

It was so peaceful when he wasn't home. Maureen and Danny came home just before dinner. Even so there was a tension in the air. Every time we heard a noise while eating, we would all look up wondering if that was the garage door. But so far tonight we were lucky. (Or were we?)

I went to my room to do my homework. I didn't have my homework finished at school today, and I got into trouble again from Sister Cecile. I was in the fourth grade at our Parish Catholic School.

I never had my schoolwork done. It was impossible to study and do homework at home. We couldn't ignore Dad when he was drunk, and he was drunk most nights. He demanded our attention. He followed us around the house either in a rage or rambling unintelligible mumblings. His mumblings were full of questions though, and he demanded that they be answered.

Usually, "Do you love Mommy? Huh? Mommy doesn't love me! Why doesn't Mommy love me? Huh? Huh? Huh?"

Finally, we'd answer in exasperation and a shrill voice, "Because you drink too much!"

Then the anger would start. "Bullshit!" he'd yell back.

We all knew it was stupid to talk to him when he was like this, but we allowed ourselves to be pushed into it. We had the disease. We were addicted to the alcoholic. This went on night after night. Who could think about school? School was just a place to go to get out of the house. My thoughts were never far away from the problems at home. I had already accepted the fact that I wasn't very smart. That's why I didn't get good grades. But in reality, how could I get good grades when all my energies and attention were directed toward the craziness at home? Our disease was our priority. We perpetuated our disease night after night. I never thought about school until I was at school, and then it was too late.

I got ready for bed and went to find my mother to say good-night. She was sitting in the dark, in the breakfast room, smoking a cigarette. That was her big vice. She was still the "good girl"—forty years old and hiding her smoking from her father. He never came around this late at night anyway, but she could deal with it better hiding in the dark, in the back of the house.

"Good-night, Mommy. I love you," I said.

"Good-night, honey," she said. I noticed her hands were shaking holding the cigarette. "I love you, too, sweetheart."

I lingered for a moment. Sometimes I needed more from my mother than she could give me. It wasn't that she wouldn't give me what I needed emotionally, nor was it that she couldn't; but the disease had turned all her energies inward trying to cope. Mother was in so much pain herself, she couldn't know the pain I was in. She felt guilty, she felt sorry for all of us and dealt with it by praying. She prayed for God to help her husband.

I awoke from a deep sleep at the sound of the doorbell ringing loudly and incessantly.

"Do you have to wake up the whole house?" I heard my mom yell in a whisper.

I looked at my clock. It was midnight.

"It's my fuckin' house and I can do whatever I want!" he yelled.

"Watch out, you're going to knock over the table," my mother shouted.

"Why? Did your father give us the fuckin' table? Big man! He gives you four hundred dollars every Christmas and a bunch of rancid meat!" he slurred.

It was going to be a belligerent night. I started to cry. It scared me and made me so nervous when he was like this. I was so afraid he'd hurt my mother. He wouldn't hurt her on purpose; but when she was trying to pick him up or get him into bed, he'd throw punches into the air and sometimes he'd connect. He was really drunk tonight. I could hardly understand anything he was saying. He wasn't making any sense. Just a lot of bad words seemed to come out clearly. Mom got Dad into the bedroom and closed the door. I could hear his muffled drunk sounds and my mother's suppressed shouting.

"Would you shut your mouth," Mom said angrily. She was exasperated and tired.

"I will not!" he answered drunkenly.

All of a sudden their door opened. Oh no, I thought. He's going to come in here. Maybe I'll hide in the closet. My dad stumbled into the bathroom. Thank God, I thought. Maybe he'll just pee and then go to sleep. Through the wall I could hear him peeing. Then some more stumbling. He didn't flush the toilet. All of a sudden the overhead light flipped on in our bedroom.

"Where's Maureen?" he shouted. He went over and sat down on Maureen's feet. "You're gonna get knocked up," he said to Maureen. "I know what that Kilmartin wants, the big galoot!" Kilmartin was what he called Maureen's boyfriend, Bill Gilmartin. He was jealous of Bill because he was big—six feet tall, two hundred pounds; and, also, because he was taking out Maureen. Dad didn't like anyone who wanted to go out with Maureen, especially big ones. My dad is a little guy. He must have hated being small because he talked about it a lot when he was drunk.

"Would you get out of here and shut up!" Maureen shouted.

My mother came running in. "Get out of here! Leave them alone!" she said. She started pulling him off the bed.

"I will not!" he shouted. He pushed her away. He was strong. She landed on the floor.

"Stop it!" I screamed. I couldn't stand to see my mother hurt. Mother started crying.

"You're crazy!" Maureen shouted. She stood up and tried to push him off the bed.

I got on the floor to keep my father away from my mother. He was swearing. Maureen was screaming. My mother was crying. I was sobbing. Danny came running downstairs.

"You asshole," Danny screamed.

"Don't, Danny. You'll only make things worse," my mother said desperately. "I'll get him in bed," she said. She dragged my father down the hall. He stumbled and swore and punched at the air.

I lay in bed and listened to him swearing and cussing at the darkness for a long, long time. I couldn't stop shaking and crying. Maureen was crying, also. I suspected everyone in the house was crying. Except him.

Ring! The alarm went off. I jumped. Morning already. I felt like I hadn't had any sleep at all. I didn't hear any noise in the house. I walked into the living room. My mom was asleep huddled in the corner of the couch with her coat thrown over her shoulder. I often found her sleeping on the couch. It didn't seem abnormal. I understood why she was afraid to sleep with him. He kicked, yelled and punched at the air.

"Daddy's not up yet, Mom. He's gonna be late for work," I said. My dad never missed work, no matter how drunk he'd been the night before. I got some stability out of that. If he could make it to work every day, then he wasn't all that bad. Missing work meant he really was a drunk and, also, we'd be poor. There would be no food, and someone might come and take our house away. I worried a lot. Mom got off the couch and went to the bedroom.

"Holy shit," I heard him say. He sounded like he was still drunk. He sounded mean. "Get my lunch ready," he demanded. He slammed the bathroom door. I heard him coughing up terrible things and making awful noises with his nose. He slammed open the bathroom door, got dressed and went into the garage. Ah, peace, I thought. *Slam!* "Where the fuck is my car?" he ranted. "Did Danny steal my fuckin' car?" Danny was only thirteen years old. How could he take the car?

"How should I know where it is. Where did you leave it?" my mother asked angrily.

His drunkenness made him do stupid things like lose the car. Dad never remembered anything about the night before. He knew we were all mad at him, so he used reverse psychology. He turned it all around. Now he was mad at us! Somehow in his twisted, wet brain *we* had wronged him. Now he could justify yelling at us and ordering my mother around. It also justified the drinking he would be doing during this day.

"I musta left it at Newell's Bar. Drive me down there," he ordered.

My mother grudgingly ran to get the keys to her '50 Chevy. Then they were gone. I grabbed a Twinkie and some chocolate milk for breakfast.

Danny came into the kitchen. "He's such an asshole," Danny said.

"I hate him," I said.

Maureen came in and said, "I can't wait till I get married and get out of here." She was so lucky. She was a senior in high school. At the end of this year she could get a job, get married, leave home, do whatever she wanted. It seemed like I'd never get out of that house.

There was nothing more to say to each other. It had been a typical night in a typical week of our lives. The pattern was firmly established.

2

My dad, Francis Stanislaus Mahoney, was born in November 1911, the son of hard-working Irish immigrants. Dad was the youngest of thirteen children, the baby of the family. Premature and underweight (he weighed in at two and a half pounds on a scale his father brought home from the slaughterhouse), "little Frankie" didn't look like he would make it through the week. His father, Mike Mahoney, announced with his usual good humor, "Mae, if that's the best you can do, I quit."

Little Frankie was the darling of the family. His twelve brothers and sisters adored him, especially his brother Vin. My dad was a skinny little kid with straggly blond hair and blue eyes, and he followed Vin everywhere.

At age fourteen my dad was working with Vin on their uncle's ranch in the Santa Inez Valley when he received an urgent letter. "Come home right away. Pa's real sick." By the time my dad got to him, his father had died of a heart attack. It was a terrible blow to little Frankie. He was an extremely sensitive kid, and he held all his hurt inside. Vin took over as Frankie's dad. It wasn't the same, but it was all he had.

Dad was an outstanding athlete; and by the time he was eighteen, he made all-city baseball. Because of his impressive athletic achievements, he won a scholarship to the University of San Francisco at a time when only the elite could afford a college education.

Dad played second base for USF; and in his first year, he was the major reason the team won the championship. He was riding high. In his second year, the Jesuits (expecting the impending Depression) decided to drop baseball from the roster completely. Money was tight and something had to give. Dad was devastated. He had to scramble if he wanted to stay in college, so he went into intercollegiate boxing and showed such skill he was given another scholarship for boxing.

Then the Depression came: 1929. The family needed everyone to pitch in to make ends meet. Dad got a job at the same slaughterhouse where his father had worked and stayed there until Prohibition ended in 1933. He then went to work at the brewery. He made forty-one dollars and twenty cents a week, which was good money. The college graduates were only making seventy dollars a month. Dad said, "For Chrissakes, why should I go to school?"

He didn't want to give up on sports, though. He had dreams. Professional baseball, professional boxing. He needed a sponsor, but there was no money available for young athletes during the Depression. Some "bigshot judges" got my dad into the Olympic Club, where he could work out and train. The Depression will have to end one of these days, they thought, and then this kid will be ready. Dad kept in shape, joined the city baseball team, never giving up his dream, hoping someone would spot him and single him out.

During this time, Dad met my mother, Marion Elizabeth Turner. She was born in San Francisco during the 1915 World's Fair. Her father, George Turner, was a butcher; her mother, Nellie Keating, was a legal secretary. Both of my mother's parents were of Irish descent. Mom was a very shy, introverted, pretty young girl with long red curls and freckles. She blushed easily and became more shy when teased about blushing.

Mother lived a very orderly, traumaless life. She had two brothers and one sister. It was a happy family. They had Sunday dinners with all the finery. Afterwards they'd sing around the piano with Mom's mother playing. Mother vicariously lived through her father, the butcher. He made deliveries at all the mansions and described them in detail to her. My mother's aunt (who worked as a governess) told stories about all the fine goings-on at Nob Hill. Mother was a dreamer and she could imagine herself living in one of those beautiful mansions with silk and velvet clothes to wear.

Mother wanted to grow up and "be somebody, not like everyone else." She wanted to "have her own style." She also wanted to live in a beautiful white house with dark green shutters and a white picket fence.

At Cogswell Industrial High School, she played piano for the glee club and was one of the best pianists in her class. Then she went to Lux Junior College, where she studied costume designing, millinery, fashion designing and interior decoration. But she was easily unnerved; and when she was told she couldn't be a designer unless she had a European background, she abandoned the whole idea.

After one year of junior college, Mom went to work. Times were hard and the family needed money. She was hired at Moffitt's Wool Pullery and did exactly that: she pulled burrs out of wool.

Mom's sister, Helen, started at Moffitt's on the same day. Helen went home for lunch and never came back, but Mom "stuck it out." Her sense of commitment would not allow her to quit, no matter how unpleasant or tedious the work. The job was seasonal and soon ended.

Mom's next job was at a dog-food company. She'd stand along the assembly line in her apron and ladle dog food into cans. It was while doing this that she decided she'd rather be an office worker.

She enrolled in Dorothy Durham's Secretarial School at night and worked days at Kraft Cheese to pay for it.

Now she was on the mayonnaise assembly line. She stood there taking jars off the conveyor belt and putting them in boxes. The quart jars were heavy and her arms got tired. If she stopped to rest, the jars would pile up and start falling off the belt. The assembly line had to be shut off many times because of Mom, so the foreman decided to move her to pints. She didn't do much better with the smaller jars, and finally she was moved to cream cheese. She could handle these little containers more easily. She stayed at Kraft until she finished her schooling a year and a half later.

Now that she could type and take shorthand, she landed a job at the Social Security Board of San Francisco. She enjoyed her work and there met Dot, who would become one of her best girlfriends.

Mom had no idea she was pretty. She had thick, shiny, strawberry-colored hair, barely visible freckles on her arms and back, clear green eyes, pale skin, and straight white teeth. Her figure was beautiful; small waist, great legs and a large bosom that embarrassed her, so she dressed to camouflage her breasts with high necks and loose-fitting tops. She never liked to call attention to herself—shy and quiet, a "good girl" who went to church regularly and lived with her parents, her sister Helen, and two brothers, George and Ralph.

Mother was introduced to Dad by her brother George (whose nickname was Red) at a Native Sons dance. Dad was instantly smitten.

Before long they were dating. Dad knew everyone in town, including
the "upper crust," through his association at USF. Dad was young and
handsome, in great physical condition and "the life of the party." Every-
one wanted to hang around Ducky (his nickname) Mahoney. Mother
was intrigued by him, his associations and his lifestyle. He took her to
USF dances, introduced her to people, brought her "out of her shell."
He was a great dancer and Mother loved to dance. They danced in the
Gold Room at the Fairmont Hotel and at the Palace Hotel to the Ted
Fio-Ritz Orchestra. It was the era of the big band, and they loved it.
Dad could do anything—the foxtrot, the waltz, the twirl, the dime jig!
Everyone would stop to watch and clap when Dad really got going. He
was small and agile and his dancing had humor and style, like that of
Jimmy Cagney. Mom and Dad would change partners, but she could
never wait to get back to him. He would glide her across the dance
floor and twirl her around. She followed him perfectly. He'd dip her
down; and when he lifted her, she'd kick her leg out behind her.

They hung out with Chili and Ann, Dot and Al, Sonny Fieber and
his girl. The guys had all been on the USF baseball team with my dad.
They were the number-one team in the league when they played; and
as alumni, they were always being given dinner dances in their honor.

They loved these dances. Dad would twirl Mom all over the dance
floor to "Twelfth Street Rag." The room would spin. Mom would throw
her head back and laugh. No one could twirl like my dad. He made
Mom's life exciting. There was no drinking at that time because it was
Prohibition. Sometimes they'd get hold of a little bootleg booze, but it
was scarce and hard to obtain.

When Prohibition was over, they started going to bars. Dad drank
highballs (whiskey and water), Mom sipped whiskey sours; they went
to the Kit Kat Club and The Black Cat. Every joint had its dance floor
with a band and a singer.

They took Sunday rides in Chili's car. Mom and Dad sat in the rumble
seat and necked. They went on picnics and to barbecues. Dad was the
instigator. He loved to put parties together. He loved people; he loved
to make them laugh. They were entertained by his jokes and his dances.
Everyone wanted to be around him and he was the center of attention
wherever he went. He knew everybody all over town. "Hey, Ducky,"
they'd yell. Ducky was the most popular guy, and Mom basked in the
glory of being with him.

On the rare Saturday night that there wasn't a dance or a party, they would go to a movie. Again, Dad would know everyone standing in line. Soon, he'd have them all laughing and Mom was proud to be with him.

Dad was the unanimous choice for second base for the All-Star City team. His friend Chili also made the team, so Mom and Dad and Chili and Ann would go out to dances and victory parties after the games. It was a glorious time; an innocent time.

Dad drank quite a bit when they went out, but he was fun "with a heat on." Occasionally, he'd get a "little out of hand," but Mom was sure it was nothing to worry about.

They went together for three years before he asked Mom to marry him. Mom's mother told her daughter "to be sure." Dad had started not showing up for dates "because of drinking," and her mother was worried. But Mom rationalized that "life with him would be fun," and "anyway," she said, "when we're married, he'll stop drinking."

After their honeymoon at Dad's uncle's ranch in the Santa Inez Valley, Mom and Dad returned home to San Francisco to start their life.

Dad didn't drink much during the first year of their marriage. It was their happiest time. He started working two jobs to get Mom her "dream house." He loved her a lot and wanted her to have everything she wanted.

First they lived in the Portola District in San Francisco were they rented an apartment on top of Mr. Switzer's beautiful white house with a gabled roof. Their apartment was in the gable. They had lots of friends and entertained often. Every week the group would go to one another's house and they'd play cards, talk, dance and drink.

During that time my father made one hundred dollars a month between his two jobs, and Mother took home forty dollars a month from her clerical job at the State Relief Board.

Within the first year, Mom was pregnant with my sister Maureen. Dad worked harder than ever trying to get together the down payment for the new house before the baby was born.

On the first anniversary of their marriage, they signed the papers for their new house; and in June they moved in.

It was beautiful; everything my mother ever dreamed of: It was on Crystal Springs Road in San Bruno, California. A little white house with dark green shutters and a white picket fence. San Bruno was a small town with one main street and was located on the "Peninsula" about thirty miles outside of San Francisco. Across the street was a beautiful park with playgrounds and a baseball field. A creek ran through the park and beyond into the woods. Dad devoted himself to turning his house into the best-kept, most beautiful home in the entire town. His lawn was mowed to manicured perfection. He planted flowers and shrubbery, an arbor of yellow wisteria leading to the back yard. Snapdragons and stock, climbing roses and lilacs lined the garden beds. He was meticulous. He kept extra cans of paint in the garage in case the fence needed a touchup and he constantly repainted the green front door so it would have a deep silky quality.

Mother was equally absorbed with the interior of their home. While Dad cut and trimmed the yard, Mom painted and polished the insides. She made curtains for the kitchen and the new baby's room. They were proud and happy.

The Mahoney slogan was "First buy a house, then have your children." That is what they did. They were on top of the world, the envy of all their friends. They had done everything right. Everyone in the gang wanted to have a life just like Mom and Dad's.

On January 28, 1940, my sister Maureen was born. Mom and Dad decided to give a big party. They had lots to celebrate; a new house, a new baby, a new life.

Dad never showed up. He was too drunk and was picked up by the police in South San Francisco.

Mother was mad. "How could you do this to me?" she asked. He felt terrible and apologized over and over. The "making up was nice," my mother said, and Dad swore he'd "never drink again." He was twenty-five.

The disease had begun. The insidious disease. It creeps up. Dad drank only on weekends at first. He still had two jobs and was able to get a case of beer for a "buck and a half" from the brewery. Every Friday he'd bring home a few cases; one for himself and the rest he'd get for his pals at his price. His friends would come by on Saturdays to pick up their beer while Dad was mowing the lawn. He'd stop to cool off and have a beer with each of them. It was fun. It was social. They'd laugh and reminisce.

Dad signed up to play second base for the San Bruno Athletic Club. When the announcer said Ducky Mahoney's name over the loudspeaker, the crowd cheered. They knew they were going to get a show. As he warmed up at home plate, he'd say things to the umpire or the pitcher loud enough so it could be heard in the grandstands. The crowd would roar with laughter. He was a showman. He swung his bat and did his little dance. He made the game fun.

Afterward the "gang" would walk across the street to Mom and Dad's house for beer and a barbecue. Dad was where the action was. The little white house with the white picket fence was the social center for all their friends and family. Father and my grandmother would come by, Auntie Helen, Uncle Dave, Betty and Roy, George and Lorraine, the Baldwins. One by one all their friends from Butcher Town followed my parents' lead and moved to the Peninsula.

For Maureen life was great. All the friends and relatives showered attention on this darling child. They brought her gifts, took her on rides, bought her pretty clothes. She had everything. Her room was all done in blue-and-white gingham. Maureen thought her dad owned Lucky Lager Brewery and Lucky Strike cigarettes. Anything that started with the word *lucky*, she thought was his. Lucky Ducky. Dad was her hero; the most wonderful guy in the whole world. He was "it." Whenever she was around him, she felt happy, secure and confident.

Now Mom and Dad added a whole new set of friends from San Bruno. It didn't take long before they knew everyone in the town. Mom got involved with the local Catholic church. She was deeply religious and attended Mass regularly. She joined the Parish Ladies Club and took flowers from their garden for the altar at Sunday Mass. Dad went out of his way to make friends. He'd help the ladies carry their groceries, pitched in to help the neighbors move into their new house. He was a terrific guy, a real asset to the community.

Every week the Athletic Club gave dances and dinner parties. Having Dad at the party ensured its success. He was an entertainer, the life of the party. They went dancing at the Turf Club and the American Legion Hall. They went to a lot of ball games. Dad drank beer and would go out again after he brought Mom home; "but it seemed like social drinking," Mom said.

Two and one half years after moving into the new house, their second child, Danny, was born on August 13, 1942. Everything was perfect. Two darling children, a happy family. Then the war came. Blondie was the first of their friends to get drafted. Dad gave him a big going-away party at the firehouse. Uncle Dave was called next, then Uncle George shipped out. One by one the gang started breaking up because of the war.

In 1944 my father was called to serve his country. He joined the Merchant Marines so he could make more money. Dad was stationed in the Pacific and had "the lousiest job on the ship—loading ammunition down below." If his ship got hit, there was no way out for him. He worried a lot about being killed and dreamed constantly of getting back home to his wife and children.

While Dad was gone, Mom wanted to do her part for the war. She knitted stockings for the soldiers, wrapped bandages at the community center, and she saved cans to be recycled for scrap metal. She was lonely but kept busy.

With Dad away Mom was having difficulty making ends meet, so she went to work at Bazzurri Accounting, leaving Maureen and Danny at nursery school. She hated leaving them.

Mom prayed every day at Mass for the safe return of her husband, her brothers, friends and relatives. Every night as she tucked Maureen and Danny into their twin beds, they repeated their litany. "God bless Daddy, God bless General MacArthur, God bless Uncle Ralph, God bless Uncle George," and on and on.

To Maureen war was fun. They had blackouts and parades and everyone had a flag. She thought her dad was a general and told everyone she met.

When the war was over, Dad wrote Mom a letter. "I'm comin' home, darlin', and I want to have another baby."

Coming home was one of the happiest days of his life. He remembers coming through the Golden Gate. "Jesus Christ, what a feeling." The band was playing *California, here I come, right back where I started from.*"

Mom didn't know when he was arriving, so she was on a picnic at the park. He dropped his gear at home and walked across the street. "I was the hit of the picnic that day," he said.

Mom spotted Dad coming up the creek. Maureen ran up to him screaming, "My daddy's home." Dad put her on his shoulders.

Mom ran up to him filled with emotion. "It was a great day, I'll tell you that," Dad said later.

Shortly after Dad's return, I was conceived. I always felt good about that. I was wanted. I was planned; born to this charmed life; the fair-haired child; the baby of the family. I had special meaning to my parents. I had brought Dad home from the war.

I was born October 16, 1946. Mom and Dad threw a huge christening party and invited everyone they knew. The little white house bulged with people; laughter oozed out the windows. Dad was the life of the party again, on top of the world. He had survived the war and nothing was going to separate him from his family *ever* again.

Dad got plastered at my christening, but it was fun. He kept a life-size rag doll in the attic; and after enough drinks and coaxing from "the gang," he dragged her out, attached the elastic from her feet onto his shoes and started dancing. The doll wore a bra and panties, nylon stockings, a garter belt and a cheap, trashy dress. Her hair was a strawberry-blond mess, makeup was heavy and lips askew. The doll looked as though she had had five drinks too many. Dad twirled her limp body around while reaching under her dress and "goosing" her behind. Everyone shrieked with laughter. He'd dip her down over his knee then bite her on the bra. It was hysterically funny. Soon all the guys wanted to dance with the doll. They played catch, her flaccid form flying through the air. The party peaked with excitement; more music, more drinks, more laughter. Dad urged everyone to "stay a little longer" or "have another beer." He hated for the party to end; but one by one they filed out, exhausted and happy. He stumbled to his bedroom and passed out. The dancing doll lay on the floor of the kitchen in a crumpled heap. The house went quiet. It had been another great night at the Mahoneys'.

We were a perfect little family, each child developing his own individual personality. Maureen, eight years old and the eldest, was still the darling of all the relatives, even though she put them through the test with her temper. "Little Iodine" they called her. She needed a lot of discipline and structure. She used so much energy each day with her gymnastics and attention-getting antics that she still required a nap. She got sick a lot and had trouble breathing. It was diagnosed as asthma. School was a difficult adjustment. She didn't want to attend and had great difficulty relating to children. She was the youngest in her class by almost a year and felt "out of it."

Danny, four years old, was so good; always laughing, undemanding, a peaceful child, never any trouble. Everyone loved him.

As a baby (I've been told), Dad loved me more than anybody. I could do no wrong. I loved being the object of his attention. I can remember adoring my dad, sitting on his lap and playing with his face, pulling his lips. He thought I was "a little doll."

The cost of living was rising, but Dad's salary was not. It wasn't as easy to have as much fun as before. Besides working at Lucky Lager Brewery, Dad took a night job at Newell's Liquor Store. He also played on the company baseball team; so on Sunday the whole family drove to San Francisco to watch him play ball. He was our entertainment. After the game there was usually a party at someone's home with lots of drinks.

I grew up thinking that all "dads" got drunk. Some of the "moms" did too. Except mine. I didn't like when my dad drank. Of course, I couldn't understand alcoholism at this age. All I knew was he smelled bad, talked real loud and played rough if he drank too much.

His drinking was starting to become a problem. Mom was mad at him a lot of the time. One Sunday morning he wanted to take me in the car to visit some friends. He had worked late the night before and then sat in the bar next door drinking until 2 A.M. To calm his nerves, he started the morning with a boilermaker (beer and whiskey).

"You are not going to take her in your condition," my mom said sternly.

"Bullshit! I can do whatever I want," Dad yelled back.

He grabbed me. Mom pulled me out of his arms and I started to cry.

"Son of a bitch," Dad yelled. He was mad and acting crazy. He picked up a chair and threw it on the floor.

I screamed in fear. Maureen watched this whole scene in shock. Dad was changing and she didn't like it. It was a big blow to her to see him so out of control.

Dad scared me. Now when he came toward me, I ran to my mother and hid behind her skirt. This made him angry with me. I had been his little pet. He wanted me to favor him, but he was unpredictable. One moment he'd be laughing and joking, the next moment he'd be mad. Sometimes he was sober, sometimes he was drunk. It was too inconsistent for me. Too confusing. I liked him a lot when he was funny. Whenever friends and relatives were over, he would be a lot of fun. As soon as they left, his mood would change. He'd get angry and yell. Mom's face would turn hard and she'd get real quiet.

Dad's disease progressed during my infancy. My sister and brother remember a lot of good times; parties, laughing; but during my first few years, Dad was becoming a different person. Booze was taking on more importance in his life. Maybe at this time he realized his dream of a career in sports was becoming less attainable. He wasn't going to be a star. Life was hard work. A wife and family were a big responsibility. He was overworked and cranky. Maybe he used booze to drown his woes, coupled with the X factor, the allergy within him. He had crossed over the line; unconsciously made the choice to fuel the craving within him. The more he fed this craving, the more it demanded. He couldn't get enough. Now he was drinking heavily almost every day, but his life was not yet unmanageable due to alcohol. He was a good father to his children, in spite of his unpredictability. Dad wanted to be the best. Deprived of his "pa" at such an early age, he wanted to make up for it by being the father to us that he never had.

I remember a lot of good times during those years. Every summer Dad took us on a two-week vacation. We went to the Russian River in the Northern California wine country until I was four years old. I loved it there. We rented a small cabin on Mr. Hartman's property near the river. It smelled of redwoods, oak and pine. Danny and I slept in bunk beds on very thin mattresses. I remember he wet the bed and pee dripped down on me in the lower bunk.

In the mornings Mom and I would pick fresh blueberries for pancakes. In the afternoons Dad would take us rafting on the river. He was strong; so no matter how fast the current, I knew he would take care of us and protect us. I was proud of my dad and especially liked him on vacations because he didn't drink so much.

Mom didn't work when I was little. We had a wonderful routine together. Every morning after breakfast when Maureen and Danny went off to school, we'd listen to the radio while she'd clean house. Our favorite program was "The Breakfast Club" with Don McNeil. The program began with shrieks of laughter from the audience. I later learned it was because the announcer would drop his pants just as the show started. At a quarter before the hour they would have "the breakfast march." I would watch the clock excitedly until the big hand was on the nine. Mom and I would each have two pot lids ready; and when the music began, we'd march around the house clanging our lids together and singing.

After the household chores were finished, we'd walk downtown to Main Street to buy groceries. Even at this young age, I can remember hoping Dad would be in a "good mood" for dinner.

I took a nap every afternoon while Mom did the mangling. The house always smelled like freshly ironed sheets when I woke up. Sometimes after dinner before Dad left for his second job, Mom would play the piano and we'd all sing. My favorite was,

> *Dearie, do you remember*
> *When we waltzed to the Souza Band?*
> *My, wasn't the music grand?*
> *Chowder parties down by the seashore*
> *Every Fourth of July*
> *Test your memory, my dearie.*

She'd also play "Turkey in the Straw." Dad proudly watched us, taking it all in. He loved "Mommy." He thought she was so beautiful and told her so all the time. He was very encouraging of our talents.

"Sing out loud, honey," he'd say to me. "You've got a damned good voice."

I enjoyed being with my dad as a small child. He taught me to tell time. He was a good teacher and had a lot of patience. He'd line up all the colors in front of me and say, "This is green, this is blue, this is yellow and this is red. Now you tell me."

I'd try so hard. "This is green, this is red . . ."

"No, no," he'd say. "This is green and this is blue."

On and on we went, but I learned them.

Even though Dad drank every day, we didn't think he was an alcoholic. Our lives seemed normal to us. Oh, Mom and Dad fought sometimes, but all parents did that. Mom took us on picnics in the summer, and in winter, she'd take us to the Ice Follies or the musical theater; and every Christmas season we'd get all dressed up and go Christmas shopping in San Francisco. It was magical; the giant tree in the rotunda of "The City of Paris," the smell of soaps and perfumes on the first floor of I. Magnin; the cable cars.

Mom was mad at Dad a lot during the holidays. He received whiskey as Christmas presents, and he would be much "drunker" than when he only had beer.

"Watch out for the tree," Mom would yell.

He was always stumbling. He did fall into the Christmas tree and knocked it over, but we were able to pick it up again. Not much damage, just a few smashed branches and some broken ornaments. At five years old I already accepted this behavior as normal.

I adored my sister and brother and had a good relationship with both of them. Maureen was a lot of fun, always doing cartwheels on the front lawn. I'd try to imitate her, but didn't have her athletic prowess. She'd try to help me, but it was no use. Maureen laughed a lot; and at night when we were going to sleep, she'd tell Danny and me stories that she would make up.

Danny was very shy as a young boy. "I just couldn't think of anything to say," he told me recently; so he kept quiet.

Danny was also real good to me. He loved me a lot and thought I was special. Finally Danny was older than someone. He was my big brother and felt it was his duty to take care and protect me. One summer vacation when we went to Yosemite and hiked to Vernal Falls, Danny ran as fast as Dad to catch me from falling over the edge. Danny felt protective of Maureen also. After all, he was the other man in the family. Children of alcoholics have an accidental suicide tendency. Their pain is so deep on a subconscious level they would like to die to be rid of it. They put themselves in physical jeopardy to accidentally kill themselves. Some children run out in front of moving cars and some, like myself, try to sit on the edge of waterfalls.

I remember one Christmas when Danny saved his allowance money and occasional quarters given to him by Father for buying presents. He had five dollars—one dollar per person, he thought. The first present he bought was for me; a wonderful miniature swing set with a little slide and two little dolls. It cost five dollars. He spent all his money on my present and didn't have anything left to buy for anyone else. I'll never forget that Christmas morning. He was so proud. It was my very favorite toy.

Danny idolized Dad and loved to watch him play baseball. He wanted to grow up and be just like him. He respected him. Dad took Danny to baseball games at Seals Stadium and to football games at Stanford University. When Santa Claus asked Danny what he was going to be when he grew up, he proudly answered, "I'm gonna work in a brewery just like my dad." When Dad heard this, he cringed.

My father was still the instigator, putting people together to have fun. In the summertime he planned family picnics. We'd get up at 7 A.M. on Sundays and go to early Mass, then drive fifty miles in our brand-new 1950 Chevy Deluxe to the Almaden picnic grounds. These were wonderful times. Everybody in the family went to these picnics; Uncle Dave, Auntie Helen, Uncle Ralph, Auntie Ann, George and Lorraine, the Baldwins, Uncle George and Father. We'd cook breakfast outside; bacon, fried eggs and sourdough toast. The men played baseball; the women set the tables for lunch. Father was in charge of the barbecue for dinner; and we children ran wild from the creek to the baseball field to the picnic tables. At night after dinner, we'd dance to the jukebox on the old outdoor dance floor. These were special times. Dad would get "a heat on," but everyone liked it. He was funny.

If we didn't picnic on Sunday, we might take a ride. We were real proud of our new car. It was two-tone green with a push-button radio and a real backseat. No more orange crates like our old car.

We'd visit friends and relatives. Dad would have a few highballs while Maureen, Danny and I would explore everything. We couldn't understand why adults liked to sit and talk and drink whiskey. (Mom didn't drink.) On the way home Mom would yell at him about his driving. He'd swerve all over the road. I'd sit in the backseat and cry because I felt so nervous.

Mom didn't want her children to grow up shy and afraid like herself, so she signed us up for all kinds of lessons. Maureen took tap dancing, jazz and elocution lessons. Danny took piano. I was still too young, so I would sit on the floor next to Mom at Maureen's dancing classes. (Mom was the pianist.) When I was five years old, Mom let me take tap from Imogene Woodruff.

Dad seemed to be jealous that Mom spent so much time with all of us kids. She was den mother for Danny's class at school, assisted at Cub

Scouts, drove us all to our various lessons, played piano at dance classes. Dad wanted her all to himself, like it was in the beginning. He didn't like sharing her. He even seemed to be jealous of Father and mocked the compliments Father gave to Mom. Dad wanted to go out with their friends and have parties; but every time they did, he got drunk and then mean. After the last guest left, he would keep on drinking whiskey until his mood changed to belligerence. They went out less and less; their parties became more infrequent.

As a family, we continued to have regular mealtimes, church on Sundays (Dad didn't go), summer vacations in Yosemite National Park; but a darkness was coming over our little white house. Something ominous, sad. I was too little to really understand. I just knew when Daddy got drunk, the house felt cold. "Good ol' Ducky" was becoming hostile, sometimes violent. Mom was becoming angry. I was afraid.

At thirteen, Maureen's asthma was still real bad. She had trouble breathing, her nose was always clogged. "For Chrissakes, go blow your nose," Dad would yell at her. His nerves were raw from all the drinking.

Mom went back to work as a secretary to pay for Maureen's medical treatment. Also, the nearest parochial school was thirty miles away. It was important to Mom that her children attend Catholic schools, so she needed the extra money to send Maureen. That's when things really started to change around our house. I was with a babysitter all day. Mom had to leave early in the morning and got home at dinnertime. She was tired at the end of the day, too tired to play the piano anymore; so the music and singing stopped. I played by myself more and more in the room I shared with my sister. It was hard on Maureen. She had to expose her oncoming teenage private life with Danny and me always around. We giggled when she struggled with her first garter belt and nylon stockings. We laughed when she tried to fit her teensy bosoms into her first bra. I was not easy to share a room with. Our room was a mess because I made countless paper dolls and paper clothes for them. Little bits of paper and glue were everywhere. My dolls and their paraphernalia littered the corner. The dolls, in my fantasies, were always nurses who took care of everybody. I thought being a nurse would be wonderful.

I turned our room into a series of forts; blankets over orange crates, blankets hanging from the ceilings. Little, small, safe places to crawl into. It was a good way to stay away from Dad. I didn't like to be around him when Mom wasn't home. If he was drunk, he scared me; and if he wasn't drunk, he might be in one of his bad moods, and that scared me, too. He didn't like coming home to an empty house. He didn't like that we didn't have enough money from his salary to pay for Maureen's treatment and tuition. These were sufficient reasons to have a beer, then another and another.

I missed my mom. She was my best friend. Soon I would be in the first grade and I, too, would have something to do all day. With Mom gone, the house didn't look as nice, the laundry would pile up until Saturdays, we ate leftovers more often.

"What the hell is all this shit in the refrigerator?" Dad would yell. Little plates of leftover potatoes, salad, vegetables. He was probably frustrated. This wasn't the way he had envisioned his life. This wasn't the way Mom had envisioned it either. She didn't like being back at work. She enjoyed taking care of her home, creating a nest, being a perfect mother. But work was now a necessity. They couldn't make ends meet without it. Somehow the brass ring was slipping through Dad's fingers and he was frustrated.

He started taking it out on us. Danny was "a dummy," he said often. Of course, there was nothing dumb about Danny, but Dad's disease was progressing. "Stinkin' thinkin' " is a part of the disease. Maybe in his boozed brain the children were the problem between himself and our mother. The more Dad drank, the more Mom immersed herself in her children, her church and her work. She found lady friends to pass the free time; playing bridge, working at the church, going to rummage sales. It was no longer fun for her to go out with Dad. He wasn't interested in dancing anymore. He would make a beeline for the bar and drink himself into a stupor. He'd use bad language and embarrass her. She'd often come home by herself.

Dad would pit Maureen and me against each other. Maureen was a great athlete, so he'd tell me, "You can't run worth shit." Maureen and Danny didn't get good grades in school. They had trouble concentrating. Dad would tell them they were stupid; "big dummies." "Suzanne's the smart one," he'd say. He wanted his kids to do well so he'd try to draw us out through humiliation. Maureen was just entering adolescence. She was skinny, flat-chested and had asthma. She needed building up, not running down. All she wanted in her young life was to please Dad. What better way than to be good in sports. She was a great third baseman. She carried her baseball mitt wherever she went and could throw a ball farther than Danny (a fact that Dad never let him forget). In eighth grade she was asked to join a women's team in Salinas.

"For Chrissakes, why do you wanna go play ball with a bunch of dikes?" Dad responded.

Maureen was dumbfounded. It had been an honor. She thought he would be so proud. She felt confused. Nothing was ever good enough for Dad.

Maureen admired Dad. She was also embarrassed by him. She remembers sitting on the front porch watching him mow the lawn. Some friends drove by. "How're you doin', Ducky?" they yelled.

"Aw, it's colder than a witch's tit in a brass brassiere," he yelled back.

It was part of his humor, but Maureen wished he wouldn't talk like that. It was so embarrassing. Yet when Mom and Dad would fight, Maureen would get mad at Mom. She felt if Mother wouldn't get so mad at him, he wouldn't drink. She wrote her a letter saying, "Mother, if you and Dad get a divorce, I'm going to live with Dad!" She felt she could manipulate Mom so they wouldn't fight anymore. She tried to please Dad more than she tried to please Mom. We were all like that. He made each of us want to be his favorite, including Mom. We were what he thought of us. One day we'd be smart, one day we'd be dumb. One day we'd be clever, one day we'd be useless. Dad was our barometer. Without his approval, we were nothing.

Danny, already quiet and shy, could easily be convinced he was a "big booby." He already thought he wasn't very smart. Dad told him so. Danny believed him.

Too bad we didn't understand Dad was an alcoholic. Whatever he said was the opposite of what he really felt. In reality he loved us all. He needed our love and respect. He feared losing us, so he controlled us. But the disease forced us (including Mom) to push away from him. It confused us. I loved him. I liked him. I hated him. I was afraid of him. None of us understood that the disease was taking hold of the whole family. We were all controlled by the addict. If he was happy and in a good mood, we were happy. If he was upset, we were upset. We had all become co-addicts. I was five years old, a co-addict and didn't even know what an addict was.

By the time I was in first grade, I was having nightmares regularly. The same thing every night. Snakes. I was positive I saw them. I'd cry in my sleep for my daddy. "They're in my room," I'd whine to my dad.

"Go to sleep," he'd yell back from his bedroom down the hall.

"They're going in my mouth," I'd cry.

"Well, close it," he'd answer gruffly.

Snakes were scary and unpredictable. You never knew when they were going to strike, just like my dad; yet my dad was who I called for in the night.

Dad's life was out of balance. Too much work, too little play. He was overtired, but the idea of quitting his second job or backing off on chores on Saturday was abhorrent to him. He wasn't a quitter. He had to find a reason, so he did; his boss was an "asshole" and a "dumb son of a bitch." The "hates" were beginning. He started to hate anyone who was doing better than he. He hated any man who was bigger than he. His drinking escalated. People in the community would see him walking home from work drunk. When he realized this, he "hated" them. He'd stay out until two in the morning regularly and come home full of hate and anger. My mother was a "lousy housekeeper" he said; so he'd turn on all the lights and start cleaning. He'd throw things around, dishes would break, doors would slam. He'd stumble and fall and swear. The noise was frightening. I'd lie in my room and tremble. I'd wet the bed and wake up all wet and cold and afraid to get up for fear he would see me. The disease was rotting him. He was hating himself and us, and we were hating him.

Maureen entered high school idolizing Tippi Hedren and Grace Kelly. She thought they were pretty and glamorous and wished she could be like them. She wished she could be anybody but herself. She thought she was ugly and stupid. Her breasts hadn't really sprouted yet so she felt further isolation as the only girl in the class still wearing an undershirt. Her only route to popularity was athletic. She was so proficient that the boys allowed her to play baseball with them. Soon she was "one of the guys;" but in the summer of her junior year her bosom grew to 32D. Suddenly she was curvy; boys were noticing her in a different way. Bill Gilmartin took one look and decided she was the girl for him. They started going steady. Bill was Maureen's first boyfriend and the only man ever to be in her life.

All three of us had trouble concentrating in school. Maureen was a dreamer; Danny was, too, but in his dreams, he "knew he couldn't do it." He was already feeling shot down. Maureen was always trying to be something that she was not. The alcoholism at home was affecting our self-esteem. We stopped believing in ourselves.

Maureen was also a "good girl" and didn't like anything to do with sex. She didn't like Elvis Presley. She thought he was immoral and didn't think "good girls" should be watching him gyrate. She wished Dad's drinking would disappear; and because he was so unpredictable, she spent more and more time with her friends in Burlingame, thirty miles away. She could pretend to herself that Dad was the guy in her fantasies; reliable, lovable, funny and talented; the guy he used to be.

I felt like I didn't fit in at school. I didn't know why, I just thought everyone was better than me. I longed to be part of the gang, but I always felt like I was tagging along. I was too young to fit in with my brother and sister; my father scared me and my mother was preoccupied a lot of the time.

My first few years of grammar school were lonely. Besides wetting the bed every night, I sucked my thumb until a huge welt appeared above the knuckle. I retreated further into my small spaces—the corner of my room, my closet—safe little places where I could concoct my fantasies of life and how I would like it to be. I got a cat named Mitzi and spent hours talking to her, petting her. She was my friend, my ally. She understood. I craved attention. I would do outrageous things to get it. During the Pledge of Allegiance in the schoolyard each morning, I would catch Danny's eye and do things to make him and his friends laugh. Obscene finger gestures that I saw the older boys do. Danny would crack up. I would get into trouble from the nuns. I had no trouble learning. I just wasn't very interested, except for singing. I'd rather fantasize. I dreamed I would one day talk to the Russians and tell them our countries shouldn't fight, and they'd say, "that's a good idea," and I'd save the world. I would lie to my friends that my dad was very strict when, in fact, he usually didn't know where I was or what I was doing and didn't care. His life was booze now. Every day. He'd be drunk and Mom would be mad. Night after night.

At thirteen Danny finally found a way to feel like something. The girls thought he was darling. He loved to "make out" and there was no shortage of girls who wanted to do it with him, but he was shy and didn't know how to make the first move. He found if he had one or two of Dad's beers, he could muster up his courage easily. His first drunk was in the park with his friend Mike. They got hold of a case of beer and a case of doughnuts and drank and ate until they both threw up. Mom and Dad never found out; they just thought he had the flu.

"Why'd you ever marry Dad?" I would ask my mother, bewildered.

"He was so much fun and such a good dancer. He was funny," she'd say sadly.

I knew what she meant, but I rarely got to see that man. Now he had three phases; sober, a little drunk and plastered.

When he was sober, he was awful; edgy and angry. Everything made him mad. "Just a little drunk" was my favorite mood—the almost normal part. That's when I liked him; after about two beers. He'd be funny. He wouldn't be edgy. He'd think I was cute and smart and tell me so. Everyone liked him when he was like this, even though we knew it would only last an hour or so. If he kept on drinking, he'd get plastered; and we never knew what mood that would bring.

Plastered brought one of two forms; the "Do you love Mommy?" sloppy mood or the mean, raging, "you cocksucker," belligerent mood.

Even at this early point, Mother was overwhelmed by what her life had become. She never wanted her marriage to be like this. Her dreams had been like fairy tales; the perfect husband, the perfect family, happy little children. Reality was an *imperfect* husband, imperfect family life and confused, insecure children. She never planned on a life of violence, fear and shame. I felt so sorry for my mom. She was caught; caught between her faith and her unhappiness. She didn't know where or how to get help. She believed in the Catholic church, and the church looked negatively upon divorce. Life was about sacrifice in order to get to Heaven. The church told her it was infallible. What the church said was right, and you were *not* to question the church. Accept what it says. Have *faith*. Have faith in God that everything will turn out right. My mother had complete faith. I know of no one closer to God. She believes that prayer always works, but she never really asked God to make it work for her.

Everyone loves my mother. Her goodness flows out of her like a light. At times she almost seems to glow. She is shy and quiet about her religion. It's a very private matter with her. She is sweet and gentle by nature, very unpretentious, never has a bad thought about anyone.

The person my mother was turning into at night was so out of character. She had not been raised with any violence. She and my dad were complete opposites, but my mother had made a commitment in marriage; "In sickness and in health, till death do us part." This, too, made divorce impossible. She had to do everything she could "to keep the family together." She would stick by her family. She would try to provide a normal life for her children.

Mother felt so guilty, afraid somehow she was responsible for her husband's condition. She felt guilty that she had brought children into a life like this. As the wife of an alcoholic, her self-esteem suffered badly. She felt responsible for the alcoholism and, therefore, didn't feel good enough or worthy enough to expect more from her life. She prayed to God to help her husband get better, but she never asked God to help her.

So here we were. My parents' dreams were slowly fading. The marriage was no longer ideal. We kids were suffering emotional trauma with no one to understand the signals. We all wanted Dad to stop drinking, but we never realized it was also affecting us.

3

I woke up with a start. I didn't know where I was. Then I realized that everyone in the class was laughing at me. Sister Cecile was standing over my desk. "Miss Mahoney, what *is* the capital of Montana?" I couldn't think. How long had I been sleeping? "Maybe we should talk to the principal about why you can't stay awake in class. Don't your parents make sure you go to bed on time?" she questioned. If only she knew the truth.

I was so tired from the night before, but I couldn't tell her that. It was my secret. I couldn't let anyone know my secret. How could I tell her that we were up all night with screaming and yelling and hitting? How could I tell her I finally cried myself to sleep at 5 A.M.? How could I tell her how nervous I was? How could I tell her this was a normal part of my life; that most nights were like this?

No teacher ever asked me if there was something wrong. They just assumed I was one of those lazy students. I'm not even sure if they *had* asked what I would have said. I was already, at nine years old, used to covering up; pretending that life inside our house was as pretty as the outside. Any house with a front lawn that perfect must house a perfect family. How could I tell anyone, "I don't know what normal is. I go to sleep on time, but night after night I'm awakened by my father's drunkenness and violence. I hide in my closet most nights. I never know what's going to happen. I'm scared. I'm sad, and I need help."

"I'm sorry," I said. "I'll go to bed early from now on." I always felt so stupid in class. I never connected my so-called stupidity to our alcoholism. I blamed myself. I had a hard time concentrating. I'd try to do my schoolwork, but I just couldn't think. I daydreamed a lot. I fantasized. I'd dream of something wonderful like being a big star on Broadway and my mother would be sitting in the front row so proud and happy. Or, I'd daydream that Debbie Reynolds and Eddie Fisher had car trouble, and they came to our house to use our phone, and we invited them to stay for dinner, and they just loved us (especially me), and my dad would be so funny and fun. The life of the party.

At 3 P.M. the school bell rang. School was out. Thank goodness. Instead of school being a place to escape the trauma of my home life, it became another kind of prison. I was dumb and stupid in school. I hid from my dad at home, and I hid from my teacher at school. I always tried to sit at the back of the room out of Sister Cecile's eyesight. I would panic when she called my name. I was never paying attention. The kids in my class made fun of me. I wasn't smart and I was skinny. Boney Mahoney they called me. I had big blue eyes, long eyelashes and chin-length blondish-brown hair that my mother combed into a page-boy. She told me I had beautiful hair. "It's so thick and shiny," she'd say. I always wore a belt to keep my uniform skirt from falling right off my waist. I wasn't "in" with the popular kids. Sandy was my only friend. She seemed to understand me; and when she saw my dad drunk, she didn't ask any questions. Even so, I avoided having her come to my house too often. Her dad drank also, but not as much as mine. Sandy and I looked alike—both blond, short and skinny. We were best friends. We lived about a half hour's walk from one another so we weren't able to play together every day; but we hung out at school. Sometimes on weekends, I'd stay overnight at her house, but my fear of wetting the bed prevented me from staying too often. When I did stay, I didn't sleep well. I'd try to keep awake to make sure I wouldn't pee; but after hours of trying, I'd get so exhausted I'd fall into a deep sleep. It was always then that my bladder let loose. It would be so embarrassing the next morning. I didn't want Sandy to know, but there was no way to cover it up.

I skipped home from school one afternoon and changed out of my uniform. After grabbing my roller skates, I went out to play. My neighbors, Janie and Johnnie, were on the sidewalk in front of my house, so I started to skate with them. We tied our sweaters around our waists and held on to each other and played whip. It was so much fun. I didn't like being the tail though; it was too scary. About five o'clock I saw our green Chevy coming down Cypress Avenue. I hoped Janie and Johnnie wouldn't notice my dad. I hoped he wasn't drunk. I felt so nervous. As the car got closer, I could see it swerve down the hill. Dad made a left-hand turn onto Crystal Springs Road. He ran over two corners. For a minute I thought he was going to do a complete circle at the intersection, but at the last moment he straightened out the wheel and proceeded left on Crystal Springs Road. He turned left again into our driveway, sideswiped the oak tree and scraped against the picket fence. He didn't put the car in the garage. Instead, he rolled out of the passenger seat (he couldn't get out of the driver's seat because the fence was in the way) and stumbled to the front gate. The gate would stick onto the concrete front path, so to open it, you had to lift it up. In Dad's drunken state he forgot and leaned over to open the latch from the inside; he lost his balance and fell over the top of the gate. There he was, impaled on the pickets, legs and arms waving drunkenly. I was mortified. Janie, Johnnie and I all acted like we didn't see him. I suggested manically that we go skate up the hill. An hour later it was dark. If I didn't get home, my mother would be worried.

When I reluctantly walked in the back door, I knew it was not good. Dinner wasn't ready, the table wasn't set. No one was around.

Then I heard my mother yelling, "I hate this. I can't stand it anymore! I'm going to get a divorce!"

Oh, please don't get a divorce, I thought. He isn't that bad. Even the thought of divorce at that time was awful. I didn't know anyone whose parents were divorced. How could we live? I felt so scared. So terrified. What would happen to our family?

I heard my dad laugh. "You're not going to leave me, Mommy," he said drunkenly. He was right. "Mommy" threatened divorce a lot, but she never went through with it.

I ran into their room. "Please, please don't divorce him, Mommy. I love Daddy. I want us all to be together. Please!" I started crying.

My dad called me over. He was drunk, but it was a lovey-dovey, mellow drunk. He was probably exhausted. All of us were and our nerves were raw.

"Mommy wants to leave me. Do you think she should leave me? Huh, Suzanne? I love Mommy," he said. "Isn't Mommy great?" Dad loved Mother a lot and said it over and over when he was drunk. He thought she was a saint. Deep down I'm sure he was terrified that she'd leave him.

"Yeah. Well you sure have a funny way of showing your love," my mother said angrily.

"Don't talk to him that way, Mommy." I was so afraid they'd break up. I just wanted everything to be nice and happy. A perfect family.

"Well, he's driving me crazy. I just want to get out of here forever!" my mother screamed.

"No, no. Please don't leave him," I cried. "I'll be so good. I'll never do anything wrong ever again; just please stay together."

My father lit a cigarette, took a swig of beer with the other hand and started mumbling unintelligibly. He was almost asleep. Mom and I went to the kitchen. I set the table and made the salad dressing. Mom made hamburgers, lost in her thoughts. Danny and Maureen came home. We sat down to eat.

Suddenly, Dad started yelling from the bedroom, "Shit! Fuck!"

We all ran to him. Dad had fallen asleep with the lighted cigarette and started a small fire. He had burned his finger and the mattress was smoking. Dad poured the rest of his beer into the smoking hole in the bed. The sickly smell of beer and smoke filled the room.

"See what you do! I can't stand it! I can't stand it!" she screamed hysterically. "Get your things, all of you. We're leaving! Now." She didn't lose it like this very often, so we knew she meant for us to get our things. I grabbed my uniform and my pajamas and got into the car. Maureen and Danny got into the backseat.

"Where're we going?" I asked.

"To a motel till I know what to do," my mother said. She was trembling.

I felt so scared and so sad. We were going to be the first divorced family in San Bruno. We went to the El Rancho Motel. The clerk asked my mother for her credit card.

"I don't have any credit cards," she said wearily.

"I'm sorry, ma'am. You can't check in without a credit card."

Mother felt so helpless. The one time she tried to break out, the one time she mustered the courage to try to save her dying family, she was stopped. She couldn't function financially on her own.

We all piled back into the car. My mother just sat at the steering wheel and started crying. It was nine o'clock. There was nothing to do but to go back home.

Dad was in bed talking in his sleep; the usual "cocksucker, asshole," etc. Mom got into bed with me and we both immediately fell into an exhausted sleep.

At 6 A.M. the following morning our door slammed open. "Rise and shine for the dollar line!" my dad belligerently yelled at the top of his lungs. He flipped on the overhead light. "Get outa bed, you lazy slobs." This was the semisober general. He was feeling righteous and angry for having slept alone. "Well, isn't this cute," he said. "All the girls in one room; and there's Mommy with her little favorite."

I couldn't move because I had wet the bed and didn't want him to know. Dad loved to yell at me for wetting the bed. My mother got out of bed. She didn't say anything about me peeing all over her.

Mom went to church that morning as she almost always did. It was part of her daily routine. Mass before work, always praying to God to make life like it used to be. She didn't want more, she just wanted the love and laughter that she once had back in her life. She wanted to keep the family together; she wanted the terror and sadness to be gone from her children's eyes. There was no other place to turn. She prayed for it to be God's will.

4

Dad didn't drink as much on weekends. He had a strong sense of morality about spending money. He always brought the entire paycheck home to my mother every Wednesday. He was not one of those drunks who spent the family money on booze. Instead, he chose to work in a brewery where he could drink as much as he could get down for free. He always filled his lunch pail with extra bottles of beer, so in time he had quite a stash piled in the garage.

Saturday mornings Dad emerged as the solid, hard-working head of the family and gave us our orders. *No leaving the house till all the work was done.* Danny worked side by side with him on the lawn and garden. Everyone who walked by commented on our beautiful lawn. Dad was a perfectionist on Saturdays. If a chore wasn't done perfectly, we had to do it all over again. He was also pretty hung over and shaky by Saturday, so his patience was nil. He would fly off the handle at the smallest thing. If we weren't working our asses off, he would yell. He had the most terrifying yell. I would actually jump.

I was very afraid of him. I think we all were. I worked alongside my mother. We vacuumed and moved all the furniture to really get things clean under, on top and all around. I enjoyed doing this. I loved my mother so much. There was no one I would rather be with. Maureen usually got the ironing detail. She would get into it and do a real professional job.

Drunks are either dependent or bullies. Dad was a bully. I don't know what we thought he would do to us; but as I said before, as co-addicts, we were controlled by him. It never dawned on us to say *Shut up!* or *Who do you think you are, treating us like this?* Our self-esteem was so low we felt we deserved his bullying. He was no longer acting in a way to deserve our respect; yet as head of the household, we gave it to him.

Around lunchtime Dad would go into the garage to cool off and have a beer. After about two or three beers his mood would change, and then it could actually be fun around the house. He'd joke at my mother. I would follow my mother everywhere she went; and he would say, "Don't stop short, Mommy, Suzanne will run into you."

Anyone looking in on this family, in this darling, well-kept little house, would think everything was perfect.

On Saturday afternoons Mom and I would go shopping, mostly to look but sometimes we did buy something new for ourselves. We imagined buying new clothes would send Dad into a rage, so we were careful to hide our purchases in the trunk of the car until we could sneak them into the house later on. Actually, we never really gave him a chance on this one. I can never remember saying, "Look, Daddy, at the new dress Mommy just bought for me." He might have been pleased; but we were so terrified of him we couldn't take the chance. Two weeks later, when I'd walk out in my new outfit, he'd say, "When the hell did you get that?"

"Oh, this," I'd answer nonchalantly, "I've had it a while." Lying was easy. It was a way of life for all of us.

Sundays were our most predictable days. Mom and I, Maureen and Danny would walk to church in the morning. Dad rarely went with us. Maybe he felt guilty. We all washed our hair, wore our best clothes and personified the happy little family.

In the afternoons we'd often go visiting relatives. It was a good excuse for Dad to drink. Mom always invited her father for Sunday dinner, so around three o'clock she'd start telling him we'd have to get going home. He didn't like his socializing or his drinking to be interrupted, especially for his father-in-law; so the ride home and the evening meal were usually very tense. The best Sundays were when we just stayed home. Then Dad would hardly drink at all. We'd sit on the front porch watching the cars go by while Mom fixed dinner. It was my job to set the table. We ate in the dining room with a tablecloth and the good china. We always had roast beef, mashed potatoes and gravy. Mom, Dad and Father all had a little wine. No one ever mentioned what had gone on all week. The secret was buried so deep we never even mentioned it to each other.

But we knew what tomorrow would bring. The pattern was predictable. Mondays Dad would be drunk but not violent. Tuesdays and

Wednesdays he was drunk and belligerent. (Father never came on those nights.) Thursdays (the day after payday) Dad would be roaring drunk and violent. He had money in his pocket on Thursdays, which allowed him to spend the evening at a bar drinking whiskey.

Whiskey made him very mean, and he would return late in the evening plastered and violent. These were the nights when fists would fly and furniture would get broken. The violence was terrifying. We all spent a lot of time hiding in our closets.

Fridays Dad would be drunk and sometimes sick. A body can only take so much abuse. He'd feel mean and ugly.

This was the typical pattern of our week; but, of course, the pattern was always subject to change. That is what made us all so nervous. Just when we'd make plans for a Saturday night (because he was usually sober), he would get roaring drunk. Events and holidays seemed to bring out the worse in Dad.

I'd have expectations . . . "I can't wait until Christmas," or "I'm so excited about Easter," or "My birthday is next week." But these things never turned out the way I dreamed they would. Something would always happen. His drinking would always mar the occasion. He couldn't help himself. The more he tried to resist, the greater his need.

This went on week after week, year after year. It was the norm. We didn't like it, but we accepted it because it was all we knew.

This Tuesday, Dad was roaring drunk again. I came home from baseball practice, and he was sitting in the breakfast room with this terrible-looking man; a carpetbagger, a bum. He scared me. His eyes looked crazy. His hair was gray, scraggly and unwashed. His clothes and hands were filthy, and he smelled. My dad and his "friend" were drinking whiskey. I ran to my mother and asked who he was. She was visibly upset. "Some bum he picked up at a bar," she said.

"Is he staying for dinner?" I asked.

"The guy gave Dad some ox tails, and he expects me to cook for them."

"Are you going to?" I asked nervously.

"Of course not. I won't even go into the kitchen," she said.

I was hungry. I wanted dinner. I went to the kitchen to listen to them. They were both laughing so hard no noise was coming out. Dad seemed to be in one of his "good" drunk moods.

"Daddy," I said, "Mommy has to cook dinner now, so it's time for your friend to go home."

"He will not!" he roared. "He's gonna spend the night."

My mother came running out. "If this man stays, I leave," she said.

She was shaking. "I will not put up with this. It's bad enough you disrupt our lives night after night with your drinking, but I will *not* put up with bringing your low-class bar friends home! Now get out. *Now!*"

"Like fuck we will. I'll bring home whoever I want," Dad said.

Mom grabbed their bottle of whiskey and broke it in the kitchen sink. I saw Dad's eyes go into a rage. We all knew one thing. *Never* take Dad's "bottle" away from him while he was awake. But to break it! Oh, no!

"Son of a bitch!" he roared. "You asshole," he screamed at her. He ran his arm across the table. Everything fell to the floor, their beer bottles, ashtrays, the butter dish.

The sound of breaking dishes made me feel crazy inside. The smell of beer, whiskey and old cigarettes was all around me. I felt rage inside. I hated this. I ran to my dad and kicked him as hard as I could in the shins. He grabbed me by the hair. "Stop it," I screamed. "You're hurting me."

My mother started screaming, "Leave her alone! Get out of here. Both of you!"

Dad's friend, the bum, said, "Man, let's get the fuck outa here."

My dad followed him, swearing all the way out the door. They knew they had to go. There was no booze left. The house went quiet. Another wonderful night.

At three o'clock in the morning the sound of a car pulled up to our house. You could hear the engine running and a lot of muffled talk. I ran to the living room to peek out the curtains and found my mother already there peeking through the peephole in the front door. It was a taxi. The driver and my dad were arguing. My dad was very drunk. The car door opened. I heard my dad say, "I don't have any fuckin' money." The cabdriver got out of the taxi and started walking to our front door. Dad fell out of the taxi and was lying on the curb in front of the house. "Cocksucker," he was mumbling over and over. I was mortified. I hoped none of the neighbors would wake up and see him. The doorbell rang. Maureen ran out of our room to see what was happening. Mom paid the taxi driver the eight dollars Dad owed, and the taxi drove off. Dad was still lying on the curb yelling terrible words. Mother called Danny downstairs to help pick him up and carry him inside. When they finally dragged him into the house, he got a new surge of strength. He started punching and kicking at the air. He took a swing and punched my mother in the breast. She screamed. He really hurt her.

Danny went crazy. "You asshole!" Danny kicked him.

Maureen punched him in the head. Then Danny threw him against the piano. He landed right on the corner of it; and by the groan he let out, we knew he was hurt.

I was crying and screaming. Danny was shaking. Maureen was crying. My mother was crying and saying over and over, "I hate this, I hate this."

Mother took Dad to the hospital. Danny, Maureen and I sat huddled together and shaking in the living room. Things were bad and getting worse. Mom got home at 5:30 A.M. Danny had broken Dad's ribs. He was still drunk, but subdued. Mom told us all to go to bed; we'd have to get to school soon.

The days after these "terrible nights" were in their own way just as bad. Violence is such an exhausting experience. Even at my young age I couldn't bounce right back. We all felt so depleted. There was nothing to say, just a terrible black feeling in the bottom of my heart. There was no one to talk to; not even Sandy. How could I explain to anyone that nights at our house were so terrifying.

We all moved quietly about the house, lost in our own thoughts. Maureen dreaming about getting married. Danny and I trying to figure out how we could make it better. If only he'd stop drinking, I thought. I was so afraid my parents would get a divorce.

Dad didn't work the next day because of his broken ribs, no sleep and a bad hangover. He was very quiet. Maybe he was angry, maybe he was guilty, maybe he was just sick. Danny felt so sad. Somehow, when Dad was sober, he didn't seem so bad. We all knew what he could be like when he was good (even though we rarely saw that man); and knowing that kept us going.

Mom didn't know what to do anymore. She was trying her best to give us some form of normalcy. She thought she was doing everything she could. She would hide Dad's whiskey and take his car keys. She would drag him to bed and clean up his vomit. She would try to hide him from our friends if he was real bad. She didn't know she was enabling him to continue drinking. She was a good Irish Catholic woman who had made a commitment and was going to keep her family together, even if it killed her. Tonight her family had gone over the edge. How much of this could we endure?

Mother went to church the next morning, praying for a miracle; "Dear God, please make him stop drinking." Her faith and her Catholicism was her sustenance. It kept her from going crazy. It was the one thing that was keeping her alive. She couldn't risk being cut off from her church. Without it, she would wither emotionally.

There was also the question of money. How could she take care of and feed her children? Women were severely underpaid. With her skills at that time, there was no way she could make enough to provide for us. She didn't know that alcoholism was a disease. The church didn't provide any answers. She didn't know she could get help. She kept her secret to herself.

5

*T*he broken ribs didn't slow Dad down for long. Booze seemed to anesthetize his pain; so instead of a little respite, he drank more than ever. The nights continued to be long, loud and ugly.

We all tried our best to carry on with our lives. Mother felt so hopeless. In the 1950s there was no information about addiction, no respectable place to go for help. The Catholic church provided only spiritual guidance. No one in the clergy was trained in substance abuse and dealing with the family as co-addicts. We all went inside ourselves to find the answers. Each of us blamed ourselves. "Maybe if I were a better person, this wouldn't happen." "Why is Dad so unhappy and mad? It must be my fault." Our lives were centered around an alcoholic. Dad was our focus.

Mom's heart was breaking, but she created diversions for herself. She joined ladies' clubs and church groups.

The church was an important part of all our lives emotionally, spiritually and socially. Mom belonged to the Mothers' Club and Dad belonged to the Fathers' Club. These two organizations were the core of our social activities. The annual church bazaar, the spring fashion show, Easter breakfasts, the softball team, sports assemblies. These were events not to be missed but to be looked forward to—the only cloud being our nervousness that Dad might show up drunk.

Mom was very active with the Y.L.I. (Young Ladies Institute). She had held every office and was the club pianist. She went to Y.L.I. one night a week. She also belonged to a bridge club. There were ten ladies who met every week at one another's houses to play bridge. Every tenth week you had the bridge party at your house. Whenever my mother's turn was coming, she would get very nervous. She had a case of psoriasis to begin with; but when her turn to give the party came around, it would get real bad.

"I'm having the bridge club next Thursday night, and I hope you will behave," she said to my dad. She would say this to him a couple of times a day to be sure he knew and could prepare himself to be sober and stay out of the ladies' way. She was setting him up. Setting him up to be sure to be bad. The seed was planted.

On Saturday my mother and I gave the house an especially good cleaning. On Wednesday night after dinner I helped her put up the card tables in the living room. We covered them with tablecloths and flowers and put out her best antique china cups and plates. Dad was very drunk, and we hoped he wouldn't knock over the tables. He was stumbling a lot and insisted on following us everywhere.

"Would you be careful?" Mom's voice was strained.

"I will not!" he roared; the tone came from the back of his throat.

At least he isn't belligerent tonight, I thought. Mom went to the kitchen to make molded Jell-O salad and the fillings for tea sandwiches. I loved helping her do this. I filled the candy dishes with chocolate-covered nuts and mints from Shaw's Candies.

Naturally, Dad came home from work very drunk on Thursday. My mother had such a pained look on her face. "Maybe he'll fall asleep after I feed him dinner," she said. Her hands were shaking again.

He didn't want to eat. "Gimme a beer," he said.

"You've had enough," she said. "I asked you to please stay out of my way tonight. Just eat dinner and go to bed."

"Like hell I will," he said.

Things were not going well.

At eight o'clock the doorbell rang. The first lady was there. "Suzanne, quick, bring Dad to the bedroom and try to get him to stay there," my mother said nervously.

By this time Dad was sitting at the breakfast table with his beer and cigarettes. He was slurring under his breath and half asleep sitting up. Beer didn't knock him out this way. He must have found the whiskey.

"Dad, come with me. Mom's friends are here," I said.

"Wha' the fuck?" he said drunkenly.

I pulled and pushed him, all the while he was slurring, stumbling and swearing. I thought my mom would cry.

"Hi," she said manically to the first lady.

Dad lay down on the bed. I pulled off his shoes. Maybe he'll fall asleep, I thought.

"Gotta take a piss," he said.

Oh, no. I didn't want the ladies to hear him. I waited outside the bathroom door to be sure he didn't go into the living room. I steered him back to the bedroom. The ladies were all here now. I could hear their reserved laughter counterpoint with an occasional "cocksucker, asshole" and other slurred drunk talk coming from the bedroom. Around nine o'clock I went to my room. Dad was asleep. Thank God, I thought. Mom is in luck tonight.

At ten o'clock the door to the living room slammed open. "What's this?" Dad roared drunkenly to all the startled ladies. "Can I join you girls?" he asked. Dad sat in my mother's chair. "I know you," he said to one of my mother's friends. "You're the one with the bulging eye-balls." He sat there using the most shocking words he could think of.

One by one each lady left. "Thank you, Marion, it was a wonderful evening," they all said.

"What? Is the party over?" Dad slurred. "Stay and have a beer with me," he yelled as they were leaving.

"Oh, be quiet," my mother said as she closed the door. "You ruin everything!" She was humiliated.

"I love you, Mommy," he mumbled.

"Well, I don't love you," she said. "You make me sick."

6

I was still wetting the bed every night. I would try so hard to stop. I wouldn't drink any liquids after dinner, but it didn't seem to help. Danny was wetting the bed every night, too. We never associated our bed-wetting with the trauma and stress of our family alcoholism. We just thought there was something wrong with us. Danny and I were both at the washing machine putting our wet and smelly sheets into the washer when Dad walked by. "Well, if it isn't pisshead and pissant—two pissheads."

Yeah, well, you're a drunk, I thought. Anger had set in. I hated him. I loved him. It was so confusing.

Danny's room was upstairs. Actually, it used to be our attic until Dad and Uncle Dave converted it into Danny's knotty-pine bedroom. I was real glad when they did that. Up until then Maureen, Danny and I all shared one small bedroom. There was just enough room for two twin beds and a crib. I stayed in my crib until I was almost five years old. With Danny's move, I took over his twin bed.

Danny wet the bed every night also; but being upstairs, he couldn't push his mattress out the window anymore to air out. Consequently his room always smelled.

Dad was not on a binge right now, but he was drinking enough to wake up with the shakes and real edgy. On these mornings he'd vent his anger by waking us all up with slamming doors and his loud booming voice. "Get up!" he'd yell, slamming the door and flipping on the overhead light.

One night Danny heard Dad in the kitchen. He thought, Ha, ha! When Dad comes up here, I'm going to be all dressed in my school uniform with my bed made and everything. Danny was always trying to please Dad. He'd do anything to make him happy. Dad didn't come up right away. Danny was still a little sleepy, so he lay down on his freshly made bed in his clean uniform. He didn't realize it was midnight.

"Get up, pisshead!" Dad yelled the next morning. Poor Danny had peed all over his uniform and the bed and bedspread. I thought it was funny. Danny didn't.

My mother wrote him a note excusing him for not wearing his uniform. Danny was such a good and loving person. Everyone liked him. He liked peace. He liked to get along with people; not make trouble. It was very disturbing and distressing to him when he lost control and got violent with Dad. It wasn't in his nature. He didn't like fighting. He would be depressed for days after those "terrible nights," but he couldn't help it. He was dealing with Dad's insanity, and there was no other way to deal with this insanity except to go insane yourself, especially when you are only thirteen and don't realize that your dad is a very sick man.

It affected us all that way. It would be embarrassing the next day with the realities of what had happened the night before. We would feel ashamed. But we were driven to rage night after night. We were getting increasingly tired and less and less tolerant.

Typically, bad things happened on Thursdays, when Dad would have the allowance he gave to himself to spend. Not much, thirty-five dollars a week, but naturally, he spent his money on booze. Booze was everything to him. It was the most important thing in his life.

This Thursday was especially bad. Father was his target during dinner again. He left with my dad calling him a pig. By midnight things were real scary. Maureen and I were hiding in our closet. He kept coming into our room screaming, "Where the fuck are they?"

Mom sneaked in our room and whispered, "Come up to Danny's room." Danny wasn't sleeping either. Dad was on a rampage, breaking things, throwing food out of the refrigerator. We all got into Danny's closet. There was a latch on the inside, so we could lock ourselves in. It was big enough for the four of us plus an old cedar chest and a chest of drawers. We all huddled together listening to the crazy man downstairs. There was a crack in the floor, so we could watch Dad when he stumbled into the garage to get another beer.

"When I grow up, I'm never going to drink," I said.

"Me neither," Danny said. "Never."

"When I get married, it's going to be so wonderful," said Maureen.

Mom was silent. What was she going to do? She had little choice. She was caught in this pitiful situation; caught between her sense of honor, commitment, faith and reality.

We heard Dad come into Danny's room. I got so scared, I started hyperventilating.

There were two other closets. He opened them both. "Wha' the fuck?" he said. "Mommy! Where are you?" he ranted. He came to our closet. He tugged at the latch. We were all shaking. He couldn't open the door. It didn't enter his mind that we were in there. "Fuck this. I'll just sit here and wait!" We could peek at him through the crack in the door. He sat on the end of Danny's bed, his legs wrapped around each other, his beer in his hand. We stayed in the closet most of the night. I sort of liked it in there. Inside the cedar chest were wonderful treasures. Lots of old Japanese kimonos my dad had brought home from Tokyo after the war. There were quilts and tablecloths. I made a little bed for myself in the corner. Maureen, Danny and Mom slept sitting up on the cedar chest.

Dad fell into a mumbling sleep. Just when you'd think he was out, he'd wake with a jump and start yelling, "You asshole, prick."

Mom would let out a pained little high-pitched "Oh." She hated swearing, yet it was all around us. The insanity would cause us all to say things we knew were bad.

Dad started coughing. We all woke up. He would start coughing and coughing and coughing till finally no sound would come out. We peeked through the crack in the door. His body was in a convulsion. He put his hands over his head to let some air into his chest cavity. Saliva dripped in long strings from his mouth and nose. His face was beet-red and sweaty, the veins in his neck protruding. He lost his balance and fell back onto the bed still coughing incessantly. He looked like he was going to die. Mom was just about to run out and help him, when he stopped. I felt relief and disappointment. I knew I was bad for having these thoughts. I didn't want him to die; and, yet, I did. I loved him, but life would be easier without him. He had these "coughing jags" a lot. I guess between two packs of cigarettes a day and all the booze, plus his practically nonexistent diet, something had to give. There must be a lot of nutrition in beer, because he lived on it and little else.

Around 4 A.M. Dad got up and stumbled downstairs. He had given up on us. He passed out in his bed. We all sneaked into our own beds. Mom got into bed with me. I went to the bathroom first.

The next night Dad didn't come home at all. At 3 A.M. the phone rang. My heart pounded. No one ever called this late. It was the police. "We have your husband down here at the station. He's been booked on a 502—drunk driving. Do you want to come pick him up or leave him here?"

Of course, Mom went to get him. That was her job. Pick him up. Keep the secret. If he stayed in jail, it would be in the papers, and then everyone would "know." Couldn't have that. His humiliation would be our humiliation. As long as he did not get caught, as long as Mom and the family covered up for him, we continued to enable him to drink. We made it easy.

Mom was becoming a nervous wreck. "You've really done it now," she said angrily to Dad. "This is it. I mean it. I've had it."

Something in her tone must have made Dad believe that *this* time she might really mean it. Dad promised he would stop drinking. He was "on the wagon."

7

The nights became peaceful again. My bed-wetting was down to four nights a week instead of seven, but the days were nerve-racking. Dad was tense and edgy. His body was in pain and craving booze. He yelled at us and still demanded perfection. He would not accept a "half-assed job." After about two months of sobriety he was starting to become civil. We had Thanksgiving at Auntie Helen's, and Dad didn't have a drink.

I looked forward to Christmas. I loved putting up the tree and wrapping packages. I loved the music and the food. It was magic to me. Dad was feeling pretty good. He even bought Mom a Christmas present from his allowance money. We always had Christmas dinner at our house. We had Auntie Helen and her family, Uncle Ralph and his family and, of course, Father. All together there were about eighteen people. Dad was getting a free turkey as a bonus from the brewery. On Christmas eve we planned to go to Midnight Mass, even Dad. We all had new outfits. I was so excited. Dad only had to work a half day on Christmas eve.

When six o'clock came around and he still wasn't home, I started getting a sick feeling in my stomach. He wouldn't, I thought. The house looked so pretty and peaceful. This was going to be the best Christmas ever! (Or was it?)

At 10 P.M. the doorbell rang long and loud. It was unmistakable. No one else rang it that way. "Ho, ho, ho," he slurred.

Oh, no, I thought. Why tonight? Dad was sloppy drunk. There had been a Christmas party at work. He had not been able to resist. I now know he couldn't have resisted.

Dad missed Midnight Mass. He passed out in the kitchen. Christmas morning he started drinking eggnog laced with whiskey. After present opening, he went back to bed feeling sick. At 2 P.M. he woke up feeling mean. Father was the first guest to arrive. "Don't ya have anywhere else to go?" my dad asked edgily. "First one here, first one to finish dinner. Huh, George?"

Father said nothing. He didn't want to rock the boat. Mom and I felt nervous. It was awful when Father was Dad's target. Everyone else arrived. Dad was the perfect bartender. One for you, one for me.

Mom asked Father to carve the turkey. (Dad was too drunk.)

"Look at the way he butchers the meat," Dad said. "It's because he's in such a hurry to eat it. Gulp, gulp, and he'll be back for seconds."

We all pretended not to hear. Dad ate nothing. He drank. He left the room a lot, which meant he was drinking whiskey. By the time everyone left that night, Dad was looking and sounding real ugly. My mother was putting leftovers in the refrigerator.

"What! Are ya saving a few potatoes? Throw them out," he shouted.

"No, they'll be good tomorrow," Mom said.

"I don't want any fuckin' leftovers in my refrigerator!" *Slam!* He threw the potatoes against the wall.

"Stop it! Please!" my mother screamed.

I don't know how she put up with it. It was the first of many times Dad would try to quit. We had had such expectations. Did we really believe in our hearts that he wouldn't drink? He had let us down so many times before. Dad was ill with a chronic, incurable disease. We just thought he didn't love us enough to stay sober.

8

The year continued as before. Dad was drunk most nights. We were getting very little sleep. Danny graduated from eighth grade. Maureen graduated from high school. Dad didn't make Danny's graduation. Danny got a camera. Maureen got a stereo. Dad also gave Maureen a fifty-dollar bill which he had saved from his allowance. He was good about things like that. He told her she could spend it on anything she wanted. She bought a pair of fifty-dollar shoes. None of us could believe that any pair of shoes could possibly cost fifty dollars. Maureen won an award at graduation for typing and shorthand. Because of her skills and the fact that she was a real knockout to look at, she landed a great job on her very first interview. She became executive secretary to the president of Pacific Southwest Airlines. Dad was real proud of her and bragged to everyone about her job. He liked his kids to do well. She was happy. She had some money to buy clothes and cosmetics. She cut her hair short in the latest style and bleached it platinum blond. (I later copied her hair color.) I remember walking down the street with her one day. She was wearing a baby-pink sheath and high spike heels. She had enormous breasts, small hips and a flat stomach. She was literally stopping traffic.

Maureen was "feeling her oats." She looked good, she felt good, she was happy. She was no longer the skinny, flat-chested jock with the runny nose. Now she was beautiful, popular and in love with a great guy. She had been head cheerleader her last year of high school, which brought her out of her shell. Her circle of friends comprised the best and the brightest in the neighboring towns of Hillsborough and San Mateo. They all liked to be around Maureen with her quick wit and infectious laugh. She loved to dance and have fun.

She didn't bring her friends around our house at all, but she was always running and going here and there—Bimbo's 365 Club, The Top of the Mark, the Tonga Room at the Fairmont Hotel. I'd hear her talk about Roberta and Jerry, Jim, Pat, Phil and Sandy. They went out to dinner, dancing, ball games. Maureen was having a wonderful time.

I was real proud of Maureen. We had shared a room all our lives, but we weren't as close as I would have liked us to be; not like we are today. I was the bratty little sister, always peeking, always in the way. My things always took over the whole room, and she complained about it a lot. Dad must have felt threatened by her sexuality, because when he drank these days, she was always the target. He didn't like to see his girls grow up. She looked better than she ever had. Up until now she always wore her Mercy High uniform; but suddenly, in one summer, she was transformed into this blond bombshell. Dad suddenly realized that every man in town was looking at her, and it made him real crazy.

Maureen continued to have a grand time. She and Bill were inseparable. I would peek out our bedroom window when I would hear them come home and watch them kissing and kissing and kissing. I loved to watch them kiss. Bill was crazy about Maureen. I liked Bill. Maureen was going to have a nice life with him.

Dad must have been peeking, too. He didn't like what he saw. He hated Bill. Maureen came in one night after one of her dates with Bill. She was in love. She looked beautiful. She was wearing a powder-blue tight wool sheath and high spike heels. There was a shawl at the collar that created a turtleneck look and then the rest of the shawl draped down her perfectly shaped backside. "Where've you been?" Dad asked belligerently. "Kilmartin getting his jollies with you?" he asked.

"Oh, be quiet," Maureen said.

"Bullshit!" he roared. "You're gonna give it all away, you asshole," he said. "He doesn't care about you. He just wants to cop a little feel."

"I love Bill," Maureen said.

"Oh, she loves him." He was making fun of her. "Isn't that sweet! You asshole! He'll just take what he wants and then leave you high and dry!"

"You're just drunk," Maureen said; and she brushed past him.

"Drunk! My ass!" he roared. He hated to be called a drunk. He followed her into our bedroom. Maureen was starting to get undressed.

"Get out! I'm getting undressed," she screamed.

"I will not!" he roared.

"What! Do you want to see? Is that why you came in here?" she said hysterically.

"You little cunt," he said. He didn't want "to see." It was just his way of keeping her in her place by beating her down. Maybe then she wouldn't leave him.

My mother screamed. "Stop that language."

"I hate him! I hate him and his filthy mind!" Maureen yelled. "I can't wait to leave this house."

Dad lunged toward Maureen. She tried to stop him. He was too strong. She scratched at his face with her long fingernails. He was bleeding. He grabbed for her hair.

I screamed, "Stop it!" at the top of my lungs.

Mom tried to pull Dad back. Maureen went for him scratching, hitting. He fell to the ground. Maureen kicked him hard, screaming, "You ruin everything! I hate you." Dad groaned. Something was hurting him real bad. Mom started to drag Dad out of our room. Maureen was sobbing and hysterical. She had lost control and hated herself for it. She loved Dad, but he had pushed her to the edge. I couldn't stop shaking. It was like a nightmare that never went away.

As long as Maureen was out with her friends, life was wonderful. As soon as she came back home, reality hit. Around Dad she was "nothin'," a "big zero." When she was with her friends, she was terrific. No wonder she couldn't wait to get out. Bill was her ticket to heaven. Life with him would be everything that life with Dad was not. The thought of leaving Mother alone with Dad gave Maureen great pain. As the eldest she felt it was her responsibility to protect Mom from the life that was surely killing her. Mom was suffering badly from the constant emotional beatings. She often told both Maureen and me to "stand up straight, stomach in, chest out. Good posture is important," yet she walked with her head held down in shame, her eyes averted from any direct contact. She wanted no one to see the pain and sadness she carried with her.

Maureen dreamed that after she married Bill she'd be able to afford to take Mom out of her environment. It was becoming increasingly clear that Mom had to get out or she would die. None of us ever realized how strong and committed Mom really was. She could and would take a lot more before she gave up.

Dad's ribs were fractured again. Mom dragged Dad to the bedroom. She had been through this before. At least there was something she could do. She wrapped Dad's ribs with an Ace bandage and put him to bed. Tomorrow they would go to the hospital for an X ray to be sure it was nothing worse.

Maureen didn't apologize to Dad. She was angry. She was upset over what happened but felt Dad had "asked for it." Who could blame her? We were all pushed to our breaking points night after night. It was natural that it sometimes erupted into physical violence.

Maureen and Bill went out every night. It was her escape. I wished I had somewhere to go at night, someplace to get away. Maureen and Bill would sit in Bill's '52 green Chevy across the street. Bill called it the "Green Weenie." You can imagine how my dad felt about that. He didn't want Maureen around *any* "weenies," especially green ones. I watched them kissing more and more often and discovered that Danny had been peeking out the breakfast room at them also.

"Did you see Maureen and Bill making out last night?" Danny asked me. "I don't know when they come up for air." Danny laughed. Maureen's sexuality had us all curious and confused.

I wondered what it must feel like to be kissed. A couple of girls in my class had already been kissed. I didn't think it would ever happen to me. It didn't even feel right to think about it. Kissing was all tied up with sex, and I had the definite impression that sex was bad. I wasn't supposed to be thinking such things at my age. It wasn't normal; although I really didn't have a clue as to what "normal" was.

Without my cat Mitzi and my friend Sandy I would have had no one to talk with. They both provided sanity to my life. At ten years old, Sandy and I shared our dreams and most of our secrets. We still looked alike; the same height and weight (both skinny). We both had streaked blond shoulder-length hair that we now wore in high bouncy ponytails. We each had straight eyebrow-length bangs that we cut ourselves. (Sometimes we'd put hair-setting lotion on our bangs and style them into one large stiff curl on our foreheads.)

At school we wore the same uniform, we had exactly the same purses with handles made from safety pins we had linked together. We thought our purses were really cool. We tried to dress the same after school as often as we could; and for our Sunday clothes, we both chose the same Simplicity pattern and the same fabric and had our mothers make us exactly the same dresses. Father Monagle, our parish priest, called us "Fric and Frac."

Every summer I took Sandy on our family vacation with us. We spent two weeks in Lake Tahoe camping at Camp Richardson. I didn't have to worry so much about my dad with Sandy. She understood that he was edgy and angry a lot of the time. She also understood when he was drunk.

Dad was a great camper and taught us a lot; how to put up a tent and dig a trench around the outside in case of rain. That way the water would run off instead of seeping into the tent. We used railroad spikes instead of tent stakes because they were stronger. We learned to use a Coleman stove and helped to hang painting tarps from tree to tree to ensure privacy. We hung mirrors on trees for shaving and combing our hair. I admired Dad at these times. He knew a lot; he had common sense. Our campground was always the coziest and best looking. It was homey. Dad would try to "keep a lid on" his drinking when we were camping, and most of the time he was fun. He'd usually stay in that "just a little drunk" stage, but inevitably he'd go beyond and get plastered. I would be humiliated when this happened. Campsites have no walls in which to hide family secrets. Everyone in the campground could hear my father drunkenly carrying on. "You cocksucker" and "that asshole" sounded much louder and uglier in the outdoors.

Sandy and I would leave when he was like this. If it was daytime, we'd go to the beach and stare at all the dreamiest guys. They never noticed us. We were in our awkward stage, still in our first decade, skinny and chestless.

If Dad got drunk at night, we'd move our sleeping bags to another part of the woods and pretend we didn't know him. With Sandy I could laugh about Dad; I could tell her I hated him. She was very important to me. We had good times together. We did little-girl things, innocent, mischievous.

One day around Christmastime of that year Sandy and I sneaked my sister's bras out of her drawer. We put them on and stuffed them with Kleenex. I loved how I looked with bosoms. We had a plan.

"Mom?" I asked. "Sandy and I want to take the bus to San Francisco and go Christmas shopping. Honest, we'll be all right. The bus takes us right to Market Street. We'll get off and walk straight to the Emporium and then to Macy's at Union Square."

"I don't know," my mother said reluctantly.

"Please! We'll hold hands all the way," I pleaded. My mother gave in.

That Saturday Sandy and I put on our best Sunday outfits and took the bus to San Francisco. We got off the bus and went to the ladies' room. We both went into one stall together. I reached into my purse and pulled out two bras and two pairs of high-heels. We both put on the bras and stuffed as much toilet paper as we could fit into them.

"You look great," I told Sandy.

"So do you," she said to me.

We emerged from the bathroom with huge breasts and wobbled in our high-heels down Market Street to the Emporium. "Let's go see Santa Claus," I suggested. I was really hoping for a Vogue doll with a bunch of really neat doll outfits that year. We waited in line. My turn finally came. Even though I didn't believe in Santa Claus, I always got excited to see him anyway. It was my turn. I was sitting on Santa's lap with my huge, lumpy breasts and high-heels (with stuffed toes). I looked up, and there in front of me was Auntie Helen. Helen couldn't take her eyes off my brand-new breasts.

"Hi!" I said sheepishly. Auntie Helen never mentioned a thing. She was cool. She told us to be careful and have a nice day. Sandy and I ran to the bathroom and threw out all the toilet paper. We took off our high-heels (our feet were killing us anyway), and went back to being ten years old.

9

Every spring Dad coached the varsity baseball team for St. Robert's Catholic Grammar School. He was a great coach. His life had been about sports, and he really knew how to whip the boys into shape. It was one of the few times each year that I was really proud of him. Just before the team was picked, all the boys in my class would be real nice to me. I guess they thought if they got in good with the coach's daughter, they'd have a better chance of getting on the team. I had no influence with my dad at all, but I enjoyed the attention from the boys. Dad sobered up pretty much during baseball practice. On the sober days, of course, he would be real edgy with his players. Nobody was good enough for him. No matter how hard they tried, they were "a pack of assholes." They all tried to please him. They would stay at practice till it got dark. They all tried harder and harder; and, consequently, Dad had the best team in the league. Some days Dad would show up for practice drunk. The boys on the team were young and didn't understand that Dad was an alcoholic; they thought he was real moody. They knew the best thing to do was to put out 100 percent during practice so he wouldn't yell at them so much. If Dad was sober, I would come to practice and sit in the grandstands and watch. Even though he would yell and call them terrible names, there was something beautiful about watching him pull the performance out of the boys. He had one star . . . his protégé. His name was Wally, and he was an incredible pitcher. Wally lived around the corner from us, and we played together all our lives. Wally really liked my dad; and because he was such a great athlete, Dad couldn't find any reason to yell at him. Wally was the first to arrive at practice and the last to leave. Whenever we drove past Wally's house, he was out front throwing a baseball against the porch and catching it. At practice Wally would throw and Dad would hit to all the players at their positions. It was catching practice.

One day Dad arrived at practice very drunk. He started hitting balls to the boys. In his drunkenness he took a swing and knocked himself off balance. The bat whipped around and hit him full force on the heel. He fell to the ground. "Son of a bitch," Dad groaned as he fell on home plate. The boys panicked. One of them ran across the street to our house.

"Mr. Mahoney's been hurt," the boy said excitedly to my mother.

Mom and I ran over to the park. Dad was still lying on the ground. Mom had some of the boys help her carry him to the car. She took Dad to the hospital. He had broken his heel. He was put in a leg cast, and he was not able to work for the next six months.

The first few weeks Dad was home were awful. He was in pain with the broken heel and his entire body ached from alcohol withdrawal. He was restless and angry, mad at himself for getting hurt, and he lashed out at us because we were around. After a month his body stopped demanding booze and we started to settle into the most normal period of my childhood. It was wonderful to feel so relaxed around the house. Dad took over the housework and he was good at it.

Sober, Dad was a perfect housekeeper. The house looked neat, the laundry was folded, the garbage tied in tidy little packages and placed outside. The windows were washed, and every night Dad made some wonderful stew or meatloaf concoction. We started singing again. Dad was still very demanding, but we were more eager to comply. We were getting good sleep at night and weren't feeling exhausted during the day.

Dad hung a calendar and gave us our orders for chores. We were rated on speed and excellence. Danny got up at 6 A.M. to trim the lawn and water the plants. Maureen and I were awakened at the same time. Maureen ironed for an hour and I cleaned our room and the kitchen. At the end of each week Dad put a gold star on the calendar next to the name whose output was the best. We all wanted to please Dad, so we each put out our maximum in order to win the star.

I loved Dad a lot during this time. I hoped it would last forever. It was great to be a normal family. I invited Sandy to sleep over a few times just to show off. Mom was a lot calmer and she started playing the piano again. She even seemed to be liking Dad.

During this time Dad, though on crutches, continued to coach the baseball team. They won the championship. Dad was a real hero at that last game. All the team members threw their hats into the air and picked him up and carried him on their shoulders in a victory march. He looked genuinely happy. I was so proud I cried, and Dad was sober.

10

It was 1957, the "normal year," because Dad was sober. I was eleven years old and starting to feel relaxed; not so nervous. I had tried hard during this time to improve my grades. It was easier to study at home when he wasn't drinking and the nights were quiet. My grades got better, and Dad told me if I got straight A's, he'd give me five dollars. I worked really hard at school and got all A's and one A minus. Dad wouldn't give me the five dollars. God! It ticked me off! I thought he was very unfair. After all, my A minus was in application. How much more could I have applied myself? No one I ever knew of got straight A pluses. He promised and he broke his promise. There was no way to please him. If only I could get his approval, maybe he'd be happier and wouldn't want to drink again.

Shortly after baseball season Mom announced she was pregnant. I couldn't figure out why she wasn't ecstatic. Besides being well into her forties, she hated bringing another child into this house of horrors. Even though Dad had remained sober during these last months, we all knew deep in our hearts his sobriety wasn't permanent. We were right.

"Son of a bitch," Dad said as he stumbled into the house. My heart sank. The calm was over. Dad was back at work, and the temptation of being surrounded by all those bottles of beer was too much for him to resist. Mom's face looked pained. She was six months pregnant.

The long, loud, ugly nights returned. We were back into our reality. This was normal. Sobriety was abnormal. My bed-wetting became an every-night event again. On August 20, 1957, mother gave birth to my new brother. Dad drove her to the hospital, and he was drunk. The baby was named Michael Patrick Mahoney. Dad was proud of the name because it was so Irish. I was excited. Maybe Dad wouldn't drink so much now that we had a new baby, I thought. While Mom was in the hospital, Dad visited every friend and relative we had, to have celebratory drinks over the birth. He came home plastered.

I couldn't stand the idea of staying alone at our house with Dad being so drunk. In his drunkenness he wouldn't do the little things, like turn on the lights. He'd sit in the dark at the back of the house drinking, smoking and talking to himself about all those "big assholes." I spent the next night at Sandy's; Danny stayed with his friend Mike; Maureen spent the weekend with her friend Roberta.

I was fascinated with my new little brother. Mom nursed him, and I loved to watch. It was so beautiful. Mom always hid in her bedroom when she nursed, because she was so shy. She probably didn't appreciate my barging in on her, but I was too curious to stay out. Dad continued to drink but was not as belligerent as usual. The baby had a slightly calming effect on the family.

It wasn't a great environment for a new baby nor was it a good environment for a mother with a new baby, but it did seem good for Dad. Now Dad had someone to listen to his all-night mumblings. Dad sat next to the crib with a beer in his hand and talked to baby Michael for hours. Michael listened attentively and appreciatively. He never talked back, he never argued, he never became frustrated or angry. The baby accepted Dad as he was. He liked his company unless Dad started yelling; then Michael would cry. But usually Dad just talked on and on and on. Michael could sleep through it; and when he awakened, Dad was still there droning on in his drunkenness. Michael was Dad's new friend; his only friend. It was some consolation to Mom. She felt so bad about bringing another poor child into this life; but she knew it was God's will, and she would do the best job of raising Michael she knew how.

Michael was a darling baby. He had blond hair and big blue shiny alert eyes with luscious long eyelashes. I just loved him. But now there were new pressures at home. Mom stopped working to take care of Michael. Without Mom's salary, there was no money for extras. Dad's paycheck only covered the essentials. We had new rules: Use only a little butter; save the butter wrapper to be used for greasing pans, do not waste anything; all leftovers are to be eaten; turn off all lights if they are not necessary. We were forced to eat Father's rancid meat. The smell made me sick and drove Dad into a rage. He seemed to relish having reasons to be angry with Father. Dad was the big bully again. Mom was more trapped than ever.

Again I retreated into a fort in the corner of my bedroom. My paper dolls were replaced by a phonograph and two albums—*Gypsy* and *My Fair Lady*. I played them over and over until every pause was memorized.

> *Look at her, a prisoner of the gutter*
> *Condemned by every syllable she utters*
> *In fact, she should be taken out and hung*
> *For the cold-blooded murder of the*
> *English tongue.*

I was Rex Harrison, complete with accent, or Ethel Merman (my favorite star).

> *Some people can be content*
> *Playin' bingo or payin' rent.*
> *That's peachy for some people*
> *Who don't know they're alive.*
> *But I-I-I at least gotta try.*

I sang both musicals over and over. I escaped into their stories. I was Eliza Doolittle pulled out of the gutter and placed into that fancy house, or Mama Rose fighting to make a better life for her kids.

As friends and relatives dropped by to see the new baby, Dad would force me to sing for them. 'Stand up, Suzanne, sing 'All I want is a room somewhere.' '" I didn't want to. My musicals were a private fantasy to me. Alone in my room I had no limitations. In front of the relatives

I felt naked. They couldn't hear what I heard in my head. They couldn't hear the orchestra swelling and the chorus of voices behind me. They couldn't see the costumes and the lights.

"Please don't make me, Daddy," I pleaded.

"Oh, for Chrissakes. You can't shut her up in her room, and now she clams up," he said disgustedly. I ran to my room crying and embarrassed.

This happened over and over. Sometimes I'd sing, other times I wouldn't. Dad liked to show off his children. He was proud of us, but I was at that vulnerable age; just entering adolescence and very unsure of myself.

I did enjoy my new little brother, Michael.

Sandy and I would take him for long walks in his stroller after school. It was a great excuse to get out of the house, as well as a good excuse to stop and talk to people. The neighbors would stop me and say, "Oh, isn't he cute," or, "How old is he now?" The same worked with the boys in town. I would push Michael in front of Wally's house. I always knew he'd be out in front with possibly the bonus of the other school "Dreamboat," Mike.

"Let's take a look at coach Ducky's new kid," Wally said.

"Yeah, I have to take him on a walk every day," I said. I didn't have to. I was just too insecure to tell them I wanted to. Wally was so cute and I had a big crush on Mike.

"Hey, Mahoney," Wally said. "I hear you know Phyllis and Judy." They were hot stuff at the nearby public school. They both had big breasts and wore tight sweaters and lots of lipstick. I had met them recently and was thrilled when they seemed to take an interest in me. I thought they were wonderful. My mother thought they were fast.

"Yeah, they're good friends of mine," I lied.

"Fix me up with them. Okay?" Wally said.

"Sure, I'll see what I can do." I wished Wally would have been interested in me, but this was better than nothing. At least it gave me a chance to talk to him. Why would he be interested in me anyway? I was skinny and stupid.

11

On Christmas eve, 1958, Bill came to ask Dad for his daughter's hand in marriage. I was twelve years old, Michael was two, Danny was sixteen. It wasn't exactly as Bill had planned it, although he'd been around the family long enough to understand the unpredictability.

Christmas eve was never a good night for us. "Silent Night" was usually more like "Violent Night." Dad came home after the brewery Christmas party plastered. He stumbled and fell into the Christmas tree, as usual. Mom and I ran to catch his dead weight before he ruined everything. "Son of a bitch," he slurred. We pulled and dragged him to the couch. Danny came running downstairs to help. His face looked tight and pained.

"Maybe he'll pass out," Mom said desperately.

"Wha' the fuck! Gimme some whiskey," he demanded. He was out of it, didn't know where he was or who was around him.

I felt so nervous. Mom and I were trying to prepare for the big Christmas dinner tomorrow night but afraid to put the good china on the table for fear he'd fall into it or deliberately break it.

Maureen's hands were shaking. This was to be the biggest night of her life and it was not starting out well.

At 8 P.M. the doorbell rang. Maureen raced to the door. "Hello, gorgeous," Bill said to her. He was beaming; full of anticipation and excitement. This was the most important night of his life also. "Where's your dad?" Bill asked enthusiastically.

"Well," Maureen stammered; then she stepped aside. There in front of them lay my dad passed out on the couch with his false teeth lying on his chest. He was snoring loudly and mumbling obscenities. With each breath his lips quivered and flapped together.

Bill stood over Dad bewildered and deflated. He had wanted to do this properly. A formal request to the father was now out of the question. "Maybe you should ask my mother instead," Maureen said sheepishly.

Mom was upstairs in Danny's room sitting alone in the dark, smoking a cigarette and holding her rosary beads. She lifted her head as Bill entered the room and turned on the light.

"I'd like permission to ask your daughter to marry me," he said to my mother.

Her eyes went liquid. "How wonderful," she said softly. "I wish you both every happiness." Then she hugged him. "I couldn't ask for a better son-in-law."

Mom was truly happy for her daughter. Now Maureen could have a normal life. She would live the type of life Mom had dreamed of for herself.

12

Things were getting exciting around our house. Maureen and Bill were getting married that June and we were starting to make all the arrangements. Bill came from a family that was everything we were not. Bill's father owned his own business. They lived in a beautiful, sprawling house in Hillsborough with lots of trees and acreage. Hillsborough was where all the rich people lived. They even had a swimming pool. Bill's mother had platinum hair and wore beautiful clothes. They drove a Cadillac. They seemed so perfect. My parents had never met Bill's parents, but the time was now coming when this event had to take place. I'm sure Maureen had been avoiding it as long as possible. My mom arranged a dinner party at our house. Oh, God, I thought. This is going to be awful.

My dad had been saving money from his allowance to pay for Maureen's wedding. They also planned to take out a loan from the bank. Irish people place a lot of value on weddings and funerals. My dad was not going to be outdone by anyone. Maureen's wedding was going to be the best. It also gave him lots of reasons to celebrate. He would buy "a round for the house" at Newell's Bar "to celebrate my daughter's wedding." Good ole Ducky! He'd come home good and drunk every night. "I love you, Maureen," he'd say sloppily. "I told all my pals how much I love ya."

Maureen would tick off another day on her calendar. The countdown to freedom had begun. Not only was she getting out, but she was going to be "doing it." I was just starting to feel sexual stirrings in my body, and Sandy and I spent a lot of time wondering what "doing it" was and what it felt like. I knew my sister was a virgin and would be until her wedding night. We were all real Catholic, as was everyone we knew. Sex before marriage was forbidden; it just wasn't done. There was no sure-fire form of protection in those days; so even if you could somehow *morally* rationalize premarital sex, the risk of pregnancy was too great. Besides, it was better to save yourself for your husband; to prove yourself a virgin by the bloodstain in your conjugal bed; the stain of proof. You were his and only his till death do you part. It was all part of the romance I was raised with. The importance of being a "good girl." More than anything I wanted to be a "good girl," and my sister, coming from the same mold, was a "good girl" too.

The wedding showers started. Maureen received the most beautiful gifts; new towels, toasters, kitchen equipment. She had registered her china, crystal and silver patterns at the gift store in Burlingame; and because she was the first child to be married in the whole family, everyone went all out. Maureen was moving to a whole new life. No longer would she live "the secret." She would have respectability and beautiful things, and I was happy for her. I fantasized that she would let me live with them. Maureen was working and living at home, so she was able to save money to buy new furniture. (Dad did make her pay room and board. "A dollar a day." It was a saying we had come to hear often in his drunken tirades.) Maureen and Bill would go to Sloane's Furniture store in San Francisco and pick out their new furniture. After shopping they would go out for a drink. Maureen discovered that she "loved" martinis. "Martinis are okay," she said. "Only bums drink beer."

The big dinner between the Mahoneys and the Gilmartins was coming. My mother was beside herself with nervousness. She wanted to make a good impression on Maureen's new in-laws. What if Dad acted up? Bill knew about Dad but hadn't told his parents about him. They were a little uptight to begin with. Mother and I both secretly felt that coming to our house in San Bruno was a come-down for them. We were easily impressed with anyone who seemed to have a normal life, let alone people who had money.

Mom had Father get us a beautiful prime rib roast. With it she would serve mashed potatoes and natural juices, fresh shucked peas, broiled tomatoes and her special lemon icebox dessert. Please don't spoil it, Daddy, I kept saying to myself over and over. I wanted it to be perfect for my mother. Her life was so difficult. I wanted her to be happy.

The evening arrived. The Gilmartins were on time and dressed beautifully. Both fathers wore suits. My dad brought out a bottle of chilled champagne. "Let's toast to the happy couple." Oh, no, I thought. Everyone sipped champagne and made polite talk. Mr. Gilmartin said how proud and happy he was to be gaining such a beautiful new daughter into his family. I loved him right away. He had a gentle twinkle in his eye. He looked like he must be the most wonderful father. My dad didn't say anything about Bill. Dad was "on" though, and he was funny. He had the best sense of humor and the ability to charm the entire room if he wanted to. He told the joke about Elizabeth Taylor waking up one morning, yawning and saying, "I feel like a new man." Everyone laughed. A lot of his other jokes had punchlines that made fun of ethnic groups; niggers, wops, gooks, shines, dagos. He was a real Archie Bunker, but everyone laughed. I didn't like the ethnic humor; but I had been raised with this language, so I didn't react to it.

The dinner party made its way from the living room to the dining table. By now, everyone had had a couple of glasses of champagne, except me and Danny and, of course, Michael. Dad opened the wine. His eyes were starting to get a little glassy, but he was still under control; and he was being so nice.

"Mrs. Gilmartin, you look so beautiful," he gushed. "May I pour you some wine, Mr. Gilmartin," he said.

"Please, call me Gil, Ducky."

It was going well. Dad was trying real hard. I loved him for that. Mom was flushed. She had red blotches on her neck, so I knew she was concerned; but she looked beautiful. Her skin turned a beautiful pink when she was flushed; and her once-red, now-turning-white, permed hair made her look like a creampuff.

The prime rib was delicious. Everyone was enjoying himself. Mr. Gilmartin made a toast. "To my darling children, may you have health, happiness and a long life together."

My father made a toast. "Here's to getting it up and keeping it up."

Ha! Ha! Ha! Ha! we all laughed nervously. Maureen turned white. Dad was getting drunk. Danny and I kept kneeing each other under the table. I got up to help my mother clear the dishes and get dessert. We were coming to the finish line. So far, pretty good. Dad was entertaining the Gilmartins with old Butcher Town stories. Something about his ol' buddy Beechie Bozio. "That son of a bitch could beat the shit outa anybody," I heard him say. "So I said, 'Kiss my ass!' " Dad said. Dad was starting to make my mother nervous. We all knew that any moment he'd start telling the story about the woman with the big tits.

Mom ran into the dining room. "Dessert, everyone?" she asked manically. Her face was now beet red. "This was my mother's recipe. I've always loved it. The kids love it, too. It's made with Pet Milk, so it's not too fattening." She was talking a mile a minute, trying to not leave any openings for my dad.

Father had been quiet all evening, trying not to "rock the boat" with Dad. "This is swell, Marion," he said. "Such a nice dinner." Everyone agreed.

"Wonderful."

"Lovely."

"Delicious."

"Do you like Mommy?" Dad asked. His jaw was starting to get loose. He was now talking to anyone. Danny and I pushed our knees together. Oh, God, here he goes, I thought. "Sometimes Mommy doesn't like me," he slurred. "Then I have to give her a little poke in the twat."

Oh, God! Oh, no, we all thought. "I'm tired," I said loudly. Immediately everyone at the table started.

"Yes, me too," Mr. Gilmartin said. "What a lovely evening. Delicious. Oh, yes, I've got clients first thing in the morning. Have to get home and get some shut-eye. Ho! Ho!"

"Thank you so much, Marion," said Mrs. Gilmartin. Then they left.

"Good-night, Marion. I love you," Father said.

Maureen went out with Bill. Danny and I helped Mom with the dishes.

Dad sat at the dining table looking mean. His mood had changed. "Mr. Kilmartin can go shit in his hat," he said. Then came his ultimate putdown. "Two kind words! Big 0."

Dad thought he could wipe out Mr. Gilmartin by calling him a zero. In his drunkenness he always retreated to that deep dark place inside him, where we all go to bury our ugliest thoughts and deepest fears. What brought these feelings and emotions to the surface when he was drunk? That is the puzzling part of alcoholism. The self-hate disguised in accusations of others. Everything said to others is meant for themselves. When my dad would yell, "You're nothin' " or "Big 0," he really meant himself. He thought of himself as *NOTHIN'*. He dealt with it by drowning his low self-image with booze.

The evening was over. (Or was it just beginning?) We thought dinner was a success.

Dad went to bed, but we knew within three hours he'd be up again. Alcoholics can only go without a drink three to five hours before their bodies start to crave more alcohol. The craving awakens them. They need their fix.

After we finished the dishes I got into bed as fast as I could. My mother and I were both exhausted from the energy we had expended for the dinner. I wanted to get as much sleep as I could before Dad started in again. I didn't realize how little I expected from my life.

13

The night before Maureen got married, she cried and cried and cried. She was still feeling guilty leaving my mother alone with Dad. As the eldest she felt Mother needed her. She was afraid of what would happen to Mom when she wasn't there anymore. What she didn't understand, what none of us understood, was that Dad wanted to have Mommy all to himself. At one time he was the apple of her eye. When we came along, she gave more and more attention to us until, finally, there was a seething jealous rage inside him. He loved us but wanted things to be "the way they were in the beginning." He was the "baby" in a family of thirteen children, so he had never learned to be mature. Probably, if he weren't a drinker, my mother would have given her attention to him rather than to us; but as an alcoholic, he did not make himself very attractive. His natural maturation stopped the day he became a drinker. So, at fifty, he had the maturity of a twenty-five-year-old.

We all thought Maureen was crying because she suddenly wasn't sure about Bill. I was hoping she wouldn't change her mind. I was looking forward to her wedding. Mom had made me a beautiful white dotted-swiss dress with a lace empire waistline with pink ribbons running through it. I had pink satin pumps with a low heel and my first pair of nylon stockings. I also borrowed Sandy's sister's bra to wear under it. I didn't need one, but with everyone being so excited, I knew Mom wouldn't notice the bra strap showing through the back of my dress. She didn't.

The wedding was lovely. A big splash. A Nuptial Mass and reception at the Burlingame Women's Club. There was a live band and waiters walked around with hot canapés. There was cake, champagne and an open bar. Bill danced the wedding dance with Maureen with his lips planted on the side of her head. They were so much in love. Maureen looked radiant. Her wedding dress was all Alençon lace with a long train. Then Maureen changed into her going-away suit of watermelon wool with a big white picture hat and white kid gloves. They left for their honeymoon to Cuba. Airfare was cheap; she worked for an airline.

After the reception we had a big party at our house. Dad was plastered, but so were all the other relatives. Even my mother got a little tipsy. Danny had a couple of glasses of champagne. He liked it.

I went into "my" room and started to move my sister out. I couldn't wait to be alone in there. I had never had a space of my own.

Nothing changed much after Maureen's wedding. The nights continued to be loud and awful, but now there was one less person screaming. I loved having my own room and would stay in there for hours listening to my forty-fives and dreaming. With my dollar-a-week allowance I would buy the hottest record of the week; and as a result, I had quite a collection of forty-fives. I loved Tommy Sands and the Four Freshmen, the Everly Brothers, Ella Fitzgerald and Doris Day. I bought more soundtracks—*Camelot, Pal Joey, Oklahoma*. I would listen to them over and over till I knew every word, every nuance, every bit of dialogue. I loved music. It was my escape. I always excelled in music class, and it was the only part of my schoolday that I looked forward to. I was in choir and sang at Mass every Sunday and each Christmas. We sang Gregorian chant and Handel, "Dona Nobis Pacem," "Ave Maria" and The Hallelujah Chorus. Handel was my favorite, so joyous and exciting. I could hear the trumpets even when they weren't there. I felt full of love and peacefulness. I could forget my pain and sadness. I focused on only good things, "the good dad," my wonderful mother, our laughter and singing and dancing. I always got the lead in the Christmas play. I was the Blessed Virgin Mary. I spent hours daydreaming of being an actress and singing and dancing; but no one from San Bruno had ever done anything like that, so I kept my dreams to myself. Besides, my low self-esteem didn't allow me to ever seriously contemplate a career. That was for other people.

I couldn't wait to be through with eighth grade. I was still skinny and flat as a pancake. After much begging, Mom bought me a bra, but it was a training bra and made my already flat chest even flatter. I was the only girl in class who didn't have her period yet. The girls made fun of me. The boys laughed at my figure, especially Tommy.

"Hey, Mahoney," he'd say, "nice shape." He'd make a circle with his thumb and index finger and run it straight down through the air as if to say, "straight as a stick."

In 1959 Danny was seventeen and in his last year of high school. He was gorgeous. I adored Danny. He had the blond good looks of a Troy Donahue and was one of the nicest people in the world. Everyone liked him, especially the girls. He liked to laugh a lot.

Danny seemed to have it all; looks, charm, great wit and personality, fabulous physique. But Danny was troubled and full of self-doubt. He didn't think he was as smart as the next guy. He grew up being told he was a "big booby" and a "dummy." His inability to concentrate in school was evident in his grades. This further convinced him of his inadequacies.

Danny had the weight of the world on his shoulders. With Dad "out of it" so often, Danny felt responsible for the rest of the family. He was the peacekeeper, the rescuer; always trying to prevent the violence that erupted so frequently at home.

Danny still idolized his dad but needed some assurances from him. Just an occasional "atta boy" or a pat on the back to let him know Dad approved of him. But Dad's disease was too far gone. He was lost in his sea of booze and was unable to know his son needed him for reassurance. If Dad *wasn't* an alcoholic, he would have been there. Sober Dad would know and understand, but drunk Dad was selfish and thought only of himself and the next drink.

"You're such a natural athlete; why don't you apply yourself more?" Danny's basketball coach asked him.

"Oh, I just don't have the time," Danny answered. He couldn't believe in his heart that he might be as good an athlete as Dad. If he was, Dad would be more supportive. But Dad never came to one of Danny's games, and Danny took it as a signal that he wasn't very good. He was easily shot down, easily discouraged.

I was still wetting the bed every night. It was just another of those embarrassing secrets I kept to my self. To me it was normal, but by this time Danny had stopped.

Danny got the lead in his high-school play, *My Sister Eileen*. He walked around the house singing "Hell of a Wreck from Georgia Tech."

Mom and I went to opening night of the play. We were so excited. Danny was great. He was just as likable on stage as he was in person. We all applauded like crazy; and when it was over, everyone came up to my mother and told her how talented Danny was. It was great for Danny's self-esteem.

My mother was so proud as she accepted the compliments. "Thank you," she said. "Danny has always been such a good boy."

After the play Danny and a couple of friends stopped by our house to change. They came in the back door (Danny knew Dad was passed out in his bedroom) and went into the garage. I heard them and ran to tell Danny how good I thought he was in the play. He didn't like me barging in on him. They were all sitting on the stair drinking Dad's beer. I was surprised. "Get outa here," Danny said.

"If Dad knows you're drinking his beer, he'll be furious," I said.

"How's he going to know?" Danny asked.

I smiled. "I'll never tell." I was so crazy about Danny, I'd never do anything to get him into trouble. I also had big crushes on all his friends. Nope! My lips were sealed. I wouldn't even tell Mom.

Danny took a job that summer working nights at the Lucky Lager Brewery. He soon found out what Dad had always known: beer was free and everybody drank it. Danny wanted to make extra money to take some of the financial pressure off Mom. He was a good boy; kind and sensitive. He had inherited Dad's sense of fairness—everyone should do his part to contribute. He no longer wanted to ask Mom for money.

Nobody recognized it yet, but Danny had also inherited Dad's fondness for alcohol. He found there was lots of free time at the brewery. Three guys could do the job of one. They'd take turns; one guy would handle the line and the other two would go to the beer room and play cards. Danny joined the Dixie Cup Gang. By contributing five dollars a week, you could have whiskey whenever you wanted. Danny invited his friends to meet him after work. Free beer and whiskey. The next day they'd laugh and brag about not remembering. Danny had no idea blackouts were a sure sign of alcoholism. The disease had begun; but like all disease, you aren't aware of it at first.

Dad's baseball team won the championship again that year. It was a real triumph. Wally had graduated the year before and everyone thought it doubtful my dad could pull off another winner without him. But he did. He hollered and pushed and demanded perfection. Those boys that couldn't take it dropped out. The tough ones stayed. You had to be tough to stand up to Ducky Mahoney. But if you hung in there, he would occasionally give you a little pat on the back. Not much, not a big deal, but it was so hard won that the smallest display of encouragement would feel incredibly good. He liked winners. He didn't like "the pissants that give up." Something about his personality made you want to succeed for him. It was a look in his eye, something in his tone and body language. It was enough to make you work harder and harder. I craved it, too. In spite of everything. In spite of all the long, drunken belligerent, violent nights, I craved his approval. It was so hard to get. There was something about him that I knew, and Danny knew and Maureen knew that was great. We all loved him. We all hated him. We all wanted to be nothing like him and yet we wanted to be just like him. Because in this man, not the drunk man, but the man you rarely got to see, was an extremely talented, sensitive and funny person. When he wanted to, he could entertain a crowd, have them laughing from their bellies. After the Awards Night at St. Robert's school, everyone came up to me. "Gee, your dad's the greatest. He's so funny," they said. Yeah, I thought, a bundle of laughs. But I was proud. Oh, I wish he hadn't used the word *asshole* in front of the nuns, but the naughtiness of it made everyone laugh hysterically. I'm sure he did it on purpose. He confused me terribly.

14

I was really starting to like boys now, but they weren't very interested in me. I was "Ducky's daughter." I walked by Wally's house. His friend Mike was out in front with him. I had such a crush on Mike.

"Hey, when are you going to fix us up with Judy and Phyllis?" Wally asked.

"Why don't you come to my backyard Friday night," I said. "We're going to sleep outside in my tent."

"Hey, great," they said.

Now that I had committed myself, I had to invite Judy and Phyllis to stay over. I never invited anyone to stay at my house except Sandy. But it was worth the risk to spend time with Wally and Mike even if they weren't exactly coming to see me. Please, God, don't let Dad be drunk. Friday night came and Dad was snockered. I had a new crisis to deal with.

I told Judy and Phyllis that at the last moment my dad got real sick so we wouldn't be able to go inside to use the bathroom. Everything was going wrong. It was ten o'clock. Wally and Mike hadn't arrived. Terrible noises were coming from inside our house. "Oh, poor Dad. He's throwing up," I said nervously.

"That son of a bitch doesn't know his ass from a hole in the ground," Dad hollered from the kitchen.

"Ha! Ha! Ha! Ha!" I laughed manically.

"For crying out loud, will you just shut up!" my mom yelled back.

"Would you excuse me, please," I said too sweetly to Phyllis and Judy. I ran inside. "Mom! Please keep Dad quiet. We can hear everything he says outside," I whispered loudly.

"I'm trying to! He won't stop yelling, he won't go to sleep. He drives me crazy." She was exhausted.

Oh, God, I thought. I can't wait for this night to be over. I was so nervous about what Dad might do.

At midnight Wally and Mike arrived. It was real dark and all our candles had burned out. "Shhh! Be real quiet," I said. "If my parents know you're here, I'll really get into trouble," I said. My dad had finally passed out and I didn't want him to wake up. Every once in a while he would yell "cocksucker" or some other choice word from his sleep, but we all pretended not to hear him.

"Wanna make out?" Wally asked.

"Sure," I said. All of a sudden the tent went quiet. I couldn't see anything, but I could hear the sounds of inexperienced kissing. Lots of suction sounds, heavy breathing and little m-m-ms and o-o-ohs. I didn't know who was with whom. I do know that I ended up with the tent pole. I danced with it, held on to it, joked with it. The tent pole was my partner. I felt so humiliated being left out, I used the tent pole to make jokes. "Wow, you're a good kisser," I told it. "Stop that," I scolded. "Wanna dance, big boy?" I was dying to be kissed, but it wasn't going to happen that night.

For eighth-grade graduation Mom made me a beautiful white eyelet dress, lined with baby-pink polished cotton. I got a gold ankle bracelet that said SUZANNE. I loved it. I was happy to be finished with grammar school. Dad was too drunk to come to my graduation. I won the music award.

Danny joined the Navy that summer. Now Michael, two-and-a-half years old, would have his own room. It depressed me to see Danny go.

Now I'd be all alone. I loved Danny and knew I was going to miss him; but I understood his wanting to get out of the house. He signed up for a two-year stint. As a lark he tried out for the Navy basketball team. He was good; a natural. They drafted him. He couldn't believe it. After boot camp he would be transferred to Hawaii, where the team was based. He was excited. He had never traveled before; and when he got out of the Navy, he would have all the military benefits. With the G.I. Bill he'd be able to buy his first house.

We had a big party to send him off. All the relatives came. Dad got pretty drunk. He kept putting his arm around Danny and saying, "You're a good kid. I'm proud of you, son." Dad got very teary that night; and by the end of the evening, just looking at Danny would make his voice quiver. I went to my room and sat in my closet and cried. I felt so alone. Danny and Dad stayed up late drinking beer together. Danny wanted to be Dad's friend. What better way than to get drunk with him?

15

*A*dolescence was an exciting and confusing time for me. I enrolled in Mercy High School in September 1960, the same school my sister had attended. I was almost fourteen years old. Mercy was an all-girls Catholic school run by the Sisters of Mercy. Sandy enrolled at Capuchino, the public high school in San Bruno. It was upsetting to be separated from her. Sandy was my only friend and the only outsider who "knew" everything.

Mercy was a real culture shock for me. The school was an old converted mansion. The grounds were breathtaking; beautiful groves of oak trees, meticulously manicured rose gardens, fountains, statuary. I had never seen anything so beautiful. The school building seemed like a complete fantasy. The halls were oak paneled, chandeliers hung from the ceilings. The theater was the former ballroom with balconies and the most wonderful stage. I loved it. My mother went back to work to help pay for it.

I was thrilled with my new surroundings. What an opportunity. Here I was with all new people. A new city. No one knew that my father was the town drunk, and I was determined that no one ever would. Now I could have some dignity. I wasn't prepared for the type of wealth to which I was now exposed. My classmates would be delivered and picked up in limousines by their family chauffeurs. Everyone had a Cadillac. All the girls bought their clothes at Saks and I. Magnin. Most had received graduation gifts of jewelry; their first diamond or a ruby heirloom ring. I was intimidated. I pretty much kept to myself. I had no friends. How could I make friends? Eventually, you have to invite friends to your home. I was never going to do that. If they knew the truth, there would never be a chance of anyone liking me. Occasionally one of the girls would give a "tea" (they were big on teas at Mercy High). I was overwhelmed by the opulence of the homes of my classmates.

Most of them lived in Hillsborough, a wealthy area of the Peninsula, where Bill had grown up. Long driveways, gardens, multiroom mansions with staffs of people catering to their every need. So, this is how the other half lives, I thought. I wanted it. I wanted my biggest problem in life to be monthly cramps. It seemed as though rich girls got severe cramps every month. One of my classmates would scream and cry and lie on the floor writhing in pain each month with her period. Her parents would come running to school, as though she had malaria, to take her home to stay in bed until the pain subsided. That never happened to me. I wasn't allowed to stay home from school unless my illness took some drastic and unmistakable form, like chicken pox. I was invited to a couple of slumber parties. I was dying to go, but what if I wet the bed at one of those fancy houses?

Mom decided to help me do something about my bed-wetting. She called the Nite-Dri Company. "Bed-wetting is just a habit," the representative said. "We've figured out how to break this habit. You put this screen covered with a pillowcase on your bed. The screen is so sensitive to moisture that one drop will set off the alarm bell and the lightbulb. You will wake up, turn off the alarm, run to the bathroom, urinate, wash your face with cold water (to be sure you are really awake), then change the pillowcase on the screen, turn off the light and go back to sleep. After this happens for a period of time, you will become conditioned to waking up before you urinate; and then you will no longer wet the bed," he stated proudly.

I felt uncertain but was willing to try. The idea of wetting the bed at a friend's house horrified me. What if I still wet the bed when I was married? I had to try this, crazy as it sounded.

Wouldn't it have been wonderful if the sales rep from the Nite-Dri company *really* understood the problem? That bed-wetting is an indication of some buried trauma; a cry for help and attention. Wouldn't it have been wonderful if he could have suggested (in addition to his bed-wetting machine) that I also go to therapy or to a social worker or to Alateen? If this man had been properly informed, he might have been able to not only help me cure the effect, but also get to the cause. But no one understood therapy back then. You only went to a shrink if you were a schizophrenic, suicidal or had been "shell shocked" in the war. No one realized you could get shell shocked by living with an alcoholic.

To my surprise, in two short months a lifetime habit was broken. The crazy screen/alarm contraption worked! I stopped wetting the bed at last, but the disease was going to find another outlet.

Mercy was a tough school academically. I had been able to pull off decent grades at St. Robert's Grammar School, but now our all-night drunken tirades were having a real negative effect on me academically. We had four hours of homework a night. I was unable to keep up. I would fall asleep in class and be awakened by a hard rap on the knuckles.

"Miss Mahoney, that will be a demerit," Sister Jean said sternly.

We were on a demerit system. Seven demerits and you were expelled. Demerits were given for bad conduct, missed homework or breaking uniform codes (no short skirts, no substitutions, no dirty shoes, *no wearing makeup*). I couldn't keep up with the homework. I loved French. My teacher said I had a wonderful accent. "Why won't you do your homework?" she asked. There was no quiet place in the house to memorize the French words. I started cheating. I didn't want to get thrown out of this wonderful school. I learned to peek from under my hair to the side and look at the paper of whoever was sitting next to me and copy the answers. I figured anyone was smarter than me. I was managing a low C average. Enough to keep me in school, but nothing to garner the favor of my teachers. I became more and more isolated. Not only was I "out of it," but I was also getting labeled "the dummy" or "stupid."

Where could I go at night to find four hours of quiet to study? Even if I sat in my closet, I could hear Dad's drunkenness through the door. Eventually, I would run out to see if everything was okay.

My closet was such an important place in the house for me. I felt safe in there. Secure. I had been hiding in my closet all my life. It protected me from the violence. Dad was usually too drunk to remember to look for me there. It was the place where I could sit and fantasize; I wish life were different . . . I wish Mom and Dad wouldn't fight . . . I wish I were smarter . . . I would dream in my closet.

To this day I feel best when I am in a small room. I now see myself as a sad little girl in her closet, but I was safe there. I could sit in the quiet and the darkness and try to figure things out. I always felt so responsible. I felt it was my job to try to "keep the peace," keep Mom and Dad from fighting; keep them from doing something awful to each other.

I wanted so much to be a good student. It was so humiliating to be thought of as dumb. It affected my self-esteem badly.

Because I wore a uniform every day, Mother would indulge me in one good outfit every season. We would go to Joseph Magnin, and I would be allowed to buy a cashmere sweater and a pure wool skirt. She would buy me a good pair of shoes and accessories. I loved her sense of quality. She always said, "It's better to buy one good thing rather than a lot of junk." So, if a school event came up when uniforms weren't required, I looked and felt presentable. In fact, often I noticed that my one outfit was more tasteful than those the rich girls were wearing.

Father-daughter night came up. I couldn't risk bringing my own father. I didn't even ask him. If he was drunk, it would be awful; and if he happened to be sober, I wouldn't know what to talk to him about. I went with Judy, a girl from school who lived nearby and her father. So went the first year. I had few friends, I was isolated, my grades were bad, my self-esteem at an all-time low, my father was drinking more than ever. Our home life was like a bad movie. The incongruity of it all still amazes me. The darling little white house and the white picket fence with all its blackness inside. Two different lives—the one we presented on the outside; the one we lived on the inside.

By my second year of high school, I finally started to develop breasts, thank God. I was the last in my class to need a bra. I was completely flat-chested my freshman year and was teased constantly by the other girls. During that summer my breasts began to grow—and grow! I began year two with large bosoms. This immediately started rumors that I wore falsies. It wasn't until spring of that year when we started swimming in gym class that the rumors stopped. I made it a point to take long showers in the communal shower so that all the girls could see. Of course, the boys at the nearby Catholic high school were not privy to seeing my ample breasts; and, girls being girls, none of them took time to correct the rumor.

On New Year's eve the entire class was invited to Peggy Coyne's house for a gala party. Peggy lived at the "Coyne Estate." I was excited. I invited a boy I had met at Serra High (an all-boys Catholic school). His name was Declan. I really wanted to invite Mike, but he now acted like he didn't remember who I was. I couldn't get him to notice me.

Naturally, this made me long for him. I would fantasize about him and imagine being married to him. Declan was a cute Irish guy who drank a lot. At least if he saw my father drunk when he picked me up, I could say he was just celebrating New Year's eve, and he might understand.

My mother bought me a new (my first) cocktail dress. It was a white brocade sheath with a tight-fitting over-jacket with fake fur trim on the sleeves. I also got my first pair of high spiked heels and white elbow-length kid gloves. I loved it. It was such a grown-up outfit. When I was finished dressing, I walked into the kitchen to get my mother's approval. My dad was sitting at the table very drunk and talking to himself. He looked up at me. His eyes went mean.

"Get that lipstick off," he slurred.

"You look beautiful," my mom said, beaming. I did look good.

"Who does she think she is?" my dad said drunkenly. "She looks like a little tramp."

"Oh, stop it," my mother said. She didn't want him to ruin things for me.

"Where do you think you're going dressed like that?" he slurred angrily.

"I have a date," I said meekly.

"Like fuck you do," he screamed. "You're going nowhere."

I ran to my bedroom. My mother came in. I was trying not to cry.

"Hide in the closet," she said, "and when your date arrives, I'll hold Dad down in the kitchen and you can run out."

It was the beginning of a little war Mother and I were waging with Dad. We couldn't control his alcoholism, but we could take advantage of it. Mother could distract him in the kitchen; and because he was in such a fog, he wouldn't know I had left. It was the only way we could fight back.

Dad had an irrational reaction to both Maureen and myself growing up. Again, I can only surmise it had to do with leaving him. He loved us a lot. He didn't want to be left. He knew he couldn't take care of himself.

I felt on edge. I had had very few dates in my life, and this was my first "dress-up." I stayed in my closet and peeked out the little window. When I saw Declan pull up to our driveway, I ran out the front door and met him at the gate. It was embarrassing to meet him like this, but it was better than getting "caught."

The party was everything and more. Peggy had a live band and dancing in the ballroom. There was a huge Christmas tree and everyone was dressed beautifully. The house reminded me so much of my high school; oak paneling, chandeliers, balconies and countless bedrooms. I was happy just to be there. After we arrived, Declan made his way onto the dance floor. I was shy and told him I'd join him later. I stayed in the foyer just looking around. There was a group of boys standing to the side of the foyer and I could feel them looking at me and laughing. I felt embarrassed. I tried not to notice them, but I could feel my face flush. They must be thinking I'm skinny, I thought. I wished I could leave. I felt so "out of it." All of a sudden, one of the boys, Leroy, came over to me and said, "We all voted and think you are the best-looking chick in the place. Do you want to dance?" I was shocked. I was thrilled. I couldn't believe it. After dancing with Leroy, I danced every dance with every boy at the party. When midnight came and everyone was kissing "Happy New Year," there was a line waiting all around me. I kissed them all. It was wonderful. Each one told me how "cool looking" I was. I had always thought I was ugly and skinny. It was a magical night.

After that I had dates galore. I was so happy. I had no girlfriends, but I sure had boyfriends. It drove my father crazy. He couldn't stand to see me become a sexual being. My mother and I continued our "dating strategy." I would wait in my closet till I saw my date pull up in front of the house. Then my mother would keep my father in the kitchen till I ran out. It became a game. I wasn't going to let my father intimidate me the way he had my sister. My dad became increasingly crazy with my sexuality. If I walked out of the bedroom in my babydoll pajamas, he would yell, "For Chrissakes, put some clothes on." He couldn't stand it.

One night Dad was very drunk and I was his target again. "Where is the little cunt?" I heard him yell.

"Please be quiet and go to bed," my mother whispered loudly.

Bang! My bedroom door slammed open. "You think you're somethin', huh? Mommy's little favorite, huh? I'll show you! You're nothin'!" he ranted. He walked toward my closet. "Mommy been buying her little pet some new clothes, huh? Huh, pisshead? New clothes for all your boyfriends? Huh, cunt?" he screamed. At that he pulled my favorite dress out of my closet and started to rip it.

"Stop it!" I screamed. I ran to him and tried to pull the dress from his hands. He grabbed my wrist and twisted it till I thought it would break. "Mommy, make him stop!" He threw me to the floor. He took another skirt. *Rip.* "I hate you," I screamed at the top of my lungs. I tried to pull the skirt away from him. He threw me aside.

My mother screamed. "Are you crazy?" she yelled. She tried to stop him. He pushed her to the floor.

"I'll show you two. You're *nothin'.*" *Rip!* went another dress.

"No! No! No!" I screamed. "Stop it, please!" He wouldn't stop. All my clothes were on the floor. *Rip! Rip!* He wouldn't stop. I jumped on him. He threw me off. My mother pulled at him.

"Stop it, you crazy man!" she yelled hysterically.

I couldn't stand it. I felt a rage I had never felt before in my life. I didn't know what to do. I felt crazy. Out of control. He was hurting my mother, he was ripping my clothes, he was stronger than both of us. I grabbed my tennis racquet and with all my might I banged the wood side down on the top of his head. I felt the wood connect. I heard the sound of breaking flesh. Blood spurted out the top of his head like a fountain. Blood was everywhere. It wouldn't stop. He groaned a deep, low, guttural sound.

"Oh, my God," I wailed. "I'm sorry, I'm sorry, I'm sorry," I screamed. My mother cried out, "God help us."

My father fell to the floor. My mother ran to the phone to call the hospital. "I didn't mean to," I cried over and over.

"You watch Michael," was all my mother said. Thank God he couldn't hear what was going on from his room.

My mother dragged my father from my room through the hall, through the living room, out the front door, down the path to the car. She pulled his dead weight into the front seat. I was hysterical. Immobile. In shock. "I've killed Daddy," I sobbed over and over. I ran out the back door not knowing where I was going. "I killed Daddy," I kept screaming over and over. I ran along the side of the house. My mother was backing out of the driveway and Dad was slumped in the front seat. My mother didn't look at me. She looked pained. In shock. "I'm sorry, I'm sorry, I'm sorry," I sobbed, I screamed. They drove off. I lay on the ground crying and crying. "I didn't mean to. I'm sorry, I'm so sorry." For over an hour I lay there sobbing. It was 4 A.M. Finally, I went back into the house. Blood was everywhere, so I started cleaning it up like a madwoman, washing and washing. I wanted to get rid of it. It was too crazy. My head was spinning. "Please don't let him die," I said out loud over and over to no one. Within an hour I fell asleep on the floor of my closet, the place where I felt the safest; and I didn't wake up until I heard my mother in the driveway. I peeked out my closet window. She was walking my dad toward the front door. Thank God. He's not dead, I thought. I felt relief. I felt remorse. I felt guilt. I felt sorry.

Dad had a concussion and eight stitches.

I could hardly live with myself after that. I felt like such a bad person, so shallow. How could I have gotten so crazy just because he was ripping my clothes? Were clothes so important to me that I would become so violent? Was I mentally ill? These thoughts lay at the base of my brain.

A darkness, an ache; there was no one with whom I could share these thoughts. Sandy and I were drifting apart since going to different schools, and there was no one else I trusted. There was so much to hide. We never talked about it at home.

Mother understood the craziness to which we were all driven at times. She couldn't condone what I had done, neither could she accept it. I mistook her silence about it as condemnation. In reality, her silence was shock. All her energy was focused on the crisis with which she was trying to cope. Mother kept turning to her church for help, praying for a miracle and forgiveness.

Dad wouldn't look me in the eye anymore, and I couldn't look at him. We were two strangers together. Observing one another only when we couldn't get caught. Wary. Like two animals, not knowing when the other might strike.

My clothes had been my equalizer. In my mind when I wore one of my "good" outfits, no one could tell where I was from, no one could figure out my dark secrets. No one knew anything about me other than that I looked respectable. I went to a fancy private Catholic girls' school, and, therefore, I must be respectable; and that is exactly what I wanted everyone to think. Ripping my clothes removed my cover. I was living in a fantasy world and I didn't want to get caught. I was sick and I didn't understand. I fantasized as a defense. I protected myself from the hurt. When I left my house the hurt didn't exist. I would later learn that it was a dangerous fantasy, but for now it was survival.

16

It was now 1960 and Maureen was pregnant with her first child. Michael was four years old. Mom and I would visit Maureen quite often before dinner. Maureen felt relieved to be married and on her own. She knew exactly what to expect when she got home; the house would look and feel as she left it. After all the years of uncertainty and nervousness, this new environment was a great luxury. She still felt bad for Mother and hoped in time she would be able to help her out of her desperate situation. It was so nice at Maureen's house. It was peaceful. She was always cooking something wonderful for dinner. When Bill got home from work, they would both have a martini or two made with Tanqueray gin. They were proud of that. It was the best gin you could buy. We would never stay too long; after all, they were still newlyweds. It was just nice to get away from Dad, who was drunk most nights.

I got the lead in the school musical, Gilbert and Sullivan's *H.M.S. Pinafore*. Thank God for music. It was the only thing keeping me in school. I got A's in music. I loved concert choir and singing church music. I loved Gregorian chants and Sister Suzanne was the only nun in the school who "took" to me. She encouraged me musically. We learned to sing in Old English. We harmonized. I was second soprano.

I did well in any class that didn't require homework; music, drama, sewing. (I was in advanced sewing class.) Over the years I had learned a lot about dressmaking by watching my mother. She taught me about cutting on the straight of the grain, fitting and finishing. I enjoyed it. Any creative activity absorbed me. It was escape.

For my term project, I designed a white silk suit with underarm gussets. It was a tight-fitting, single-breasted jacket lined with pink flowered China silk that matched the blouse. The skirt was straight with a back kick pleat. I was quite proud of my creation. I finished all the buttonholes and topstitching by hand. My teacher said I had "a real flair for fashion" and chose my suit to be in the senior fashion show. Mine was the only entry made by an underclassman. I felt good about that. I wasn't a total loser.

But the rest of my grades were awful. I had given up, convinced I was stupid. I still hadn't made the connection between alcoholism and bad grades. Instead of paying attention in class, I would daydream and write little love poems. They would usually be written to or about Mike, although I was never going to actually send them to him. It was my fantasy. I would practice writing his name over and over. When the teacher walked by, I would quickly stick the poems or doodles into the back of my book and act like I was real busy.

Near the end of the second term of the second year I was called to the principal's office. I hadn't done anything wrong that I was aware of; nonetheless, my body started to shake and sweat. Sister Jean didn't look like the other nuns. She had mean eyes and she frightened me. I also instinctively knew that she didn't like me. I was asked to wait in the waiting room and told that Sister Jean would call me when she was ready for me. I sat for what seemed like an eternity. "You can go in now, Miss Mahoney," the secretary said. To my surprise my mother was sitting in the corner. It looked like she had been crying.

"Sit down," Sister Jean said sharply.

I felt scared. What could be so bad that they called my mother to come, I thought.

"I went through your locker this weekend, and guess what I found?" Sister Jean sounded sarcastic. I didn't understand. "What!" she demanded.

"I-I don't know," I said meekly.

"Louder."

"I don't know," I said again.

"Well then, I'll just have to tell you," she said. "I found all sorts of notes. Notes are against the rules. Don't you know that?" she demanded.

"I really don't know what you mean," I stammered.

" 'Dear Mike,' " Sister Jean read, " 'How much I love you and wish you were in my arms.' Isn't that sweet?" Sister Jean said sarcastically. She read on and on. She had a whole pile of my notes and she read them one by one. " 'How I would love to make love to you all night long,' " Sister Jean read. "You cheap little girl," she said. "Aren't you ashamed of yourself?"

"Sister, honest, I never . . ."

"Quiet!" she read on. " 'I want you to kiss my breasts and my back.' "

I had tears running down my face. "It never happened. I was never going to send them. I made it all up," I said desperately.

"Hush, you bad girl," Sister Jean said. "Mrs. Mahoney, aren't you ashamed of your daughter?"

My mother was crying. She didn't know what to believe. Her life was one big crisis. It was getting harder and harder for her to cope. Mom was of a generation that didn't question authority, especially the authority of the church. A nun was just under a priest in terms of church status, the priest was the link to the Pope and the Pope had a direct line to God. The Pope was infallible; therefore the church was infallible. If Sister Jean told my mother I was wrong or bad, how could my mother question her? Sister Jean's authority came from a higher source. My mother had a rigid sense of right and wrong. She had to accept Sister Jean's appraisal.

"We can't have bad girls like this at our school. Mercy High School is for ladies, not little tramps."

"But I'm not," I cried. "Honest, Mommy, honest. I've never done anything like that."

"I'm sorry, Miss Mahoney, but I'm going to have to expel you. You broke the rules, now you must pay the consequences."

I couldn't believe it. Expelled. For what? For notes? For sex? I'd never had sex with anyone. I would kiss my dates good-night, but never anything else. I was a good girl. Or was I? I didn't know what or who

I was anymore. I knew I was capable of being crazy. Somehow I felt I deserved to be expelled.

My mother and I drove home silently. I cried to myself. "Go to church and ask God's forgiveness," Sister Jean said as we left. Why should God forgive me, I thought. I was too bad . . . but I wasn't. Sister Jean had taken advantage of the situation to get me out of her school. I didn't have any of the things that counted. I didn't get good grades and I didn't have money. And I suspect, my natural sexuality must have been threatening to these women in black robes who had chosen celibacy.

I hadn't connected my poor academic showing with the conditions of my home life. I hadn't thought of my sexual stirrings as natural, but as something that was bad, dirty, wrong. I thought I was the only one with sexual curiosity.

As time went on, I thought less and less of myself. I was only fourteen years old; too young to have the proper perspective to understand what was happening to me. I was in the early stages of the disease that would try to destroy me later in life.

I never saw any of the girls from Mercy ever again. I was too ashamed. I never knew anyone who had been expelled. I knew they were all talking and laughing about me. Word was out. I was expelled for writing dirty notes about sex. It wouldn't be the last time my fantasies would get me into trouble.

I enrolled in Capuchino High School to finish the last two weeks of year two. I didn't know anyone in any of my classes. By this time friends had been made. Cliques had been formed. I was "out of it" again. I did find the schoolwork a lot easier than at Mercy. That was good.

17

My sister was pregnant again. Her first baby, Billy, was only two months old! Maureen was a good Catholic so she wouldn't and couldn't practice birth control. Nevertheless, she had hoped for a little more of a breather between babies.

Maureen was getting disenchanted with marriage. She looked to Bill for approval and encouragement. Her self-worth was tied up in what he thought of her. But Bill was obsessed with becoming a success. All his energies went into his business. He wanted to make it big. No longer was Maureen his total focus. He no longer lavished his attention on her. She felt wounded and cast aside. Money was tight; Maureen had quit her job to raise the baby and Bill worked for real-estate commissions. Some months were better than others; but mostly, in those beginning years, they were behind. Bill's esteem lowered. It was important to him to be a good provider. Starting a new business is difficult and time consuming. Bill put in more and more hours each day to speed the process. Maureen found herself alone much of the time.

Maureen found the best way to get her husband home was to invite people to their house. She started organizing parties. Everyone liked to go to the Gilmartins. The gin flowed freely. Maureen, coming from an unrealistic environment, spent money they couldn't afford to entertain. She wanted to have fun. She wanted to be with her husband. Bill would relax after a couple of drinks and they would talk about their dreams and plans for the family. This was their quality time. For the moment he was hers again.

I babysat for her a lot. It got me out of the house and let her spend time alone with Bill and their friends. Besides, I loved little Billy. He was so cute and sweet. I would hold him and feed him; and in return, he would laugh and coo at me. Whenever I saw Maureen, she either had just had or was having a drink. Either a martini or "just a gin and tonic." I wish Dad could drink like that, I thought. Just a little here and there, now and then. Just enough to get happy. When Maureen drank, she had fun. Whenever he drank, even when he promised he was only going to have "one," he always got drunk. When he woke up in the morning, he would have a boilermaker. That was beer with a whiskey chaser. His body craved alcohol. He couldn't be without it.

None of us understood alcoholism. We just thought Dad was a jerk. Why won't he stop, we kept asking. If he had been epileptic or mentally retarded, we would have understood. If he had sores or pain or fever, we might have been able to understand. When Dad was sick in the mornings, we all thought, "It serves him right." If he wouldn't drink so much, he wouldn't feel so bad. No one ever told us he had a disease. If a person has cancer, you get him help immediately, but because we didn't perceive alcoholism as a disease, we did nothing to help Dad get better. I think now how tormented and helpless he must have felt inside. No one wants to act so terribly. He loved his family. He didn't want to hurt us. He didn't want us to be so miserable. If we had known that the whole family gets sick together, that a family is only as strong as its weakest link, we might have been able to help ourselves. But we didn't.

In my third year of high school I met Bruce Somers. We met on a blind date and got along great from the first moment. He went to University of San Francisco on a baseball scholarship. He was "the life of the party." I moved into his social life. I had no friendships established at Capuchino High, so my free time was spent at USF fraternity parties. It was a lot of fun. Bruce was such a nice guy; everybody liked him. Even my dad. Bruce was the first boyfriend I could bring around the house. My dad was always happy to see him. They had so much in common. They would talk baseball and boxing. They would share a "couple of beers" together. I didn't have to go through all the hiding in the closet waiting for Bruce to show up for our dates. I gradually let Bruce see more and more of the reality of my life. My dad was a drunk; and besides Sandy, Bruce was only the second person I ever told. I was more relaxed. If Dad was plastered when Bruce arrived, I didn't care. Bruce came from a pretty eccentric family himself. For starters, his mother followed Johnny Cash all across America. She would actually sleep outside in her sleeping bag in front of the ticket office to be sure she got good seats. She also liked to stay up all night reading novels and drinking scotch with milk, but she wasn't an alcoholic. She was simply unique. Not PTA fare. She was an interesting woman and a graduate of Smith College. She was the first person I'd ever heard talk about Lou Rawls and an "interesting new singer, Barbra Streisand." I became very fond of his mother. Because of her I bought the soundtrack to *Funny Girl*, which became my favorite new album. I would close my bedroom door and vamp in front of the mirror, complete with Barbra's accent:

> *I'm the greatest star,*
> *I am by far*
> *But no one knows it!*
> *Wait! They're gonna hear a voice*
> *A silver flute—toot, toot, toot, toot!*

I'd grab the curtain to use as my boa and flip it over my neck.

> *Hey, she's terrific!*
> *I'm a natural Camille*
> *As Camille I just feel*
> *I've so much to offer!*

It was my dream, my fantasy to perform, but that is all it would ever be. I kept it to myself. The best I could do with my life was find a good husband and raise a family.

I wasn't thinking of marriage yet, but Bruce was certainly a step in the right direction. He was the type of guy who could offer a nice life.

Bruce kind of understood coming from a "different" family. We laughed a lot and kissed a lot; and before I knew it, we were going steady. Bruce made me appreciate the importance of a college education; and it was because of his influence I decided not only would I go to college, but to a Catholic college. I never mentioned to him that I was the class dummy.

Maureen had her second baby; another boy. His name was Timmy, and within months she was pregnant again. She was frustrated. She loved her children, but she wasn't happy to be having a baby a year. She went to our parish priest to convince him to let her practice birth control, but the answer was no. "Abstinence is the only approved form of birth control. The marriage bed is for procreation." So be it. Three years, three children. The good old church!

Bruce and I were dating every weekend, usually both nights. We would dance and laugh. Bruce always drank beer and I ordered Coca-Cola. I liked Bruce so much, but sex became an issue. The end of each date was a wrestling match. He would reach under my blouse. "No," I said. He would try to put his hands up my skirt. "No, please." I felt hot. I would get aroused and excited, but I was a good girl. I had to save myself for marriage. It was how I had been taught. If I gave in, he wouldn't respect me. Things were different then.

In my senior year the school musical tryouts were posted. The play was *Guys and Dolls*. God, how I wanted the part of Adelaïde. I knew every word, every song. I practiced and practiced. For a month I thought of nothing else. I had my friend Diana, who was a majorette, teach me one of her dance routines. I wasn't very well known at the school, so no one even considered my getting the part. Everyone was sure the part of Adelaide would go to Suzie Mills. The night of tryouts Dad was very drunk. I didn't care. He could rant and rave. I only had one thing on my mind. I was Adelaide.

"Suzanne, you're next," said Mr. Bates, my drama teacher.

I had a crush on Mr. Bates. I also had a crush on Mr. Mielenz, my music teacher. I craved approval from older men. I craved love and approval from my dad, but I hardly ever got it, so I transferred my cravings to these two men in the form of crushes. It's not abnormal for young girls to fantasize about their teachers. I noticed other girls in my class would act giddy around them also. Besides, they would never notice me. It was just a secret fantasy.

As I walked to the stage, I felt nauseated, my insides were shaking. "Concentrate," I said to myself. "Don't screw yourself up." I stood on the stage and began.

> *The average unmarried female*
> *Basically insecure*
> *Due to some long frustration*
> *May react . . .*

I was starting to relax. I loved this song.

> *In other words,*
> *Just from waitin' around*
> *For his plain little band of gold,*
> *A person can develop a cold.*
> *A-a-choo!*

Then I did my little dance, and it was over.

"Ver-ry nice," said Mr. Bates.

I went back to my seat. The rest of the auditions seemed an eternity. Mr. Bates and Mr. Mielenz went outside to deliberate. Finally they reentered the room.

"The part of Nathan Detroit is Rich Scuitto."

"Yea," everyone yelled.

"Sky Masterson is Gordon DeVol."

"Yea," everyone cheered.

"Sister Sara will be played by Yvonne Camper."

"Great, terrific," everyone said.

"And the part of Adelaide . . ."

I held my breath. I promised myself I wouldn't cry when he read Suzie Mills' name. She was better. She'd been at the school longer. She and Mr. Bates were good friends.

Mr. Bates announced, "Suzie,"—I knew it would be her, I thought, I knew it—"Mahoney," he said. Everyone gasped.

I couldn't believe it. It was the most wonderful thing that had ever happened to me. I cried big tears. "Mr. Bates," I said, "thank you so much. I promise to be the best Adelaide you've ever seen."

I totally immersed myself in the musical. I was first at rehearsal and last to leave. I loved every minute of it. The auditorium was an impressive one-thousand seater. It would excite me just to think about it; singing, dancing in front of a live audience! I couldn't believe it. Mr. Bates was so supportive. I'd stay late, and he'd tell me what a natural talent I was. He'd give me a little pat on the behind whenever he got the chance. We wore somewhat skimpy costumes for "Take Back Your Mink," and I would catch him looking at my legs, or my breasts. It made me uncomfortable; and, yet, it was exciting. He was an older man and I wanted his approval. I enjoyed the attention from him.

Things were getting strained between Bruce and me. He wasn't enjoying the joy I felt with my accomplishment. The musical was taking all my attention. It was all I wanted to talk about. It was all I could think about. I was stagestruck. Bruce would park across the street from my house after our dates. We would kiss for a while and then he'd suddenly turn into an octopus. Hands everywhere. "No, please," I demanded. He didn't listen. It was so hard for me to resist. It felt so good, but I didn't want to. Only the "loose" girls did things like this. "Stop!" I said faintly. "Please don't." With all my strength and will-power I pushed his hands away. "No! No! We can't."

"Why not?" he said. "I love you. Don't you love me?"

"Yes," I said. To say no would end everything right then. I didn't want to do that. "It's not right," I said.

Honk! Honk! Vroom! Vroom! We both stopped.

"What's that?" Bruce asked.

I looked up. There was Mike driving by and revving up his motor. The mood was broken.

"Who's that?" Bruce asked.

"Just an old boyfriend."

I couldn't figure it out. Lately, Mike was acting like a jealous lover. Here I'd had a crush on him all this time; and now that I had a boyfriend, he was finally showing an interest.

"I'd better go inside. I'm sure my mom is looking out the window."

"Okay," Bruce said reluctantly. He walked me to the door. "I love you," he said.

"Uh huh, I love you, too." I ran inside as fast as I could.

Mom was sleeping in my bed. She hadn't had a good night. I went to the bathroom and washed for a long time. I felt guilty.

18

O pening night of *Guys and Dolls* was so exciting. I loved putting on the makeup. I loved getting into my costume. The orchestra was tuning up and the audience was arriving. Both of my parents came, and Dad wasn't drunk. I couldn't believe it. Maybe he did care about me. There was a loud hum coming from the audience through the stage curtain. I was nervous, but I wasn't scared.

Mr. Bates came up to me. "You're gonna be great, Mahoney."

"Thank you, Mr. Bates."

The overture started and the audience applauded. I felt so emotional. There were tears behind my eyes. Then the music started.

> *When you see a guy*
> *Reach for the stars in the sky,*
> *You can bet that he's doin' it*
> *For some doll*

the chorus sang.

I made my entrance on stage and I was home. I felt comfortable. The first act went perfectly and the audience loved it. The second act had "Take Back Your Mink" and "Sue Me." I was in heaven.

Then the chorus sang loudly,

> *That the guy's only doin' it*
> *For some dol-l-l.*

The end.

The audience leaped to their feet. One curtain call, two curtain calls, six curtain calls. Then Mr. Bates came on stage. He was with a man I had never seen before. Mr. Bates went to the microphone. The man came over to me and whispered in my ear.

"Ladies and gentlemen," Mr. Bates said, "this has been an exciting night. We've witnessed some extraordinary young talent. With me to-night is a man who is no stranger to show business. He has been so impressed with this production that he has asked that we run one extra performance to donate all proceeds to the Damon Runyon Cancer Fund. Ladies and gentlemen, I proudly present Mr. Walter Winchell."

So that's who he was, I thought.

After removing my makeup, I went home to change my clothes for the cast party. My dad was sitting in the living room. We hadn't really talked since I hit him on the head with the tennis racquet almost two years ago. He had a look in his eye I had never seen before.

"You were damn good," he said, his voice trembling.

I was taken aback. He rarely praised. His eyes showed astonishment, pride and emotion.

"Thank you, Daddy." I was flabbergasted. It meant so much to me.

"What'd the guy say to you?"

"You mean Walter Winchell?"

"Yeah," he said.

"He said, 'You're going someplace, sister!' "

Bruce and I left the *Guys and Dolls* cast party early. He wasn't having any fun.

"Please! Stop! We can't!" The wrestling match was on again in his car. I had so much feeling. "No! No! Don't!" I pushed his hands away. He put them back. I pushed them away again. Back and forth, back and forth. He pushed his body on top of mine. I could feel him pressing himself on me through my skirt. It's getting so out of hand, I thought.

Sex made me feel so guilty. It was wrong. The nuns had been telling me that for years. Just writing about it got me expelled from school. Why couldn't I control myself. Bruce knew by now that my "No! No!" really meant "Yes! Yes!" I wanted to be a perfect person. I was so imperfect, but it felt so incredible. The fact that it was wrong made it more exciting. I knew one thing though. I would never, *ever* let him go "all the way."

19

Money was getting real short around our house. Dad was a Teamster, and his union had been on strike now for three months. We were really starting to feel it. Tickets to Grad Night were seventy-five dollars apiece. The price included dinner, dancing, games and breakfast. Mom told me she just couldn't afford it. I was heartbroken. Everyone was going. Mr. Mielenz, my music teacher, found out about it. As a graduation gift, and to show his pleasure with my performance in *Guys and Dolls*, he gave me the tickets. Mom told me she would make me a new dress if it wasn't too expensive. I had seen the most beautiful dress in the window of a very expensive store in San Mateo.

"Do you think you could copy it?" I asked.

"I think so," Mom said. She was a wonderful seamstress.

It was beautiful. It was a full-length gown of pink-and-white crepe. The top was a white blouson style, sleeveless, with a low round neck and two rows of pink rhinestone and pearl jewels that followed the bustline. The bottom was pink straight down to the floor. Mom did an incredible job. You really couldn't tell the original from the copy. She even lined it in China silk, so it felt like a dream when I was wearing it. The store price was twelve hundred dollars. My mother made my dress for forty-seven dollars. My sister gave me long white opera-length kid gloves. I loved clothes. I couldn't wait to wear this gorgeous new dress.

Bruce picked me up in his tuxedo. He didn't really enjoy any of my high-school events. After all, he was in college, but he was good-natured and knew that it was important to me.

"Wow! You look beautiful," Bruce said.

"Thanks," I said self-consciously. Bruce couldn't take his eyes off my protruding breasts. This was the first time I had ever worn a low neckline. Oh, dear, I thought.

The party was okay. Those events are always more exciting in anticipation than in reality. I still didn't have many friends at school, so I didn't know who to sit with or who to talk to. I knew a lot of kids from the play, but Bruce didn't want to hang out with them. My short-lived acting career was a tense spot between us. It threatened him. We stayed for a couple of hours. Bruce wanted to go. He had some gin in the car, and wouldn't it be fun to have a drink? I knew it had more to do with my lovely young bosom than with thirst. We left and drove to our favorite parking spot.

"No! Don't!" I said. He had never had such easy access to my breasts. There they were in all their glory, sticking right out in front of his face. He was kissing me and pulling my straps down at the same time. "Please stop it," I said. It was getting harder to resist. "We can't," I said weakly. His hands were trying to find their way up my skirt. I didn't want him to. "No!" I meant it. "It's never enough for you, is it?" I felt angry. I was always the policeman. Always the one holding back. The mood was ruined.

Bruce took me home. "I'm sorry," he said at the door. "I just can't help myself."

"I know," I said. "It's hard for me, too."

I graduated from high school that June of 1964. Dad was too drunk to come to the graduation. I didn't care. It was easier if he didn't come. I wouldn't have to worry about him. I received a five-hundred-dollar music scholarship. I had been accepted at Lone Mountain College. It was an all-girls Catholic school run by the Sisters of the Sacred Heart. It was also right across the street from USF, which at the time was an all-boys college and the school Bruce was attending. It was a real good school with tough entrance requirements. It was also a school where money and status counted. I knew I didn't have the grades to get in, so I spent a lot of time fabricating a fascinating background for myself. It was easy. By the time I finished, you would have figured I was next in line to the throne. But it worked. One day a letter arrived saying I had been accepted and they were "looking forward to my arrival." Oh, boy!

"How are we going to afford this?" my mother asked.

"I'll get a job this summer and every penny will go toward my tuition and board, plus the five hundred dollars from the scholarship. Please, Mom, please?"

I got a job that summer selling dresses for the House of Nine. They sold to small women, sizes 3, 5, 7 or 9. I was determined to sell a lot of dresses. Going away to school was a way out.

I liked my job. I liked working. I didn't enjoy taking the bus every day, but I didn't have a car. In the first week on the job, I ran into Mr. Bates. He lived in that area.

"Hey, Suzie," he said. "You look great."

I was wearing a dress I borrowed from my sister. It was a navy-blue sheath with high navy-blue spiked heels. Maureen couldn't get into any of her old clothes right now because of all her pregnancies. It depressed her. She had always been so proud of her beautiful figure, but she was a "good girl" and an obedient girl and wouldn't disobey the rules of the church. She now had three baby boys, ages one, two and three. I could feel Mr. Bates looking me up and down.

"Want to get a cup of coffee with me?" he asked.

I didn't drink coffee, but I would learn. "Sure," I said. Why did older men excite me so much?

"You've got a dynamite body," he said.

I didn't know how to react. I liked the attention, but he was my teacher. *Was* my teacher. That's right. I no longer went to that school. We went to the Colony Kitchen.

"Do you take cream?" he asked.

"No, thank you." I felt jittery sitting next to Mr. Bates. He had a way of looking at me that made me uncomfortable. I knew it must be my imagination, but it felt like he was coming on to me.

"Hey, I've got a couple of tickets to *The Rainmaker* at the Geary Theater Wednesday night. Do you want to go with me? I think it would be good for you to see some theater."

"I'd love to," I said eagerly. Oh, my God! How exciting!

"It's not a date!" I screamed at my mother. "He's my drama teacher. He just wants to take me to a play. God, I can't believe you, Mom." My mother didn't like this situation at all. I didn't care. I was going, even if I had to sneak out.

"You're stupid, Suzanne," my sister said. She was visiting us. "He's just a dirty old man. Why does he want to go out with a sixteen-year-old girl anyway?"

" 'Cause he wants to expose me to the theater," I said defensively.

"Oh, really? What else does he want to expose?" Maureen was laughing.

"Oh, shut up." I stomped off.

"He's almost fifty years old," Maureen yelled after me.

20

"Hi," I said nervously when Mr. Bates came to the door. My mother was positively cold. "Well, bye-bye," I said. I wanted to get Mr. Bates out of the house as soon as possible. I knew this time my mother wasn't going to keep my dad hidden in the kitchen. This was one date she was completely against. But I was out of high school now and "knew" everything. Being a typical teenager, I felt Mom was just overreacting. I didn't allow myself to acknowledge that Mom was right. Mr. Bates was coming on to me. Mr. Bates was too old for me. I was feeling giddy with infatuation for him. Bruce had gone home to San Diego for summer vacation; after all, what was I going to do for the next three months? Stay home and live like a nun?

What a wonderful evening. Mr. Bates drove a white Cadillac with big fins on the back. He treated me differently from when I was his student—almost flirtatious. Very flirtatious.

"God, you have a great ass," he said as I was climbing into the car. I didn't know how to react. I giggled. I wore a camel and charcoal-gray sheath. The top was camel and tight fitting with a high neck and long sleeves. It fit tight to my hips. At the hip line was a camel belt and a short tight charcoal-gray skirt fell to just above my knees. My shoes were camel spike high-heels with gray detailing on the toes and charcoal-gray heels. I liked the way I looked in this outfit.

He was easy to be with. Even though I was very nervous, he kept the conversation going, talking about people and subjects we both knew. We talked about my talent and how I should continue to cultivate it. The possibility of having a career hadn't entered my mind. No one from San Bruno had ever done anything like that. Besides, I didn't feel I was good enough. But it was a wonderful, heady experience to be with someone who liked to talk about theater and audiences and the thrill of performing; so unlike my conversations with Bruce. With him, the mere mention of show business and acting would ruin the evening.

We pulled up to the Geary Theater on Sutter Street in San Francisco.

Mr. Bates gave the car to valet parking. I felt giddy. Valet parking! I was not used to such luxuries. Our tickets were for front and center. I had been to this theater before, but always in the last row of the third balcony. Over the years my mother had taken me to all the musicals that played San Francisco. I loved the theater. I'd brought a pair of binoculars but realized this time I wasn't going to need them. I could practically count the cavities in Inga Swenson's teeth! Inga Swenson (a regular on the television series "Benson") was one of the stars of *The Rainmaker*. When the main character, called Starbuck, went to kiss her, he pulled a hairpin from her hair and the most beautiful, long, silky blond, lustrous hair fell to below her bottom. It was so romantic. After the play we went to the Pam-Pam Coffee Shop and Bar down the street. I had chocolate cake and a glass of milk. Mr. Bates had a drink— bourbon and soda. We talked and talked. He told me about the characters in the play, who was good, who was not. It was wonderful. When we reached my house, Mr. Bates got out of the car and opened my door for me. He walked me to the front door, just like a real date.

"I had the best time. Thank you so much," I said.

"Hey, Suzie, it was a pleasure for me, too. I'd like to do it again," he said.

Then he lifted my chin with his finger and kissed me on the lips, softly and briefly. I gulped. "Good-night," I said.

"Bye, Mahoney." He waved and drove off.

21

My brother Dan wrote home to tell us he would be returning from the Navy this summer. It would be so great to see him again. He had enjoyed his time in the Navy. When he wasn't playing basketball, he worked as a bartender at the officers' club. He couldn't get away from booze. It was an arena he understood. All the officers liked him. He'd laugh and joke with them. He'd pour their drinks nice and stiff. They found him (as everyone did) a real pleasant guy to have around with a great sense of humor.

Also working at the officers' club as a cocktail waitress was Mardi, a beautiful Yugoslavian girl who had lived around the corner from us in San Bruno—twelve houses away. She had gone to Hawaii for a two-week vacation as a graduation gift and liked it so much she got a job and stayed.

She screamed with excitement when she saw Danny the first time. She missed home, and he brought it back to her.

Before long they were dating steadily and were madly in love. On Christmas eve a year and a half later they impulsively got married. Dan called home to tell Mom. She was happy for him. Like all parents, she would have preferred they wait and marry at home with the family; but it was too late and she gave him her blessing.

Mardi's father was very unhappy. He felt he should have been consulted.

Danny and Mardi returned from the islands jobless and penniless. They moved in with us. Why Danny would subject his new wife to Dad's alcoholic and outrageous behavior was a mystery to me. Danny's system of denial was well at work. He convinced himself Dad wasn't as bad as he remembered. They both would be reminded soon enough.

Mardi was breathtakingly beautiful. She had an exotic face and gorgeous figure: tall and tan and thin. I wasn't thrilled to turn my room over to them. I had to sleep upstairs in Danny's old room where five-year-old Michael now slept. We shared Danny's old peed-up twin bed. I had no place to escape; no place to fantasize or listen to my music; no privacy. But it was wonderful having Danny back again. I missed him a lot while he was gone.

He and Dad were getting along better than they ever had. They would stay up late and drink together. They both liked beer. Danny also liked gin. Dad liked having someone to drink with. Maureen came over to visit Danny and his new wife and brought her three kids.

"Suzanne, will you keep an eye on the children for me?" Maureen asked.

Maureen sat in the back room with Danny and Dad. All three of them drank gin together. No one saw any danger in their behavior, not even Mother. It seemed like social drinking; a way to connect; a way for Maureen and Danny to get close to Dad.

No one was aware that Danny had already experienced blackouts. No one realized deep inside Maureen was a bashful, insecure person; and alcohol made her feel confident, glamorous. She felt she was more interesting after a couple of drinks. It also took away her anger at feeling deserted by her workaholic husband.

But it was strange. I remembered so vividly hiding in the closet with Maureen and Danny on so many nights when all three of us vowed, "When we grow up, we're never going to drink." Oh, well, at least they'd never become alcoholics like Dad. *Never.*

It didn't take long for Mardi to lose her special status as the newcomer into our household. She became a "dumb son of a bitch" like the rest of us. If she and Danny argued over anything, Dad would say, "For Chrissakes, quit whining." He did think she was a good worker though. The house was clean again, the laundry up to date and she made Dad's lunch for him every day. Her sandwiches were nice and thick, not "goddamn shoe leather" like Mom's. Mardi soon fell into the pattern that we had of craving his approval. He had a way of telling you he liked your sandwiches that could make your day. Dad had no compunction about yelling at Mardi; and many an evening she ran from the dining table crying.

Mardi and Danny stayed with us a few months, then they moved into their own apartment. Danny was working as a carpet layer. Within the year their first baby was born; a boy named Sean.

Sunday dinners transferred from our house to Maureen and Bill's house. It was Maureen's way of helping Mom. Everything was getting too difficult for Mother. She was so nervous and rattled all the time. She couldn't remember to take the buns out of the oven; or she'd forget to turn on the meat. Her psoriasis was constant; her hands always shook. Dinner at Maureen's was a time and place for Mom to relax and unwind. Besides, Maureen liked to have a house full of people. Her house became the core of the family. She felt responsible for everyone, and we all loved to be there.

Around 5 P.M. everyone would arrive. Mom and Dad, Michael, myself, Mardi and Danny with their new baby, Maureen's three children, Father and sometimes Auntie Helen and her family. Maureen drank gin and tonic; so did Danny. Tanqueray gin, of course. Only the best. Maureen could put out a wonderful dinner all the while sipping on her drink. Maureen's husband, Bill, drank straight gin on the rocks; but he could handle it because he was such a big guy. Bill could almost finish a whole fifth of gin all by himself. Everyone was very loud. It was fun. Suddenly, with everyone drinking, Dad didn't stick out so much. The louder he talked, the louder everyone else talked. The drunker he got, the drunker everyone else got. There was a lot of laughing, a lot of singing. The babies stayed up later than they should. Little Timmy came into the kitchen carrying a poop-filled diaper. Everyone laughed.

"Suzanne, I think Timmy wants his diaper changed," Maureen said.

I took Timmy to his room, cleaned him off and put on a fresh diaper and clean pajamas, the kind with the feet. He was so cute with his red hair and freckles. I went to the kitchen and filled his bottle with milk. He grabbed the bottle from me along with his blanket. His little eyes rolled back into his head, and I knew he was on his way to sleep for the night.

When I went back to the kitchen, everyone was having after-dinner drinks, crème de menthe on the rocks. Yep, dinner at Maureen's was a lot of fun.

22

Mr. Bates stopped by the House of Nine where I was working. "Hi," he said. God, I found him attractive. "Would you like to have some dinner with me after you finish work tonight?" he asked.

"I'd love to," I said.

"I'll pick you up at seven o'clock," he said.

I called my mother and told her I was going out with some friends and I'd be home late.

Mr. Bates took me to a romantic little Italian restaurant. He ordered fettucine Alfredo for me. I had never had that before. He also ordered a glass of red wine for me and a bourbon and soda for himself. The wine made me feel so relaxed.

"You have the most beautiful eyes," he said. "Bedroom eyes."

I didn't know what to say. "What are bedroom eyes?" I asked. I really didn't know.

"The best kind," he said.

After dinner Mr. Bates asked if I would like to see where he lived. I knew I was treading in dangerous territory, but being adventurous, I said sure.

His house was a cabin in the woods of Belmont. Lots of wood, a large stone fireplace. He started a fire and put some Johnny Mathis music on the stereo. The only light was from the flames in the fireplace. Mr. Bates had another bourbon. We sat on the couch and talked and laughed. I had never been alone with a man before. Bruce and I had spent a lot of time in the car together, but this was different. I felt nervous; and, yet, I wanted to be there. We talked about acting and college. There were no other areas of conversation I was capable of handling.

Mr. Bates brushed a wisp of hair from my eyes. My hairpin fell out, my hair came falling down. "Just like Inga Swenson," he said. "You look beautiful with your hair down and messy," he said. Then he leaned over and kissed me; the longest, sexiest kiss of my life. I didn't want it to be over. We kissed again and again and again. We kissed for over an hour, then his hand moved to my breast. I immediately pushed his hand away.

"Don't, please," I said softly. I was frightened. I couldn't handle this.

"Don't worry, Suzie," he said. "I won't push you to do anything you don't want to do." I just sat there looking down at the floor. I couldn't bring myself to look into his eyes. "Are you a virgin?" he asked.

"Yes," I said quietly.

"I can wait," he said. "One day I'll ask if you're ready and you will be and it will be beautiful."

The next day there was a letter waiting for me under the door when I arrived at work. It said, "To the beautiful girl with the loose hair and falling bobby pins. I can wait for a long time."

I continued to see Mr. Bates over the summer. I never told my mother. I knew she would hate it. When September came, I quit my job and got ready to move my things to school. I was excited about college. It was such a new adventure. I felt bad leaving my mother and Michael alone with Dad. Things had gone from bad to worse with my dad. After twenty years of working at the Lucky Lager Brewery, he was fired for being repeatedly drunk on the job. It was amazing that he had lasted this long. Dad was angry and disgusted with himself. He would drink until he was plastered every day, all day, all night. My mother looked so weary. Not only was Dad's drinking escalating, but also there was no money coming into the house. I worried about my mother. How much stress could she take? I could hardly handle any more, and I was only sixteen years old.

Dad stumbled into my room while I was in the midst of packing my things for school.

"Where the fuck are you going?" he mumbled.

"I'm going to college," I said. "Lone Mountain."

"Lone what?" he asked. "Bullshit," he said drunkenly before I could answer.

He didn't have any idea what I was talking about. It didn't register. He didn't know if I was going to college five miles away or five thousand miles away. He was lost in the drunken corridors of his mind. He didn't know the name of the school nor did he care. His illness was reaching terminal proportions.

The next morning Mom and I packed the car for school. I felt excited—a new beginning. Lone Mountain College (also known as San Francisco College for Women) was only thirty minutes away in San Francisco, but to me it was a lifetime away. I could make friends now because everyone lived away from home and no one would be inviting anyone home to meet her parents. I loved the idea of being back in Catholic girls' school. It represented class. I liked being "classy." When I think about my education, the time I spent at Capuchino Public High School has had the most profound effect upon my career today; but I felt ordinary at public school. An ordinary girl from a crazy family. I wanted to be extraordinary. I felt going to a fancy private girls' school would help me achieve that. Even if I did have to pay for it myself.

Lone Mountain was beautiful. It was another of those old mansions turned school with beautiful paneling and chandeliers. The furniture was antique, the kind you see at Versailles—Louis XIV, Louis XVI, Louis XVIII. Louis was a busy guy. My mother and I were greeted by the nuns of the order of Sacred Heart. I wish we had a nicer car, I thought. Our car was, thanks to my dad, a beat-up '58 Chevy Biscayne.

The nuns showed me to my room. It was wonderful. It was small with an antique dark wood twin bed, a mahogany chest of drawers, an antique bed table and a mirror. I immediately set upon the task of decorating. Earlier in the week I had turned in all my mother's books of S&H Green Stamps and gotten myself a pink plaid quilt and a pink rag rug. These things, along with cherished items of mine from home, made the room look really nice. My mother beamed. She was happy for me. All she wanted out of life now was for her kids to be happy. Behind her smile was also the ever-present tension. How can we afford this? she was thinking.

"Don't worry, Mom," I said. "With the money I've saved this summer and working every weekend, I'll be able to pay for it.

Mom wanted to believe it. She didn't want to ruin my fun.

Mom left and I ventured out of my room to start meeting the other girls. They were from all over the United States, from Mexico, from South America. I could sense money about them. Diamond studs in their ears, gold graduation watches, heirloom ruby rings. I didn't miss a thing. Everyone was excited, everyone was really nice. I was so happy.

"Hi! Where're you from?" the girl asked. She was sitting next to me in the auditorium during our first assembly.

"I'm from the Peninsula," I answered. It wasn't a lie. San Bruno *was* on the Peninsula. Of course, so was Hillsborough, the wealthy area.

I loved school. Life was so orderly, three meals a day, at the same time each day. No one was drunk, no one was throwing food, no one was running off in tears. I was so happy. When I would think of my mother and poor Michael all alone with Dad's craziness, I would feel sad and guilty. But I became expert at pushing away my feelings.

Bruce and I went to fraternity parties and college basketball games. On Sunday afternoons there would be softball picnics in Golden Gate Park. I loved it.

Saturday mornings I would get up real early and catch a train to the Peninsula for work. Mr. Bates came by most Saturdays after work. If there was nothing doing at the school that night, I would go out with him, usually to a restaurant for dinner then his house for romance. He moved very slowly with me, knowing how easily he could scare me away. Sometimes he would get very drunk and sad looking. He was lonely. I never thought he was an alcoholic, though. He wasn't belligerent, he wasn't crazy, he wasn't anything like the drunks I knew. The excitement of having an older man interested in me was wearing off a little. I liked being with him, but sometimes I would look at him and he would just seem "old." The guys at the fraternity were more fun, more energetic. They talked about their dreams, their plans, the future. In time I started pulling away from Mr. Bates. I was spending more time with Bruce. Mr. Bates realized this and it made him crazy. He started sending daily love letters to me. I would receive long-stemmed flamingo roses two and three times a week. He called on the pay phone in my dorm and let it ring and ring and ring until someone would answer it and come and get me. He was becoming a pest. It was embarrassing. The girls started asking me about it.

"Who is he? What does he want? How old is he?" "Forty-seven years old! You're kidding."

Bruce didn't know anything about him. It was typical of the way I handled my life. Secrets. I had been keeping secrets for so long it was a way of life. Finally, I cut it off completely with Mr. Bates. I told him

I was in love with Bruce and I didn't want to see him anymore. He drove to school drunk and demanded to see me.

"Suzanne, there's a gentleman in the lobby to see you," Sister Ernest said.

Oh, great, I thought. I went downstairs. He looked pathetic. Old and drunk and sad and lonely.

"I love you, Suzie," he said. "I'll take you any way I can. Just see me sometimes. That's enough for me."

I felt nothing except discomfort. "Please go away," I said. "It's just not right. We want different things. My life is just beginning. I don't want to have to make any decisions about my life right now. Please go. Please," I said earnestly. "I like you a lot, but please don't call me, or write me or send me flowers. Please," I pleaded.

He just stood there looking at me sad and lonely. I left the room. There, I thought. I felt awful. It's finally over and done with, but still I felt sorry for him.

23

"God! Bruce! Stop! Please." Bruce and I had been at a fraternity party—a beer party. I hated beer. The smell of it reminded me of my drunken dad. Bruce loved beer. He also loved me and I liked him a lot. We spent a lot of time necking after fraternity parties. It was always out of hand though. I wanted it, but it was a sin. What a Catch-22. If I gave in, I'd be known as a "loose" girl. By not giving in, my evenings with Bruce would end in a fight. At the very best, tense.

I wanted sex. I loved kissing. I could feel myself aroused. It was hard to say no, but the consequences of saying yes were too much to bear. I was a "good girl." It was the only part of me I was proud of. I was a virgin. I wasn't a tramp. It was hard enough going to confession and telling the priest I had engaged in heavy petting.

"Just what does that mean, my child?" the priest asked.

"Um, my boyfriend touched me in impure places," I said.

"Where?" he asked.

"Well, um, my breasts," and then I mumbled, "and other places."

"Do you love this boy?" the priest asked.

"Y-yes," I said hesitantly. There was a long pause, then the priest began his sermon.

"You know, my child, God created sex for the purpose of making children. Sex is a very serious event in the lives of a man and a woman who are devoted to spending their lives together. God asks of you to be chaste until you find the man you intend to marry. That is all God asks of you. Can't you do that for God?"

"Yes," I stammered. I felt so ashamed of myself. I vowed that I would be strong with Bruce. Kissing only. Nothing more. Ever.

I became more and more dependent upon my relationship with Bruce. I needed his friendship. I had trouble making friends with the girls at my school. I didn't know why. Of course, now looking back on it I know exactly why. They could sense there was something about me that didn't ring true. They could sense my insecurity. They could sense my awe of them. I didn't feel good enough for them. I told them my dad was a manager of a large corporation. Just too busy to come to any school functions. I told them I left all my jewelry at home. I didn't want to have to even think about it being stolen. I was so afraid they wouldn't like me if they knew who I really was —an ordinary girl from a sick family with a drunken father. I had to keep my secret at all costs. Even if it meant I had no friends.

One night all the girls on my dorm floor met in one room. Everyone except me. I knew I had been intentionally excluded. They were in there for over an hour. All of a sudden one of the girls came rushing out. She looked upset and disturbed.

I asked, "What's going on in there?"

"Oh, they're just a bunch of gossips," she said.

"Why?" I asked.

"Oh, I really don't want to tell you. Your feelings are going to be hurt." She paused, then continued. "They're making fun of you because Sherry told them you're poor and live in a little crackerbox house and your father is the town drunk."

I was embarrassed. I had tried so hard to keep the truth from them. I had tried so hard to "be somebody" in their eyes. I always knew if the other girls found out about me, they wouldn't like me. This incident confirmed my feelings. I was right to keep my secret.

It never dawned on me to question the character of these girls who had nothing better to do than gossip and ostracize those less fortunate than themselves. As usual, my low self-esteem condemned me. I wasn't "as good as" the next person.

When I think about it now, I wonder why I wasn't relieved. One less secret to keep. I was now starting to feel the ramifications of our family alcoholism. My secrets, my fantasies were starting to create problems for me in my life. But I didn't see it that way then. My disease clogged all my thoughts.

Tryouts for the school musical were coming up. I hoped to get a part and immerse myself in it. The musical was *The Boyfriend,* and I easily won the part of Maisie. The theater at Lone Mountain was nothing like the Capuchino High School theater. It was smaller and less professional. It had no real lights to speak of. Just the essentials—On and Off. But I was happy to be back in an arena where I could excel. Everyone was astounded by the strength in my voice. Everyone else in the musical was there "just for the fun of it." My drive was stronger. I wanted to be great. I sang with everything I had. I danced with everything I had, and I acted out the part as if I were on Broadway. The director took me aside one day and explained to me that this was an ensemble piece and I stood out too much.

"Would you mind bringing your performance down?" he asked.

I obliged. I didn't want to be thrown out of the play.

"You wanna go out for dinner tomorrow night?" Bruce asked.

"That'd be great," I said.

"Wear dress-up clothes. I want to go somewhere really special," he said.

I looked forward to it. I loved good food and any excuse to dress up. We had dinner at Alfredo's. It was a beautiful Italian restaurant at the top of Broadway. Everything was in ice-blue satin brocade with crystal chandeliers. I've always loved beautiful rooms. We dined on limestone salad, veal Oscar and the house special dessert, fried cream. We drank red wine and said lovely things to each other. I was really enjoying myself. Bruce worked construction on weekends, so he had extra money to take me to special places, but this was fantastic. After dinner we got into Bruce's Volkswagen and kissed for a while. Then he started driving.

"Where're we going?" I asked.

"It's a surprise," he said.

Bruce drove in the direction of San Bruno. We took the San Bruno exit. We drove a few blocks and then he turned off and pulled up in front of my sister's house.

"What are we doing here?" I asked. I was confused.

"This is the surprise." He reached into his pocket and pulled out a small box. "I love you, Suzanne, and I want us to be engaged." He opened the box and there was a lovely marquise-shaped diamond engagement ring. "I told your family I was going to ask you to marry me tonight, and they are all waiting inside to celebrate with us."

I didn't know what to do. I didn't know what to say. I felt so pressured. I didn't want to hurt Bruce's feelings. He would feel so humiliated if we walked inside and had to tell everyone I turned him down. I don't want to be married yet, I thought. I'm only seventeen years old.

Bruce took the ring out of the box and placed the ring on my finger. "I love you," he said.

"I love you, too," I answered quietly. We went inside.

"Congratulations."

"Oh, what a beautiful diamond."

"Look at her ring."

"Isn't it wonderful."

I tried to act enthusiastic.

"Bruce will be a wonderful husband," my sister-in-law said.

"I know," I answered.

Only my mother wasn't gushing. It was as if she could read my mind. Too soon, too soon, I thought. I wanted to see what else was out there. I felt trapped; and, yet, I acted happy. More secrets.

All the girls at school gushed over my ring.

"You're so lucky. When're you getting married? Isn't it beautiful."

There was no one I trusted enough to bare my soul. I didn't want to be married.

I immersed myself in rehearsals. I wanted to be great in this musical.

The next Friday night Bruce and I went to another crazy fraternity party. Lots of drinking, lots of dancing. Girls were throwing up in the bathroom, and some of the pledges passed out from consuming too much "punch." The punch was a concoction of every conceivable kind of liquor—gin, whiskey, vodka, all mixed together with orange juice. It was vile tasting; but you felt that immediate "buzz," and that was the whole idea behind it. I never looked at all of us as tomorrow's alcoholics. In my mind, these were just kids having a good time. I've often wondered how many of those who attended that party are lost in a sea of booze today.

Bruce and I stayed till the end. When we got in the car, passion overcame us both; and soon the car windows were fogged up from the heat our two bodies generated. I looked at the clock and panicked. It was 1:30 A.M. "Oh, my God! They lock the school doors at one o'clock. What am I going to do?"

"Why don't you just tell them you went home for the weekend and forgot to sign out," Bruce said.

"Yeah, but then what? Where will I stay tonight?"

"Let's get a hotel room," Bruce said.

"We can't," I answered.

"Why not? We're engaged. It'll be okay. We won't do anything wrong," Bruce assured me.

I knew I was making a mistake. I knew I was being real stupid and creating a crisis. Go back to school, I thought. Face the consequences. So what if I get grounded. But the sensible side of me didn't win out. The next thing I knew Bruce and I were checking into a crummy San Francisco hotel.

"Here's your key, 'Mr. and Mrs. Somers,' " the desk clerk said.

I was sure he could tell we weren't really married. I already felt guilty.

Upstairs I sat on the bed and started to remove my stockings. I was wearing garters. "Let me watch," Bruce said. "I've been waiting all my life to see this."

Soon we were rolling and writhing on the bed together. I left my underpants, bra and shirt on. Bruce tried to remove my panties.

"No!" I said. I wouldn't let him. We pushed and pressed against each other. I couldn't let him inside me. I wanted to, but I couldn't.

"I love you! I love you!" Bruce frantically said over and over. He pressed against me. I could feel him getting too close. It took all my self-control not to let him push all the way inside.

"Oh, my God," Bruce yelled.

Then it was over. My panties were wet, covered with stickiness. I felt so embarrassed. It had never gone this far. It had to stop. Thank God I didn't give in and let him go "all the way."

Two months later my breasts became very sore and swollen. I figured I must be getting a humdinger of a period. When was my last period? I wondered. The soreness didn't go away. My breasts were growing larger.

"I don't know what's wrong with them," I told Bruce.

"Maybe you should go to a gynecologist and find out," he said. "Maybe you're pregnant."

"Pregnant! How could that be? We didn't go all the way. I left my underpants on." I felt panic.

"Yeah, but we got pretty close. Maybe something slipped inside—a sperm or something."

"No way," I said. "I've never heard of anything like that."

By the next month I hadn't had a period yet. My breasts were gargantuan and I woke up feeling very nauseated. Oh, God, I thought. I feared the worst.

Bruce made an appointment with a nearby gynecologist. I sat in the doctor's office on the verge of tears. Fat, pregnant women on all sides of me. Baby magazines, pictures of all the newborns on the bulletin boards. All the mothers-to-be talked excitedly about their aches and pains.

"I felt it kicking today," one said.

How wonderful, I thought sarcastically.

"I hear if you rub Vaseline on your stomach every night you won't get stretch marks."

Stretch marks! Kicking! Vaseline! I felt crazy.

"The doctor will see you now, Mrs. Somers," the nurse said. I followed her into the examining room. "Just remove all your clothes, Mrs. Somers, put on this gown and lie down on the table," she said cheerily.

I was so scared. I had never had a gynecological examination before. The nurse left. I removed my clothes, folded them neatly and hid my underwear on the bottom. I took the paper gown. It had no buttons, so I put it on with the opening to the back. I lay down on the table. I was all alone.

"Hello, I'm Dr. Martin." He had a nice gentle face, thank God. "Let's see now. Let me get a little history on you. How long have you been married?"

"Uh, six months," I lied.

"Okay, and how old are you?" he asked.

"Um, eighteen," I lied again.

He looked up at me. "When was your last period?"

"Three months ago," I said.

He then asked the usual questions; have you ever had polio, rheumatism, scarlet fever, measles? I just lay there answering a litany of no's thinking to myself, Dear God, please don't let me be pregnant. Please!

"Okay," he said. "Let's just put your legs up here in these stirrups."

Suddenly my legs were wide apart so he could see right up where I'd never let anyone look before in my whole life. Not even me. The stirrups were cold metal. He then started to insert a large metal tube into my vagina. It hurt me. I started getting teary. "Just relax," he said. He continued to push. "Relax, Mrs. Somers. It'll be okay." Then he pushed real hard. I screamed. It hurt so bad I started crying. I had never felt so miserable, so humiliated. I cried and cried.

I wasn't a virgin anymore. Technically, anyway. I lost my virginity with a stranger on a cold table with my legs in the air! I wanted to die. I covered my face with my hands. I was so confused. What was virginity? What was sex? I had tried so hard to be good.

"You poor child," the doctor said. His eyes were soft. "I'm sorry. I didn't mean to hurt you."

"I know," I said sobbing.

The doctor continued with his examination, his fingers inside me poking, prodding. "Hmm," he said. Then he removed my legs from the stirrups and put them back together. He opened the top of my gown exposing my breasts.

"You have the gown on backwards, dear," he said gently.

I looked away. He examined my breasts. "Are they tender here?" he asked.

"Yes," I answered.

"Here?"

"Yes."

"Here?"

"Yes."

"Have you had any morning sickness?" he asked.

"Yes," I said.

"Well, I'd say you are definitely two and a half to three months pregnant. Congratulations. Do you have any insurance?"

"No," I said.

"Does your husband?"

I just sat there looking at the floor. Suddenly my shoulders started shaking, convulsing. I was sobbing uncontrollably. "I-I don't have a husband," I stammered. "I'm not married. I don't know what to do." I cried till there were no more tears.

24

"What are we gonna do?" I asked Bruce. "Maybe we could go horseback riding," I said frantically. "I hear that bouncing around is very bad for you when you're pregnant and can cause you to miscarry. Or I could sit on the marble stairs and bounce all the way down. That would probably do the same thing."

Bruce sat there looking down at his feet. There was suddenly a lot of responsibility for him to bear. The one thing we never discussed was abortion. It was out of the question. It was a sin. Against all church rules.

"We have to tell my mother," I told Bruce. I dreaded telling her. How much could one woman take—the humiliation of her drunken husband and now me. I was terribly upset. I walked around in a kind of daze. My thoughts were crashing in my head. I felt so ashamed of myself. Angry with myself. Angry with Bruce. I wouldn't let Bruce kiss me or touch me. He repulsed me. Bruce felt so bad. He tried to comfort me.

"We'll get married," he said. "Everything will be okay. I can work part time and go to law school. I'll take care of us."

That weekend there was a play at Capuchino High. I called my mother and asked if she would like to go with Bruce and me. I never heard one word of the play that night. All I could think of was how hurt my mother was going to be when we told her the news. During intermission I told Bruce, "I can't do it. You'll have to tell her for us. I can't bear to look in her eyes."

After the play we went back to my mother's house. She was making tea and cake. Dad was passed out in their bedroom. I went into my old bedroom to hide.

Bruce came into my room and said, "It's okay. I've told her. Everything is okay." I walked timidly into the kitchen. Mom looked at me; her eyes were moist, and she was trying her best to smile. I felt so awful.

"I'm so sorry, Mom. I didn't mean to hurt you. I'm so sorry."

She looked into my eyes and then she put her arms around me. "It's okay, darling. I understand. I really do." She hugged me and patted me on the back. "Everything will be okay. Don't cry, honey. I love you. Everything will be okay."

My mother told Maureen, who told Bill. They told Dan and Mardi. Bruce called his parents and told them. My mother also told my dad I was getting married, but he was drunk and it didn't seem to register.

My sister called me at school. "Bill and I want to come up to the city and take you and Bruce to dinner."

So Monday night Maureen, Bill, my mother, Bruce and I all went to Phil Lehr's Steak House for dinner.

"Well, well, well. Gonna have a shotgun wedding, huh?" Bill joked. "No sense waiting. How far along are you?" he asked.

"Three and a half months," I said quietly.

"Well, we better get on with it then," Bill said. "It's gonna be hard enough telling everyone the baby's premature as it is. Ho! Ho! Ho!" he laughed. "You really did it this time."

So, over gin and tonics, a bottle of wine and five steaks, my fate was decided. "Today is Monday," Bill said. "How about Thursday? Thursday is a good day to get married. Then you guys can leave on Friday for a long honeymoon weekend." Settled.

My mother came to school the next day to take me shopping for a wedding suit. "Maybe it shouldn't be all white," she said. We settled on an off-white wool Chanel-style suit with blue silk lining, a blue silk shirt and a matching blue silk pillbox hat. We had shoes dyed to match in the same blue. Normally I would have been ecstatic, but this was a bittersweet purchase for me. I had a hard time fitting into my usual size. My breasts were embarrassingly large, and I couldn't button the waist on the skirt. We then went to the lingerie floor at I. Magnin's where she bought me a mint-green silk nightgown and matching peignoir.

My sister found a cabin for rent in Lake Tahoe for our honeymoon. My mother and my sister planned a wedding reception. It would be a dinner for the immediate family at the Mark Hopkins Hotel on Nob Hill in San Francisco. So! The arrangements were made. I packed up a lot of my belongings from school and quietly moved them to my mother's car. I didn't tell anyone what I was doing. I felt so sad leaving school. I had wanted to stay there four years and graduate. The dream was over now. My life was over. I was going to be a housewife with babies just like every other woman I had ever known.

I couldn't bring myself to tell the director of *The Boyfriend* the truth, so I just stopped showing up for rehearsal. In time, I thought, he'll hear that I had to get married. The part of Maisie required running around in a twenties bathing suit. It wouldn't look good to be pregnant.

Bruce's parents arrived the day before "the big day." "You'll need a car," they said. As our wedding gift they bought us an old Ford Falcon. It wasn't in the best of shape, but it was a generous thing to do; and we were grateful.

Wednesday night I stayed at home as a single girl for the last time in my life. My dad was roaring drunk. The whole week had been like a nightmare; but now, being back in this drunken reality was more than I could bear. Dad was sitting at the breakfast table with a beer in one hand, a cigarette in the other. His legs, as usual, were wrapped around each other and he was looking real mean. He must have been drinking whiskey. He looked at me and smirked.

"Two kind words," he slurred drunkenly. "Big 0! You're nothin'."

I couldn't take it. I ran to my room. My mother was already sitting in there fixing the straps on my negligee. My dad followed me into the bedroom. I wish he would leave me alone, I thought. Dad took one look at the negligee and his eyes went wild.

"What's this for?" He spit as he said it.

"I'm getting married tomorrow in case you don't remember," I said angrily.

With that he turned and glowered at me. His face was red. "You little tramp! I knew you'd get knocked up! You little cunt."

"Stop it! Shut up," I screamed back.

The veins in his neck were popping out. "I always knew you'd get knocked up," he said again.

My mother shouted, "Get out of here. Things are bad enough as they are without you making it worse." She pushed him out the door.

"Like fuck, I will! Tell *her* to get out, the little cunt!"

"I will! I will," I screamed. "I'm getting out tomorrow and I'm never coming back. I'll never have to live with you again!"

I slammed my door and lay on the bed crying. My mother came in and sat down patting me on the back.

"Oh, Mommy, Mommy!" I sobbed. "I don't want to get married. I'm not ready. I don't love him. I've made such a mistake. I don't want to pay for it the rest of my life."

My mother sat there silently for a long time. She felt bad for me and wished she could undo it, but she couldn't question the authority of the church. The church said it was wrong to have premarital sex. I disobeyed the rules. I created the crisis; now I must be responsible for my actions, regardless of my feelings toward my new husband-to-be.

Finally, my mother said sadly, "You've made your bed, Suzanne. Now you must lie in it."

25

April 14, 1965, my wedding day. Hardly the way I'd always imagined it. We didn't even tell Father or Auntie Helen. I've always felt bad about that. But, it was our way. Keeping secrets. Don't let anyone know the bad things. Pretend everything is wonderful.

The house was very quiet that morning. I woke up and looked at my wedding suit hanging in front of me. I heard Dad coughing up terrible things in the bathroom. At least I don't have to listen to that anymore, I thought. It sure felt different from Maureen's wedding day. Her day was filled with pride, excitement, anticipation. Today felt dark and shameful. I bathed, washed my hair and shaved my legs. I used Dad's razor. That was his pet peeve. It made him crazy. He'd even gone so far as to leave the razor twisted open three and a half times so he'd be able to catch me if I used it. But I had figured it out. Leave it twisted open three and a half times, dry it off perfectly, put it back in its box standing straight up, and he couldn't figure out why his razor was always dull.

Mom was in the kitchen making bacon and eggs. Dad was still a little drunk from last night. He sat at the breakfast table reading the paper and drinking a beer. No one mentioned "the wedding." The only reference to the day's coming event was, "What time are we going to get going?" Get going—that meant marriage.

I put on my new suit and stared at myself in the mirror. I looked chubby. I was chubby. The chubby little bride. Mom wore a blue knit suit with green trim. It wasn't new. In fact, she had worn it quite often. Dad wore a suit. Everyone got lost trying to find the church. At least it wasn't dark yet, I thought. None of us had ever been to this church before. None of us had ever even met the priest before. It was the parish in the district where Bruce and I went to school. If I had gone to my own church in San Bruno, word would have gotten out, and then everyone would know I "had" to get married. I hoped I could keep it a secret. It was April. The baby was due at the end of October or beginning of November. The doctor wasn't sure. It would be pretty hard to keep it a secret once the baby arrived.

The ceremony was brief. There I was. I couldn't believe it. Monday, just another college girl; Thursday, a pregnant married woman.

"I pronounce you man and wife."

Just like that! Done! Married! Well, I might as well make the best of it, I thought. We left the church and drove to the Mark Hopkins Hotel, Bruce and I in our "new" car. No tin cans dragging behind us. No JUST MARRIED signs. No indication that something festive had just happened.

Everyone met at the bar. "Gin and tonic," my sister said.

"Gimme a shot of whiskey and a beer," my dad said.

"I'll have an old-fashioned," said my mother.

Bill made the toast. "Well, here's to the bride and groom."

"Yes. Hear! Hear!"

We stayed at the bar around forty-five minutes. At the dinner table there were more drinks. Champagne for everyone.

"I'll have a scotch with milk," my mother-in-law said.

"Yeah, I'd rather have gin and tonic," Dan said.

"Me, too," said my sister.

Everyone was starting to get real loose. Dad's eyes were already gone. No focus. He had a way of staring right past you when he was drunk. My mother was trying her best to look happy. I must have looked manic. Smiling too much. Laughing too hard. Ha! Ha! Ha! Ha! Ha! We ate roast beef and Yorkshire pudding. Dad didn't eat.

"Gimme another shot," he ordered to the waiter. Dessert was wedding cake, one layer. There was a combo playing on a small dance floor in the room. Someone must have told the singer we had just gotten married because he said, "Let's have the bride and groom dance their first dance together as man and wife."

"Yea," everyone cheered.

I looked around for my husband. I didn't know where he was.

"Come on," my new brother-in-law, John, said. "I'll dance with you."

Everyone thought it was hysterically funny. I was laughing too. On the outside. My insides felt broken.

The bill came to my dad. "I don't have any fuckin' money," he yelled belligerently at the waiter.

My mother turned crimson. "Sir," she whispered, "it's already been arranged for you to mail us a bill."

"Fine," he said, "but I will need your husband's card."

"What card?" my dad slurred. "Want my fuckin' library card?"

Oh, God, I thought. How humiliating. Get me out of here. "We should leave now," I told Bruce.

"Good-bye," they said. "Good luck."

"Have fun. Don't do anything I wouldn't do," Bill said. "Ha, ha."

"I love you, honey," my mom said.

I felt like crying, but I had a *big* smile on my face.

The valet brought us our Ford Falcon. Well, this is the beginning, I thought. (Or is it the end?)

26

We spent our wedding night at the San Francisco Hilton. I went into the bathroom and washed my face for a long time. Then I put on my new negligee set. Jesus, I thought. My breasts are huge! I came out and Bruce went into the bathroom. Twenty minutes later he came out dressed in a terrycloth bathrobe. I was lying in bed. I wished we could just go to sleep. It had been a long, exhausting week. Here I was. A pregnant, married woman; and I had never made love to a man.

"Well, here goes," Bruce said. Right in front of me he took off his robe and stood there completely naked. I was shocked. I had never seen a naked man before. I averted my eyes. I didn't want to see. Bruce lay down on the bed and held me. I liked that. Then he started kissing me. I felt my body turn to stone. I had no feeling anywhere. Too much pent-up emotion. Too much repressed anger. It felt nothing like it did when we necked in the car. Suddenly, sex was demanded of me. I hated the idea of "having" to do anything, especially give away my body.

"I'll go downstairs and get some Vaseline," Bruce said.

He was trying to be understanding. He was stressed also. Great, I thought, and when we're finished, I'll rub it on my stomach so I don't get stretch marks! Bruce got up, got dressed and went downstairs to purchase the Vaseline.

The next day we drove to Lake Tahoe for our honeymoon. I had morning sickness for the first few hours. I was not happy. I realized I was probably going to have to do "it" again tonight and it made me feel weary.

I got up early our first morning in Tahoe. I stood at the door of the bedroom looking at my sleeping husband. I gotta get out of this, I thought to myself.

We spent the rest of our honeymoon driving around the lake. We drove to Virginia City, Nevada, and had our picture taken under the BUCKET OF BLOOD SALOON sign. We took a ski-lift ride. Those were the good times. Bruce was a real nice guy, and we talked a lot. I always enjoyed talking to him.

I tried real hard to get over my depression; but when nighttime came, my insides felt cold. I would stall going to bed. "Gotta do the dishes," I said. "Let me just put away this food. I'll be right out. I just want to take a hot bath." Anything to avoid my new "wifely duty."

27

We rented a furnished apartment in the Richmond district of San Francisco. Bruce had two months to finish his third year of college. We had enough money for two months rent and food. Then he would get a summer job. We needed to save four hundred dollars to pay for the hospital and another two hundred fifty to pay the gynecologist.

Dan and his wife Mardi said they would loan us their bassinet and old baby clothes. Mardi also had some maternity dresses when I could no longer fit into my own clothes. My breasts were growing a lot faster than my stomach. I had to buy new bras. I was wearing a 34D cup. When I walked down the street, horns were honking. This wasn't the kind of attention I wanted. I saw no one during this time. I avoided my family. I avoided my school chums. I sat around the apartment and watched television. I also cleaned a lot. The apartment sparkled. The rest of my day was devoted to making dinner. I enjoyed that. It was creative. Bruce liked my food, and that made me happy.

By July we had to move out of our apartment. We couldn't afford it anymore. We found a real cheap place on the Peninsula near to the House of Nine, near to where Mr. Bates lived. I hoped I wouldn't run into him. Our new place was a garage turned into a studio apartment. It was 120 dollars a month. The garbage cans were right in front of our front door. It smelled and there were a lot of flies. I tried to get my job back at the House of Nine, but they liked people who could wear the clothes; and in my condition, it just wouldn't look right.

Bruce got a job working in construction. He came home at night real tired. I got a job as an Avon lady. "Ding dong! Avon calling," I would say. I trudged along, up and down the hilly streets, with my big fat stomach and my sample case. I must have looked pathetic. Everyone invited me into their houses to "sit down and have a glass of water." I didn't sell much Avon, although I was just glad to have anyone to talk to. People who didn't know me. People who wouldn't judge me.

"Well, I bet you're real excited about the baby," they'd say.

"Oh, yes," I lied.

"You look so young to be having a baby! Why, you look like a baby yourself."

I heard that one a lot, too.

By September Bruce and I moved back to San Francisco. Bruce needed to be closer to school. He'd also gotten a job as a claims adjuster for an insurance company. They were giving him a company car. Things were looking up. We rented an old flat on Turk Street right across from Lone Mountain College. I had picked up some old furniture from my Avon customers.

"What are you going to do with that old couch in your garage?" I'd ask. Or "Would you like to get rid of that old table?" Soon I had collected a couch, dining-room table, six chairs, two end tables. My sister gave me her old bed. Danny gave me some baby furniture. My mother gave me her old green rug. I got into decorating.

My dad (yes, my dad) came up one afternoon to help me paint the apartment. We never mentioned the baby or my big stomach. Just once when I was teetering on a ladder painting the ceiling he came over and said, "Hey, you shouldn't be doing that in your condition."

I borrowed my mother's sewing machine and made curtains for the dining room and the baby's room. The baby's room was fun. I painted the walls aqua and my borrowed bassinet was pale yellow organdy with a curtain over it that hung from the ceiling. My mother gave me some more S&H Green Stamps so I was able to get a fluffy four-by-six-foot aqua floor rug and a baby lamp that was also a music box.

I became a perfect little housewife. My house was spotless, no ring-around-the-collar for my husband. I read cookbooks voraciously and presented my husband such delicacies as beef stroganoff and beef Wellington. I was craving celery and strawberry sundaes, all the while my stomach and my breasts grew. It was like a contest. One day my stomach stuck out more than my breasts, then the next day my breasts outdid my stomach. Stretching, stretching. The baby kicked nonstop. It was like having a football player inside me. My cheeks were chubby, my arms were chubby.

"You look so beautiful pregnant," people would say. "Radiant."

Oh, sure, I thought. I had no feeling for the little life inside me, just resentment and anger with myself. Boy, did I screw things up, I thought over and over.

28

I waited and waited, and on the morning of November 8, 1965, I woke up feeling like I had to go to the bathroom real bad. I kept running to the toilet, but nothing came out. I also had cramps, but nothing major. Could this be it? I wondered. Bruce had already left for school (or was it work? I can't remember at this point). I called my doctor.

"Not yet," he said. "You'll know."

A few hours later I knew. The pain was excruciating. I called my mother. "Can you come up and stay with me, Mom?" I asked.

"I'm leaving now," she answered.

I wanted my mom more than my husband. By the time my mother arrived, my water had broken. The doctor told me to get to the hospital immediately. I called Bruce. It hurt so bad. Like something was ripping out my guts from the inside. Bruce looked excited. The reality hit us both. For the first time we realized we were going to have a baby. A human being.

I was wheeled into the delivery room, praying to God—no more of these pains, please!

"Ow-w-w," I screamed. "Make it stop. Make it stop."

"You look so young," the delivery nurse said. "How old are you?"

"Nineteen," I lied. I had just turned eighteen the month before.

"Isn't that something," the nurse said. "A baby having a baby."

"Ow-w-w!" I yelled.

"Better give her the spinal," the doctor ordered. "She's ready."

"Bear down, Suzanne. Push. Push harder."

I pushed with all my might.

"Push again, Suzanne. Look in the mirror. See the head?"

I was mesmerized. The head! A real head of a person.

"She's too small," I heard the doctor say.

I watched him cut open my vagina with a pair of scissors. I felt nothing. The anesthetic killed the pain. I just felt tremendous pressure like I was having the most giant bowel movement of my life.

"Bear down," the doctor said. "That's a good girl! Here it comes. Here it comes. Push! Push! Push!"

Flap! Amazing. I heard and felt my skin slap against my bones. The pressure was over.

"Here's your little baby boy, Suzanne."

They laid the little baby on my chest and I realized the real miracle of birth. For in that moment, I felt the truest, purest, most honest love of my life. I loved my baby. My darling little baby. I cried. I put my arms around him and cried. "I love you, baby," I said. "I'm going to make a real good life for you."

Then they took him away to clean him off. I felt like I was in heaven. I felt like I was on an astral plane soaring into light and love and beauty. I loved God, I loved myself, I loved my baby.

We named the baby Bruce.

"I'd sure be proud to have my son carry my name," Bruce said.

I never really liked the name Bruce, but it was okay. Bruce was feeling left out of this whole birth process. It was the least I could do for him.

29

I loved the baby. Little Brucie. He was so cute. I loved to give him his bath. I'd comb what little hair he had into a curl on top of his head. I'd put him in new little outfits. Relatives gave him "welcome to the world" presents, so he had little sweaters and little suits and little hats. It was like dressing up a doll. I took him for walks as soon as he was able to go outside. I felt none of the shame I felt during my pregnancy; none of the embarrassment. I felt proud of my baby. Happy, even.

"Isn't that sweet! Sister taking her new little brother for a walk," the lady said.

"Yeah," I answered.

I started taking birth-control pills right after Bruce was born. I had been watching my sister have baby after baby. I wasn't going to let that happen to me. I felt guilty about it. Birth-control pills were against church rules, and here I was breaking them again; but I couldn't afford to have another baby right away, emotionally or financially. I'll have to find a way to live with my guilt, I thought.

Bruce was real busy working all day and going to school at night. On weekends he played golf and watched football. I still liked him a lot, but there was no excitement, no passion. I'd sit in the window of my apartment and watch my friends coming and going from school. Often my friend Nora and her friends would use our house to dress for the night's social event.

Nora was the only girl at my school who kept in contact with me. Again I had left a girls' school in shame. I was grateful for Nora's friendship. She loved little Bruce and was always bringing presents— little coats and jumpsuits, darling little designer outfits—things I could never afford myself.

"You should come with us tonight," my friend Nora said. "We'll have a lot of fun." She was putting on mascara. I was dunking poop-filled diapers into the toilet.

"Naw," I said. "We like to stay home." Who could afford a night out and a babysitter?

I felt restless, discontent. "I'm going to modeling school," I announced. "Then I'll be able to make some extra money for us and not have to leave the baby. I hear you can earn sixty dollars an hour, and it would be exciting." I signed up for a 110-dollar modeling course at the Grimme Modeling Agency. We learned how to walk, how to sit, ramp modeling, makeup and photographic modeling. I was a good student. This could be a way out for me. I knew I wasn't going to stay married. I just hadn't figured out how to get out of it. I learned how to do the latest hair styles, I wore a flattening bra (the Twiggy look was in), I wore individual false eyelashes.

One day the owner of the agency walked by me and said, "She'd be good." What? What? I wondered. "Do you want to work tomorrow?" Jimmy Grimme asked.

"Do I? Do I? Yes," I said eagerly.

"Okay, go to the Palace Hotel tomorrow morning at seven o'clock. It's a fashion show. Ask for Adeline Ross," he said.

"Great. I'll be there." I was ecstatic. A job! A job! My first job!

I stayed up late that night practicing my ramp walk. Pelvis thrust forward, cheeks tight (as if you were carrying walnuts in your ass), little baby steps, cross left leg over right foot and turn as if you were floating on air. Over and over, up and down my hallway. I set my hair in rags (very uncomfortable) so my hair would be in long curls, and packed up my model's case with makeup, every pair of shoes I owned, ribbons, dress shields, hair spray, rubber bands and anything else I could think of. I arranged for a babysitter to arrive when Bruce would leave for work.

I arrived at 7 A.M. exactly. I went to the designated place. No one was there. I sat down and waited and waited. At 8:30 the models started arriving. They piled in with their bags and plunked themselves down on chairs that were lined up in front of the makeup mirrors. They had done this a thousand times before. I decided to do whatever they did. I sat down. I lined up all my shoes on the floor. I laid out my makeup, hair spray and ribbons. I started putting on more makeup and fiddling with my hair. Adeline Ross came up to me. "Who are you, dear?"

"I'm Suzanne Somers. I'm so happy to meet you, Miss Ross. I'm very . . ." She cut me off.

"You're not a model, you're a dresser."

A dresser! Oh my God. I felt so stupid. The models around me started to giggle. I picked up my shoes, my makeup and my ribbons and stuffed them back into my bag. I felt like a fool. I spent the rest of the morning pressing clothes and helping the models in and out of their pretty outfits.

30

*B*ruce graduated from USF that June of 1966. I sat with the baby and listened to the dean of boys give the valedictory speech. Little Brucie was fidgeting. He kept pulling my hair, tugging at my earrings. Then his face went beet red and he pushed out a big smelly poop. It was hot and stuffy in the auditorium. The people on both sides of me reacted to the aroma. I felt so embarrassed. This was my life now, I thought. It revolves around baby spit-up and messy diapers. I wanted more than that.

I got a job as a nurse's aid at Kaiser Hospital. I would work from 2 P.M. until 5 P.M., come home, feed the baby, cook dinner for Bruce and me, then go back to the hospital until 10 P.M.

I loved my baby, but I was frustrated. My husband was going to law school now. Every free moment he spent poring over his books. I wanted to do something. I wanted excitement. I felt trapped. It made me feel crazy. I was tired. My schedule was exhausting. I would wake up real early, make my husband's breakfast, pack his lunch, change the baby, feed the baby, bathe the baby, do the dishes, clean the house, take the baby to the park for a swing, do the grocery shopping, pay the bills, work all afternoon at the hospital, cook dinner, put the baby to bed, go back to the hospital, come home, put myself to bed and start all over the next day. I was eighteen years old. I felt like life was over before it ever began.

My husband was working real hard too. He had dreams and ambitions; but our life together was boring. We had no sex life to speak of. It wasn't Bruce's fault. I just had so much anger at being trapped in this situation that I blamed Bruce. When it came time for us to have sex, my body turned to ice. I felt nothing. I wanted to feel nothing. Now, in retrospect, of course, I know it wasn't Bruce's fault. We created the situation together, but I was young, naïve and stupid. We never went anywhere. We had no money. I wanted out! I wanted out! No one I knew was divorced. Divorce was still fairly uncommon in 1966. I was frightened to consider it.

One day I picked up a piece of paper. On it I wote, "Dear Mr. Bates, I'm ready!"

Just like that! Impulsively I mailed it. I knew I had done something major. I knew by that one action, five little words, that I was altering the course of my life. I knew what that note would lead to—although at the time, I was not thinking of the future. It was immediate gratification that I wanted. I got it. Four days later my phone rang.

"Hi, Suzie," Mr. Bates said.

"Hi," I answered. My palms felt sweaty, my heart was racing.

"What does this note mean?" he asked.

"Oh, I just thought it would be nice to see you," I answered nervously.

"When?"

"How about . . . tonight? I get off work at ten o'clock. I can meet you outside. I'll tell my husband I have to work late."

"Great," he said. "I'll see you at ten. I still have my white Caddy. Bye."

"Bye," I answered. I just sat there staring. What have I done? What have I done? I thought. It suddenly felt so wrong. I went into the kitchen. I put together a really great dinner for Bruce. The Last Supper. My last dinner as a faithful wife. My hands were shaking. I took a bath and washed my hair. I rubbed Chanel body lotion all over my legs and arms. I didn't use it every day. It was too expensive, but today was special. Oh, God.

I went into little Brucie's room. He was so darling lying in his crib cooing. "Hello, little baby," I said. He looked at me and smiled a big toothless grin. He gurgled. Goo, goo, ga, ga. He couldn't talk yet. His room smelled like Johnson's Baby Powder and baby lotion. I twisted the music box. "Lullaby and good-night," it sang. I gently shook the mobile on his crib. He smiled and gurgled some more. "Go to sleep, baby. Have a nice nap. Mommy loves you so, so much." I touched his soft little face, pulled the little yellow quilt up around his neck and tiptoed out of his room. My head was a mess of feelings.

I couldn't think at work. My job was in the Multiphasics Department at the hospital. It didn't take a genius to do what I did. Multiphasics was a complete physical, including psychological tests. I handed out the psychological tests. In turn the patient would hand me a full urine-specimen cup. "No, no, Mrs. Krupnik. It's supposed to be a *urine* specimen!" Oh, God! Some days it was hard to take. The patient would then hand me back the psych test, and I would give it to the computer operator. The computer decided if the patient was sane or crazy.

"I'm not answering some of these questions. They're too personal," the patient said.

"It's up to you," I said cheerily; and so my day went.

My heart was palpitating. Nervous rushes shot from my toes to the top of my head. I was dropping things.

"Are you all right?" asked LaDonna, the computer operator.

"Oh, yes," I said nervously. "Just got a lot of things on my mind today."

At five o'clock I ran home to make dinner. I set the table real nice.

"Hey," Bruce said, "what's the occasion?"

"Nothing, really. Just thought it would be nice," I answered. I was flushed. Bruce looked at me, but in his wildest dreams he couldn't have imagined the truth. Little Brucie was crying.

"Oh, dear," I said. "I'd better give you a bath, honey. You're a mess." Brucie didn't want to waste time in the bath. He wanted dinner. He cried and kicked and splashed. My nurse's uniform got all wet. My hair got wet in front and went completely straight. I looked at myself in the mirror. I didn't look like the girl Mr. Bates had last seen. I wanted to cry. I was so nervous. So guilty.

"Come on, baby," I said to little Brucie. "Mommy will dry you off, then you can have a nice dinner."

Babies always look so cute when you take them out of the bath. I wrapped him in a fluffy little aqua baby towel. I dried him and rubbed baby powder all over his bottom. It always made him quiet. I put him in clean diapers and clean little pajamas with feet.

I looked at the clock. Oh, my God! It was 5:40 P.M. I had to be back at the hospital at six. I rushed the baby into the kitchen, put him in his highchair and fed him his three jars of baby food, lamb, vegetables and fruit. Brucie hated the lamb. I'd spoon it in his mouth, he'd spit it out. Then I'd mix it with the carrots and he'd swallow.

"You'd better start eating," I said to my husband. "I'm running late and I don't think I'm going to have time for dinner."

Bruce ate beef bourgignon, mashed potatoes and string beans. I had no appetite. When the baby finished his dinner he looked like he needed another bath.

"Could you clean him off and put him to bed?" I asked Bruce. "It's five minutes to six. I'm going to be late as it is." I kissed them both good-bye. I felt like Judas. Then I ran off.

I kept sneaking to the bathroom at work that night trying to make my hair look decent. I put on makeup. I normally didn't wear makeup to work, but tonight was different. It was hard enough trying to look sexy in a white nurse's uniform. I wanted to look good tonight. I looked at the clock: 9:30 P.M. I gulped. In one half hour I would become an unfaithful wife. Was sex going to be a part of this evening? I hadn't confronted the reality. Don't be naïve, Suzanne, I thought. You're no longer the blushing virgin. You're used goods. Nothing to save yourself for. Boy, I've really turned out great, I thought sarcastically.

At ten o'clock my knees started to shake. My legs felt like Jell-O. I walked the long walk down the hallway to the side exit like I was walking to the electric chair. Nothing was ever going to be the same again.

"Hi, Mahoney," Mr. Bates said.

"Hi." I felt embarrassed. We just sat there looking at each other for a couple of minutes. I could feel my body temperature rising. Suddenly, Mr. Bates reached over and grabbed me. He kissed me fiercely. There was an animal quality about it. He smelled of bourbon. His tongue was pushing into my mouth; farther, farther; as far and hard as it could go. I felt so unbelievably excited. So did he.

"Let's get out of here," he said. He grabbed me and pulled me to sit close to him in the front seat. He kept his arm around me, rubbing my face, my neck, my shoulders. His hands kept running through my hair messing it.

We drove into the Pacific Heights area of San Francisco. We pulled up under a large tree in front of a mansion, and then we let loose. He was all over me. I loved it. I had never felt such passion. His legs pushed against the steering wheel. The horn started honking. We didn't stop. Hot tongues; lips, wet, frantic, frantic, frantic. Oh, my God! It was the best, the most exciting. It was over, but I didn't want it to be over. I wanted it to go on and on and on. I felt like a woman for the first time. Now I'd had excitement. It was 12:30 A.M.

"I have to go," I said with my lips on his. I couldn't get enough. I kissed his neck all the way back to my car.

"When can I see you again?" Mr. Bates asked.

"Tomorrow," I answered without hesitation. "Tomorrow, same time, same place."

"I can't wait," he said.

"Me neither," I answered.

I got into my crummy car. I was now driving a beat-up old Volkswagen. The car was cold. I looked at myself in the mirror. I was a mess. My hair was a mess. My makeup was smeared. My lips were swollen.

My dress was a wrinkled mass. I tried to straighten myself out. Oh, God, I thought. I hope Bruce is asleep.

I tiptoed into the house. It was dark and quiet. I slipped into the bathroom. Have to take a bath. Have to wash my face. Get rid of this dress. Put it in the laundry hamper. I was a combination of stress, fear, guilt, excitement, exhilaration. I don't want to get caught, I don't want to get caught, I kept thinking. There was no future, only tomorrow night and maybe the next. I had to have more. I couldn't stop. I wanted more.

I got into bed, all the telltale signs of love washed away. I smelled like Noxzema and Dial soap. Only my throbbing genitals could give me away. Bruce never woke up.

When I opened my eyes the next morning, my husband was gone. I heard the baby talking to himself in his crib. "Hello, little baby," I said gently. Brucie was all wet. "Poor little thing." I bathed him and changed him into one of his little outfits. During his breakfast the phone rang.

"Hello, sexy," Mr. Bates said. "You were great last night. I told you you'd be ready one day," he said.

"I can't stop thinking about you," I whispered.

"Tonight," he said.

"I can't wait," I answered. The baby started crying. "I've gotta go."

That night was more of the same. Sexy, frantic, unbelievably passionate. It was hard for me to believe. I was now an eighteen-year-old adultress.

Three weeks later my husband said, "You have to work late again?"

"Yes," I lied. "So many people are taking multiphasics, we're staying open late every night." It was getting precarious, but I was good at it. The lying, the secrets; it was like déjà vu!

My affair with Mr. Bates got serious real fast. We wanted to see more of each other. We dreamed of being able to spend the entire night together. I wanted to do the normal things that lovers do; walk on the beach, go out to dinner, go away for a weekend. I kept thinking if I hadn't been so stupid in college, I wouldn't be in this horrible, deceitful situation right now. I felt awful lying to Bruce so much; always covering, always on the verge of getting caught. It would have been so easy for him to find out. One quick ride over to the hospital at 11 P.M. and he would have found the Multiphasics Department completely closed up. I was living on the edge—never knowing when I came home if this would be the night of discovery. I grew up living on the edge. It had always been that way. I was used to operating within crises. Without crises life was not exciting. So, I continued my affair.

"There's a baby shower Saturday night for Pat," I told my husband. Pat was a pregnant girl I worked with. There was no baby shower, but it was one of the many stories I concocted to get out of the house. I was so excited. Mr. Bates and I were going out to dinner and then to his house. Until now our time together had been spent in the front seat of his car. The baby shower was a flimsy excuse. Ladies never stayed at those things past ten or eleven at night. I knew with dinner and romance I wouldn't get home until well after midnight.

On Saturday I fed little Brucie his dinner, bathed him and put him to bed. I sat down and ate dinner with my husband, trying not to eat too much. I was looking forward to my second dinner. I dressed in a black knit dress with gold earrings and black silk pumps. I even went so far as to wrap an empty box with baby wrapping paper to make my lie believable.

"Well, good-night," I said. "Don't study too hard." I looked at Bruce and felt overwhelmed with sorrow and guilt. This is such a terrible thing I am doing to him, I thought. He doesn't deserve this kind of treatment. He's been good to me. I felt so awful, I considered breaking the date. But I didn't. Mr. Bates would have become crazy. I wouldn't be surprised if he came banging on my front door. He didn't care if he broke up my marriage. He wanted it to break up. He was already talking marriage to me.

"What time will you be home?" Bruce asked.

"Oh, eleven or so. Bye!" Then I left.

I'm such a shit, I thought. All my life, I've worried about being a good girl, and now here I am the baddest of bad girls. My father was right. I am a tramp. I did get "knocked up." I was an adulteress. Oh, God, help me, I prayed!

My car pulled into Mr. Bates' driveway. I reached in my purse and pulled out some sparkly rhinestone earrings and replaced the gold ones with them. I sprayed myself once more with Chanel Number 5. I looked great. I felt awful.

"You look gorgeous, Suzie," Mr. Bates said.

"Well, I feel terrible. I just can't help it. I feel so guilty. I can't stand lying all the time. I'm afraid of getting caught. I'm a nervous wreck," I said.

"I know, I know, it's difficult. I feel sorry for you too," he said. "I know how hard it is. Here, have a glass of wine. You'll feel better."

We sat in front of the fire, all the while Mr. Bates telling me how beautiful I was. "I love your hair. You've got great eyes, your legs are fantastic."

Pretty soon I was feeling a lot better. We went to a fancy, expensive Italian restaurant. More wine, veal, pasta, all the while looking into each other's eyes. Long, dreamy looks. People in the restaurant were staring at us. I looked so young, he looked so old, and they noticed. They also noticed that we were lovers. You couldn't miss it.

We had no dessert. We knew no dessert could match what we'd be doing as soon as we got back to Mr. Bates' house. It was incredible. Gentle, tender, then fierce, urgent, passionate.

I looked at the clock. Oh, my God, 2 A.M. "I've got to go." I was terrified. For sure I'd get caught tonight. I drove home like a maniac. Gotta think up an excuse, I thought. No baby shower could possibly last this long. Thank God, Bruce had never thought to ask where the shower was being held, and he didn't know Pat's last name. I felt panic. Maybe he'll be asleep. Please, please be asleep. I drove up to the house. The lights were on.

"Where've you been?" Bruce asked icily.

"Well," I said, "we were drinking a lot of punch at the shower. I guess we got a little drunk and suddenly we all looked at the clock and noticed that it was 1 A.M. I drove LaDonna home; you know, she lives way out in the boonies, and after I dropped her off, the car just stopped. I got out and started fiddling with the engine. I pushed the carburetor thing up and down. I think it was jammed; and finally, I got the car working, and here I am!" Please believe me, I thought. Please believe me.

Bruce just looked at me. His eyes were hard. After a long pause he said, "Next time you should call me."

Whew! I thought. "I will, I will. I promise."

That was close, I thought. What would I have done if he caught me? Would we get a divorce? Would I be the first divorced person in my family? In my whole town? Could I handle it? What would I do? How could I make money? I hadn't had a single modeling job yet. I should stop seeing Mr. Bates. It's too heavy.

The next day, Mr. Bates said, "I love you, Suzie. You can't stop seeing me. I know you want me. Leave him! Divorce him. Marry me. I'll be a wonderful father to little Bruce. I've always wanted a child. I want to see you tonight." He was pleading. Desperate.

"All right, tonight we'll talk about it," I said.

Mr. Bates picked me up after work. We went to our usual spot in Pacific Heights. After two minutes of protesting we were back at it again. Hot, desperate lovemaking. I couldn't stop seeing him. I couldn't bring myself to leave Bruce. The dilemma was too much to bear. Don't think about it now, I thought.

Tension was building at home. Bruce didn't know what was wrong, but he knew it wasn't right.

"I'm not happy in our marriage," I finally told him. "I'm bored."

"Maybe you should go talk to Father Schallert," Bruce said. "He's a sociologist. One of the foremost in the country. Maybe he could help you."

I obliged. I made an appointment with Father Schallert. I told him about my boredom and feeling trapped. I told him I never wanted to be married in the first place. I told him I got pregnant without ever having penetration. I told him I felt that life was over for me, that I was unsatisfied, that I wanted more out of life; a career even. I told him I didn't love my husband; I liked him, but I didn't love him and that I had told my mother this on my wedding night. I told him I was afraid of divorce. I never told him about Mr. Bates.

Father Schallert thought for a while. "When you and your husband make love, how long does it take?" he asked.

"About five or ten minutes," I answered.

"Okay," Father Schallert said. "Next time you make love, I want you to set an alarm clock for twenty minutes. Do not stop lovemaking until the alarm goes off. Next time you make love, set the alarm clock for twenty-five minutes. Every time you make love, increase the time by five minutes until you work up to an hour."

I sat there. I waited for more. He said nothing.

"Don't you want to talk about everything I've told you?" I asked.

"Don't need to," he said. "Divorce is out of the question. You'll be excommunicated. I think the alarm clock will do the trick. Try it!" I was dismissed.

Simple. Screw for twenty minutes, save your marriage. I laughed as I left the rectory. What an asshole, I thought. If this is the church to which I've devoted my spiritual self, I'm a fool. *Excommunicated!* They're the ones who told me I must get married. I never wanted to. Shit!

What a waste of time, I thought. No way am I going to make love to an alarm clock. My failing marriage had nothing to do with sexual duration. I couldn't believe it. I pour my heart out to this so-called expert and he tells me to screw for twenty minutes! What about feelings? What about love? Aren't those important elements in a marriage?

I walked home. The only message I got out of meeting with Father Schallert was the realization that this church no longer worked for me. I was and am a very spiritual person. I believe in God, but *my* God.

All these years I had been watching terrible things happen at home; the violence, the craziness, the guilt, the shame; and the church never provided any answers for us. Have faith, they kept telling my mother. She accepted their simple solution. I couldn't. Suddenly I could see the difference between my mother and myself. She would have set the clock. She would have obeyed the priest. I wasn't proud of my reaction, but I knew I couldn't do that.

31

"*H*ow did it go?" Bruce asked.

"Fine," I said. "I feel a lot better." More lies, more hiding, more secrets.

I was getting so much pressure from Mr. Bates. "Leave him," he said. "I want you to tell him about us. You don't belong in that marriage. You belong with me. Grow up, Suzie. Make a decision," he repeated over and over.

I kept stalling Mr. Bates. I knew I had to make a decision, but I also knew I was not going to marry Mr. Bates. The decision I had to make was to abandon both of these men. It was painful. It would leave me all alone. I was scared. I wished I could love Mr. Bates enough to marry him. Life would be so much easier. But I knew my main attraction to him was physical. When I considered the day to day, I knew he wasn't enough for me. I wanted more. I was attracted to the illicit excitement of my affair. Even at this point, with all the pressure and fear of getting caught, I couldn't give it up. I thrived on the crisis. Crisis was part of my disease.

I was a nervous wreck. Bruce was becoming very suspicious. Every time the phone would ring I would jump.

"Who was that?" Bruce asked.

"Uh, some blind people selling lightbulbs," I lied. I could tell Bruce didn't believe me.

"You've got to stop calling me when Bruce is home," I whispered to Mr. Bates on the phone. I still called him Mr. Bates.

"I won't, Suzie," he said. "I want him to know about us. You've got to tell him. This has gone on long enough. I'm tired of sharing you. I want you all to myself. Tell him tonight," he demanded.

"I'll try," I answered.

Pressure, pressure. Too much pressure. This pressure was making Mr. Bates very unattractive to me. I wanted it to be the way it was in the beginning. Sexual. Animal. Now all he talked about was marriage. Get out of this marriage. Jump into another marriage. That's the last thing I wanted to do. I don't want to be anybody's wife, I thought.

Mr. Bates picked me up at the hospital that night. My nightly liaison had gone on so long that Bruce thought I had new working hours. I worked till midnight, I'd told him. He either never noticed, or never wanted to ask why my paycheck didn't reflect the new hours. I guess he was afraid to know the truth.

"Did you tell him?" Mr. Bates asked.

"Not yet. I need more time," I told him.

We drove to our usual spot in Pacific Heights. It was cold and rainy outside. I wasn't in the mood. The whole thing was making me feel cheap; like a tramp. Suddenly, making love in the front seat of his car felt so sleazy.

"I'm just worn out," I told Mr. Bates. I needed time to think.

When I arrived home that night the lights were on. I shivered. Thank God I'm not all messed, I thought. I pulled the car into the driveway. My heart was racing as I walked up the stairs. I opened the front door. Bruce was sitting at the kitchen table. There was a beer in front of him.

"Work hard tonight?" Bruce asked. He looked strange. His face looked hard.

"Yes, it was real busy tonight," I said warily.

"Really," Bruce answered. He sounded sarcastic. "I went over to the hospital to see you tonight," Bruce said. My heart stopped. This is it, I thought. I'm getting caught. "Yes, I stopped by the Multiphasics Department and guess what? It was all closed down. The sign said it closed every night at ten," he said accusingly.

My mind was racing. I felt like a trapped rabbit. "Didn't you go up to the tenth floor?" I asked.

"What do you mean?" he asked.

"Well," I lied, "at ten o'clock we move the whole operation upstairs, something to do with security in that part of the building. Didn't I tell you about that? I guess I didn't think it was important. Gee, I wish I had seen you. That would have been fun. It gets so boring up there." More lies.

Bruce just looked at me. "I don't believe you," he said quietly.

"Why?" I asked indignantly. "Why would I lie? Do you think I enjoy staying out this late each night? What do you think I'm doing?" My voice had elevated. I felt panic.

"Are you seeing someone else?" he asked.

This is my chance, I thought. A chance to get out. Start over. A new life without lies, deceit or anger. "No," I answered incredulously. Why did I say that, I wondered.

"If I find out that you are, I'll kill you," Bruce said. He looked mean. He walked down the hall toward the bedroom.

I was cornered from every direction.

"Tell him," Mr. Bates said on the phone the next morning. "If you don't, I will," he threatened.

"No, please! I'll tell him myself," I said desperately.

"Will I see you tonight?" Mr. Bates asked impatiently.

"I can't. If Bruce catches me, he's going to do something awful to me. Give me some time. Please!" I pleaded. I couldn't stand it. I had gotten myself so trapped. There was no place to turn; not even the church. My church, that had given me so much solace all my life, now told me that whichever direction I took, I would no longer be welcome as a member of its congregation. I had broken the rules. The Catholic church only works if you follow all the rules. So, now I couldn't even pray. I would have to figure this one out by myself.

I stayed home that night feigning sickness. I was afraid to go to work for fear that Bruce would now go to the tenth floor at ten o'clock and find out that I had lied. We spent a wordless night together. I couldn't eat. I couldn't sleep. It was all crashing in on me. I wished I were dead.

The phone rang at eight the next morning. "Well? What did he say?" demanded Mr. Bates. "Did you tell him?"

"Yes," I lied. "He is very upset and says he wants to try to work things out." It was all a lie. I needed more time. "I have to give Bruce that much," I said. "After all, he is my husband. I have to act like I'm making an attempt to save our marriage," I lied some more.

"Shit!" said Mr. Bates. "I don't want you sleeping with him. How long is this going to take?" he asked irritably.

"I'm not sure. A couple of weeks or more," I said.

"No! I can't wait that long. I've been waiting for three years!" he yelled. "Two weeks. No more! I mean it. I want to see you tonight. It's been two days."

"I can't," I screamed. "I don't want to see you for two weeks. I just can't take any more pressure. I can't tell any more lies. I feel like I'm going crazy. I don't even know if I want to see you anymore! This isn't any fun. You put so much pressure on me. I'm just not sure how I feel about you anymore." Finally, some semblance of truth was coming out of me.

Mr. Bates went quiet. "Suzie, you love me, don't you? Tell me you love me." He sounded desperate.

"I don't know anymore. Please, just leave me alone for a while."

I felt such a relief to get Mr. Bates off my back. I went back to work that night prepared to hang around the tenth floor till midnight just to keep my cover. I was depressed. It was hard to keep a cheery disposition at work with such a heavy heart. I drove home at 5 P.M. to make dinner for Bruce and the baby. I walked up the stairs trying to remember if I had a fresh vegetable in the refrigerator to serve with the baked chicken. I opened the front door. I gasped. Oh, my God! There, sitting on my living-room sofa were Mr. Bates and my husband. I wanted to run. My heart was pounding, and I was hyperventilating. Both men looked up at me. The room felt black, ominous. Bruce had hate in his eyes. Mr. Bates looked pathetic. He was drunk.

"Mr. Bates just finished telling me that you fucked him on every street in San Francisco," Bruce said icily.

I felt crazy. There was no getting out this time. It was over. Caught. Anger and fear welled up in me. I lunged at Mr. Bates. I grabbed his neck and dug my fingernails into him. "Get out of here, you asshole," I screamed at him. "Get out of my house. I never want to see you ever again." I kicked him, hit him, scratched him. He drunkenly made his way to the front door, all the while trying to block my attacks. "I hate you! I hate you! I hate your guts," I screamed after him.

The baby began crying from the other room. I started to run to him. Bruce grabbed me. "Stay away from that baby," he said. He slapped me hard across the face. He slapped me again on the other side of the face. He grabbed my hair.

"I'm sorry. I'm so sorry," I screamed.

"You slut!" Bruce threw me to the floor by my hair. He kicked me. "Get out of here," he said venomously. "Get out of here right now or you'll never see your baby again."

"Oh, no! Please don't do that! Please! Please! The baby needs me. Please," I cried. "I promise I'll be good. I know I've been stupid. Please forgive me. I beg you. Please!" I felt so desperate.

"Go back to work," Bruce said. "I need time to think." He looked broken.

I felt worse than I'd ever felt in all my life. If it weren't for the baby,

I would have jumped off the Golden Gate Bridge. I became what my father had always said. I was a worthless, immoral tramp.

I trembled as I pulled into the driveway after work that night. I'll sleep in the baby's room, I thought. I can't sleep with Bruce anymore. He's too disgusted with me. I didn't know what to expect. Bruce hates me now. I can't blame him. I wish I could start my life all over again. I'd change everything. I wouldn't change the baby though. I loved little Brucie so much. He was the only good thing in my life.

My mother answered MY front door. "What are you doing here?" I asked. I was bewildered.

"Your husband has left you. He's taken the baby," she replied. She looked shaken.

"Oh, God! No! No! No! Where are they? Where did they go?" My worst fear had been realized. I felt an ache in my heart as if I had been stabbed; like someone had just ripped out my guts. "Oh, my God! Oh, my God," I cried. "Mother, please tell me where they are," I cried again.

"I don't know," Mother said. "Bruce called me and told me everything. He said I should come up here because you might try to kill yourself. I'm so ashamed of you, Suzanne. How could you? Didn't I teach you anything?" My mother looked at me disgustedly. It was the lowest point of my life. I had lost my husband, lost my baby and now I had lost my mother. My mother! The two people I most cared for; my mother and my baby. The two most important people in the world to me; and I had lost them both. Life wasn't worth living. I had totally botched things.

I hid my head in my hands. I sobbed, "I'm so very sorry. Please forgive me." I cried uncontrollably the entire night. Please, please, dear God, give me another chance, I prayed. Please forgive me. Let me start over. I'll stay married to Bruce. I won't get a divorce. Please let me have my baby back.

Mr. Bates called first thing in the morning. My mother answered. "Get out of our lives, you dirty old man," my mother said. "You've brought nothing but heartache and shame to us." My mother hung up. The phone immediately rang again. We let it ring and ring and ring. I didn't want to talk to him. I hated him. He made me sick.

By the second day I no longer wanted to kill myself; but I felt desperate. I called everyone in my family. "Have you seen Bruce and the baby?" I asked my sister.

"No," she answered. Her voice was cold and accusing.

"Have you seen my baby?" I asked Dan. Same response.

My family had turned on me. They were ashamed of me. Whatever had gone on throughout our lives, there had always been strong moral overtones. We had been a good Catholic family. Dad always brought the entire paycheck home. No matter how drunk he became, he never picked up with other women.

I had done the unthinkable. Both Maureen and Danny were morally outraged. How had I sunk so low? I understood how my sister and brother felt and was ashamed of myself. But I didn't care. I was so desperate I called them over and over. I didn't go to work. I couldn't work. My mother went home. She was worried about Michael. She had left him with friends because my dad had been drunk and belligerent.

I was glad she left. Her presence made me feel worse. She couldn't understand me. She had stayed by my dad all these years through his drunken, belligerent tirades; and I couldn't even stand by my husband of one year for the simple reason that I didn't love him. She was very angry with me.

"Life doesn't always go the way we want it, Suzanne," she said as she was leaving. "We are put on this earth to make sacrifices so we can earn our perpetual reward in Heaven." Then she left.

More church bullshit. Weren't we put here to be happy? I thought.

Four days went by. No word of my baby. Mr. Bates called incessantly. "Leave me alone," I said. "I never want to see or hear from you again." I hung up. The last time he called he was very drunk.

"I love ya, Suzie," he slurred. Ugh! It made me sick. He sounded just like my drunken father.

I continued to call everyone in the family. I called my sister. I called my brother over and over. My brother said, "They're not going to come here, Suzanne."

No one had any idea where the baby was. "If you see them, please call me," I said desperately. No one had any empathy. I deserved what was happening to me. I had no tears left; just a dark, empty feeling inside. I didn't comb my hair. I didn't eat. I couldn't sleep. I prayed. I prayed to the God that didn't want me anymore. I begged his forgiveness. I was all alone; an outcast.

On the fifth day Bruce and little Brucie walked in the front door. Little Brucie smiled a big grin at me. He outstretched his arms. "Ma, Ma," he said. I grabbed him. I hugged him and squeezed him.

"I love you, I love you, I love you so much. My baby, my baby, my sweet little Brucie," I cried over and over. "I missed you so much." It felt so good to touch him again; to smell him. I felt so much emotion. "Please don't take him from me again," I pleaded to Bruce. "Thank you so much for bringing him home." I was truly grateful. "I can't live without him," I said.

"What about me?" Bruce asked. "Can you live without me?"

"I don't know," I answered honestly. "I'm willing to try to make it work."

"I've done a lot of thinking," Bruce said. "I'm really hurt. I don't know if I can ever get over it. I don't know if I can forgive you; but as a family, I think we've got something here. I'm willing to try." Then Bruce put his arms around me and the baby. The three of us stood there hugging in the hallway.

"I'm sorry," I whispered.

The baby started fidgeting. We broke our embrace. Life was fighting to return to normalcy.

"By the way," I asked Bruce as I was bringing the baby to his room, "where did you stay while you were gone?"

"At your brother's house," he said.

32

I n 1967 we moved to Novato, California. Bruce and I decided to start anew; erase all the memories. Novato was a suburb of San Francisco where you could get a lot of house for little money. It was a "tract" development out in nowhere. There was no town to speak of, just a brand-new shopping center. We had Ralph's Supermarket, Thrifty Drug Store, a Laundromat, dry cleaner and a Sears catalogue store. The only place to go out at night was the bowling alley. The area was halfway between San Francisco and Napa and it was hot. Sticky, sweaty, hot.

"Watch out for those rattlesnakes," our new landlord told us. "Ever since they come in here buildin', the rattlesnakes got all moved around and ya never know where they're gonna show up," he said. Oh, great, I thought.

Bruce was working in San Francisco as a claims adjuster, so he would have a fifty-minute commute every morning. Bruce had decided that law was not for him; so he dropped out of law school and decided to pursue a master's, then a Ph.D. in sociology.

Our rented house was a typical tract home; two bedrooms, two baths, living room, kitchen-breakfast-room combo and a two-car garage. It also had a small backyard. The outside of the house was a nondescript green. The inside was dark. I painted all the walls white. I spent days stripping the cabinets and antiquing them a popular green color. My brother Dan got us a "good deal" on some wall-to-wall celery-colored shag rugs.

We also bought ourselves a speedboat. We couldn't afford it, of course. We bought it on credit—fifteen hundred dollars with a one-hundred-dollar down payment and forty dollars a month after that for the three years. The San Francisco Bay ended in Novato, and there was a nice area to launch our speedboat right near where we lived. I had always loved water skiing and Brucie loved to sit up front next to his dad and play the little captain. It was all part of "starting a new life." Bruce and I were determined to start over—put the past behind. We wanted to make it work—new area, new house, new friends, new rules. Even a new boat. So we moved in. It wasn't going to be easy. There were a lot of bad feelings left—a lot of anxiety. Trust had been violated and it was very difficult to trust and believe again.

Bruce and I were very tentative with each other. I was trying too hard to "feel." I wanted it to work. I was overwhelmed with guilt; so to make up for it, I became the perfect wife, the perfect mother, the perfect homemaker. All the while, gnawing away inside me was discontent. I knew I could do so much more.

Lovemaking was courteous. I tried to be the perfect lover, also. I tried to feel the excitement that wasn't there. Bruce touched the right places, but my nerve endings were dead. I faked ecstasy.

One morning after Bruce had left for work, the doorbell rang. It was a neighbor from down the street; a woman in her twenties who had the smell of matronliness about her. She was holding a coffee pot.

"Hello," she said. "All the ladies on the block get together every morning for a coffee klatch, and we'd like to invite you to join."

"Oh, how nice," I said. I thought I would barf. Here I was in this nondescript tract home development, married to a man with whom I felt frigid, being invited to the block coffee klatch. Is this all there is? I thought. Is this the prison to which I've condemned myself at age nineteen? Shit!

I went to the coffee klatch. One of the ladies was married to a fireman, one lady's husband sold food-freezer plans. We talked about diaper services and how great baking soda is to remove the sour smell of baby throw-up.

33

I went home and called my modeling agency. "Don't you have any work for me?" I was begging. "I'd be happy to do catalogues or conventions." Shortly after that phone call I was booked on my first job. It was for the American Medical Association; hanging in traction for three days at their convention. I was thrilled.

I was the perfect traction model. I arrived each morning on time, and dutifully had my arms and legs strung up. The doctors at the convention would pass by me all day long. "When this job is over, you're gonna be two inches taller. Yuk, yuk," they all said. I laughed each time as if it were the first time I'd ever heard the joke. My employers, the traction company, were delighted with me. They even called my modeling agency.

"She's terrific," they said. "What a cheery personality," said another. "We'd like to book her for next year."

Because of the recommendations, I quickly got another job. This time it was for the American Walnut Association. All I had to do was dress up in a squirrel suit and pass out nuts on Market Street in San Francisco. "Wanna nut?" I'd ask perfect strangers. I felt like a dope in the outfit, but it was work.

"I'll show you my nuts if you show me yours," one wise guy on the street responded.

Hey, what the heck. I made 150 dollars a day. It was worth the come-ons and the verbal abuse.

My work was upgraded a bit. I was hired as the pretty blonde you can barely see in the Chevrolet ads. These were shot in Carmel, California. I was hired because I was blonde and because I had a nice personality. I'd be fun to go on location with.

One night on location in Carmel, the photographer, Charlie, banged on my motel door. "Can I sleep in your room? I'm locked out of my room and I don't want to wake up Pete. I'll sleep on the floor," he said, trying to reassure me.

"No," I said.

Between my husband's salary and the little I was making in my modeling, we just couldn't make ends meet.

"I'll get a full-time job," I told Bruce. I was qualified for nothing.

I applied for a job as a cocktail waitress at the Villa Roma Cocktail Lounge in Fisherman's Wharf, San Francisco. The hours would work out. Bruce would be coming home from work about the time I needed to leave. Little Brucie would never have to be left with a babysitter. I got the job. I lied about my age.

"Oh, sure," I said. "I've worked a lot of cocktail lounges."

The bar manager thought I was cute and had a nice personality. He hired me without checking my references.

Being a cocktail waitress was more than I had anticipated. I thought I knew everything about booze. I grew up with whiskey, beer, gin and tonic, vodka on the rocks and an occasional old-fashioned. I wasn't prepared for planters' punch, brandy Alexanders, Manhattans, martinis, daiquiris, gin fizz and a hundred others. But I even got used to those. It was the tables that said, "I'll have a bourbon and seven, bourbon and water, scotch and water, scotch straight up and whiskey over."

I'd say, "Okay, bourbon and water, scotch and seven, whiskey and soda?"

"No!" they'd yell. "Whiskey over, scotch and water!" I'd get so confused.

One man said, "I'll have a pinch straight up."

I got indignant. "I'm sorry, sir. They don't pay me that much here." I didn't know "Pinch" was a very good brand of scotch. I also learned that I wasn't very good with money. I'd get so confused making change that often at the end of the evening I'd end up with less money than I started with.

Months went by. It was an exhausting schedule. I didn't get home till 3 A.M. and Brucie would wake up at 6 A.M. wanting breakfast and a bath; but we needed the money, so I continued my nightly commute to the bar.

Here I was again watching drunks get drunk. My life story. It was interesting. There were a group of regulars who would come to the bar every night at the end of business—between five and six. They were well-dressed, middle-income people who would start drinking politely, making conversation with those around them. By nine o'clock they'd pair off and drink till they were plastered; and somewhere around ten thirty or eleven they'd leave in couples "to grab a bite to eat," which really meant "to get laid." It fascinated me. The only two people in the bar who weren't drinking were myself and the bartender. The regulars kept sending drinks over to me, but I'd tell the bartender to give me the cash instead.

One of the regulars became fascinated by me. He was a young, good-looking, junior-executive type. He would sit in his chair all night nursing his drinks, all the while trying to make eye contact with me. I avoided his eyes, but I couldn't help the feelings that were stirring inside me. One night after work at 2 A.M. he was waiting outside for me.

"I don't know what else to say," he said. "I have got the maddest crush on you."

Oh, God, I thought. "Please don't," I said. "I'm married. I plan to keep it that way."

"Lucky guy," he said and walked away.

I knew then that it was only a matter of time before I'd be bored to tears with my marriage. I didn't want to get into another illicit situation. It was time to get out.

Bruce wasn't surprised when I told him. "It's just not working for me. I've tried, but I just don't feel what I want to feel." Bruce moved out.

It wasn't working for him either. We never should have gotten married in the first place. We were good friends who married each other for the wrong reason. We had both been forced into a situation that placed huge burdens on us. The environment removed the friendship, and then we had nothing. We both felt tremendous sadness that day. We tried and we failed. Still in our teens, we now had to start anew with our first major failure hanging over our heads. I was to be a "divorcée." At that time people considered divorcées desperate, sexually starved women. Bruce had to live knowing his ex-wife had played around on him. We both felt terribly burdened and depleted. It was a low point in both our lives. I wished him well. He kissed my forehead and gave little Bruce one last long hug. I fought to hold the tears back as he walked out the front door.

I now lived alone with little Bruce in this mundane, colorless house. I started dating the guy from the bar where I worked. He took me to nice places. I enjoyed him. Nothing else.

Ours wasn't an angry divorce. We had tried, but deep in our hearts we both knew it was over. Bruce didn't seem angry with me, and I was happy about that. He visited our child as often as he could; then the lawyer got involved.

We had to have grounds for divorce, and there was the question of custody. I had never considered that Bruce might want custody. When he tried to get it, bitterness grew up between us and escalated to name calling. All of Bruce's repressed anger toward me rose to the surface.

The grounds for my divorce were adultery. I was an adulteress. I thought about wearing a big scarlet A around my neck. I asked for one dollar a month alimony and 150 dollars a month child support. I didn't get the alimony.

On the morning of the court divorce proceedings, I sat there listening to Bruce's lawyer talk about my mental cruelty to him; that I was an adulteress. My neighbor (the husband who sold food-freezer plans) testified on behalf of my husband that I was an adulteress. He testified to a green Pontiac Firebird that he observed in my driveway all night long.

"And when did you last see this car parked in the driveway?" the judge asked.

"This morning," my neighbor answered.

"And was it there all night?" the judge asked again.

"Yes," replied my neighbor.

"That will be all," the judge said.

The car, in fact, did belong to my friend from the bar. So there it was in the public records for all to see. I was officially recorded as an adulteress. But it was over. I felt a bittersweet elation. I was now on my own for the first time in my life. I got custody of my child, which was all I cared about. Bruce had not fought very hard for it. I would, somehow, some way, make a good life for my baby and me; just as I'd promised him on the day he was born.

Part TWO

34

As I look back on this next part of my life, I wonder how I ever made it through. I was totally unequipped emotionally and intellectually for the challenges that lay ahead. I had no knowledge of the disease within. I simply had the desire to survive. I wanted to redeem myself in my family's eyes. I wanted my mother, brother and sister to be proud of me again; I wanted to provide a happy home life for my child. But how was I going to do it? The reality of having no money really hit me. Up until now Bruce and I had had problems making ends meet, but there was always enough to pay for rent, gas and electricity, telephone and food. Bruce moved out in August 1967. It was now September and I didn't have the money to pay this month's rent. I quit my job at the Villa Roma Cocktail Lounge. I couldn't leave little Brucie alone every night. Also, I didn't earn enough to pay for a babysitter and keep a household going. The first thing I had to do was move back to San Francisco. I needed an apartment with two bedrooms and someplace safe to keep a child.

Finding an apartment in San Francisco was not easy. Everything was so expensive. I had been looking constantly for four months. I was behind in my rent, I hadn't received any child-support payments yet, and my landlord told me I had to get out.

I was still casually dating the man I had met at the Villa Roma Cocktail Lounge. His name was Fred.

"I'm going to be commuting to Newport Beach from now on," he said. "I'll only be home on weekends. Do you want to share an apartment?"

I really didn't want to, but sharing the rent was very appealing, especially since Fred was a salaried person and I knew his portion would be on time. Besides, I was feeling desperate.

We found a nice little place on Lake Street in San Francisco near a park. We had to tell the landlady that we were married. It was easy to convince her that we were a happy little family. More lies. The rent was

400 dollars a month. I was sure that I'd be able to come up with 200 dollars. The big downside was the bedroom situation. There were only two bedrooms. I told Fred I would sleep on the couch on the weekends. Sex was no longer a regular part of our relationship. We moved in.

I immediately found that I resented Fred's presence. I hadn't thought it through. I hadn't thought about mealtimes and the dailiness of sharing an apartment. Dinner was for three. Breakfast was for three. We watched television together. We went to the store together. I was back in the same old rut; just one of the faces had changed. I had also forgotten that Fred was a drinker. Tanqueray gin. He'd start early afternoon and drink until he was whacked. Then he'd chase me around the apartment. Now that he had companionship, he no longer needed to go to the Villa Roma. He drank at home. I counted the hours until Monday when he'd have to leave.

During the week it was peaceful and lovely. I took Brucie to the park every day. I'd push him on the swing. We'd ride the merry-go-round, I'd slide down the slide with him. We were two children together. Little Brucie was my best friend in the whole world. At night I'd read him a story and lie next to him until he fell asleep.

My mother called and invited me to dinner on Sunday. It was a good excuse to get away from Fred. I didn't know about seeing my family. I felt awkward, guilty and ashamed. Ever since the "Mr. Bates affair," I had avoided my family; but it would be good for Brucie to get together with his five cousins, I thought, so I said, "Yes, we'd love to come."

I borrowed Fred's car to drive to my mother's house. The Volkswagen that Bruce and I owned had long since disintegrated and Bruce drove a company car. I was "without wheels." I hoped that in time I could earn enough to buy a car, any kind of car, and pay my monthly expenses. Money was such a problem.

I didn't invite Fred to go with me to my mother's. I didn't want to invite him. I couldn't invite him. "My dad is dead," I told him. It was part of a new fantasy I had created for myself. I was on my own now. No one knew anything about me, so I decided to kill off my dad. Why should I continue to live with the shame of my drunken father? I told anyone who was interested that my dad was a doctor, had a stroke and died. No one asked me any more questions after that. Having a dead father who was a doctor, combined with all my fancy private schools, painted a more respectable picture of me. I had spent my life "not feeling good enough" for anyone. I was going to create a new me from the bottom up. It was the beginning of a very dangerous time for me mentally.

Little Brucie and I walked in the back door of my mother's house. Everyone made a big deal over Brucie.

"He's grown so much."

"Look at all his teeth."

"What a cute little sweater he's wearing."

"How old is he now?" my brother asked.

"Two and one-half," I answered.

Everyone (including myself) acted as if nothing had happened during the past years. We didn't mention the divorce or Mr. Bates. I'm sure they were trying to be polite, let "bygones be bygones"; but burying problems had always been our family way of dealing with them. No one had ever said to my dad after one of his "terrible nights," "You were awful."

The rules were firmly in place. No one asked me anything about my life. No "How're you making out?" because the rest of the sentence would be, "since the divorce." No "Do you have enough money to get by?" or "Where are you living these days?" These were my problems. I was responsible for any mess I made. That was also our way. We had been told since childhood, "Once out of the house, you're on your own." I never questioned it.

In turn, I didn't ask them how they were doing. It never entered my mind that their lives could possibly be messed up. I had no idea that as adult children of an alcoholic they could be suffering the residual effects of a childhood riddled with fear and anxiety.

I couldn't know that Maureen's drinking was starting to cause problems at home. I had no idea that Mardi and Danny argued over the residual effects of his alcohol consumption—late for dinner, dents in the car, hanging out with the guys. Mom and Dad's problems were obvious, but what was happening to Michael? We all had new secrets to keep. Everyone was there—Maureen, Bill, and their three children, Billy, Timmy and Joey. Danny, Mardi and their two children, Sean and Erin, and, of course, my mom, Dad and Michael. Bill and Maureen brought their own gin, which they shared with Danny. Dad drank beer, but I'm sure he had a bottle stashed. His face had that peculiar shine that whiskey gave him. Everyone laughed a lot. It was nice to be together again. I hadn't realized how lonely and cut off I had been. The kids ran around like crazy. They made forts in every room. Brucie's face was red, flushed and sweaty from the excitement. I hadn't realized how little time he had spent with other children. Dinner was roast beef, mashed potatoes, gravy, fresh peas and my mother's famous zwieback torte. It was a concoction of peaches and custard with a zwieback cookie crust.

It was delicious. I loved this dinner. It made me feel secure. Sunday-night dinners had always been less tumultuous than weeknights, especially if Father wasn't there. I noticed that Mother hadn't invited Father tonight. I guess she didn't want to take any chances.

I had never seen my sister really drunk. It scared me. Maureen, Bill and Danny had finished off the entire fifth of gin; then they drank wine with dinner. Maureen's eyes lost focus. She would look at me, but her eyes looked right past my head.

Bill got very boisterous. He would pick up all three of his little boys at one time and throw them around. They would scream hysterically, but they liked it.

Danny got very quiet and melancholy. His eyes lost focus also.

Bill started making fun of Maureen, calling her a dummy; and she got angry. "Oh, stick it."

Suddenly there was a new kind of tension at our family dinner table. It was still drunk tension, but the players were changing.

Maureen was physically exhausted from taking care of three little babies. Her nerves were raw, and any verbal attack by Bill was enough to send her over the edge.

She was angry with Bill for leaving her alone so much. She did nothing but clean house, change diapers and listen to screaming babies all day. She had mounds of laundry to contend with. Bill was still immersed in his work and didn't get home until late each night. Maureen found she couldn't wait until five o'clock each night. (That was the hour she deemed respectable to have a drink.) After two martinis life got calmer, funnier, relaxed. She was hooked and didn't know it. Two martinis made her drunk. The next day she'd feel so guilty, she'd work like a dog to have the cleanest house, the shiniest kitchen, scrubbed and polished children. She did not want to be found out.

On the nights that Bill came home for dinner, they often had cocktails until 9 or 10 P.M. She'd forget to cook dinner or worse, burn what she had been cooking. Danny stopped by often because he knew he could get free booze at their house. Out of his salary he took a twenty-dollar-a-week allowance that he'd usually spend on beer or gin the first day. The rest of the week he'd have to scramble for his fix. Maureen's house was a good place to do it. Booze was plentiful and the company was good. After 5 P.M. Maureen's house was always a party.

"Have some coffee," my mother said nervously to Maureen.

"Michael, go in the garage and get me a beer," my dad ordered.

I started feeling my old gut ache. It was time to go home. I bundled

Brucie in his little jacket. It was cold outside. It was damp and foggy; typical weather for January in the Bay Area.

"Good-bye, everyone. I'll see you soon." Everyone was lost in his own little world.

All the way home I thought about Maureen and Danny. "It'll never happen to me," we all had said over and over when we were children hiding in the closet. Well, Maureen and Danny aren't alcoholics, I thought; but I was surprised to see them drink so much.

I also felt sorry for Michael. He was essentially an only child living with our crazy dad. Mom seemed more stressed than ever. I wasn't sure if Dad was even aware that we had all been there for dinner, such was his stupor. Michael seemed introverted and nervous. He had hardly talked at all. His eyes didn't have the same brightness and alertness they once had. Well, maybe he was just tired tonight, I tried to rationalize. But I felt sad. There seemed to be a distance between everyone; so much repressed feeling. We didn't know how to talk to one another anymore.

If it weren't for Mom, I don't think any of us would ever have returned home again. There was nothing to say to Dad. He was a blob. He made no sense, he had no awareness. It was Mom who kept us together. She was the reason we came back.

35

My modeling agency called. "We've got a booking for you with Passport scotch."

"Great," I answered.

"You'll have to wear a costume, a Scottish kilt," said my agent. A kilt sounded simple after wearing the squirrel costume on Market Street. "Also, they want you to sing a little Scottish song. You sing, don't you?"

"Oh, yes," I said.

"The pay is one hundred dollars a day, and they want you to work for four days."

Four days! It was like money from heaven. Four hundred dollars would cover two hundred for this month's rent, about one hundred would take care of food, gas and telephone, and I'd still have a hundred left over to put toward a new apartment. I was thrilled. Things were going to be okay after all.

In my excitement I never asked exactly what my job with Passport scotch entailed. The job was for Tuesday morning. I arrived on time.

"Hello, Miss Somers," said my employer. He was an older fellow with a red face, the kind you have after drinking all night. He smoked nonstop and his hands were very shaky. But he seemed like a nice enough guy. "If you'll kindly change into this outfit, we'll go to our first location."

We drove to the nearest gas station and I went into the ladies' room to change. I stood in front of the mirror looking at myself. I was wearing a little plaid tartan skirt, a peasant-looking little velvet jacket that laced up the front, a tartan sash that draped across my front like a bathing-beauty banner and a tartan hat shaped like the ones the Army G.I.'s wear. I looked stupid. The man I was working with was a liquor sales-man. All I had to do was walk into a liquor store in my little outfit, do a jig and sing the Passport song.

"Here we are," he said.

Suddenly I realized what a dumb thing I had been hired to do. I nervously walked into the liquor store. The man behind the counter looked up.

"Well, well! What you got under your kilt, lassie?"

I felt like such an ass. I wish I had some bagpipes, I thought. Singing a cappella in a liquor store with a bunch of strangers milling about is not easy. I began to sing to the tune of the Highland Fling:

> *I'm here to tell you 'bout something new*
> *Passport scotch will be good for you.*

I continued singing and dancing the jig. I felt like a moron.

Those were four of the longest days of my life. I got through them by thinking of the money. We went to ten liquor stores a day. Every time I finished my little performance, I would think, Well that's another ten dollars.

The liquor salesman passed out free samples at every store. "Well, up ye're kilt," he'd say to the customer, and they'd both bang down a shot. By the end of the day my employer was looped. I ended up driving him from location to location. Boy, I thought, I just can't get away from booze.

I got another modeling job. It was to pose for a cutout for supermarkets. All I had to do was wear a bikini, holding a frying pan in one hand and a box of Rice-A-Roni in the other. It paid seventy-five dollars. I wished I could get jobs like the other girls at the agency. They were all tall and skinny with no bosoms. My curves seemed to dictate my work. Blond hair, big bosom, curvy body. There would be no runway work for me; no high fashion. I was definitely the sexy-girl type. Every once in a while I'd be the young mother holding a box of soap.

The next month I was hired as a photographic double on a movie called *Daddy's Gone A-Hunting,* starring Paul Burke and Carol White. I looked very similar to Carol White, so I got the job. I was asked to lighten my hair to match hers. Up until then my darkish blond hair had been natural. I didn't realize that "lightening" my hair would become a life-long chore. I did it cheerfully. I had always loved my sister's blond hair.

It was a month's work or more at thirty-five dollars a day and extra pay for doubling work. I would double Carol White when a scene required getting beat up, messed up or was dangerous. When I wasn't doubling, I put on different wigs and played "background." I loved everything about making movies. I studied Carol White. I learned the "lingo." I was on time, cooperative.

I drove Brucie to my sister's house early every morning and picked him up late each night. I hated leaving him. His lower lip curled up and tears filled his eyes when I said good-bye; but I had to work. We had to have money.

The director was Mark Robson. He walked over and talked to me for the first time. "This is the big scene tonight. Scott Hyland is chasing you. You crawl out the window and start climbing up the fire escape of the Mark Hopkins Hotel. You climb and climb till the stairs end. Then you work your way over to the windowsill, pull yourself up and climb onto the roof. When you reach the top, we'll cut."

"Will there be a safety net?" I asked.

"Naw. It isn't dangerous," he said.

I gulped. Climb to the top of the roof. I was scared. I went over to the assistant director. "How much am I getting paid to do this?" I asked.

"An extra sixty bucks," he said proudly.

The star, Paul Burke, overheard. I saw him go over to the director and talk animatedly. Paul Burke then came over to me. "I got them to pay you six hundred dollars."

"Wow! Thanks," I said. Now it was worth it. Six hundred! What a bonanza.

They dressed me in a full-length leopard coat. A makeup man worked on my face. The hairdresser did my hair exactly like Carol White's.

When they were finished, I couldn't believe it. I had never been professionally done before. I looked really pretty.

"Okay," the director said. "Action!"

I did as I was told. I climbed and climbed. I never looked down. I was terrified. It worked for the scene. I was supposed to look terrified.

"Cut!" the director yelled when I had reached the top.

I looked down. Oh, my God! I didn't realize how high it was. Below me was all of San Francisco. I felt dizzy. Don't think about it, I kept saying to myself over and over.

"Come on down, Suzie," the director yelled.

Thank God, it's over, I thought. Coming down was scarier than going up. I had high-heels on and they kept slipping on the tiles of the roof.

"Have her take off the coat," the wardrobe mistress yelled up at me.

Right! Let's not wreck the good coat, I thought. We can always get another blond double, but good coats are hard to find.

I took each step carefully. It took me a half hour to get down. The ground felt like it was swaying. My legs were unsteady. My heart was pounding.

"We're gonna have to do it again! Camera problems," the director said.

Oh, no! I thought. We did it six times that night. It never got any easier. I just kept thinking of the money to distract myself.

I didn't get any work after the movie for six months. Nothing. Not one single job. My money had completely run out. Fred was very perturbed that I could not come up with my half of the rent. Bruce had not made a single child-support payment.

I had been ordered by the court to sell the speedboat that Bruce and I had bought during our marriage as part of the divorce settlement. We owed fourteen hundred dollars. I put an ad in the *Free Press.* No response. People who read the *Free Press* in the sixties were not interested in speedboats.

I remembered that the bartender at the Villa Roma Cocktail Lounge talked about boats a lot. I decided to phone him.

"Hi! Are you still looking for a boat? If so, I've got a great deal for you."

To my surprise he was not only interested, but also bought the boat. I went down to the bar and he gave me a check for fourteen hundred dollars. Sold.

"Where's the pink slip?" he asked.

"I just have to pay off the bank loan and they'll send it to you," I said.

I deposited the check into my account. God, it felt good to have money, even if I couldn't spend it.

I got a notice from the telephone company. YOU HAVE 24 HOURS TO PAY YOUR DELINQUENT BILL OR YOUR TELEPHONE WILL BE DISCONNECTED. Oh, God. Without a phone I'll never get any work. Well, I'll just write a check and next time I get paid, I'll deposit the money so the balance will stay at fourteen hundred dollars. I should write the check to pay off the boat loan, I thought. But I didn't.

YOUR GAS AND ELECTRICITY WILL BE DISCONNECTED IF PAYMENT IS NOT RECEIVED WITHIN 24 HOURS. Oh, God. I wrote another check. We had no food in the house. I mean *no* food. I'll just go to the grocery store and write a check, I thought. Just the essentials. After all, we have to eat. I went to the grocery store and filled the cart way up to the top. Brucie was so happy. He sat in the little seat of the grocery cart eating a box of animal crackers.

It was raining as I put my groceries in Fred's car. I didn't care if I got wet. When I got home I filled my freezer with meat and poultry. My cupboards were full of wonderful ingredients; flour, sugar, breakfast cereal, spices, corn meal, olive oil, cooking oil, cans of tomatoes, tomato sauce, spaghetti. I bought onions, potatoes, garlic, fresh vegetables. It was wonderful. I couldn't wait to cook. I'll make a roast for dinner. I'll make cookies for Brucie; maybe a lemon cake, too. I was excited. I had spent almost two hundred dollars.

Brucie really needed some new shoes. The ones he was wearing were getting too small and I was afraid it might affect his walking. I took him to the shoe store. He needed corrective shoes the salesman told me. His feet were turning in. Corrective shoes would force him to walk straight.

"Of course," I said. "Can't have him walking crooked."

For the new shoes and socks and a new pair of "play" shoes, I wrote a check for ninety-six dollars.

Bruce also had asthma. He coughed at night and had a lot of congestion. He had trouble breathing. I took him to the doctor. "You'll have to get a vaporizer and keep it going in his room every night," the doctor said.

"Right," I answered.

The doctor also gave Bruce his innoculations and a prescription for his congestion. I wrote a check for eighty-five dollars for the visit and shots. I wrote another check for Bruce's medicine and another check for the vaporizer. God! Life is so expensive, I thought.

"You have got to have an answering service," my agent said. "I can't tell you how many times we've called with interviews and couldn't find you."

Wow! I thought. I'd better get an answering service or I'll never be able to make any money. The answering service was sixty-five dollars a month with a deposit of one hundred dollars. Tracer calls would be extra. I wrote a check.

Rent was due again.

"You better have your share this time," Fred said.

"I do, I do." Another check: 200 dollars.

Telephone was due again, so was gas and electric. In ten days the answering service.

"Where's my pink slip?" demanded Joe the bartender.

"Didn't you get it yet?" I lied. "I'll call the bank and find out."

Oh, God. What was I going to do? I had spent 950 dollars of the fourteen hundred. The bank was sending nasty letters about the loan and adding late charges.

"Where's the money from the sale of the boat?" Bruce demanded.

"I have it," I lied. "Where's my child support?" I asked accusingly.

"I can't afford it," Bruce answered.

Bruce and I had reached that stage in our divorce where we were angry with each other all the time. We never stopped to think why. We were young and immature and responded in a way that was expected. Once divorced, people expected you to dislike and be angry with one another. We had forgotten it had been an amiable divorce; that we had tried to work out our young marriage; that we hadn't been able to; and we mutually agreed to divorce. We were into "habit hating."

Bruce resented paying child support. When he couldn't get custody of Brucie during the divorce proceedings, coupled with his feelings about my adulterous behavior, he became bitter. I was slowly beginning to realize that I was never going to get child support. I was still so racked with guilt over the way I handled our marriage that I didn't feel right about pressuring him for the money.

Bruce had already remarried. Talk about rebound! His new wife didn't like me or little Brucie, and she certainly didn't want any of "their" money going into my household.

The pressure was building. Money! Money! Money! Pay me! Pay this! Pay that! I felt so overwhelmed. Everything about my life was so insecure.

"You have to get some new pictures," my agent said. "I can't get you any print or commercial work with the pictures you've given me. You have to spend the money and get a real professional composite shot."

"How much will that cost?" I asked.

"About two hundred fifty dollars, plus another hundred for printing costs. Without a composite we just can't get you work."

It was a Catch-22. Oh, well, what's another 350 dollars, I thought. I'm so far behind now. Maybe if I spend the money, I'll get work, I can pay off my debt and get out of this mess. I wrote another check for 350 dollars.

IF YOU DO NOT PAY YOUR SCREEN EXTRAS' DUES WITHIN 5 DAYS, YOU WILL NOT BE PERMITTED TO WORK! I wrote another check for sixty-five dollars to pay SEG dues.

I had a hundred dollars left.

"I'm sick and tired of your excuses," Joe the bartender said. "I want my pink slip by tomorrow or you're gonna be real sorry."

I was scared. I couldn't ask Fred for money. I already owed him for rent from the month before. I was too proud to ask anyone in my family.

I've got to find a real job, I thought. I went to an employment agency.

"What are your skills?" asked the woman. "Do you type or take shorthand?"

"No," I said.

"Can you file?" she asked.

"No," I answered again.

"Can you operate a switchboard?"

"No."

"Well, there's really nothing I can do for you," she said. "You're not qualified for office work."

Well, I didn't want to work in an office anyway, I thought.

I applied for work at the phone company. "Sorry, you're not qualified," I was told.

I applied as a waitress at Denny's. "Can you stack?" I was asked. I didn't know what they meant. "How many plates can you carry?" the man asked impatiently.

"Well," I said, "I'm sure I could carry three or four at a time."

"Sorry," he said. "You're not qualified."

"Pay me, or you'll be sorry you didn't," said Joe the bartender.

"Please give me a little more time," I said to him. "I've spent the money; my husband hasn't paid me; and I'm looking for a job."

"Shit," Joe said. "I knew it. I knew you were trouble."

I sold my diamond ring; the ring my ex-husband worked construction all summer to buy me, for six hundred dollars. I gave the money to the bank. Now I owed eight hundred dollars. The bank turned me over to a collection agency, and they in turn pursued me relentlessly. They called me on the telephone, they sent me nasty letters, they showed up at my house; and I still had to pay Joe.

Slowly, I began to eke out a living with my modeling. Nothing spectacular, barely enough to get by, but I was able to move away from my roommate, Fred, and start paying off my bills. I rented a little carriage house behind a lovely home in Jackson Heights in San Francisco. There was a long alley in which Brucie could ride his tricycle and a little grocery store on the corner. All I thought about was money. If only I had enough money to do this, or if only I had enough money for that, I would dream. I dreaded the first of the month. That was when rent was due. I never had enough and was always scrambling to pull the two hundred dollars together.

"Do you think I could get an advance on the Ford job?" I'd ask my agent. "I did the job six weeks ago, so they should be paying me any day."

My agent would sigh disgustedly. Sometimes he'd give me the advance, sometimes he wouldn't.

I had a couple of commercials running on television, so occasionally I would get small residual checks in the mail. The money was usually spent before I received it. Every month the telephone company would send me threatening letters; so would the gas and electric companies. Somehow, I would dig up the money to keep a roof over our heads and the lights on.

I took every job that was offered to me. I was not proud. I was the pretty girl who handed out pamphlets at the conventions. I sang and danced in industrial shows. I was an extra in every movie filmed in San Francisco during the sixties; and, of course, I had my true-blue account —the traction company. I hung in traction at the American Medical Association convention for two weeks every year. I was getting by. I lived alone with the sweetest, most adorable little boy in the world. I had my freedom. There was no drunk in my life, no husband, no one telling me what to do. I was broke, but somehow I was getting by. Brucie didn't know we didn't have any money. He had dinner every night, shoes on his feet and a nice bed to sleep in. He spent very little time with babysitters because I didn't work very much. Our time together was special. We went everywhere together. I took him on my job interviews. He loved riding the buses and cable cars in San Francisco. I took him with me when I worked "extra" on movies. There was so much sitting around and waiting, we would talk and play games. Usually, the movie company would welcome the look of a mother and child in the background; and as compensation, Brucie was allowed to have a free lunch. Bruce developed a wonderful personality. He would sit on the bus and talk to all the other extras. They thought he was darling. I would watch him and beam. I loved being Bruce's mother. When I looked at him, I didn't feel that I had failed. When I looked at my child, I felt determined to accomplish something in my life. I wanted to give him the best.

"You've been hired as a prize model on 'The Anniversary Game,' " my agent told me.

I screamed! "Oh, my God! Oh, that's so wonderful."

I had interviewed for the job a month ago and had heard nothing. *Television!* It was like a dream come true. I had always wanted to be on television. I couldn't believe it.

"Go to KGO-TV Monday morning at seven A.M. and ask for Alan Waterson," my agent said. "They will have wardrobe and makeup for you."

It meant so much to me. A job. A glamorous job. More than I'd ever dreamed of. Up until now I would fantasize about being a weather girl on a local news program, but this was incredible. At twenty years old, being a "weather girl" seemed like the top of the world. "The Anniversary Game" was on the network! It was shown at the same time, on the same night, in every city in America.

I had a friend drive me to work that Monday morning. (I still didn't have a car.) I felt like I was in a dream. This could change my whole life, I thought. Little did I know *how* different my life would be as a result of this job.

I felt nervous and insecure walking into the TV studio. I met Alan Waterson and he told me to sit down until it was my turn to rehearse. I recognized two girls who were on the stage—Barrie and Louise—two of the loveliest models from the agency. They had already been hired as regulars on the show. With them was a very slick, good-looking man; and by his voice and demeanor, I guessed he was the game-show host. He was wearing brown bell-bottom pants, the back cut longer than the front, and a red alpaca sweater. I had never seen pants like that before. He was about six feet tall with sandy-colored hair. His hair looked like it was curly, but blown dry to look straight, and then sprayed to death. It was the fashion for men in the sixties. Men were wearing their hair longer and straight. I'm sure it had something to do with the Beatles. The game-show host was definitely the center of attraction. Everyone hung around him.

"Hey, Al," they'd say. "What-a-ya think we try this?" or "How do you feel about that?"

The host had an answer for everything. Everyone was trying to be clever for him; make him laugh.

"Can I get you anything, Al?" they'd ask.

"Did ya hear the one about . . ."

"Ha! Ha! Ha! Ha! Ha!" they all laughed.

The game-show host was cool; very confident. You could tell he knew his way around television, and he was used to being the center of attention.

I sat quietly watching him in the front row of the theater seats waiting to be told what to do and where to go.

"Let's take five," the stage manager said.

The game-show host was talking with the producer and his assistants. I was trying not to stare, but I couldn't help myself. I couldn't take my eyes off him. He looked over at me. He smiled; then he walked toward me.

"Hi, I'm Alan Hamel," he said. "What's your name?"

I felt nervous. I was reacting to his voice, his eyes, his strength.

"Suzanne," I answered. "I've been hired to work on this show."

"Hey, that's great," he said.

I felt so little. I had never met anyone like him before. He was such a man. So sure of himself, so powerful, so sexy. This only happens in the movies, I thought. Every feeling inside me was stirring. I kept imagining what it would be like to be with him. He was incredible. Those eyes! His eyes were so blue; so liquid; so soft. Forget-me-not blue eyes. His voice was deep, compelling, and musical. He was articulate. I could tell he was smart. He had savvy. I was overwhelmed.

He asked me lots of questions; where was I from, how old was I, what did I do, did I travel much, all the while his eyes seemed to devour me; kind, gentle, sensitive, sexy eyes. I loved his eyes. He was funny. He made me laugh. I loved to laugh.

At twelve o'clock lunch was called. Suddenly the studio was deserted. The lights were turned off. It went quiet. I looked around. I was all alone. I didn't know where to go. I didn't have any money to buy lunch. Alan Hamel, the game-show host, was in his dressing room talking with the producer again. I didn't want to seem like a pest. I decided I'd go for a walk.

It was raining. It rained so much in San Francisco. Lucky I brought my umbrella, I thought. I couldn't stop thinking about Alan. He'd never be interested in me. He's been around too much. I'm just a small-town girl. I don't know anything. I'm only twenty years old. I'm sure he thinks I'm a child. Oh, well, it's fun to dream.

I walked back into the TV studio. The first person I saw was Alan lying on the couch in his dressing room with the door open.

"Hi," he said immediately. He sat up.

I felt my face get hot.

"Where'd you go?" he asked. "I was looking for you. I thought maybe we could have lunch together," he said.

Shit! I thought. I missed my chance. "Oh, I was real busy, had an interview," I lied. I didn't want him to know I was broke and couldn't afford lunch. I just stood there looking at him. The silence was awkward.

"Could you get me a cup of coffee?" Alan asked. As the star of the show, he was used to people fetching for him.

"Sure." Anything, I thought. I didn't know where they kept the coffee. I asked a man in the hallway.

"The fourth-floor cafeteria," he answered.

I ran up the stairs. The coffee was twenty-five cents a cup. I scrounged through my purse. I've got to have a quarter somewhere. I took everything out; comb, brush, makeup, wallet, a pair of Brucie's socks, a scarf, paper clips, bobby pins, some old cookie crumbs. No money. Shit! I thought. Then I remembered I kept a dollar hidden in the secret pocket of my wallet. Aha!

"One cup of coffee, please," I said to the waitress. "To go."

I ran downstairs. When I returned, Alan was already on stage drinking a cup of coffee.

"Where'd you go?" he asked. "The coffee is right over here in the corner."

Oh God, I'm so stupid. What's a quarter, I thought. Just a box of animal crackers, or a box of Kraft Macaroni and Cheese (enough for two dinners) or one-way bridge fare. No big deal!

"It's okay," I said, out of breath. "No problem."

We rehearsed. All I had to do was stand in front of the refrigerator. When the contestant's prize was announced, I would open the refrigerator door, show the place where you keep eggs and act like I gave away refrigerators every day of my life. Simple.

At 4:30 the audience arrived. Alan went to his dressing room to change. I was whisked into wardrobe. I changed into a dress loaned to the show by Saks Fifth Avenue and then went into makeup.

I stood next to the curtain waiting for the show to begin. Alan walked up behind me and put his hand on my shoulder. It felt like an electric current. He gently turned me around to face him.

"Have dinner with me tonight," he said. He looked right into my eyes.

I couldn't believe it. I was speechless. "I-I can't," I said. I was scared.

"Yes," he said. "Yes, you can."

Then we heard the announcer. "Today, some lucky member of

our studio will compete for cash and prizes worth over fifty thousand dollars . . ."

"I have to go out there," he said. "Tonight!"

"How about tomorrow?" I answered.

"No. Tonight!"

"And now here's the star of our show, *Al-l-l-l! Hamel!*"

"Yea!" everyone cheered.

"Tonight," he mouthed.

I screwed up miserably during the show. They had told me to look at the camera when I was showing the refrigerator. I did. No one told me to look at the camera that had the red light on. I just looked at the camera that was in front of me. The stage manager was waving his arms frantically. By the time I looked over at him, they had moved the camera shot to the original camera I had been looking at. I was a real amateur, and they knew it. When the show was over, the producer walked over to me.

"I'm sorry. It just didn't work out," he said. "You won't have to report to work tomorrow."

I felt awful. I blew my big chance. I didn't want Alan to see me. I felt so stupid. I grabbed my coat and ran out of the studio to find the nearest bus home.

36

Boy, do I make a mess of things, I thought as I walked in my front door.

"Hi, Mommy," Brucie screamed. He ran to me and threw his arms around my neck. He was so darling, so affectionate.

Suddenly, the day's events didn't seem so heartbreaking. After all, what is life really about? I have this beautiful little child who thinks I'm smart and great, and we have a roof over our heads, for now.

Brucie was excited to have me home. I rarely left him with a babysitter. "So, what did you do today?" I asked.

"I rode my bike, and then we went to the park, and Joey pushed me off the swing so I kicked him and then the babysitter got mad at both of us and made us go home and take our nap, and then we woke up and she let us help her make cookies . . ." He was excited. He was rambling. I loved him so much. "And then Joey got in trouble again 'cause he peed in his pants . . ." I kept thinking of Alan. He's never going to want to see me. He must think I'm such an amateur. It was stupid of me to think anything could happen between us. I blew my chance. "But I didn't pee in my pants, Mommy, just Joey," Brucie continued his litany.

Two weeks later my phone rang. I guess Brucie (then three) had answered the phone (I didn't hear it), said hello, then left the receiver to dangle while he went off to play.

"Hello?" I said into the receiver.

"Hi there," answered the sexiest voice I had ever heard. It was Alan. "You can't believe how much trouble I've had tracking you down. I'm still waiting for an answer. Thank goodness I'm a patient guy. Will you have dinner with me tonight?"

I said yes, and we decided I would pick him up at his hotel, the Miyako.

I thought about him the rest of the day. I couldn't remember ever looking forward to a dinner date this much. I knew it was going to be wonderful. What to wear, what to wear, I thought. I tried on everything I owned; skirts thrown on the bed, shoes all over the floor, one dress after another discarded. Nothing seemed good enough for this special night. I finally settled on my new white wool pants, a tailored navy-blue gabardine tunic, navy-blue-and-white spectator high-heels that used to be my sister's and a beautiful Yves St. Laurent scarf that was navy blue and orange, a gift from Fred. I washed my hair and used extra conditioner to make it really soft and silky. I had always had good, thick hair. Luckily, coloring it blond didn't seem to damage it. I wanted to look good. I wanted to look gorgeous.

I had to borrow Fred's car. "I have a job," I lied. "Please, just one more time." Fred reluctantly gave in. God, I wished I had the money to buy a car. I felt so trapped. I couldn't even visit my family unless I took a bus.

At seven o'clock that night I pulled into the subterranean garage at the Miyako Hotel in San Francisco. I looked in the rearview mirror. I was pleased. I wore mascara, a little blush-on and very little lipstick. I was hoping to be kissed and didn't want gooey pink lips to get in the way. My hair was clean and shining straight down my back. My insides felt giddy with excitement—a combination of nerves and anticipation.

I got out of the car and walked to the elevator. I guess I go to the lobby, I thought. I hated going to hotels.

"Excuse me. Could you ring Mr. Hamel's room and tell him Miss Somers is waiting," I nervously asked the desk clerk. I looked around. Nice hotel, I thought.

"Mr. Hamel said to go right up. He's in the Japanese Suite. Room 1428," the desk clerk answered.

"Thank you." Why did hotel clerks always have that knowing little smile, I wondered. Well, here goes. My heart was beating so fast. I could feel my neck breaking out in nervous blotches. He's just a man, I thought. No, he's a famous man and he's asked me to dinner. I walked down the long hallway. I knocked on the door.

"Hi," he said, "come on in. I'm on the phone, but make yourself comfortable. Be sure to take off your shoes. This is an authentic Japanese suite."

I wonder what else you have to take off in an authentic Japanese suite. Shit! I take off my shoes and my new white pants drag four inches on the floor.

"Well, how do you like my room? Senator Percy stays here when I'm not taping," he said.

The room overwhelmed me. The bed was a large Japanese quilt on the floor on top of straw matting. Light consisted of candles everywhere and a color TV with the horizontal purposely screwed up so the picture was just a multicolor wave. The room said *sex* everywhere you looked.

"I have a bottle of saki warming in the sink," he said. "I'll get it for us."

Warming in the sink! Boy, was he smooth. Alan handed me a little cup of saki; I downed it in one gulp.

"You're supposed to sip it," he said.

God, he was gorgeous; tall, lean, very tanned, with those sexy blue eyes. The saki made me feel warm and toasty.

"Here, try this," he said. He handed me a piece of cake.

"Yuk, it tastes like dirt," I said.

"It's a brownie with grass in it."

"I've never tried it before," I said. But I ate it anyway. I didn't want him to think I wasn't "with it."

"I took the liberty of getting dinner for us," Alan said. "I went down to Fisherman's Wharf after the show and had my friend Vince cook us some fresh Dungeness crabs."

Alan laid the crabs out on newspapers on the Japanese bed. In another paper bag were lemons, all cut into wedges, and a loaf of sourdough French bread. He went to his refrigerator and pulled out a fancy bottle of white wine and two chilled glasses. We sat on his bed laughing and talking, nibbling on the crab and the French bread. The wine made me feel giddy. (Or was it the brownies?) I never laughed so much. Everything was funny. The more I laughed, the more Alan would make me laugh. I was having such a wonderful time. Alan leaned over and kissed me in the middle of a laugh. My laughing instantly changed to passion. Everything was spinning—my head, my heart, the room. I didn't want this kiss to end. The feeling was so delicious. We broke our embrace. We both went quiet. We both knew that had been no ordinary kiss.

"Is that all your hair?" he asked me.

What a question, I thought. "Yes," I answered.

"It's beautiful," he said. He ran his fingers through my hair. He touched every part of my face—my lips, my cheeks, my nose, my eyes. Then he kissed me again, a long, lovely, passionate kiss. He reached under my hair and pulled at the zipper of my tunic. Long, slow, deliberate unzipping. He pushed the material off one shoulder. He pushed at the other shoulder. My tunic fell to my waist. He ran his hands over my shoulders, my neck, my breasts.

"You are so beautiful," he said in his deep, husky voice.

He gently pushed me down on the quilt and proceeded to finish undressing me. We made the most incredible love of my life. Nothing could ever be as good again. Our bodies fit together beautifully. It was slow, gentle, deliberate. It was sensitive and sexy. It was strong, animal, passionate. When it was over, I lay my head on his incredible chest. He had smooth, thick, strong skin. His chest was very tan with a sprinkling of hair in the middle. I just lay there, thanking God for this one magnificent night. I felt lucky. I knew I'd probably never see Alan again after this. He's got so many girls, I thought. I'm sure they are all after him. I'm just glad to have had this one wonderful night. He held me and kissed my head. Then he rolled over and fell into a deep sleep. It was over.

I lay there for over an hour. My insecurities overwhelmed me. I felt nervous about looking at him when he woke up. Quietly, I got out of bed and got dressed. Quietly, I tiptoed out of his room. All the way home I kept thinking, I shouldn't have given in, I shouldn't have given in. Now he'll think I'm easy. I could hear what my mother would say if she knew. "Why buy the cow when you can get the milk for free?" She was full of those little sayings. I couldn't help myself, I thought. I wanted him, I wanted it. It was beautiful, wonderful, magical. Maybe, just maybe, he'll see me once more. I hope so. God! I hope so!

At seven the next morning my phone rang. "Where'd you go?" Alan asked. "I woke up at three A.M., reached over for you and nothing! Gone!"

"I had to get home and let the babysitter go," I said.

"You were wonderful," he said.

"So were you," I answered nervously. "I've never had such a good time," I told him honestly.

"Can you see me again tonight?" he asked.

"Yes," I said incredulously. "What time?"

"Come by my hotel at seven P.M. I know a great little sushi restaurant."

I was elated. I didn't care what we had for dinner. I wanted more dessert. My body, my entire being felt so stimulated. I thought about him all day. Brucie and I went to the park after his nap. I pushed him on the swing. Then I set him in the merry-go-round and ran along the outside as fast as I could to get it going real fast. Then I would jump on. Brucie would squeal with laughter. I loved to make him laugh.

"Let's go play in the sandbox," Brucie said.

I got into the sandbox with him and we sat there making castles and mud pies. Soon other children joined us. I was the only mother covered with mud and sand. I was happy, Brucie was happy and I knew I had a great night ahead of me.

Brucie and I both got into the bathtub when we got home. I washed all the sand off of him and shampooed his hair. Then I washed my hair. Brucie loved to play with the soap bubbles. I rinsed us both off and wrapped a big towel around Brucie. "Cold," he said. I had him stand in front of the heater while I got my robe. He was shivering.

I made Brucie's dinner; his favorite, macaroni and cheese and asparagus. He called them "sparegrass." After dinner he went to his room and played with his toys while I got dressed.

I put on a dress I had been given free in exchange for modeling. It was a camel hair sheath with red fox trim on both sleeves. I wore camel-colored high-heels. San Francisco was a dressy town. When you went out, you got dressed up. Even shopping during the day was a dressy event for San Franciscans. Women still wore hats and gloves.

I wore my hair straight down my back again. Don't want any rubber bands getting in the way, I thought. I sprayed myself with Chanel Number 5 (another gift from Fred). I was ready. I was excited. I couldn't wait to see him.

"Bye-bye, Brucie. You be a good boy and go to bed as soon as Shirley tells you to," I said.

"I will, Mommy. I love you," Brucie said. He threw his arms around my neck and hugged me tight.

"Oh, Brucie, I love you so much." As I got into my car, I noticed I had chocolate cookies scrunched into the shoulder of my dress and down the front. Shit! I thought.

I drove up to the Miyako Hotel and Alan was waiting for me. I had borrowed my babysitter's car, an old Dodge. I wished Alan didn't see me in it. Alan didn't seem to care. He jumped in.

"Do you want me to drive?" he asked.

"Sure," I said.

He jumped out and ran around the car to the driver's seat. I started to slide over, but before I reached the other seat, Alan grabbed me and kissed me passionately.

"I've been thinking about doing that all day," he said.

"I've been thinking about you doing that all day, too," I answered.

We drove to the North Beach section of San Francisco and pulled up in front of a little restaurant called Osho.

"I spent six weeks in 1964 at the Tokyo Olympics as a commentator for the CBC," Alan said. "I ate sushi every day; and ever since then, I've just loved it."

"What is sushi?" I asked as we were walking in the front door.

"Raw fish," he said.

My heart stopped. *Raw fish*, I thought! I don't even eat cooked fish, let alone raw fish. I hadn't been able to stand the smell of fish ever since I was a little girl and my grandfather brought home smelly meat and fish from the shop. I ate meat now because I bought my own, but I couldn't get past the smell of fish. How was I going to get through this dinner? We sat at the sushi bar. There in front of us was every kind of fish imaginable. Big heads and eyeballs, their mouths wide open. They looked like doo-wop backup singers.

"Have one of these," Alan said. "It's eel wrapped in seaweed."

Eel! I thought. I put it in my mouth. Ugh! It tasted awful. There was something on it that made me want to gag. My eyes started watering. I had never had such a big bite of anything in my mouth before. I chewed and chewed. It wouldn't go down. It tasted worse and worse. I started to dry heave. Oh, please. Please don't let me throw up, I kept saying to myself. More gagging. Finally, I took my napkin and discreetly spit the entire foul-tasting wad into it. Alan hadn't noticed. He was busy talking to the sushi chef about our next delicacy.

"I'd like to try the plain rice with the seaweed," I said. It was awful, too. They put some vile-smelling horseradish on it. This is going to be a long night, I thought. I can't wait for coffee. It never entered my mind to tell Alan I hated this kind of food. I was afraid he might not like me.

Alan continued to smack his lips after each little fishhead. "You like it?" he asked.

"Um-hm," I lied. I sipped wine and ate steamed rice. Finally, I had found something palatable.

After dinner we took a walk along Broadway looking at all the freaks. It was the era of topless. Carol Doda was a big item in San Francisco at that time. She had huge silicone-filled boobs and she danced topless. We went into a small club to have a drink and three girls were on stage dancing wearing enormous tophats. After a closer look, I realized I was not looking at the girls' eyes. Holes had been cut out of the tophats and their boobs were sticking out where the eyes should have been. There they were, waving in the air, keeping step to "Me and My Shadow." Thank God, I've never had to do anything like that for money, I thought.

I loved walking with Alan. I loved when he put his arm around me. Every time we'd stop to look in a window, he'd lean up against me and rest his face in my hair. His touch, just feeling him near me, sent a rush through my body. He kissed me a lot. Short kisses, but sometimes we'd find ourselves standing on a corner involved in a long, sensuous kiss. I wasn't embarrassed. I didn't care who was looking. I knew I was feeling special feelings and I didn't want even one to pass me by.

We drove back to the Miyako Hotel. I sat as close to Alan as I could possibly get. I kissed his neck, his ears, his shoulders, whatever my lips could reach. I couldn't wait. I wanted him so badly. We gave the car to the hotel valet and walked to the elevator. As soon as the elevator door closed, Alan pulled me close and kissed me passionately. I wished we were in the Empire State Building so the elevator door wouldn't have to open for a while. I felt overwhelmed with passion. We kissed while we walked down the long hallway. Alan fumbled with the keys, then we were inside. It was dark, but moonlight was shining through the shoji screens.

Alan reached into his suitcase and pulled out a chocolate candle. He lit it, walked over to me, grabbed my hand and led me to his bed on the floor. Such ecstasy. Such joy. Such happiness. Our lovemaking was so easy, so generous, both deriving such pleasure from giving. I didn't want it to end, but at 2 A.M. I knew I had to go. I had to let the babysitter go home.

Alan walked me to my car and paid the valet, thank God. "Can I see you tomorrow night?" he asked.

"I can't wait," I answered. We kissed once more, then I drove off.

The next morning after Brucie's breakfast I called my mother. "Mom! I met the man I want to marry. I'm totally in love with the most incredible man in the whole world." It was December 1968.

"How about seven o'clock tonight at my hotel?" Alan said.

"I've got a better idea," I told him. "Why don't you come to my house at eight and I'll cook you dinner. My little boy goes to sleep at eight and then we'll be alone."

"That sounds great," he said.

I was glad Alan agreed. I felt guilty leaving Bruce again; three nights in a row was too much. Besides, I was having trouble paying the baby-sitter. I hadn't had any work for two weeks. I was excited. I loved to cook. I'll wow him with my cooking, I thought. I dressed Bruce in a little jacket and hat and put him in his stroller. It's cold and damp in San Francisco in December. It's cold and damp most months in San Francisco. Great weather for your skin. Keeps it moist and glowing.

Brucie and I walked past the park to the market. It was a neighborhood corner market with an excellent meat department.

"What do you have that's special today, Simon?" I asked the butcher. "I really want to impress someone tonight."

"Well," he said, "I have a few fresh pheasant in the back."

"Pheasant! That's great! Cut one up for me and charge it, please."

I bought some vegetables, the rest of the ingredients and a box of animal crackers for Bruce.

"Cash or charge, Miss Somers?"

"Charge it."

I skipped home. Bruce loved me to push his stroller fast and make "wheelies." A "wheelie" is when you stop the stroller so fast that the front two wheels go in the air. Bruce laughed and laughed! So did I.

Alan arrived at 8 P.M. sharp.

"Hi," I said nervously. He was wearing a soft black leather sports jacket, faded bell bottom blue jeans and a white cotton shirt unbuttoned at the neck.

"Here," he said. "These are for you." He handed me a bouquet of yellow daisies. "And this is for us." It was an expensive-looking bottle of French red wine. "You look beautiful," he said. "Great house."

"Thanks. It's an old carriage house that's been converted. I like it. I feel safe back here behind the main house. Want me to show you around?" I asked.

"Sure," Alan said.

"It's small," I said as we walked up the stairs, "but it's got a lot of charm and it's just the right size for Bruce and me. The whole downstairs is Bruce's bedroom and playroom, and upstairs is the kitchen and living room. I use the dining room as my bedroom." It made a pretty room. There was a crystal chandelier and some beautiful old Chinese wallpaper. My small bedroom overlooked the lovely rose garden of my neighbor's house. I had a double bed, a bureau and mirror, two end tables, two lamps and a small slipper chair. I still had my pink quilt from college days.

"Hmm, I like this room," Alan said. He was leaning against my backside with his arms around my waist. He kissed my hair. I turned around. I put my lips on his softly, softly, then intense, frantic. I was crazy about Alan.

"We'd better stop now, or you'll never get dinner," I said.

Alan followed me to the kitchen. I sautéed the pheasant chunks with shallots in clarified butter and allspice. When the pheasant was browned, I poured in a small bottle of white wine.

"There," I said. "I'll let that steam a little while."

"Smells great," Alan said. He kissed me. I was having such a great time.

"Would you like a glass of wine?" I asked. I poured wine for both of us. "Tell me about yourself," I said.

"Well, I was born in Toronto, Canada. My parents are Polish immigrants. My mother didn't even know she was pregnant with me until her water broke."

"How could that be?" I asked.

"She had trouble getting pregnant. One day she had a terrible stomach ache, and four hours later I was born. I was two months premature and weighed two and a half lbs. [Exactly the same weight as my dad, I thought.] Everyone told my mother I wouldn't live through the week. I was too small, but I stayed in my incubator for six weeks; and when I weighed five pounds, they brought me home. Then I contracted whooping cough from my sister in the first week; and again the doctor told my mother I wouldn't live. 'If he does survive, he'll be a giant,' he said. Obviously, I made it." Alan laughed.

"I grew up in the boardinghouse my mother ran, surrounded by eight Chinese brothers, one Scottish Presbyterian minister, a Nigerian prince named Okwa Chicwa Aika Jani who attended the University of Toronto nearby, a French-Canadian woman who was a cartographer (she took me to my first burlesque show), and a blind trumpet player. There was also Mr. Landau the tailor, and an English caretaker.

"They were my family. We ate all our meals together, we laughed, we talked; we were a strange, international, colorful conglomeration."

Not as strange as my family, I thought to myself.

"I slept in the dining room with my parents till I was eight years old. Then I moved into the attic with Mr. Landau. I remember it was cold in the winter and hot in the summer, a teeny room that barely fit two army cots. The ceiling was so low you couldn't stand up straight. The snow and wind leaked through the windows and Mr. Landau had smelly feet."

I poured Alan some more wine. "Go on," I said. "I love this."

"Are you sure I'm not boring you?" he asked.

Nothing about him was boring to me.

"Well, it was a great life. I was happy, but I was a rambunctious, restless kid. Even at that time I wanted to get on with it.

"I always worked. I had my first job at five years old opening and closing the door at the grocery store across the street. I made one dollar a week and spent it on candy and comic books—forbidden items at our house.

"I didn't have any toys, but I did have a crystal set, which I put in my ear and fell asleep with every night. That's probably why I eventually became a radio announcer.

"At seven my mother made me take piano lessons at the Royal Conservatory of Music; and at eight, I started going to synagogue every day. I hated it. Both of these activities bored me, but my mother was strong. She ruled the house; and no matter how much I whined and cried, I still had to go. She wanted me to be somebody, educated and aware of my roots and culture.

"I never stopped working. At seven I was a delivery boy, had a paper route at eight and was a stock boy in the supermarket at nine."

"Why did you work so much?" I asked.

"The war in Europe was in full force, luxuries were scarce and I was restless. I remember my friend Gibby and I sneaked a case of salmon out the back window of the supermarket to bring home to our moms. Mine was furious. 'Take it back right now and apologize,' she yelled at me. I couldn't get away with anything.

"It was a rough time for my parents. Their entire families were murdered by the Germans in Nazi concentration camps. I can remember my mother going through the pictures of the death camps with a magnifying glass trying to identify her family. It was very sad."

Alan sat quietly staring at the fire for a while. Then he continued.

"There was a lot of anti-Semitism in Toronto. I got beaten up every day after school by a gang of boys who called me a 'dirty Jew.' I'd come home crying and bloody and my mother could only say, 'Who's dirty? You or them?'

"My mother reported the kids to the school, but they did nothing. My mother would wait in front of our house every afternoon to try to stop the affront, but the kids would hide on another block.

"One day they grabbed me and dragged me to an old abandoned garage. I kicked and screamed all the way, but they kept beating me. Then they pulled out a rope and tried to hang me. I was terrified. I screamed so loud that some passersby heard and rescued me. My mother was livid. She went into a blind rage—and with her apron still on and a soup spoon in hand, she marched down the street right into the house where some of the kids lived and started beating them.

" 'The dirty Jewess is beating us up,' they wailed. The parents shouted, 'Get out of here, you Jewess,' and my mother answered, 'Take me to court.'

"After that the beatings stopped, but I was confused. Here they were beating me up because I was a Jew, and yet their fathers were fighting the Germans in Europe because they were killing the Jews." I sat there looking at this man so powerful and in control of his life and couldn't imagine him as a twelve-year-old at the mercy of these bullies.

"At thirteen I was bar mitzvahed and announced to my mother, 'Now that I'm a man, I'm no longer going to synagogue.' I quit Hebrew studies and piano lessons and got a job working on the trains as a 'newsy' on the Canadian National Railway. I worked weekends during the school year and full time in summers. It was a great job. I wore a uniform and sold 'cigarettes, matches, chocolate bars, chewing gum, peanuts, biscuits and oranges.' I also rented pillows between Toronto and Vancouver and on the way back turned the pillowcases inside out and rented them again.

"When I was fourteen, I started selling ham sandwiches on the train. I made them myself and got over a hundred sandwiches out of one pound of ham. They were two pieces of white bread with one *very* thin, almost transparent slice of ham for fifty cents. I cleared between 350 and 450 dollars for a four-day week.

"I left home at eighteen and went to Ryerson Polytechnical Institute as a radio and TV arts major. During my midterm exams my professor whispered into my ear that they were holding auditions right then for a radio job and he thought I could get it. I put my pen down and left in the middle of exams. I got the job. It was a natural for me. I had studied music for so long I knew all the names of classical composers and artists, coupled with the countless symphonies my mother dragged me to. I thoroughly impressed my employers," he said. What really impressed me as I listened was his confidence. He could take the risk and miss the exam. I never could have done that.

"This job led to the next, a classical radio show I co-hosted with Carl Haas for five years. From 1955 to 1960 I lived on the Detroit River (the Canadian side), did the radio show every morning and went fishing every afternoon. I bought a boat, got married and took extra work doing commercials.

"Then my wife and I moved back to Toronto, where I became the 'busiest guy in Canadian television.' "

Wife? I thought. What wife?

"I hosted several shows at once. At one time I did eleven different shows each week. I ran from studio to studio. When I wasn't in the studio, I traveled. I hardly ever saw my wife. We grew apart before ever having a chance to know one another.

"Finally, I did a show called 'Nite Cap,' Canada's most successful satire variety show, which eventually spawned 'Saturday Night Live.' But I wanted more. So, I moved to Los Angeles—beautiful weather, beautiful girls and no career limitations. I went as far as I could on Canadian television," Alan said. "There were no more challenges left.

"What about you?" Alan asked. "Tell me about yourself."

My life was so dull next to his. What do I say? I grew up with a drunk, I was an adulteress. I'm the mother of a small child, and I can barely make ends meet? No way. He'd never be interested in me if he knew all that.

"Well," I lied, "my father is dead. Yes, he died of a heart attack a couple of years ago. It was so sad. He was a doctor. My mother was so upset by it that she took the life insurance money and has been traveling ever since. Right now she's in Alaska. I received an inheritance of thirty thousand dollars and I use that to live off of until I get my career going." (Might as well not let him think I'm broke. I have my pride, I thought.)

"Where do you want your career to go?" he asked.

"I'd like something dependable like being a weather girl or something like that," I told him. "I'd also like to sing and act in Broadway musicals, but that's kind of a dream. I know nothing like that could ever happen."

I told him about high school and *Guys and Dolls* and Walter Winchell and how I had loved the experience. How nothing since then had left me feeling so stimulated. I loved talking with him.

He told me he knew the station manager at the local ABC station and he'd be happy to set up a meeting for me. He told me he thought I'd be a great weather girl. He asked me if I was a good actress. I said yes.

"I bet you are. You've got a very vulnerable quality about you," he said.

"More wine?" I asked him, then filled both of our glasses.

I was so used to telling lies, it seemed very natural to deceive Alan. Now I was stuck with my lies, my fantasies.

As much as I desired this relationship to continue, my subconscious had decided I wasn't good enough for him. "Make it impossible," my subconscious must have said to my conscious self.

We ate dinner by candlelight in front of the fire. Pheasant in wine, lightly sautéed snow peas. We would take a bite, kiss each other, take another bite.

"You are an incredible cook," Alan said.

"Wait here," I said. "I'll go get dessert."

I ran into the kitchen and opened the oven door. Perfect! I proudly entered the living room with a hot, steaming chocolate soufflé. It had risen a good three to four inches above the edge. I ran back to the kitchen to get the bowl filled with fresh, unsweetened vanilla whipped cream.

Alan lay on the floor while I put spoonfuls of hot chocolate soufflé dipped in fresh cold whipped cream into his mouth.

"This is heaven," Alan said.

I could tell he liked my food. We pushed the dishes aside and lay on the floor in front of the fire. Alan's arms were around me. I felt so secure. I was in love. Everything was perfect.

"Does your ex-wife still live in Canada?" I asked. I wanted her to be as far away as possible.

"No, we live in Los Angeles." All I heard was "we." My eyes must have said what I was thinking. "I'm sorry," Alan said gently. "I thought you knew. In fact, I have to go home this weekend. We're giving a birthday party for one of our kids."

"How many kids do you have?" I asked, astonished.

"Two—a boy six and a girl seven."

Wife! Kids! He was not divorced. I never thought about his having a wife or kids. What a blow.

My bubble popped. Everything was so perfect a few minutes ago. Suddenly it became complicated, illicit, cheap. I didn't know what to say. I said nothing. I just lay there in his arms wishing it would go away.

Snap my fingers and there'd be no wife. I didn't mind kids. That could be fun. I wanted to be your wife, I thought. I know we've only had three dates, but I know I want to be your wife. Now there's no chance. Well, I thought, I have two choices; get up right now and tell him to leave or accept being number two. Maybe just having him is better than nothing at all. In my heart I knew I should tell him to go. That's what a "good girl" would do. But the "good girl" was long gone, wasn't she? You're no longer "Suzie, the obedient little girl from San Bruno" any-more, are you? No. Now, I was a twenty-year old divorced adulteress. It never dawned on me to question his character. Why was he with me? In my eyes he could do no wrong.

Alan fit right into my behavior pattern. I couldn't criticize or get angry with him for withholding information. I had lied to him, and he had lied to me through omission. Why hadn't I asked him the first time we were together if he was married? I must not have wanted to know. Now I was in love with him, and it was too late. I had put myself right where I felt I deserved to be. Being his mistress added to my already suffering self-esteem. I knew I wasn't good enough to be number one.

"Are you okay?" Alan asked.

"Sure," I said.

"You've gotten awfully quiet," he said.

I looked at Alan. The fire made him look golden; like a golden Adonis. He touched my face, my lips, then he kissed me gently. Gentleness turned into passion. Soon we were overcome with our desire for one another. I had made my choice.

I thought about Alan all of the next day. It was different now. He was in Los Angeles with his wife. I wondered what she was like. He said they weren't very happy. Maybe he'll get divorced and come to me. In the meantime, I'm just going to enjoy the time we get to have together. Savor every moment. I'll put no pressure on him. I'll never ask him to get a divorce. I'll never mention love and commitment. I'll take him under any conditions. I just want to be with him. Lucky I didn't blurt out an "I love you" in front of the fire last night. That would have ruined everything. It probably would have sent him running. It had been on the tip of my tongue between every bite of soufflé. No. I won't blow it. We'll just continue on as it is. Monday through Thursday he'll be mine. Friday through Sunday he'll be hers. Only three more days to go until I see him again. My body was aching already.

37

*E*very afternoon Brucie and I went to the park before his nap. As we returned home, I could hear my phone ringing. I ran up the stairs.

"Hello," I said out of breath.

"Where's my money?" It was Joe the bartender.

Oh, God, I thought. I had only been able to pay two hundred dollars since the last six-hundred-dollar payment. I still owed six hundred.

"I'm trying real hard, Joe. I haven't had any work for a while."

"I have some friends in the Mafia and I'm gonna have them break your pretty face in if I don't get money or a pink slip in thirty days! I mean it. Thirty days. No more!" He hung up.

I just stood there looking at the receiver. It was all closing in on me again. Rent was due, telephone, answering service, Joe. What was I going to do? Christmas was coming. I was going to need some money to buy Brucie's presents. I had to get some work. I also had to get a car.

I called my agency. "Hi. Anything going on?" I asked.

"As a matter of fact, I was just going to call you," said Marsha, the English girl who did the bookings. "Joseph Magnin is hiring models to work in a boutique for men only during the holidays. It's a private room where men can go to have a drink or two and pick out gifts for their wives and girlfriends. You would model the clothes and receive a commission on everything you sold."

"Sounds great," I said.

"Good! Your interview is at the store this afternoon," she said.

I was determined to get the job. It would mean almost three weeks of work. What would I do with Brucie, I wondered. I hated leaving him, but this was one job where he wouldn't be welcome.

The phone rang again. It was my mother. "We haven't seen you in so long, honey," my mother said. "Why don't you and little Bruce come for dinner Sunday night? I'll ask Maureen and Danny. It'll be fun. Do you want to bring your new boyfriend?"

"Uh, no. Not yet, Mom," I answered. "I'd love to come, but we've got no way to get there. God, I need a car so bad, Mom."

"I'll come and get you," she said. "Maybe we can talk to Father. Maybe he'll lend you some money to buy a car."

"God, that would be great," I answered.

"How are you doing?" she asked. "Are you getting work?"

"Oh, yeah!" I lied. "I work all the time. I just got a little behind for a while, so it's taking time to catch up. Soon I'll have money for a car." I didn't want her to know the shoestring I was living on. She would worry. I couldn't tell her about Joe and the boat money.

My whole family still thought I was crazy to have treated such a nice husband so badly. I was determined to prove to them that I could take care of myself. I didn't need any help from them. I could make it on my own. I didn't want them to know I was floundering.

"By the way, Mom, how's Dad?"

"Oh, don't ask." She sounded bleak.

I hadn't seen my family in weeks. None of us were too close right now. We were all caught up in our own problems. The family was going in separate directions, each person manifesting his illness in his own way.

As an adult child of an alcoholic Maureen looked to her new husband to be her savior. She had no idea she entered her marriage with low self-esteem and big expectations. As marriage disillusioned her, she found solace in alcohol. She didn't realize that using it to numb her pain and anger would lead to her total destruction.

She didn't know that as the daughter of an alcoholic, she was predisposed to the disease. "I'll never drink like him," she often said. We didn't realize Dad never planned to drink either. The disease was squashing the potential for success and happiness in all of us.

Danny drank to have fun. So did Maureen. They never questioned why they couldn't have fun without it.

We were all good people trying to do our best, trying to fight our way out of an invisible box, the perimeter being our own self-limitations. We couldn't see what was good about ourselves. We only saw what was wrong. Years of emotional batterings had us convinced of our inadequacies. It was sad and a waste.

When Maureen was sober, she was loving and giving. She provided an immaculate home for her family. She loved her husband and was a faithful wife and a good Catholic. She set strong moral examples for her children, and felt responsible for keeping the family together. When she drank, like her father, she became angry and frustrated. Unable to put her finger on the problem, she drank for clarity, which added to her confusion.

Danny worked as a carpet layer. He was a good provider for his wife and two children. Like his father, he never spent the family money on booze. He was a sensitive, emotional guy who dreamed big dreams for himself and his family. Yet, deep in his heart he knew he was incapable of making his dreams come true. He wanted life to be pretty. He liked meadows and streams, animals. Gentle things. When he drank, he felt good about himself. He was the "life of the party," always the funniest, the best dancer, best looking. But at most, there was one party a week. How could he live with himself the other six days? He started keeping a six-pack of beer in his car. The end of each work day was focused on the clock. At five he could have his first beer. Then he'd become "Fancy Dan," the guy in his dreams on into the evening. Mardi would get angry watching her husband lose his focus night after night. Danny deafened her recriminations through more booze.

Mother was desperately trying to salvage some sort of life for Michael, but he never had a chance. He never saw the sober Dad. He didn't know the good parts, the Dad who organized picnics and family parties. He never saw the dancing doll; the guy who had the audience in stitches at the school sports assembly. He didn't know the encouraging Dad; the guy who said, "You've got a damn good voice," or "You're a damn good athlete."

Michael was alone and experiencing the full brunt of Dad's disease with no other siblings to talk with. At ten years old, he had become very quiet and introverted. He had learning disabilities, which further aggravated his low self-esteem. Mother took him to private tutors, social workers and a psychiatrist. None of these professionals were able to realize that his disabilities and inability to communicate were manifestations of that which was going on in his home. Michael was emotionally paralyzed from the disease. He was unable to express it verbally. The right professional could have seen it in his eyes. But that was twenty years ago. Even the professionals didn't know the disease cripples the entire family.

My mother arrived around 1:30 P.M. to pick me up on Sunday. She looked so tired, so worn out.

"Are you okay?" I asked her.

"Oh, yes. We've just had a bad week, that's all," my mother said wearily. "Dad lost his job." He now worked for the San Bruno Parks

Department as a caretaker. "He was stopped for drunk driving in a city car," she said. "His license is being revoked. I don't know what we are going to do. He was fired from the brewery and now from the Parks Department. I'm hoping they'll give him another chance. Something where he doesn't need to drive."

My poor mother, I thought. How does she stand it? Why won't she leave him?

"Is he drinking a lot?" I asked.

"Yes, he's on another of his binges. He probably won't drink tonight since it's Sunday, his day of rest."

"What are you going to do, Mom?" I asked.

"I don't know," she said. "I think about leaving all the time. Then he stops drinking for a few days and I lose my nerve."

I could see her psoriasis was acting up again. All around her hairline was blotchy. A sure sign of stress and nerves. I wished there were some way to help my mother. But I was barely keeping my own head above water. Every month I faced possible eviction. Work was slow, my ex-husband still refused to pay child support. I was sick in alcoholic terms and didn't know it, and now I was having an affair with a married man. We were both a mess.

It was great that night seeing my brothers, sister and all the children. I had forgotten how special family times could be. My sister laughed at my miniskirt. "Suzanne, your skirt is so short, you can see the bottom of your panties," Maureen said. It was the sixties. Miniskirts were hot stuff. The shorter, the better.

Little Bruce loved playing with all his cousins. He ran around and screamed with them. They built forts everywhere out of blankets and tables while the grownups had cocktails. Mother and I each had a couple of glasses of wine. Enough to get loose. Danny, Maureen and Dad went for the hard stuff. Dad loved having drinking partners. It was like a contest. Who could drink the most the fastest. I watched Dad's patterns. He never let his glass out of his sight. He told funny story after funny story while pouring himself another drink midsentence. Soon you could see his eyes going cockeyed. When I looked at Maureen and Danny, I noticed their eyes going cockeyed also. I wonder if they could be alcoholics also. Wouldn't that be ironic. After all the times we swore as kids we'd never drink.

"You eat dinner. I'm not hungry," I heard Maureen say to Bill. Her words were slurred. She poured herself another gin. She seemed angry. It was so unlike her. She was a "laugher." She liked fun. I never remembered her being hostile before.

Danny just got happy. The more Maureen got pissy, the more he laughed. Dad laughed too. None of them were hungry.

"Come to the table," Mom demanded.

Obediently, Danny picked up his drink and went to the dinner table. Maureen and Dad followed. Bill said grace; all the children yelled "Amen" and started dinner. Bruce only wanted to eat the olives.

"Have some roast beef, honey," I said to him.

Timmy started yelling because Billy was kicking him under the table. "Stop it!" Timmy yelled at little Billy.

"Stop kicking me, you turd!" little Billy yelled back at Timmy.

"Shut your mouths and watch your manners," Bill demanded of his children.

Joey knocked over his glass of milk. Suddenly there was a big scramble. Mother jumped up to get a rag.

Maureen said, "Oh, Jesus." She sipped on her drink.

Danny laughed. His eyes were out of focus. Dad didn't seem to notice. Danny's little girl, Erin, started to cry. The noise and confusion scared her. My mother carried on as if nothing was happening.

"More potatoes?" she asked. This was calm for Mom. No violence. She didn't have to worry about Dad embarrassing her. This was a "good night."

"How about an after-dinner drink?" Dad asked everyone.

"Sure," Maureen said. "I'll have a gin and tonic."

"Me, too," said Danny.

No crème de cacao for them.

Mom and I were in the kitchen alone. "Do Maureen and Danny drink all the time?" I asked her.

"Well, I do worry about it a bit," my mother said. "But Maureen says she and Bill just have a couple of drinks before dinner every night. I don't think that can do any harm."

She didn't realize "a couple of drinks" meant finishing an entire fifth of gin. She didn't realize they were getting plastered every night. Danny was getting into the "cocktails before dinner" syndrome also. But none of us knew these were warnings signals of the beginning of addiction.

I got home around 8:30 P.M. Mom loaned me her car for a couple of days. Dinner with the family had been draining. Brucie laid his head on my lap as soon as we got into the car and slept all the way home. I carried him out of the car and into his bedroom. He sat on the bed barely awake while I put on his pajamas. His face was red, the back of his hair still wet with perspiration from all the running around. I tucked him in, kissed his cheeks, turned off the light and tiptoed upstairs.

Ring! I ran to the phone. I didn't want it to wake up Brucie.

"Hi," Alan said.

"Hi. I'm so surprised to hear from you," I answered.

"I couldn't stop thinking about you, so I came back tonight instead of tomorrow morning."

"Come over right now," I whispered.

Alan taxied to my house. I met him in the foyer. I didn't turn on the light. We just stood there kissing passionately in the dark. Alan took my hand. Together we walked up the stairs.

I awakened at 5 A.M. and stared at Alan. We were asleep on the floor of the living room. The fire was out, but there was still a little life left in the embers. He opened his eyes. "You look so beautiful in the morning," he said.

I loved his compliments. No one had ever talked to me like that before. "You're the one who's beautiful," I said. "I love your eyes, I love your skin." I love you! my insides were screaming; but I couldn't say that. He'd run away. Control yourself, Suzanne, I thought. Just enjoy the moment. There is no future. I had accepted that. In my life I had learned never to count on the future. "You better leave before Brucie wakes up," I said.

"Absolutely. Can I see you tonight?" he asked.

"You name the place. Anytime after eight," I answered.

"My hotel," he said. Then he was gone.

38

I started my Christmas modeling job at Joseph Magnin's "Wolves' Den" the following week. It quickly became clear to me why it was called the "Wolves' Den." All the junior executives from Montgomery Street (the financial section of San Francisco) spent their lunch hours at "The Den." I called them "the gray suits." They could come to the "Wolves' Den," have hors d'oeuvres, a few drinks, have a cute young model try on some clothes for them and then say they'd "think about it." When you asked one of them what size, all of them said, "about your size." I was there to make money, so I decided right away to avoid the men who didn't seem serious. I looked for the shy, insecure types who really wanted help. There weren't many.

The closer we got to Christmas, the drunker the customers. The final week was a madhouse. The men really did need help now. They had waited until the last minute and now they needed to have something to put under the tree. The store was low on stock and sizes. I was pushing fur coats. There was slight chance of the gift being returned, and usually one size fit all. "Wouldn't your wife go crazy if you surprised her with a fur?" I'd ask. The more coats I sold, the bigger my commission checks. Also, I didn't have to spend so much time trying on outfits for them. I figured if I had a husband, I'd love to find a fur coat under my Christmas tree. The commission on one fur coat was worth more than ten outfits. I sold nine fur coats that week.

The men arrived in packs. I got so I could tell who was going to spend and who wasn't. This job wasn't a game with me. I needed the money and I was enjoying myself. I liked the men and they liked me, but I wore a wedding band to discourage dates. Occasionally I'd get stuck with a customer who was interested in getting me to model the sexiest dresses in the store. Sometimes he'd even buy the dress, but I knew it would be a return. No commissions on returns.

I was running all over the store grabbing coats and jewelry. I used the stairs; the elevators took too much time. The store was eight stories, and I bet I ran up and down the stairs fifty times a day. I was the only model wet with perspiration at the end of each day.

We also had to know when to cut off the drinks with the customers. Having been around drunks all my life, I knew how many drinks to give them to get them loose enough to say "yes," then cut them off while the sales check was being completed. I wanted them to leave upon receipt of their package so I could move on to my next customer.

On Christmas eve at closing time I sold one last fur coat. I got on the bus to go home feeling very satisfied with myself. I had done well. The rent would be paid this month and Brucie would have Christmas presents. I hoped I could pay off the boat and give Joe his pink slip.

"The Anniversary Game" went on a three-week hiatus over Christmas and New Year's. I missed Alan terribly and was glad I had been so busy. He called me often, but they were frustrating phone calls. Usually he was in a phone booth at the supermarket and our talks were constantly interrupted by children's voices.

"Daddy, can I have another quarter?"

"Daddy, put me on the horsie."

Mom and Dad (*back row*, couple on the right) before they were married. Dad, being the "life of the party," as usual.

My mother and father on their wedding day, April 23, 1938.

Mom and Dad, proud and happy in front of Mom's "dream house" on Crystal Springs Road.

Me and Mom.
(I was six months old.)

Maureen, 10 years old, Danny, 6,
and me, 2. (Notice my white
angora sox.) Danny was always
taking care of me.

Me, 4, Danny, 8, Maureen, 12.
(Mom cut my bangs.)

Christmas, 1949.

Dad with the three of us
at the beach, 1950.
I was 4 years old.

Christmas, 1951.
Auntie Helen's house.

San Bruno Posy Parade, 1949.
I was 2 years and 7 months old.
Mom made my costume.

My new outfit, 1949.
(I liked outfits.)

I was Queen of the May in kindergarten.

San Bruno Posy Parade — 7 years old.

Danny, 12, Mom,
Maureen, 15, me, 8, visiting
Virginia City on our Lake Tahoe vacation.

Dad — Virginia City, Nevada,
summer vacation.

Mom and Dad at the beach, Lake Tahoe.

Mom and me, Emerald Bay, Lake Tahoe.
Mom's face looks tense.

Me, 10 years old.
Sandy and I had
the same ponytail
hairstyles.

Dressed in our uniforms,
ready for school. Maureen,
16 years old, Danny, 13, me, 9.

First-grade class picture. I am in the first row,
second from the right. My best friend, Sandy,
is in the third row, first person, on left.

My favorite picture
of Dad as a young man in training
at the San Francisco Olympic Club.

Me with my new baby brother,
Michael, 1957.

(Left) Camping at Lake Tahoe. *Top row:* Maureen, Bill, Cousin Roy, Danny.
Bottom row: Cousins Judy and Tim, Mom with Michael, Dad, me.
(Right) Dad taking care of the garden.

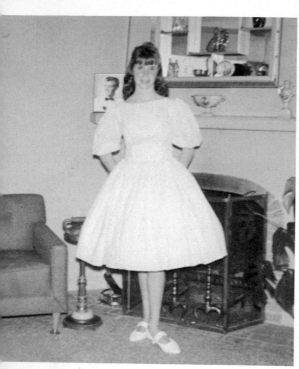

Me, eighth-grade graduation,
June 1960. Mom made my
pink-and-white eyelet dress.

Junior in high school.
Roaring Twenties dance.
Mom made my dress.

High school
class picture, third year.

My junior prom. Mom made the dress.

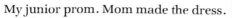

SHIELD

NOVEMBER 1961

H.M.S. Pinafore,
first year at Mercy High
Catholic Girls School.
My first cover!

Me (in white wedding
dress) as Adelaide in
Guys and Dolls with
Walter Winchell.
I was in my last year at
Capuchino High School.
Little did I know that
in less than a year
I'd be in a wedding
dress for real.

Maureen and Bill's wedding day,
June 20, 1959.

Maureen and Bill, 1958.
Maureen colored her hair and cut it short.

The family the morning of Maureen's wedding — Michael, Danny,
Maureen, me, Mom and Dad.

Mom and Michael. Mom's face is tight,
but the garden is nice.

Danny in the Navy, home on leave,
in the backyard with Dad
and Michael.

Danny in Hawaii at Pearl Harbor
Naval Base. Bartending at night
in Officers' Club; also on
Navy basketball team.

Danny and Mardi, who is pregnant
with their first child. Our yard
is not looking so good anymore.

My graduation picture
from high school.

Grad Nite with Bruce Somers.
Mom made my pink-and-white
gown for $47.

My wedding day, April 14, 1965.
Clockwise from left: Dan, Mardi,
Sharon and John Somers, my new
mother-in-law, Ardyss Somers, me,
Bruce, Chuck Somers (Bruce's father),
Maureen, friend, Mom, Dad, Bill.

Maureen, me, Mom at my wedding
shower, given by Maureen and Mom.
I am five months pregnant.

Brucie's second birthday.
I made both our outfits.

Dad (looking very thin)
and Father, 1967.
The front lawn is perfect.

Bruce (almost
2 years old) and me. I had
already started modeling.

Dad, Michael, Father, 1967.
Father's hands show tension.

Me, Bruce, Sr., Brucie,
playing in the yard.

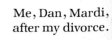

Me, Dan, Mardi,
after my divorce.

Alan and me on vacation in
Hawaii, 1969.

Alan and me in Montreal.

Alan hired me to be one of the three females to interview one male
celebrity guest on *Mantrap*. (The guest was Werner Klemperer.)

Early modeling photo.

First modeling picture.

Picture-perfect gifts ... famed-name leisure-wear

Does this girl have
a future or what!

(Top right) I got a lot of
catalog work. (I am the
first girl, on the right.)

My first *Newsweek* cover.
I received $750 for
appearing nude under
psychedelic lights.

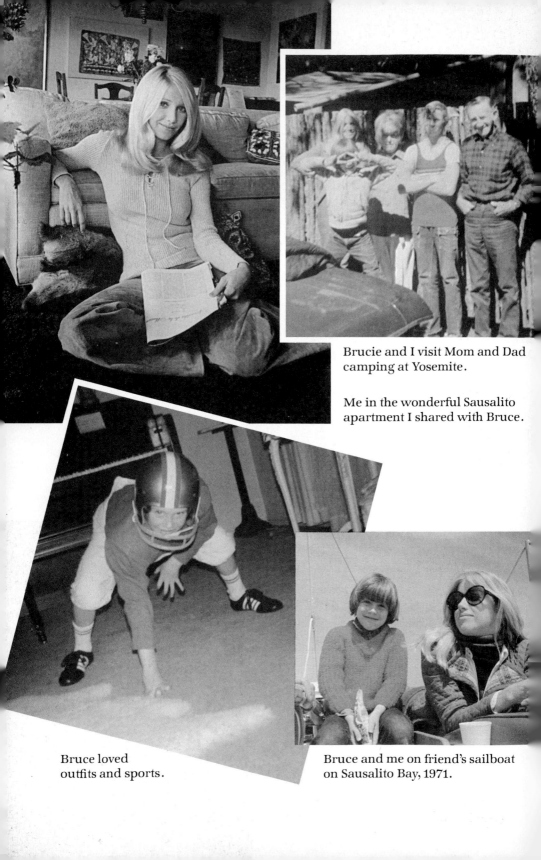

Brucie and I visit Mom and Dad camping at Yosemite.

Me in the wonderful Sausalito apartment I shared with Bruce.

Bruce loved outfits and sports.

Bruce and me on friend's sailboat on Sausalito Bay, 1971.

Me with my best friend, Bruce, summer 1974.

Me just after arriving in Los Angeles.

Self-portrait of Alan, Leslie, Stephen, Bruce and me on picnic at Joshua Tree, California, 1978.

Dad and me in Lifesaver commercial, 1977. (Dad had been sober less than one year.)

Alan and me, 1980.

Alan and me, 1986. I laughingly
refer to this picture as
"the Producer and the Showgirl."
HARRY LANGDON PHOTOGRAPHY

Alan and me today, happily married.

Michael, Maureen, Dad, Mom, Danny and
me today, all together and happy.

Mom and me today. Mom's face is
relaxed and beautiful again.

"Ladies and Gentlemen,
'd like you to meet my dad,
)ucky Mahoney," on stage,
.as Vegas Hilton, 1985.

Me and Bruce today.
MIA BEARDE

Mom and Dad today.

Bruce and my dad today.

Danny and Mardi today.

Maureen and Bill, 1985.

Maureen with two sons, Tim and Joe, at Billy's (firstborn) wedding.

Mardi and Dan with their two children, Sean and Erin, today.

Mom and Michael today.

Family all together, Las Vegas Hilton, 1985. *Clockwise from left:* Dan, Mardi, Dad, Mom, me, Alan, Auntie Helen, Maureen, Bill.

Me on stage Las Vegas, 1987.

"Daddy, can I have an ice cream?"

"Daddy, when are we going?"

Our relationship was filled with complications.

Christmas morning was wonderful with Brucie. He loved his hot cars and tracks. He got enough tracks to go all around his room, under his bed and into the hallway. Around one in the afternoon, we took a taxi to my mother's house. It cost me twenty-eight dollars.

It was great seeing all my relatives; Auntie Helen, Uncle Dave, Uncle Ralph, Auntie Ann. My dad was drunk, but jovial. Everyone enjoyed him when he was like this, even us. He got everyone all revved up. He created excitement and laughter. His mood dominated the room. If he was happy, we were happy. I loved my dad a lot. If only his mood would stay like this all the time.

Dad gave me a big kiss. "Merry Christmas, sweetheart," he said. "You look beautiful."

"Thanks, Dad. Merry Christmas," I said.

"Well, well. Look at Brucie. That's some sportcoat! Strictly north of Market." The kids all thought Grandpa was funny. Brucie adored him.

Dad continued to greet the guests. His voice got louder and louder. He served the drinks. That way he could pour them real strong. He liked to get his guests drunk. He didn't stick out so much that way.

Father came up to me and put his arms around me. "How're you doing, honey?" he asked.

"I'm getting by," I answered.

"Your mother tells me you need a car. I'd like to loan you the money for it," he said.

"Oh, Father." My eyes welled up with tears. "That would make my life so much easier. God, that's so nice of you. Thank you. I love you so much," I said.

"I love you, too," Father answered. "I want you to pay me back, but we'll make it something you can handle each month," he said.

"I can't thank you enough." I kissed him and ran to the kitchen to tell my mother.

What a wonderful Christmas surprise. I didn't tell Dad. He was always so jealous of Father. I was afraid he'd find some way to criticize Father for having done me the favor. I never understood Dad's reaction to Father. Maybe it was simply because everyone loved Father so much. He was good and kind and loving. He didn't drink (to speak of); he lived a clean life, had done well financially and loved his children and grandchildren. Maybe Dad was afraid Mom compared her father to Dad and he came up short. They were two different types of men. They were both great; my father just had a terrible disease. In his drunken state he would have been jealous.

Father told me he'd be willing to loan me around twenty-five hundred dollars for my car. I spent the next two days reading the want ads and making phone calls. I didn't know anything about cars or car engines. I didn't know what questions to ask. I found a used car, a 1968 Pontiac Firebird, and bought it on the basis of appearance. It was a blue convertible with a white top, air conditioning and an eight-track stereo system. The salesman's name was Neil Siedel (Cash for Cars), and he assured me this car was a "jewel." I was thrilled, Brucie was thrilled. Wow! Our own car. It was such a luxury. We could drive to the store, we could go for rides, we could visit with the family. I agreed to pay Father back sixty dollars a month. I was sure I'd be able to afford that.

On Sunday, I called my mother to see if she wanted to go for a ride with Brucie and me to Searsville Lake. A recreation area we went to when I was a child, the lake was about thirty miles south of San Bruno.

I pulled up in front of her house with the convertible top down. The sun was shining. I had Eydie Gorme singing at the top of her lungs from the stereo. I felt great. I felt free. Mobile. Halfway to the lake I could smell rusty water. My radiator light was on. We pulled into a gas station. Sure enough, my radiator was overheating and bubbling.

"You should get this checked," the attendant said as he was putting water in it.

Oh, God, I thought. I can't afford to have car trouble. We had to stop two more times on the way home to put water in the radiator.

On Monday morning I took the car back to Neil Siedel to have him fix the problem. He told me I'd have to leave the car with him for a couple of days. I took a bus home. On Thursday the car was ready. I still didn't have my pink slip (the document of ownership). Neil Siedel said the papers were still being processed. I got in my car and backed out of his driveway. I never saw the oncoming car. *Crash!* Oh, God. Oh, no! I jumped out of my car.

"You stupid bitch," the man yelled at me.

"I'm sorry," I said. "I didn't see you." It never entered my mind that the oncoming car might have been speeding. I just assumed the blame. I didn't have any car insurance yet.

Neil Siedel ran out to the rescue. "Don't worry, Suzie, I'll take care of this."

The other car was all banged in on the front passenger side. My bumper was a mess. Neil Siedel said his garage would take care of fixing both cars. I agreed. Two weeks later I was presented with a bill for 750 dollars. My car damage was 200 dollars. The other car was 550 dollars. I was sick. I wasn't sure how much my commission check from my Christmas job would total. Between the 600 dollars I owed Joe the bartender, rent, gas, electric, the grocery store, answering service, my 60-dollar payment to Father and now this 750-dollar bill, I could see my money was going to be used up. Now I had to worry that my check would cover my expenses.

"I can't pay you for a couple of weeks," I told Neil Siedel.

"Well, I'll have to hold your pink slip as collateral," he said, "and you'd better get yourself some insurance."

Oh, right, I thought. Another bill.

39

Alan was back in town. He made me forget my troubles. Alan didn't know I had any troubles. Remember me, the heiress? There were so many secrets I kept from him. But what's the difference? This relationship had no future. I was sure my secrets would never be found out.

My evenings with Alan continued to be magical. He moved out of the Miyako Hotel into a lovely apartment on Telegraph Hill. I was glad. No more desk clerks. More privacy. I could call him at home directly.

Alan enjoyed cooking for me. He made such wonderful things as pepper steak, oyster stew, scrambled eggs with fresh asparagus and honeyed lamb chops. He'd feed me, compliment me, make love to me. It was all so romantic. I would have him on any terms just to have him. I was hopelessly in love.

My salary and commission check from Joseph Magnin arrived. I had done well. The check was a little over twelve hundred dollars. Unfortunately, my bills came to more than that. I paid the final six hundred to Joe the bartender. Thank God, that noose was no longer around my neck. Next, rent had to be paid and I couldn't be without a telephone and my answering service. My telephone was my link to work and, most important, to Alan. Boom! Suddenly a thousand dollars was gone. I only had two hundred left. I had to buy groceries. Another eighty-six dollars. Oh, my God, I didn't have enough to pay Neil Siedel's bill from the accident. Now I can't get my pink slip. Without the pink slip I can't get insurance. Oh, right! I owe Father sixty dollars for my car payment. I can't believe it. I have fifty-four dollars left until my next job, with no prospects in sight.

I have to move, I thought. I just can't afford two hundred dollars a month for rent. Besides, I'd like Brucie to have a neighborhood to live in. Bruce's best friend was our neighbor, Jack Hanson, who was forty years old. I met Jack through Bruce.

Jack was a terrific guy. He was handsome, slight of build and had a wonderful sense of humor. He had a funny way of looking at life—very basic, gut level. I enjoyed him immensely.

Jack worked in and out of local television. He had hosted kids' shows and news shows; he had been a weatherman and now was producing documentary films for Wells Fargo. We became close friends very quickly. Jack adored Bruce, and his friendship was extremely important to me.

I decided to look for a new apartment in Marin County. It was quiet and peaceful there and less expensive than living in San Francisco. I combed the want ads and lined up all the possibilities on one day so I wouldn't have to pay the fifty-cent bridge toll more than once.

I found a lovely little house in Sausalito; a two-bedroom cottage with a small deck that overlooked the Bay. The rent was one hundred fifty dollars a month. It was perfect. All I needed was first and last month's rent and a hundred-dollar deposit. Four hundred dollars! How could I come up with four hundred dollars?

Marsha from my modeling agency called. "They are looking for a girl for the cover of *Newsweek*. It pays 750 dollars for two hours' work and you have to be nude."

"Nude!" I said.

"Yes," said Marsha, "but no one will know it's you. It's going to be shot in psychedelic lights and all you will see is the outline of your shape. It's an article on women in revolt, about the feminist movement."

I didn't really want to do it. The idea of being naked in front of a photographer bothered me a lot. But no one would know it was me, and I desperately needed the money. "Okay," I said to Marsha.

I got the job and my agency advanced me the money. I should have paid off Neil Siedel, but I wanted to move to Sausalito. It was typical of my pattern. I was creating another crisis for myself. Neil Siedel was already starting to get heavy about the money I owed him. I sent him a hundred dollars just to get him off my back for a while. I also owed for gas and electric and the grocery store. They could wait a while longer. I needed money to move and install telephones and electricity to my new house.

My brother Dan, my brother-in-law Bill and my friend Jack all helped me move. Bill borrowed his friend's truck and the three men started the process of packing my belongings into it. Around one o'clock in the afternoon when my house was half empty, my phone rang. It was my new landlady.

"I've been thinking about it," she said, "and I just don't want a divorcée living on my property."

"But I'm in the process of moving right now," I said incredulously. "I've given notice at this house and I have nowhere to live."

"I'm sorry," she said. "It's not my problem. I've already torn up your check."

I started to protest again and realized I was talking to a dial tone. She had hung up on me. What was I going to do? The house I was living in was already rented to someone else. They were moving in the next day.

I told my brother and brother-in-law to keep packing the truck. "I'm going to drive over to Sausalito and try to find another apartment," I told them. I remembered there was a new apartment complex that had just opened, called the Anchorage. I could live there until I found something better.

The Anchorage Apartments were available. I was the first person to rent. My monthly payment was one hundred twenty-five dollars, first and last month's rent and a hundred-dollar deposit. About the same as the little house, but nowhere near as charming. The Anchorage had over a hundred ugly white stucco apartments with no charm. But they had a swimming pool and a communal sauna and they were willing to let me move in immediately. I called my brother and gave him the address. Three hours later I was moved in. I had no intentions of staying very long, but it was better than being on the street.

I got Brucie's room together and that was about it. I didn't bother hanging my pictures. I didn't bother arranging my furniture to look perfect. This place was temporary.

I was saving money on rent but it didn't make much difference. Work was slow. Work would always be slow. There just wasn't that much going on in San Francisco. I'd audition for any movie shooting in town, but the most I could hope for was a line or two if I were really lucky.

Mostly, it was extra work. I wasn't tall enough to do ramp modeling and photographic jobs were few and far between.

I remained in my temporary residence for a year and a half. I never did hang my pictures, never arranged my furniture. I deluded myself into believing I'd be moving at any time, so why bother. My apartment was just like the apartment next door, which was exactly like the one next to it. They were ordinary. I didn't like feeling ordinary. I wanted to be different. I wanted everything about my life to be different. I had this gnawing feeling eating away inside me. I knew I had talent. My experience in high school had shown me that. I had never gotten over my elation of doing *Guys and Dolls*. I wanted to sing, dance and act, but I didn't know how to go about it. I had a casting agent now, but the only time she sent me on a job was for extra work and an occasional local commercial. She didn't know I could do anything else, and I didn't have any film or tape of myself to convince her.

Extra work seemed demeaning to me. They referred to us as "background," a bunch of cattle. "Don't wear bright colors," they said. They didn't want us to show up too much, just be that invisible blur behind the important people. I yearned to be one of the important people.

My financial situation went from bad to worse. I couldn't make ends meet. My car turned out to be a real lemon. Every time I took it somewhere, something went wrong. All my money was going to auto repairs. I still didn't have the pink slip. Neil Siedel was making my life real difficult. I still owed him 650 dollars from the accident and I just couldn't come up with the money.

One morning I went out to get in my car and it was gone. I couldn't believe it. I ran around the parking lot looking everywhere. Why would anyone want to steal my crummy car? I called my mother crying.

"Someone stole my car," I said sobbing.

"Oh, dear," my mom said. "You'd better inform the police."

Three hours later I received a phone call from the Sausalito Police Department. "This is Sergeant Collins. Your car wasn't stolen. It was repossessed by a Neil Siedel Used Cars."

I couldn't believe it. Neil Siedel told me that in order to get my car back I'd have to pay 650 dollars plus a 400-dollar repossessing charge and 300-dollar towing bill. All together 1,350 dollars. There was no way I could pull together that kind of money. I still owed Father 1,800 dollars for the car loan, plus my usual monthly bills. I felt humiliated, embarrassed and defeated. I had lost my car. I didn't want anyone to know how broke I was, so I told my mother, my sister and Alan that my car had been stolen and I had no insurance. (That part was true.)

I was back where I started, except now I was in a mundane apartment with my pictures sitting on the floor, unable to get to San Francisco for interviews. My friend Jack helped me immensely during this time. He had moved to Sausalito also; and on days I had interviews, I would drive with him to the city, drop him off at work and pick him up at the end of the day. It was hard on Brucie. He would get tired and cranky dragging around all day on interviews with me, but hiring a babysitter was out of the question. I just couldn't afford it. In a few months he would be starting kindergarten. That would make things easier.

I needed to provide my darling son with food, shelter and clothing. I was managing the shelter part and the clothing, but sometimes I just didn't have enough money for food. I started writing checks. I would write a check for groceries and ask the clerk, "Could I make this for fifty dollars extra?" Then I would pray I would somehow, miraculously, come up with the money to deposit in my bank account before the check bounced. For the moment I would be relieved. I would have a cart full of groceries and some extra money in my pocket. I could only buy what I could carry home or push in a borrowed supermarket cart, now that I didn't have a car. This practice of check writing was the beginning of the worst crisis I had ever created for myself. But it fit right in with my life pattern; being unrealistic, living in a fantasy. I developed a real and deep anger toward my ex-husband during this time. I could have really used the 150-dollar-a-month child support. It had been three and a half years and I had not received one penny from him. But he was angry with me, and this was his way of letting me know. Time wasn't healing the wounds. Time seemed to intensify his feelings. I felt bad, but I couldn't undo what I had done.

I was surviving any way I could. If it meant writing a bad check so we could eat, that is what I had to do. More crises. Pride is stupid, and I was too proud to go to my family, and I never, ever wanted Alan to know my real situation.

I now had a series of bad checks being held by a lot of nice people who were being "understanding." The checks were always under a hundred dollars, so no one got too frantic, but I was playing with fire. Sooner or later someone was going to turn one of my checks over to the police department.

My telephone ringing was always such a dilemma for me. It could be Alan and I didn't want to miss talking to him. It could be my agency with work, or it could be an angry recipient of one of my bad checks.

The highs and lows. My affair with Alan was my escape from reality.

Yes, it was filled with problems. He was married and I still had all the secrets I kept from him. But I couldn't give him up. I loved him too much. I enjoyed every moment with him as if it were the very last time. It was so passionate, both knowing when the weekend came he would have to go home again. He made me feel beautiful. He made me laugh and forget the realities of my life. I was addicted to him and he to me.

I had my telephone put on a jack so when Alan was over I could unplug it. I didn't want him to overhear the numerous phone calls that came in every day from those holding my bad checks. "Miss Somers, we have redeposited your check twice and the bank has sent it back again! We must have restitution in cash by tomorrow."

"Oh, I'm so sorry," I would say. "I'll take care of it right away." Then I would call my agency and beg for an advance on my last job. Living on the edge. Crisis. Sometimes I would sit on the floor of my closet and sob. I didn't want little Bruce to see me. He was happy. He didn't know anything. He got to be with his mommy all the time. He had a room, toys, clothes and food, and soon he would go to school; then he would have friends. He was so lovable, so good. He hardly ever saw Alan because I met with him after Bruce went to sleep at night. I didn't want Bruce to think he might be getting a new daddy. I knew there was no future with Alan. Because of my lies I had seen to that. I never talked to Alan about his wife and I never put any pressure on him. I didn't want to send him away. I loved him and I was sure he loved me, but neither of us could say it because it would change the relationship. I didn't want to take the chance. Besides, if he was in love with me, he was in love with a person he didn't really know. How I wished I had never told him all the lies. I was beginning to realize he would have loved me anyway. He was attracted to my naïveté. I wasn't slick, I wasn't "Hollywood" and he loved my vulnerability. He loved the small-town girl in me even though I tried to be a big-city girl. Our affair was now into its second year.

My telephone continued to haunt me. Every message ended with, "We must have it by tomorrow." I was now avoiding my family also. I felt stupid being without a car again and I didn't want to run into Father. I hadn't been able to pay him for the car for months. He would have understood. Instead, I chose to hide from him. I couldn't handle facing him and the truth. Lying was easier for me; avoidance, being unrealistic. That's how I lived my life now. I didn't know why. I didn't want to be this way, but I did it over and over again. More crises. More isolation. I carried the burden of my making all alone. I was averaging a couple of jobs a month. For San Francisco, that was considered good.

I didn't know anyone else trying to survive financially solely in the "business" in San Francisco. There just wasn't enough work. Why I didn't get an "ordinary job" as a receptionist I'll never know. I imagine it would have burst the bubble of my fantasies. In my dreams, I was a star in waiting. Someday, someone would recognize my talent. I wasn't even sure what my talent was. It was raw, untrained, untapped. But I could feel it churning inside me. I had no money to take lessons. I didn't realize I was training myself. I didn't realize the acting ability it took to continue my façade with Alan or the one I constructed for my family. The only person who knew the reality of my desperate financial situation was my friend Jack. I don't know what I would have done without Jack. He was also a good friend to Brucie. He took us shopping, loaned me his car, took us on weekend drives when Alan was at home. Jack thought Alan was a jerk for being married and seeing me at the same time. Jack didn't realize I allowed Alan to lead this double life. I put no pressure on him, I let him "have his cake and eat it too," as my mother would have said. I now know that Alan had been crazy about me from the day we met. I didn't know his marriage was rocky, and he wasn't the type to air his problems. He respected his wife and loved his children; and as long as I wasn't pressuring him it was easier for him to put off the inevitable. As long as I didn't think I deserved Alan, I wasn't going to have him. I never wondered why I thought so little of myself.

40

On Friday, the first week of August, Alan left for a three-week vacation to Mexico. I was miserable. The thought of him vacationing with his wife was shattering. He kissed me good-bye and told me he'd miss me a lot. I believed him. Our time together was so special. I wished he hadn't gone.

I tossed and turned most of the night. Finally, around 4 A.M. my brain gave in and allowed me to fall into a deep sleep. At 6 A.M., August 23, 1970, my doorbell rang. I jumped up, disoriented. My mind immediately flashed back to all the nights of my childhood when the doorbell meant Dad was home and really drunk. I felt fear in the pit of my stomach. I grabbed my robe and looked through the front-door peephole. Oh, my God! It was a policeman. He wasn't in uniform, but he flashed his shield. I opened the door.

"Suzanne Somers?" he asked. "I'm from the Sausalito Police Department. I have a warrant for your arrest."

Arrest! Everything inside me started to shake. I felt nauseated. "What did I do?" I asked.

"The charge is fraud. I can't be specific until we officially book you at the station. You'll have to come with me," the officer said.

"But I can't," I stammered. "My little boy is still asleep and I have no one to take care of him." My world was crashing in; catching up with me.

"We'll take your child into custody and put him in a foster home," the officer said.

"No! No!" I pleaded. I didn't know what to do. "I have a neighbor, officer," I said desperately. "Please let me call and ask if she will babysit. Please!" I could not hold back the tears. Thank God the officer had some compassion. I called my neighbor. I hardly knew her, but she had a little boy that Bruce played with sometimes. I had no choice but to tell her the truth and beg for help. She said luckily she was off work that day and Bruce could come over. The officer said he would wait while I dressed and got Bruce ready. He went into the living room. I could see him looking through my things. I had no rights. I couldn't say, "Excuse me, would you mind!" I got dressed, then reluctantly went into Brucie's room to wake him. My nerves were frazzled but I had to act calm. Bruce was so cute in the morning. His face was all red and his hair went cockeyed from sleeping on it. His little thumb was in his mouth. I gently rubbed his head and his little back. Tears were streaming down my face.

"Brucie, sweetheart. Wake up," I whispered. He made cute little baby noises, shifted positions and went back to sleep. "Brucie, honey, time to wake up. Mommy has to go to work."

He opened his eyes. "Where are we working?" he asked sleepily.

"No, honey. Today Mommy has to work alone and you get to stay at Brian's house."

I tried to smile and fake enthusiasm. I didn't want him to see me crying. I held him in my arms. I loved him so much. I didn't want to let go of him. He felt so good. I didn't know when I would see him again. I didn't know if I was going to jail forever. I didn't know if I'd be home tonight or a year from tonight. It was the loneliest, most terrifying feeling of my life. I dressed Brucie in clean clothes. My hands were shaking so much I could hardly button the little buttons on his shirt. I put on his warm sweater, washed his face and tried to comb his hair. No amount of water would make his hair lie down flat.

The officer was standing at Bruce's bedroom door. "We have to get going," he said.

"Do I have time to give him breakfast?" I asked. I wanted to stretch things out as long as possible. I wanted to savor every precious moment with my child, relish every last minute of freedom.

"I'm sorry. We have to go," he said without emotion.

I packed up Bruce's pajamas and his favorite toys. "Am I staying overnight?" Bruce asked. He looked concerned.

"I hope not," I said. "These are just in case I work real late," I said trying to be encouraging. "If it's real late, I'll have Grammy come and pick you up." Please, dear God, please let me be home tonight. Please hear me, I prayed silently. I couldn't bear the thought of Bruce being without his mother.

We walked out the front door; Brucie, myself and the police officer. I saw his unmarked car. It had a grille separating the front from the backseat. I felt frantic. I couldn't let Bruce see that grille. He was smart. He would know something was wrong.

"I'll walk him next door," I said to the officer. My eyes were filled with terror.

The officer paused. "Okay," he said.

My neighbor was looking out the window. "See, Brucie? See Brian in the window?" I tried to act happy. I walked Brucie up the stairs knowing that each step brought me closer to saying good-bye. I was straining to keep from crying. At the top step I hugged Bruce with all my might. "I love you, darling. You be a good boy for Mommy. Okay?"

"I will," he said. "I love you, too."

"Bye-bye, honey. I'll see you real soon." I kissed him again. Then he went inside. My neighbor was smart enough and kind enough to keep Bruce away from the window so he wouldn't see the policeman put me in the backseat and drive off.

Once inside the police car my tears froze in terror. There was the grille and there were no door handles. The officer told me that he should have handcuffed me (the rules, you know) but decided to let it go this time. Handcuffs! Only criminals wear handcuffs. The reality was hitting me. I was a criminal. My bounced checks for groceries were a criminal offense.

A blonde in the back seat of a police car attracts a lot of attention. I ducked down to avoid the stares. This was not the kind of attention I wanted.

"Do you always look that bad in the morning?" the policeman asked.

"Well, I had a hard time sleeping and I've been under a lot of stress," I tried to explain. He could say whatever he wanted. I had no rights.

We pulled up to the police department. It was almost quaint. A little red-brick jailhouse. "I'm going to have to cuff you now," the policeman said. "Don't want you running away."

He was enjoying this. I was in shock. It was like a blur around me.

"Hey, Berkhouse." (That was the officer's name.) "Got a cute one this morning, huh?"

I was the object of attention for all the policemen drinking their coffee.

"She a hooker?" one asked.

"Naw. Rubber checks."

I was nothing. They talked about me as if I couldn't hear. Couldn't feel. I sat in the corner shaking, with my hands behind me in handcuffs. My officer was filling out his report; my name, age, etc. Then I was moved to a small room with a camera.

"Look this way." *Click!* "Turn to the side." *Click!*

I now had my mug shots. Officer Berkhouse took off my handcuffs. He stuck my thumb onto black fingerprinting ink. Press. He did the same with all my fingers. I was frightened. Humiliated. Why had I been too proud to go to my family? Why had I been so stupid? Why had I messed things up so badly? I wanted to give my son such a good life. Now his mother was going to be in jail. I felt so afraid, numb. Jail! I'd seen so many movies about women in jail. They were so tough. What if I got raped? What if I got beaten up? I started sobbing. Police are conditioned to tears. They don't hear them. They don't see them.

Snap! The handcuffs were back on. I sat in another little room, this time for three hours. Then Officer Berkhouse opened the door. "Okay, let's go."

"Where are we going?" I asked.

"To the county jail. We don't have room for you here."

Back into the backseat of the police car. No door handles. No rights. No respect. We drove past beautiful Mill Valley, past Fairfax on the way to San Raphael. We pulled into an underground entrance of the large San Raphael courthouse. This was not quaint. They meant business here. I was still in handcuffs. We entered a long hallway. An elevator took us down three floors. What is happening to me? Another room. More policemen. A policewoman. Another camera.

"Is that all your hair?" asked the officer operating the camera.

"No," I said sheepishly. In my rush I had put on my long hairpiece so I wouldn't have to bother with my hair. It was the look of the sixties.

"Take it off," the officer said coldly. In front of these people I pulled off my hairpiece. "Stand over there." *Click!* More mug shots. Front view, side view. More fingerprints.

The policewoman took me to a small room. "Get undressed," she ordered. I stood there naked while she searched my body everywhere. Fingers going through my hair, my vagina. I felt numb. Hollow. I wasn't human. "Put this on." The matron handed me a gray hospital-looking dress. "You have one phone call coming to you."

I didn't know who to call. My mother? Jack? I couldn't call Alan. I remembered a lawyer I knew and called him. "Please get me out of here," I begged. "I'll go crazy if I have to stay here." I was losing it. Crisis! Crisis! Crisis! How could I have done this to myself.

After my phone call I was led to my cell. I'll never forget the sound of the cell door closing. *Slam!* The sound of heavy metal. I stood there shaking. I was all alone. I had a terrible headache. "Excuse me," I called for the matron meekly. "Excuse me. I have a headache. I wonder if I could have an aspirin." I was talking to myself. The matron ignored me. I had no rights. I was a criminal.

I sat in that cell all day, my head in my hands. I didn't know what to do. Where could I get money? I had to make more money. I had to get a job. I had to get out of jail.

Nine hours later my lawyer arrived. "You've been released on your own recognizance," he said.

"What does that mean?" I asked.

"It means they are letting you out without bail, and they trust you will show up for your court date in thirty days. I recommend you make restitution on these checks. They total a little over three hundred dollars. If you pay them, I'm sure the judge will let you off, being it's your first offense and you have sole custody of your child."

I felt so relieved. I was given back my clothes and my hairpiece. My lawyer drove me as far as the San Raphael bus depot.

"By the way," he said as he dropped me off, "my fee is seven hundred and fifty dollars. I'll need a deposit of three hundred and fifty right away and the balance in thirty days."

"I'll get it," I promised. Then he drove off.

I called Bruce from a pay phone to tell him I'd be home in an hour. The bus dropped me off a half mile from my house. I ran home up the hill in the dark. I wanted to get home to my baby and the safety of our apartment.

Bruce was asleep on my neighbor's couch. He was wearing his jacket. I knew he didn't want to spend the night there and he figured he'd be all ready to go when I arrived. I thanked my neighbor from the bottom of my heart and carried Bruce to our apartment. I hugged him and kissed him all the way. After I got him into his pajamas, I lay down on his bed with him until he fell asleep. I felt so thankful to be with him again. I had never before appreciated what freedom meant. Free will. Free to do what I want, when I want. All I have to do is obey the rules.

I sat in the dark of my bedroom determined to get out of this mess. With my lawyer's fee and bad checks, I was another thousand dollars in the hole. My back ached, my head ached, my whole being was weary. It had been a long, long day.

I fell into an exhausted sleep but awoke many times during the night in a cold sweat, panicked! A new nightmare had begun. Jail! Being dragged from my house. Brucie screaming, "Don't go! Don't go!" I would reach for Brucie, but I couldn't touch him. Agony! Big, mean, masculine women moving in on me; closer, closer. I was screaming, "No! No! No!" Then I would wake up, wet and shaking. I hated to go back to sleep. I didn't want the dream again, but my body was exhausted.

The next morning I awoke to find Brucie playing with his hot cars on my back. Captain Kangaroo was on television. Things were back to normal, for thirty days anyway. I couldn't allow myself to think of what might happen if the judge decided to convict me. I had to get the money together to make restitution on those checks. I had to get the money for the lawyer. My ex-husband owed me three and a half years worth of child support. That could save me, but I knew it was futile to ask. He was never going to pay me anything.

Who could I borrow from? When Alan was gone, I had casually been dating a man named Arthur. He was of San Francisco society and had lots of money. In fact, I had met my lawyer through him. He would loan me the thousand dollars. I didn't want to ask. Arthur was such a nice guy, but I was desperate. Better he should think I'm foolish than Alan. If only I had been straight with Alan. He would have gladly given me the money.

I hated the position in which I had put myself. I was proud. I didn't want help. I wanted to make it on my own. I called my agency.

"Nothing going on this week," my agent said cheerfully.

"I have six hundred dollars due from the Macy's catalogue, and I wondered if I could be advanced the money," I asked. Modeling was a very slow paying business. I had done the job for Macy's almost two months ago. It was impossible to plan. Never knew if the money would take four weeks or four months. Please, please, I was thinking. I need the cash.

"Okay, we can advance half the money," my agent answered coolly.

"Thanks," I said. Half is better than nothing.

I called my friend Arthur. "I'm in a bit of a jam." I told him the story. It was so humiliating.

"Sure, I'll help you out," he said patronizingly.

I could tell he thought I was foolish and stupid. He was right. I knew it better than anyone. He loaned me seven hundred dollars. With the advance I had my thousand for the checks and the lawyer. Now I had to hope the balance of the Macy's money would come in soon so I could pay for my rent, telephone and food.

41

*S*uch a low point in my life. I was filled with dangerous thoughts and self-pity. Everywhere I turned I faced crises. I was so hard on myself. It was impossible for me to understand I needed therapy, not money, to solve my problems. Someone to help me get at the root of my troubles; someone to take me all the way back to the crazy violent nights of my childhood so I could see that crises and insane behavior had been my training ground. I needed to be retrained. What was normal behavior? What was realistic? I had been taught never to lie, but our lives were a lie; always pretending things were different from the way they actually were. I couldn't cope with the truth. I couldn't accept the reality of who I really was. There was no one to talk with.

The rest of my family was in a similar crisis. Dad's illness had reached pathetic proportions. His thoughts were twisted and warped, sometimes even evil. "Good ol' Ducky, the life of the party," was gone. What was left was the darkest part of his soul. The disease had devoured everything that had been good. He ranted and raved, badgered and belittled. He told Mom she was no good, crazy and the cause of all the problems. "The humiliation and shame of being treated like this by someone who is supposed to love me creates doubts about my self-worth," she wrote in the diary she kept during those years. "I believe I am the cause and responsible and I am so lonely. I cannot make friends and there is no one to talk to," she continued. Mother was in agony; the color was drained from her face, her skin was dry and blotchy. Her hands shook, she felt hopeless. Her only solace, her only sustenance was still the church.

The disease was also bringing out a different Maureen. The person that she really was—the vibrant, enthusiastic, fun-loving, proud sister I had grown up with—was negated by booze. In its place was an unconfident, angry, jealous, frightened person. She was divided in two. The life of the party at night and the timid, guilty, repentant person by day. After two martinis she'd get wild. Maureen, Bill, Danny and Mardi belonged to the San Bruno Lions Club. It was like a fraternity. There was always a party with lots of booze and dancing. It wouldn't take long before Maureen and Danny were both the center of attraction. Maureen would take down her hair and dance for attention. Bill would get angry and leave. Danny danced and drank himself into a stupor. He never wanted to go home. Mardi would leave without him.

The next day Maureen would not remember anything but knew from the deafening silence in the house she had been bad again. She'd try to repent by working like a slave, always on her hands and knees scrubbing floors, her eyes begging for forgiveness.

Danny's house was silent also. His guilt was so heavy he'd feel terribly ashamed of himself. All the things he hated in Dad he was doing himself. He'd promise Mardi, "This is it. I'll never drink again." It would last about a week, then he'd slip.

Mother wrote in her diary that "Michael is depressed and saying he is stupid. He has no ambition, never takes care of the little important things. I am worried about the friends he has chosen. I feel so guilty that I've done nothing to change our life."

The disease had everyone in pain and turmoil. We were all paralyzed by our inability to see the root of the problem. We all needed professional help desperately. We were all walking, talking, seemingly alive; but death was around us. Emotional death and insanity.

42

I missed Alan. I needed to be held and loved so badly. "The Anniversary Game" was on hiatus for the summer. Alan flew up from Los Angeles as often as he could, but it was hard for him to get away. Now he was in Mexico.

While Alan was gone I dated other men. Nothing serious, although I'm sure some of them would have liked it to be. As long as I could afford the two dollars an hour for a babysitter, I usually said yes; but I could not leave the house until 8 P.M. That was when Brucie went to bed for the night. I was a lot of fun. I loved to laugh, I knew how to dress so they could take me anywhere. I knew how to make conversation and I was funny. I didn't think these qualities in myself were anything special. Dating was an escape, a chance to go to fancy restaurants, parties; a chance to meet new and interesting people; an opportunity to forget my problems.

There was my dear friend Jack Hanson, Arthur, Jim who was a poet, a dentist, a banker, a real-estate investor. I wouldn't go out with losers. I dated upwardly mobile or successful, accomplished men, usually around ten years older than myself. I found men my age (twenty-two) didn't understand the problems of children and babysitters. I always hoped one of these men would steal my heart, but I was in love with Alan. No other man could take his place. I didn't want to be in love with Alan. It was too complicated. Being Alan's mistress only added to my already suffering self-esteem. If I could fall in love with one of these other men, the burden of financial responsibility would not rest solely upon my shoulders; but I could never ever marry someone for the sake of finances. I had to be wildly in love; and so far the only man I had ever felt that way about was Alan. Who can explain love. Right, wrong, when you love, you love, and I loved Alan.

Our times together became more passionate, desperate. A stolen weekend, a single night. He used every excuse to get back to San Francisco. I could never get enough of him, nor he of me. When he left, I would cry. There was so much I wanted to tell him. He was smart. He could help me figure out how to get out of this legal mess; but I couldn't take the chance. What if I lost him? If he knew the real me, he might lose interest, feel betrayed, think I was sick. I couldn't risk it.

I would have to bear the burden of my impending conviction alone. I wouldn't go to my family. We were drifting further and further apart; all lost in a sea of our own personal problems. My dad was now permanently retired. He was drunk every day and every night. To support them, my mother worked full time as a medical secretary. She looked terrible; frazzled, nervous. She was paralyzed emotionally from living on the edge, living with crises, living with the constant insanity around her. Her anger smoldered deep inside. She just tried to get through each day as best she could.

The reality that her children were in bad shape added to her heavy heart. She smelled liquor on Michael's breath. (He was twelve.) Sometimes she noticed his eyes looked dead or stoned. When questioned he denied everything, but Mom's instincts were flashing a red light.

New violence was erupting at night. Michael internalized all his feelings; but when pushed to his breaking point, he erupted like a volcano. Dad would rant and rave night after night until finally Michael would explode. They went after each other physically. Not even Mother could curtail Michael's strength. The anger between them was intense.

Mom would suggest to Maureen that perhaps she was drinking too much and Maureen would lash out. "I really don't need you coming around here with your holier-than-thou attitudes telling me what to do." Maureen was racked with guilt. She did not want Mom to be "on to her." None of us wanted to disappoint Mom. We all tried to keep "our secrets" to ourselves.

Danny was the best at it. Mom would stop by their house and look in on a perfect little family having dinner. She had no idea Danny waited till everyone was asleep then would sit in the kitchen and drink a fifth of gin all by himself. He'd pass out on the kitchen floor, but always got himself up for work the next morning. His hangover, terrible stomach and excruciating headache was his penance for being bad the night before. Relief came when he repeated the process that night.

Mom wrote me letters telling me she was disappointed in the way I was handling my money matters and my life. Her letters made me feel angry and guilty. I knew I was screwing up. I didn't need her to tell me. I stopped communicating with her.

No one in the family approved of my relationship with Alan. I thought, "To hell with all of them. I married the last one because they all told me to. This time I'm doing it my way."

Now we were all cut off from one another. Alone with our pain.

43

I n the days following my arrest, my shock turned to determination. I knew I had God-given gifts; talent. I wanted to put them to use. A few modeling bookings came through. Next month's expenses would be covered. I decided to swallow my pride and apply for waitressing jobs near my home. No one was hiring. I tried the Trident, the coffee house, the Pancake House, the pizza restaurant. "We'll let you know," was the response.

Brucie was starting kindergarten in a week. That would leave my mornings free to pursue work. Ten days till my court date. I had paid off my checks. I prayed the judge would let me go free. I feared going back to the San Raphael courthouse. "Dress conservatively," my lawyer told me. I would do anything. I didn't ever want to be in a cell again.

Bruce had the usual fears the night before he was to start kindergarten. He didn't want to be apart from me. Up until now we were always together; mother and son, best friends, our mutual need was for each other. I reassured him that school was fun and exciting; he'd have lots of friends to play with. I rubbed his back and talked to him until he fell asleep. I sat there looking at him, loving him. All the world was crashing in around me, yet here I was blessed with this wonderful little boy; blessed with love. We would make it. He was having a good life. I was determined not to fail as a mother.

The next morning I woke him, gave him his bath, washed his hair and made his breakfast. He liked soft-boiled eggs. This morning it was soft-boiled egg. We only had one egg left. It was enough; he was excited. All the while I talked about school. It was fun, I told him, exciting, he'd paint, sing, play ball. My ex-mother-in-law had knitted him a darling blue sweater. I had scraped together eight dollars to buy him new sneakers. So he looked cute. New sweater, new shoes, clean white shirt and beige cords. He didn't look like his mother had to go to court in three days. We walked to school together hand in hand, sometimes skipping, singing his favorite song, "Raindrops Keep Falling on My Head." I actually felt happy. It was the beginning of a new phase for my child. I was proud of him. I was proud of us. We had made it this far.

Wednesday night was an emotional one for me. The next morning I had to appear in court. I tossed and turned all night long. Sleep brought my nightmare; leaving Brucie, jail, violence. I would awaken wet and shaking. I wanted the night to be over, yet it meant I would be closer to court. I borrowed Jack's car and dropped Brucie off at school. I then proceeded to drive to court. The last time I took this drive was in the backseat of the police car.

I wore a very conservative A-line, gray-and-white coat dress with gold buttons, white stockings, white low-heeled shoes and a white purse. I pulled my hair back into a high ponytail and wore small gold earrings. I was so scared walking into the courthouse. The sight of police officers sent shivers through my body. Police had always represented safety and security to me; now they represented everything I feared.

"*Marin County versus Somers,*" said the court clerk. It was my turn. I bit my lip. I held onto the rail to keep from falling, I felt so faint.

"Raise your right hand," the deputy said to me. "Do you swear to tell the truth, the whole truth and nothing but the truth, so help you God?"

"I do," I said quietly.

Then my lawyer spoke for me. He told the judge I was young and having a hard time making a living. He told him I was a mother caring for my child alone. He told him he was convinced I realized the seriousness of my crime and that I'd never do it again. He told him this was my first offense and that I had made full restitution on my checks. I closed my eyes and looked down at the floor. I prayed to God, help me please once more. Please! Please! Please! I never heard what the judge said. I was so lost in my thoughts. I only heard the words, "case dismissed." Relief flowed through me. I was free. I could sleep again. No more nightmares. I would never have to think of losing my Brucie again. Thank you, God; thank you. The blade had passed over my head. Someone was looking out for me, but it wasn't me.

I was waiting for Bruce when he got out of school. The sky was blue, the air was fresh with the smell of eucalyptus. I ran to meet him and gave him a big hug.

"Hi, honey! Want to go get an ice cream?"

"Yeah!" he said with a big grin.

44

*L*ife got better. Alan was back, work picked up. Everyone had put summer vacation behind and was ready to get involved in the new fall projects. Conventions came to San Francisco, and that was good news for me. Every convention meant at least a week of work. I handed out pamphlets, I was the attractive hostess for the Union Oil cocktail party (Senator Jackson came to that one). I did the Macy's catalogue, the Emporium catalogue. I was feeling human again.

I loved autumn in Marin County. The leaves turned color, the air was crisp and smelled of cedar burning in the fireplaces. I would bake chocolate-chip cookies for Bruce when he came home from school. He liked them when they were still warm from the oven. I felt happy.

Alan moved to a houseboat on the Sausalito Bay. It was wonderful. I would meet him at his place after Bruce went to sleep. Alan always offered to pay my babysitter which I gladly accepted. We'd sit on his deck overlooking Sausalito Bay and Tiburon, our toes dipping into the water, sipping white wine, laughing and talking. There was no one I'd have rather been with. Alan was golden brown after his vacation and summer in Los Angeles. He talked about his children a lot. He loved them a lot. He also talked with me about his wife. He said things were very tense around his house. He felt she knew he was seeing someone, that it was inevitable they would get a divorce, but the thought of leaving his children was so painful. He said consequently he gave all his attention to his children when he was home, which further infuriated his wife.

Alan told me how difficult it was living this double life. It forced him to lie constantly and keep secrets. If he only knew how similar our behavior patterns were at this time. Dishonesty was not a natural state for Alan. He is a scrupulously fair man who always "tells it like it is," but his double life reduced him to looking for opportunities to get out of the house to sneak a phone call or take a quick trip to San Francisco. I'm sure he felt guilty. He wanted to be a good father and a good husband and felt pained for failing.

It was the first time Alan opened up to me. I understood and empathized with his pain, but felt an elation at his mention of the word *divorce*. Maybe, after all, we did have a future. I had never seriously entertained the idea of being married to Alan. I had always accepted him on his terms. What am I thinking? Even if he does get a divorce, he's said nothing to me about a future together, I thought. I couldn't afford to get my hopes up. It would be too disappointing. We went inside his houseboat. Alan was a fabulous cook, and had whipped up a wonderful bouillabaise With lots of shellfish, saffron and fennel. We sat in a carpeted "pit" in front of the fireplace and dipped fresh San Francisco sourdough bread into the rich bouillabaise; Alan poured more white wine. Dinner was followed by beautiful love, the only light being that of the fire and the moonlight.

Two months had gone by and I was actually making ends meet. I had had enough work to cover my expenses and next month (December) I had already been hired to work at Joseph Magnin in the "Wolves' Den." If I really hustled again, I might make another twelve hundred dollars just like last Christmas.

Two whole months without a crisis. No police on my back. I was seeing Alan every minute he was free and in town. His houseboat was like a second home to me. By day I took care of one love of my life, Brucie; by night I took care of Alan, the other love of my life. I rarely put the two of them together. No sense in rocking the boat. I didn't want to confuse Bruce.

November and December were good months for me financially. I had a couple of modeling jobs, two conventions, a Rice-A-Roni commercial and three weeks work over Christmas in the "Wolves' Den." The commercial also had the potential to pay residuals. Altogether I made over two thousand dollars. It was the most money I had ever garnered together in my life. I had plans for it. First, I was going to get a car; second, I wanted to move out of my nondescript apartment and third, pay Father for my last car. I still had not hung my pictures or taken any great care to arrange my furniture. This apartment had always been temporary for me, even though I had been there over two years. A big part of me is very domestic. I love to cook. I love making "nests." This apartment made me feel "disorderly."

I had been watching buildings going up across the ravine from my apartment. They looked like mountain log cabins. I decided to walk over and see them. They were about half finished. The workers said they'd be ready to rent in about two months. I loved them. There was one two-bedroom house with a big stone fireplace, beamed ceilings, all redwood inside and out. The bathroom had a huge tub, the kind that could fit four people if you were into that. I have to live there, I thought. The house had charm oozing from every corner. I made it my business to find out who was in charge. I wanted to put down a deposit before someone else got it.

"We'll be renting this one for four hundred dollars a month," the contractor said.

In my gut I knew that was too much, but being my usual unrealistic self, I fantasized that all the rest of my months would be as lucrative as November and December had been.

"I'll take it," I said, and wrote the man a check for eight hundred dollars—first and last month's rent.

"Great," said the contractor. "You'll be able to move in around the end of February, beginning of March."

I was elated. I ran home to meet Bruce and tell him the good news. He would have a neighborhood now and other children to play with.

The following morning I woke up feeling queasy. No sooner did I have two bites of toast than I found myself running to the bathroom to have it come back up. How did I catch the flu? I had been getting lots of rest, I had been eating properly. Two hours later I felt fine. Must have been something I ate.

The next morning the same thing happened. Nauseated. Couldn't hold down breakfast. Two hours later it passed. I realized my breasts were tender. No! Oh, no! No! No! It can't be. I can't be pregnant. I've taken my pills faithfully. Every day without fail . . . except the day I was in jail. That's right. I forgot to take my pill when I was arrested. One day couldn't make that kind of difference. No one could be that fertile. I felt devastated. One thing after another. I can't have a baby. If the circumstances were different, if Alan weren't married, and if he wanted to marry me, I would love to have his baby; but in my situation I just couldn't bring another child into this world. I couldn't afford it emotionally or financially.

As the days went by, my morning sickness continued. I also hadn't had my period. I hoped that the stress of the last two months was causing a false pregnancy, but in my gut I knew. A woman can "feel" when she's pregnant. It was such a dilemma. Abortion was against my religion. Even though I no longer went to church, the rules were still indelibly imprinted in my mind. I prayed for a miscarriage. I thought of all the people who couldn't have children. I thought of having the child and putting it up for adoption. I couldn't do that. I knew I would love it too much. I knew I'd never be able to give it up. If I carried the baby full term, I would become financially destitute. Pregnant models do not get work. The only thing I could do was get an abortion and fast, while it was still a lot of tissue and not a person yet.

I prayed to God to forgive me. But it was the church that would condemn me, not God. This church had already abandoned me. I had broken its rules and it had tossed me out. My God understood my dilemma.

Alan was sympathetic and understanding when I told him. "It was my fault," I said. "I forgot to take my pill." He didn't know about jail. Alan immediately offered to pay all the expenses and said he would come with me to the hospital.

Now I had to find a doctor who performed abortions. It was illegal at the time, and I didn't want to go to Mexico and lie on a kitchen table while some butcher with a coat hanger removed the tissue inside me and risk my life.

I started asking around and found out about a doctor in the Richmond District of San Francisco. His office was old, unkempt and tattered looking. I felt uneasy being there. There were no baby pictures on the wall, no mothers-to-be proudly discussing their stretch marks. There was one other woman with a black eye who was staring at nothing. She didn't acknowledge my presence.

The doctor came out. "Miss Somers, you're next." No receptionist, no nurse. "Get on the table," he said. "How far along are you?" he asked.

"I don't know exactly," I answered nervously. "You're the first doctor I've been to."

He roughly examined me and announced, "You're definitely pregnant. What do you want to do?"

"Well, I'm not married and I don't have much money," I said sheepishly.

The doctor cut me off. "So you want an abortion," he said coldly.

"Well, if circumstances were different," I started to explain.

He cut me off again. "Listen, I'm not your priest. If you want an abortion you have to go to a psychiatrist and tell him you'll kill yourself if you don't get it. Here's the name and address of the one I use. I suggest you see him right away. The longer you wait, the more difficult the operation. The fee is fifty dollars for today. You can write a check or pay cash."

I was dismissed. I just sat there for a couple of minutes. I put my underpants back on and got dressed. What a debilitating experience. I went home and called the psychiatrist. Two days later I went to the psychiatrist and told him I'd commit suicide if I didn't get an abortion. It was the worst performance of my life. I was a survivor. No matter what, I'd never kill myself. What a selfish act. How would Bruce ever have a good life if his mother killed herself? I said the words to the psychiatrist without feeling, "I'll kill myself," the same way I'd say, "I'll have an ice cream." I didn't care if he believed me. He just had to hear the words so he could justify his notes legally. He was a creep anyway. What kind of doctor is it who makes his living this way? He gave me my piece of paper saying I was mentally unsound and should be given an abortion. The whole procedure made me sick. I grabbed my "prescription" and walked out. I went home and took a bath.

I was to check into the hospital at 6 P.M. to be prepped for the operation the following morning. Alan and I spent the whole day together. I felt very scared and sad. Alan could tell and was very gentle with me. He told me he was sorry I had to go though this. "I wish I could do it for you," he said many times. He made me lunch and then we sat on the couch holding each other. We did not make love. It wasn't the right time. I just needed to be with him, to feel that he cared. He kept stroking my head. I was overcome with emotion, and I started to cry.

I was so confused. Abortion felt wrong to me. I would love to have had his baby.

"There's something I want to tell you so badly, but I'm afraid," I said.

"What? Tell me," Alan whispered gently.

"I'm so afraid. I'm afraid you won't want to see me anymore." I was overcome with emotion. I couldn't hold back any longer.

"Please tell me," Alan said.

I whispered into his ear, "I'm in love with you." There, I had said it.

Alan held me so tight. "I know you are," he whispered. "I love you, too."

He had said it. He loved me. He *loved* me. He kissed me so tenderly. We both had tears on our faces. I didn't know if they were his or mine. All this pent-up emotion flooded out.

"I've loved you for a long time," Alan said.

"Why didn't you tell me before?" I asked.

"It didn't seem fair," Alan answered.

It meant everything in the world to me to hear those words. It took the illicitness out of our relationship. How could it be wrong when we loved each other.

Alan and I drove to the hospital. After I was checked in, I told him to go. He'd had a trip scheduled to New York. "There's nothing more you can do," I said.

"No, I'll stay," he said.

"It's not important," I said. "What can you do for me in a hotel or my apartment? Go to New York. I'll be fine. It's a simple operation. You can call me tomorrow when it's all over."

Alan was torn. He wanted to stay and take care of me; he needed to go to New York. He had just left an angry wife to come to his pregnant girlfriend. His children were upset with him for "leaving again." It was a difficult time for him emotionally. He knew he was going to have to make some choices soon. He could not go on like this.

"I love you," he said. He kissed me, touched my face. "I'll call you tonight and see you next week." Then he left.

I lay in bed that night trying not to think why I was in the hospital. All my thoughts were of Alan. Alan loved me.

My mother picked me up from the hospital the following day. She was taking care of Bruce. I had told her I was having a D & C. I don't think she believed me because she was very cold and unfeeling toward me. In the Catholic church, abortion is murder. She didn't come into the hospital. She didn't want to "know." She waited out in front in the car. If she really thought I was having a gynecological operation, she would have come in. She would have been concerned. I had automatically lied to her rather than confiding in her, and she chose not to acknowledge the truth. It was too painful for her.

I felt very weak and tired. I was bleeding very heavily and wanted to get home. Dad was drunk and I was too exhausted to put up with him.

"I know it's a long way, Mom, but could you drive Bruce and me to Sausalito? I just need a good day's rest and tomorrow I'll be fine."

The next day I wasn't fine. I still felt very weak. I woke up and I was lying in a pool of blood in my bed. It took every ounce of my strength to get up and change the sheets. I felt dizzy. I called the doctor.

"Is this normal?" I asked.

"Yes," he answered impatiently.

I got Bruce some cereal, turned on the television and got back into bed. I woke up at 6 P.M. because Bruce was shaking me.

"Mommy. Get up! You've been sleeping all day. I'm hungry."

"I'm sorry, honey. Mommy's got the flu and feels real tired."

I got out of bed and was stunned by another pool of blood in my sheets. I had only two sets of sheets. I took off the bottom sheet and used the top sheet for the bottom. I was so dizzy when I stood up. I staggered to the kitchen.

"How about a hot dog, Brucie?"

I didn't have the energy to make anything else. I gave him Campbell's chicken soup, a hot dog and a Hostess Twinkie. He thought it was great. I felt guilty. As soon as I'm better, I thought, I'll make him a good dinner.

I got back into bed. At 10 P.M. I woke up. Bruce was still up in my bed watching television.

"You have to go to bed, honey," I said.

"I want *you* to put me in bed and I didn't get my bath," he said. He was confused by my illness. It made him mad.

"I can't give you a bath tonight. I just don't feel good. Tomorrow I'll be all better."

Bruce got into his pajamas by himself. I managed to make it to his room to tuck him in.

"Good-night, sweetheart. I love you," I said.

"Good-night, Mommy. Alan called you whole bunches of times today. I told him you were sleeping."

I felt glad Alan had called. Then I fell back into a deep sleep. The next afternoon I woke up to the sound of my doorbell. The television was on so Bruce must have been waiting for me to wake up. I kept hearing a familiar voice calling my name. It was Jack. I opened my eyes, but I couldn't see. Couldn't see. I felt so weak. I fell back down on my bed. Bruce must have tried to open the door, but the chain was on and he couldn't reach it. Jack told Bruce to get up on a chair and open the door.

I was barely aware of Jack's presence. "Who is your doctor?" he kept saying. I tried to answer, but only mumbling came out. Jack got me to the bathroom. Blood was everywhere. I couldn't stand up. I still couldn't see. Jack put a cold towel on my face.

Brucie was crying. "Is my mommy okay?" he kept asking.

The cold towel woke me into coherence. "Call your doctor," Jack demanded. I told him where to find the telephone number and he dialed.

I heard the doctor's impatient voice. "Yes," he said.

"I'm feeling so sick and I keep bleeding. Blood is everywhere," I said weakly.

"It's normal to bleed after an abortion," he said.

"Well, this doesn't feel normal. There's so much," my voice was faint.

"What do you want me to tell you? That you're not bleeding to death?" he asked angrily.

"Yes," I said weakly. Tears were streaming down my face.

"Okay, you're not bleeding to death!" he said angrily. "Just stay in bed and rest."

"He's a jerk," Jack said. "I'm taking you to the hospital."

I don't remember anything after that. I was hemorrhaging. The doctor at emergency said I wouldn't have lived more than another two hours. Jack stayed with me for the next three days. I was incoherent; in a deep, deep sleep. Jack fed Bruce, changed my sheets, did my wash, fed me, changed me and nursed me back to health.

Jack answered my phone. It was always Alan. Jack didn't like Alan and felt Alan should have been there with me. But he didn't tell Alan how sick I was; nor did I.

"I can't help it," I said groggily during one of the times I came to. "I love him." Then I fell back into a deep sleep.

On the fourth day I began to feel better. I was still bleeding heavily and felt weak; but I was no longer delirious. I thanked Jack for being the best friend I had ever had in my whole life. He had to get back to work. I told him I would be fine; a week or so of rest and I should be back to normal. I had a good-paying job in two weeks and I didn't want to miss out on it. I didn't have the luxury of time to recuperate. Every dollar was important to me.

Alan flew out to see me on the weekend. He was upset at the way the doctor handled my operation. He said I should sue him. I didn't understand the law; I was afraid somehow it would turn around and I'd end up being the one in jail.

"I just don't want to get involved in lawsuits," I said. "It's over now and I'd rather just forget it."

Alan thought I was crazy. Normally, Alan would have pushed the issue, but he seemed preoccupied with other thoughts.

"What's on your mind?" I asked.

"Well, I just got news 'The Anniversary Game' has been canceled."

We both knew what that meant. We both sat silently. Things were going to be very different now. I knew in my heart it wouldn't be the end. We loved each other. We would figure out a way to be together.

"I'm producing a pilot for a new television series," Alan said. "We'll shoot the initial show in San Francisco; and if the network buys it, I'll be working here again."

At least there was some hope. I wished Alan would leave his wife. I was being pulled in two directions; I couldn't leave him and I couldn't have him.

At the end of the month Alan quietly moved out of his houseboat. Neither of us wanted to make a big deal out of it. We didn't want to acknowledge the end of our easy access to each other. We didn't want the good times to be over. We were one another's escape. When we separated, we each went back to our own individual problems. In order for us to be together on any regular basis, Alan was going to have to make some changes; and I wasn't sure he was ready to make them.

The thought of leaving his children brought him great pain. Neither of us were emotionally equipped to commit to each other. In order to do that, I would have to be completely truthful; and that terrified me. I felt sadness and insecurity knowing our situation might change. The unknown is always frightening.

45

Alan returned to Los Angeles and began the long, arduous task of putting together a television show. He had to hire a staff, get the script written and line up facilities. I talked with him by phone every day, but I hadn't seen him for over a month.

During that time he got me a free Chrysler to use. Alan knew I was frustrated without a car, and deep down he must have known I didn't really have a stash of money. He told the people at Chrysler that I was his production assistant, and I needed the car to scout locations for the television program. In return, Alan would give them commercial credits on the show. They thought it was a good deal, and so did I. For a one-line credit, they would give me two weeks with a free car. Two weeks was better than nothing, and I promised I'd return the car in two weeks. Alan gave his address and phone number as production staff headquarters, but the car had to be put in my name and driver's license number.

It was wonderful to have my own car again. Buying groceries was suddenly so much easier, getting to work was easier. I'd drop Bruce at school and take a drive just for the fun of it.

On Sunday Bruce and I went to my sister's house for dinner. Everyone was there. My sister's house had become the "core" of our family. The gathering place. I missed them. I didn't want to be cut off from them; and when I returned home, I was always overwhelmed by how much I loved all of them. They were the only people I was truly comfortable with. I understood all the moods. We had shortcomings and accepted them in one another.

I loved being around Maureen, Bill and their three children. I envied their life. It seemed safe and secure. Although alcohol was eating away at their marriage, I didn't realize the bottom could fall out and the top could come crashing down. It still hadn't dawned on me that alcohol was that potent. Their life appeared to be stable. When Maureen was sober, she was great. She had good instincts and common sense. She was sensitive, loving and supportive. Her family was my family, along with Dan, Mardi and their two children.

Mom, Dad, Michael and Father arrived after I did, and within minutes the noise level was deafening, with everyone laughing, talking and drinking. These were the good times; the first couple of hours at our family get-togethers. The booze made everyone forget and feel good. "Stinkin' thinkin'" wouldn't happen for another couple of hours.

Dad was in the first phase of his drunk—the loose phase, the funny phase. He amused us all with stories of Butcher Town and his escapades with Red and Beechie Bozio. The grandchildren all thought he was great when he was like this.

I had a glass of wine, then another. It felt so good, so relaxing. The last few months had been so traumatic. I had told no one in my family of my arrest or my abortion. More secrets. These were dark secrets. I had another glass of wine. It made me feel a little tipsy, but I didn't care. Wine made me forget reality. I laughed and joked with the rest of them. After dinner my sister coaxed me into singing "Something in the Way He Smiles." I never sang for anyone; I was too inhibited, even though I knew I had a good voice.

"Go on," Maureen urged. "Sing."

What the heck, I thought. I had had just enough wine to break down my defenses.

"Yea," everyone cheered.

A cappella I sang "Something."

"More!" Everyone clapped.

I sang another song, more wine, then another. I went through my entire repertoire from my favorite albums of Barbra Streisand, Laura Nyro, Carol King and my Broadway favorites.

Only my dad wasn't saying anything. I looked over at him. He had passed into his "mean phase." He snickered and slurred "two kind words." That was his way of saying, "You're nothin'!"

"I don't care what you say, Daddy," I said, "one day I'm going to be a big star! You'll see!"

"You asshole," he yelled. "You don't know anything."

The mood of the room was broken. The house went quiet. I felt embarrassed. I had never before articulated my dream, not even to myself. I had had too much wine and acted like a fool. I knew they were all thinking, "Who does she think she is with all her big ideas?"

I had two cups of coffee to sober up and got Bruce into the car. I wanted to get out of there.

"By the way," Maureen said as I was leaving, "when are you going to bring that boyfriend of yours around to meet us?"

"Maybe next time," I said quickly. How could I bring Alan? "Thanks for dinner." I drove off.

Two weeks later Alan asked if I would like to go away with him for the weekend. I suggested Lake Tahoe. I knew of a cabin we could rent. I asked my sister if she would babysit for Bruce. I told her I had to work. In my mind I had decided she would have disapproved of my spending the weekend with Alan. I felt she was out of touch with reality. These were the sixties. Good girls were out. This was the era of peace, harmony, free love. The "Age of Aquarius." Girls had abandoned their bras. In reality, my sister probably would have preferred I tell her the truth. It was I who was hung up on being a "good girl." Lying. Secrets. My disease, the disease that was slowly but surely doing me in.

I was supposed to return the Chrysler on Friday, the day I was to leave with Alan; but how would I drop Bruce off at my sister's? How would I pick him up Sunday night? Three days won't matter, I thought. I'll take the car back Monday morning.

Two whole nights with Alan. The anticipation was magical. We loaded up his rented car with food and goodies. He had lots of cassettes for the stereo and some of his "super brownies."

"By the way," he said when we were about an hour out of San Francisco, "did you return the car?"

"Oh, yes," I lied automatically. Why worry him? I thought. I'm going to take it back Monday.

We arrived at our rented cabin in early evening. The bedroom was nondescript so we decided to move the mattress to the living room, right in front of the fireplace. It was more romantic. We stocked the refrigerator with bacon and eggs, English muffins, Rose's Lime Marmalade and fresh sweet butter. For dinner we bought a good bottle of red wine, two steaks and potatoes for baking. I wanted to keep it simple. No tournedos Rossini tonight. Not enough time.

We had dinner on the deck. Alan barbecued the steaks. Then we lay down in front of the fire. Alan held me tight for a long time. I could tell he had a lot of feeling for me, but I also sensed a preoccupation.

"Is everything all right?" I asked.

"Yes," he answered quietly. "I'm just thinking about my children." He touched my face. "I love you a lot," he said.

The next morning Alan got up before me and said he was going "to the store." I knew going to the store meant he was checking in with his wife. This was the part I hated. It made me feel guilty and cheap. Alan's friend Hank had shown me a picture of Alan's wife, and I had been stunned to see how beautiful she was. I had always hoped she would be a mean, old, ugly troll; but the picture told the truth. She was blond and beautiful. She was also an artist.

I knew things weren't perfect between them. Alan often told me of their arguments and disagreements. He said they were growing in different directions. For my sake, I hoped they would continue to do so.

When Alan returned to the cabin his face was ashen. He looked at me sternly. "Did you take the Chrysler back?" he asked.

I felt panic. I knew I had created another crisis. Tell the truth! Tell the truth, I said to myself. "No," I said quietly.

"Why did you lie to me?" he asked.

I couldn't answer. I just stood there feeling horrible with my insides screaming at me: *You lied because that is what you've done since the first day you met him! Everything is a lie—except the way you feel.* Why did I do this? I kept asking myself. Why did I constantly keep screwing things up? I didn't have the ability then to see the broad view. I didn't realize that lying and fantasy were as natural to me as breathing. I'd been keeping "secrets" and putting on "a happy face" since I was a little girl. Always pretending on the outside that life was something it was not.

"If you had told me the truth, I could have gotten an extension," Alan said. "They called my wife looking for you and told her I borrowed the car in your name. My wife was screaming at me, demanding to know if you were the one I was having the affair with."

"I'm so sorry," I repeated over and over. I felt awful. I never wanted to create problems for Alan.

"We have to leave right now," Alan said.

We quickly gathered our things and started our wild ride home. It was a horrible trip. Alan was speeding; we didn't talk. It was such a contrast to the ride to Tahoe, when I had sat close to Alan, my arm around his neck, kissing and talking. The ride home was solemn and nerve-wracking. I sat next to the passenger door, both of us lost in the agony of our thoughts.

Alan hurriedly dropped me at my apartment and continued on to the San Francisco airport. I felt miserable. I've lost him, I thought. Through my own stupidity I've lost him. I got into the car that I allowed to bring me all the trouble and drove to my sister's house for Bruce. I felt so lonely. I knew it was over.

46

Days went by. Alan never called me. I couldn't leave the house for fear the phone would ring and I wouldn't be there to answer it. I wanted to hear Alan's voice one more time. I craved it. Maybe if we talked, he would change his mind. The idea of being without him left me feeling so empty. I wanted to tell him everything. The whole truth. I had nothing to lose at this point.

After two weeks reality set in. I had to start again. I had to get out of my house and meet new people. Other than Jack I had no friends. I had to forget. I wasn't interested in other men. They all paled by comparison to Alan. With the loss of Alan and the disintegration of my family, it was another low point in my life.

I took Brucie to swim in our communal apartment pool. He liked to sit in the sauna and get warm for a couple of minutes, then run and jump into the pool. He did this over and over. Another man was swimming also. I hadn't seen him around before.

"Why do you look so sad?" he asked.

I had no intention of pouring my heart out to a stranger; yet before I realized it, I found myself saying things like "his wife, and now I haven't heard from him for weeks." I told this man the whole story.

He was a psychiatrist from New York and had a way of getting me to talk. He told me he was in the middle of a messy divorce and came to California to escape the pain. He invited Bruce and me to have dinner that evening; and before the night was over, he had a mad crush on me. I knew that because he told me. I felt nothing. The next day roses arrived. Later on a romantic note was slipped under my door. He was nice but he wasn't my type. He came to my apartment to bring me Julia Childs' latest cookbook. (We had discussed my love of cooking.) How could I turn him down for dinner? I felt obligated; he had been so nice.

We dined at Ondine, a lovely expensive restaurant in Sausalito. It was right on the water. I loved good food; and while he sat sipping martinis and staring googily-eyed at me, I gobbled down light delicate sole quenelles, sweetbreads and asparagus tips. I ordered a chocolate soufflé for dessert. He had another martini.

"I'm leaving for New York tomorrow," he said. "I want you to come visit me."

I stopped eating and stared at him. I hardly know you, I thought. Talk about golden handcuffs! I had never been to New York before. Here I had an opportunity to have an all-expenses-paid trip to New York; but all expenses paid meant I would have to sleep with him. Ugh! The thought repulsed me. I didn't want any other man.

"I'll think about it," I heard myself saying. I kissed him politely at my front door, thanked him for the lovely dinner and went inside my apartment. I paid the babysitter eight dollars. Brucie was fast asleep with every stuffed animal he owned all over his bed. There was hardly enough room for him. I loved to watch him sleep. He snored and gurgled and had a peculiar habit of sleeping with his eyes slightly open. I pulled the covers over him, rearranged his stuffed animals and tiptoed out of his room.

I lay in bed thinking about New York. I'd love to get away. Maybe I could get an agent in New York for commercials. Brucie and I could move there and I'd make lots of money. We could start a new life. I could forget Alan in New York. Certainly in a big sophisticated city there would be a fantastic man for me. Why not take the chance! I said yes to my psychiatrist friend when he called the following day. I decided I'd figure out what to do about the "sleeping problem" once I got there.

I missed Alan so much. Every day the ache in my gut got more painful. I needed something to distract me. My mother told me Dad wasn't drinking much this week and said she'd be happy to watch

Bruce. I didn't like to leave Bruce with my dad. I didn't want him to experience the terror I had been raised with. But it seemed all right this time.

Everything was set. I wish Alan would call me before I leave, I thought. He didn't. I decided to leave a message with my answering service "just in case" he called.

"Dear Alan," I said, "I'm very sorry for bringing trouble to your life. I never meant to hurt you. I've gone to New York with someone new, hoping to get over you. Our time together has been the most beautiful, wonderful experience of my life. I miss you with all my heart and I will always treasure my memories." It sounded silly to have the operator read back this romantic message. "Good," I said. "Please make sure he gets the message if he calls."

My airplane tickets were first class. I was to go to the Plaza Hotel; the room would be under my name. I arrived at Kennedy Airport and heard my name being paged. I ran to the white courtesy telephone.

"Yes," the operator said, "an Alan Hamel is trying to reach you. He didn't leave a number."

I felt frustrated. I didn't know where he was; I didn't know how to get hold of him. I waited around the airport hoping he would call again. How did he know where I was? Why did he wait until today to finally call me? Now I felt all mixed up. Maybe I shouldn't have come, I thought. I got in a taxi, lost in my thoughts. New York unfolded before me. I couldn't help being excited. The taxi driver was speeding, the highways were jammed and there in front of me was the Empire State Building. I thought of Broadway and Lincoln Center and Bergdorf Goodman and the Museum of Modern Art. Central Park! Sardi's! I couldn't believe it. I hadn't felt this good in weeks. We were caught in a big traffic jam. I didn't care. Horns were honking everywhere. My taxi driver leaned out the window to yell obscenities at another driver. It was wonderful. Just like the movies.

The Plaza Hotel was incredible. Large Chinese porcelain urns holding huge palm trees; everything seemed to sparkle; mirrors and crystal everywhere. The rugs were too beautiful to be walked on. I tried not to step on the design. The furniture was covered with brocades and velvets. Men in crisp white starched short jackets carried silver trays of drinks to beautifully dressed people sitting at taffeta-covered tables. In the background was playing the kind of music one would expect at Versailles.

The bellman carried my shoddy-looking bags to my room. It was all ice blue. Satin, brocade, velvet was everywhere. It had a crystal chandelier and the bathroom was all sparkling white tile with a huge bathtub with little legs on it. On the dresser was a basket of spring flowers with a note. "See you tonight," it said. Oh God! I thought. My bubble burst. That was the reality. "See you tonight"! Now it would be my turn to reciprocate. He was a gentleman, I thought. Maybe he would understand and take things slowly. There was no rush. I'd be here all week.

Ring! My phone. I leaped to answer it. Maybe Alan found me, I hoped.

"Hi!" It was my psychiatrist friend. "Everything all right?" he asked.

"Oh, yes! It's just beautiful and exciting. I've never been to New York before," I said.

"Well, that's great. I'm going to enjoy showing it to you," he answered. "How about if I come over in about an hour and we'll have dinner?"

"Great. See you then."

Five minutes after he arrived the doorbell rang again. The waiter set down a silver urn and two glasses. "I took the liberty of ordering a pitcher of martinis for us."

Martinis, I thought. One martini and I'll be drunk. I didn't like the taste of straight hard liquor. Maybe it'll help calm my nerves, I thought. Josh had three martinis within a half hour. I watched his eyes go blurry. I was an expert. I had been watching eyes go blurry all my life.

The doorbell rang again. This time the waiter wheeled in a cart covered with silver trays of food. "I know how you like to eat so I took the liberty of ordering for you," he said.

"I guess this means we're eating in," I said nervously.

Josh had no intention of leaving this room. We were bunkered in for the night. A pitcher of martinis, roast quail with champagne grapes, duchess potatoes, baked tomato halves with fresh peas, mint and baby pearl onions and a silver bucket packed with fresh lemon ice cream. Another silver plate was filled with petits fours, napoleons and chocolate-dipped Florentine cookies.

I started eating. Josh had another martini. I was going to drag this dinner out as long as possible. Maybe he'll have so many martinis he'll pass out, I prayed.

Dinner was delicious. It was my first quail. I licked my fingers after every bite. Josh just watched me, smiling. Fatten her up for the kill, I was thinking. The potatoes were full of butter and shallots. I would twirl them around in the brown sauce from the quail, then I'd take a bite of the tomatoes and the peas would pop in my mouth. It was so good.

The ice cream tasted like fresh lemons and cream stirred together. I would place a spoonful on top of the crisp lacy chocolate cookies, and put it into my mouth.

I couldn't eat another bite. I wanted to get into that great bathtub and then fall into bed. I could tell my plans were not in sync with Josh's. He had stars in his eyes now and big plans to take me to the moon.

"Let's move to the couch," he suggested.

Oh, God, I thought. Here it comes. He sat next to me and started fondling my hair.

"You have such a sweetness about you and a vulnerability. I love to watch you," he said.

"That's nice," I answered.

He pushed my hair aside and started kissing my neck. I could feel him breathing heavily.

"I could love you so easily," he whispered in my ear.

Oh, dear, I thought. "I don't know how I feel," I said. "I need time." The artful dodger.

"I won't rush you," he said reassuringly.

When I came out of the bathroom, Josh was lying on my bed. Oh, great, I thought. I'm glad we're not rushing.

"Come lie next to me," he said. His tie was off. So were his shoes and socks; his shirt was unbuttoned. I hesitated. I felt so trapped. "I won't do anything," he promised.

I sat on the edge of the bed. He pulled me down and started kissing me passionately. I felt nothing. These weren't the kisses I wanted. I wanted to feel Alan's arms. I didn't fit with this man. Suddenly, he was all over me, pulling at my clothes, trying to undress me. I felt like I would suffocate.

"You are incredible," he kept saying.

"Please stop," I said quietly. He didn't hear me. His passion had drowned out all sound.

"I have to have you," he kept saying. "I've been thinking of this ever since I met you."

I couldn't stand it anymore. It wasn't worth a trip to New York to go through this. I should have thought it through. "Please! No!" I shouted. I pushed him off. "It's too soon," I said. "I'm not ready. Please!"

Josh sat up. He looked like a puppy who had been scolded. "I'm sorry," he said. "I didn't mean . . ."

I cut him off. "I know. It's all right. I understand," I said. "I didn't mean to mislead you, but I can't make love until I'm ready emotionally." Silence.

"Well, I think you're a nice girl," he said. "I'll leave now and come over in the morning and have breakfast with you."

I felt such a relief. Now I could go get into that great bathtub.

Josh arrived at ten the following morning. We shared scrambled eggs with toast points, fresh raspberries and delicious coffee. In the middle of breakfast my phone rang.

"Hi," Alan said.

I didn't know what to say. I had been waiting for him to call for so long, and now I was speechless. It was awkward. Josh was smart. He could figure out who was calling.

"Are you alone?" Alan asked. His voice was a strange combination of warm, yet cold.

"No," I answered quietly.

"I called all the hotels. I knew I'd find you," he said.

I wanted to tell him this guy didn't mean anything. I wanted to tell him I didn't want anyone but him.

"I want you to come to me today," Alan said.

"I-I can't," I stammered.

"I'm in Toronto," he said. "I just left New York, and I've left my wife."

I couldn't believe it. I'd been waiting to hear those words for so long. There was no question what I would do.

"I'll be there," I said. Josh looked up at me. Resignation came over his face. "I'm sorry," I said when I hung up the phone. "I have to go to him. I love him. I'll try to pay you back for all the expenses," I said.

"No," Josh said. "It's not necessary. You don't owe me anything. I've enjoyed the little time we've had together."

What a nice guy, I thought. "Thank you for being so understanding." Then he left.

Now I was alone, free and on my way to the man I loved. The unmarried man I loved. No longer would we have to hide. No longer would it be cheap, illicit or wrong. Now I could freely love him and he could love me. I was happier and more excited than I had ever been.

I called my mother and asked if she could take care of Bruce a few days longer. Bruce got on the phone. He was disappointed.

"I want you to come home. I miss you," he said sadly.

I felt such inner struggle. I missed him, too. I didn't like to let him down. He depended upon me for everything.

"It'll just be a few more days, honey," I said gently. "I'll be home next Saturday. Then I won't be going away again for a long time." I told him I loved him and hung up the phone feeling guilty.

I packed my bag while making airline reservations. I would have to use my San Francisco return ticket to get me to Toronto. Alan would reimburse me later.

I couldn't believe it. Soon I would be with Alan. I felt a strange combination of excitement and nervousness. Toronto was Alan's hometown. Would we have to keep a low profile? What if we ran into any of his family? Well, we'll deal with that later, I thought.

I looked at myself in the mirror. I had already washed my hair, so that was fine. It was long and blond and straight. This outfit won't do, I thought. I had dressed for Josh in an ankle-length skirt and a large, shapeless, oversized cotton sweater. I didn't want to entice him in any way. I searched through my things and chose my pale peach crepe shirt and brown velvet jeans. Alan always liked the way these pants fit. He liked to see me casually dressed. He felt that makeup and fancy clothes were "gilding the lily."

I wanted everything to be perfect. I wanted Alan to take one look at me today and know he'd done the right thing. I was madly, passionately in love with him. In three hours we would be together again. I couldn't wait.

I walked outside the Plaza Hotel. It was a beautiful spring day. The air was crisp and clear. The birds were singing, horns were honking. The breeze made my hair dance; my feet felt light as air. I was happy and excited.

"Good morning, sir," I said cheerily to the cabdriver.

"Where to, ma'am?" he asked.

"Kennedy Airport," I answered.

During the flight I kept imagining what it was going to be like. It seemed an eternity since I had last seen him. I couldn't wait to touch him. I couldn't wait to look into his eyes; his incredible, liquid, sexy blue eyes.

I looked at my watch. Thirty-five minutes until arrival. I felt flushed and hot. My hands were damp from nervousness. The anticipation was overwhelming.

"Ladies and gentlemen," the stewardess said on the intercom, "we are preparing for arrival in Toronto, Canada. Please fasten your seat belts."

I took one last look at myself in my compact. My neck was covered with nervous blotches. I could feel my insecurities surfacing. What if he decided I wasn't worth it, I thought. I felt scared and anxious.

I got off the plane and walked down the long hallway to Customs and Immigration. I felt fidgety in line. Hurry up, hurry up, I kept thinking. A driver's license was all that was necessary for entry, thank God. I didn't have a passport. I had never been anywhere.

"What is the nature of your visit?" the Customs officer asked.

"Pleasure," I answered, smiling.

"Well, have a nice stay," he said.

Oh, I will, I was thinking as I rode the escalator. Another long hallway. This time the walls were glass, and people with anxious faces were pressed against the windows looking for their loved ones. My eyes scanned the crowd. Where is he? Where is he? Suddenly, standing out in that sea of faces was his face. I stopped. Our eyes locked. We smiled. He walked with me on the other side of the glass. So near, yet so far. I looked ahead of me—another seventy-five feet to go. Then it was slow motion, as though underwater; voices were filtered and distant. We were the only two people alive. Twenty-five feet to go. We walked faster and faster. In a moment I'd be with him. Alan reached the doorway before me. I stopped. I couldn't move. Alan stepped inside and grabbed me to him. I fell into his arms. We stood there holding each other tightly, flooded with emotion from all the buildup.

"Excuse me," a voice from behind said impatiently.

Embarrassment broke our embrace. Alan grabbed my bag with one arm and wrapped his other one around my waist. Arm in arm we made our way to his car. He hadn't kissed me yet. We were both wordless and awkward. Finally, in the quiet and privacy of the car, he pulled me to him. Our lips touched softly, then passionately. All the tension left my body. I felt limp and defenseless in his arms.

"God, I've missed you," he whispered. I was still too overwhelmed to talk.

Alan and I spent three wonderful days at the old Four Seasons Hotel. He assured me there was no looking back. He had made his decision and was comfortable with his choice. For the first time I felt there was a chance for commitment. Relationships are built on steps. We were taking a step, moving forward.

Alan introduced me to his sister Cecile and her husband, Lewis. I liked them and found them very accepting of me. I was surprised at the amount of affection Alan displayed toward me in front of them. He no longer needed to be restrained. He had freed himself and was now able to demonstrate his feelings. My dream was coming true. It felt so good to finally come out of hiding.

Alan and his wife had gone through all the pain and torment two people experience when divorcing; anger, tears, resentment, sentiment. In the end they both agreed it was over and had been for a long time.

On the fourth day we flew back to New York, rented a car and drove to Bridgehampton. Alan had a dear friend there and wanted me to meet him. We stopped along the way to buy fresh Long Island ducks. Tonight we would make a feast with Alan's friend Sascha. In the car we laughed at my answering service operator's delivery of my speech. Alan said she had practiced every line, every comma, every pause. It was Ingrid Bergman at her most dramatic.

I liked Sascha instantly. He called me "Little Mary Sunshine." He was a musician, greatly influenced by, but not limited to jazz. He was creative in all aspects. He painted; he had just finished making an album. He had built his beautiful, tasteful Long Island house. I never wanted to leave that house. It was built of cedar, the kind that turns gray in the ocean air. It was one large room downstairs, angular, with lots of glass, a stone fireplace and beautiful wood stairs leading to the two bedrooms. It was furnished in the good-taste, New York sort of style; gray wool flannel sofas, ethnic rugs, a few pine antiques and carefully selected pieces of pottery. Music was everywhere. The three of us drank great red wine, dined on roast duck and danced the jitterbug until late into the night.

Bridgehampton is a wonderful place, mainly due to its inhabitants. There is great emphasis on the arts, an atmosphere of creativity that is catching.

The three of us spent the rest of the week enjoying the simple pleasures of life. We dug through the already plowed potato fields to find the little baby potatoes that were left behind because of their size. We drove to Montauk to buy fresh cherrystone clams and lobster. We sipped champagne sitting on sand dunes watching the sunset in silence. Nights were spent in front of the fire listening to beautiful classical music.

I drank it all in. This was a new experience for me and yet it wasn't unfamiliar. I felt right in this stimulating environment. It was the closest I had come to experiencing the kind of lifestyle I would like to have. Bridgehampton was both sophisticated and simple. The people were stimulated and stimulating. I wanted it; and now that Alan had left his wife, maybe I could have it.

It was a glorious week. I arrived home glowing with a bag of fresh ducks on one arm and a sack of Spanish onions on the other. Sascha had given me a book to read and a cassette of his album, an instrumental impression of Long Island. One selection was "Pheasant Walk"; another was "Montauk Bay." Through music he was able to place you in the environment so you could see, smell, hear and feel. I listened to that tape for years. It finally wore out.

I was ready to start a new life. I had a week's work for Ford trucks, and then I could move into my new house. I felt no sentiment in leaving my colorless, mundane apartment. Things had not been good there. This was the place where I had reached bottom: arrest, abortion, verge of death, fear of losing Bruce, fear of losing Alan. Good-bye! Good riddance! I couldn't wait to leave.

47

I t was an easy move. I had never really unpacked. Things were still in boxes in the living room, the pictures were unhung. My new house reminded me of Sascha's home in Bridgehampton; all wood, one large room downstairs and two bedrooms upstairs. Brucie was so excited. We arranged his furniture and placed all his toys. I got out my tools and hung the old redwood shutters I had saved from his room in San Francisco. They fit his window perfectly. We made bookcases out of orange crates and hung his favorite pictures on the walls. It looked darling.

My old furniture looked good in the living room. I had my chocolate-brown rug cut to a twelve-by-fifteen-foot size. My brother Dan gave me a foam pad to put under it. My worn linen sofa and chairs went great with the rug, the redwood floors and walls and the stone fireplace. I stripped my dining room table and chairs from my old Avon days down to the natural wood and discovered that underneath the fabric on the seats was beautiful black leather. This did not look like the house of someone poor. My bedroom was a loft overlooking the living room. I had no furniture other than my bed. I made two end tables out of orange crates and I had an old lamp for light. I didn't care. I thought it was wonderful. Later, when I had more money, I would fix my room. What it lacked in luxury, it made up for in charm and romance.

Alan came to visit the first weekend after I moved in. He loved my place. He had moved out of his home and was now sharing a house in Bel-Air with his friend Leonard.

Leonard was good friends with Alan's ex-wife (or soon-to-be ex-wife) and had already labeled me the "homewrecker." It was a new label, but I could live with it. Better than being the "mistress" or the "adulteress."

It was the first weekend I had put Bruce and Alan together. They had met many times but never spent enough time together to know one another. This was going to take a while, I could tell. Alan was cordial but certainly not warm toward Bruce. I suppose he felt guilty spending time with my child when his son, who was the same age, could not be with him. Bruce didn't know what to think of this new man who was sleeping in Mommy's bed. He had never seen me with anyone in this way and was used to having free and easy access to my bedroom. He was jealous. I will work out the problems between the two of them, I thought. It'll take time and adjustment. Soon Alan will be able to bring his children with him. Then it will be good.

In spite of the slight tension between Bruce and Alan, it was a wonderful weekend. We kept a fire going nonstop. My house smelled wonderful. The wood walls were still pungent. Outside, the house was encased in tall, old, fragrant redwood trees. I had plans to plant a vegetable garden and daisies. I wanted to make us a real home.

I cooked up a storm that weekend. Perfect cheese soufflé and butter lettuce salad for lunch. Dinner was stuffed lamb chops, wrapped in puff pastry. Alan would melt over my food. I loved to feed him, spoil him, pamper him. There were no guarantees or promises that came with this relationship. Alan never said, "Now that I've left my wife, I'm going to marry you," but it was okay. It was much easier to handle our relationship this way than when he was married.

By the fourth month of living in my new house, I came face to face with reality. It took everything I had to gather together the four-hundred dollars for a month's rent. Now I was one month behind. My landlord showed up at the front door demanding the rent immediately or eviction.

"I'm so sorry," I stammered. "My paycheck is late this month. I'll see if my employer can advance me the money. It'll never happen again," I assured him. This guy was not fooling around. He was not going to put up with any nonsense. I needed more work. Modeling was always so slow in the summer. He gave me an extension "for this time only."

I was now working to pay my rent. I needed to make at least five hundred dollars to cover my expenses, and that didn't include food. I still didn't have a car. I just need to make it through the summer, I thought. Work always picks up in the fall. I knew it wasn't going to be easy. I wished I could make money with my talent. I sing, I dance, I love comedy, I thought. Instead, I eke out a living having my picture taken in a business that is constantly telling me I'm too short, too busty, I don't have cheekbones, too blond, I don't look like the girl next door, or worse, I do look like the girl next door. If I could use my talent, it wouldn't matter what I looked like. No one was hiring Barbra Streisand because she had a great nose. If I could make three hundred dollars a week, I could live so well. I kept watching our local weather girl on TV. I could do that, I thought. Simple. Use a pointer, point to different cities, read the temperature, pick up your check at the end of each week and become a local celebrity. I was a dreamer; but deep down I knew it would never happen. Other girls got those jobs. Not someone like me.

48

Near the end of the summer I took a short vacation in the mountains with Bruce, my mother and Michael. Maureen had invited us to stay with her at her in-laws' cabin. It was wonderful to get away with my mother for a while. I rarely got to be alone with her. Traveling anywhere was a great escape for me. When Mother was away from Dad, she got very relaxed. He was on a rampage again, so drunk he probably didn't realize she was gone.

Michael had become very withdrawn and sullen. He was now Dad's scapegoat. "Michael's a dummy," he would tell anyone who would listen. By the look on Michael's face, I could tell he was believing it. I felt so sorry for him, so helpless. I invited him to stay with me as often as I could, but nothing could replace the reality of his life. He was suffering the brutal, crazy, hostile brunt of his alcoholic father. I suffered from it, and I didn't even live with him anymore.

My mother was so emotionally sick from living with Dad that she retreated into the corridors of her mind for self-protection. She was able to provide Michael with a regular schedule, breakfast at eight o'clock, lunch in a brown bag, and dinner at five o'clock. But so often dinner would turn into violence and food throwing. They were all slowly going crazy.

This little trip to the mountains was a respite for all of us; an escape from our individual burdens. We laughed and talked, ate watermelon at a roadside stand and stopped at a garage sale and bought an old squirrel fur coat for eight dollars. The coat was falling apart, but we thought it would be great to make a blanket or collars for coats. It was fun. We giggled and were happy.

It took all day to get to the cabin. When we finally arrived, Maureen, her in-laws and Maureen's three children were all on the deck beginning to prepare the barbecue for dinner. I was so happy to see little Billy, Timmy and Joey. I loved Maureen's children like they were my own. Bruce squealed with excitement at seeing them. Michael stayed in the backseat of the car and had to be coaxed out.

Nothing smells as good as chicken grilling over an open pit. We sat on the deck overlooking the redwood trees and sipped before-dinner cocktails. My mother and I had white wine, Maureen had gin and tonic. I could tell she had already had a couple before we arrived. So what, I thought. She was on vacation. Maureen had a lot of pressure; three little boys so close in age. They were a lot of work. We had another drink. It felt good. I enjoyed feeling "high." My mother was a little tipsy, also. I was glad. I liked to see her relax. She would rarely drink around my dad. I guess she knew that someone had to be in control. Maureen poured herself another drink. I noticed she filled the glass halfway with gin, added a little tonic and then threw in a couple of ice cubes. Stiff drink, I thought. Her eyes were getting blurry. The children were running in circles, screaming and squealing; but she didn't care now. She was very relaxed. Maureen hardly touched our delicious dinner. She had another drink; and while we all had coffee, she had another drink.

Mother, Maureen's mother-in-law and I did the dishes and cleaned up. Maureen stayed out on the deck sipping her gin in the cool mountain air. Mom and I went outside when we were finished to say good-night and see if Maureen was going to bed.

My whole body tensed when I looked at my sister. She was drunk. Plastered. And to my horror, she looked exactly like Dad. Her eyes had the mean, hostile look that he got when he was drunk.

"Maybe you should go to bed now," I said to Maureen.

"I will not!" she roared.

It was like déjà vu; only the hair color was different.

"Would you like some coffee?" Mother asked.

"I don't need you two taking care of me," Maureen said belligerently. Mom and I didn't know what to do.

"Come on, honey. Come to bed," Mother said gently.

"Leave me alone," Maureen slurred. She got up out of her chair and pushed Mother away.

"Stop that," I yelled at Maureen. "Don't be this way." I was shaking.

Maureen started yelling at us, "Just get out of here. You both think you're so good, don't you. Goody two shoes. I don't need you around here telling me how good you are. I'm sick of you checking up on me, so get out of my life and quit saying your goddamn novenas for me."

Maureen was hysterical, screaming, having a real wingding. The children were all peeking out the window.

"Get back to bed right now," I yelled at them.

Maureen went running off into the woods. Mom followed her. I ran after the two of them. I couldn't believe what was happening. We caught Maureen and started pulling her back to the house, all the while she punched and kicked and staggered. When we finally got her inside, she started sobbing.

"I love you, Mom," she kept saying. "I'm no good. Just go away and leave me alone." Finally she passed out.

I couldn't believe it. Poor Maureen. She had inherited a terrible disease. She had unconsciously made the choice to give in to it and have some fun times. But the "fun times" were the bait, the irresistible feeling that got you hooked. I lay in bed thinking about what had happened. It was an exact repeat of our childhood! Drunk, vicious and violent. Just the face had changed. I now knew Maureen was an alcoholic.

Maureen didn't drink the rest of the weekend. She felt too guilty. Of course, we never mentioned what had happened. Mother and I acted like everything was normal and wonderful. We had had years of practice.

49

*A*utumn came. Bruce, now six, was back in school in the first grade, and I had a few conventions lined up for work. I found an old Volkswagen for sale and in good shape. It cost nine hundred fifty dollars. I asked my mother if she would co-sign a loan for me; and to my surprise, the bank accepted the application. I finally had a car. My payments were forty-six dollars a month; and I could drive for a week on five dollars' worth of gas. This time I wasn't going to lose this car.

Bruce made friends with a little boy down the street whose name was Thomas. He was a sweet little blond boy, very skinny with huge horn-rimmed glasses. I just loved him, and soon he and Bruce became inseparable. Thomas' mother was a terrific lady named Doris and her husband was Don. They both soon became dear friends and an extended family to us.

Alan was back East in New York a lot these days. He was trying to sell his television show on the barter system, so much of his time was spent making contacts. He would have liked me to stay with him the entire time he was gone, but my responsibility as a mother would not allow me to do so. I visited him as often as I could. It was such an emotional tug-of-war. I missed and craved Alan so badly; but whenever I left, Bruce's lower lip would quiver and tears came down his cheeks. I couldn't stand to be without either of them.

I felt bad leaving Bruce to see Alan, and I felt just as bad when I couldn't see Alan because of Bruce. I had worked out a babysitting arrangement with Doris, Thomas' mother. She needed the money. Bruce was real comfortable in their house, and his life and school schedule was not disrupted.

My life was such a contrast. In New York with Alan, money was no object. We went out for dinner to the best places. We saw Liza Minnelli at the Persian Room, Benny Goodman at the Rainbow Grill. We hung out with Alan's new business partner, Dick Clark, and the three of us shared a beautiful apartment in Gramercy Park. While Alan worked, I spent my days combing Madison Avenue and all the wonderful little boutiques I had read about in *Vogue*. Alan would give me money to buy something for myself, but I always tucked it away in my wallet, knowing this would take care of the babysitter or the electric bill.

My family was silently critical of my trips to New York. They didn't know who this "Alan" was that I was always running off to see, but he must be after "one thing and one thing only," because he sure wasn't making any overtures about marriage.

"He'll never marry you," my sister slurred drunkenly at one of our Sunday dinners.

There was nothing I could say. I honestly didn't think he ever would either. I didn't believe I was good enough. But I loved him and was willing to take him under any conditions.

50

December came and I was working in the "Wolves' Den" at Joseph Magnin again. The same guys came back every year; and, as usual, my goal was to make as much money as I possibly could during the three weeks.

Alan came up to visit me one weekend; and while I was busy preparing dinner, he sat in the living room in front of the fire. Even though I couldn't afford this house, it was a lovely place. The fireplace was huge and the whole house glowed when the fire was blazing. You could smell redwood and pine. Carol King was singing "You're So Far Away" in the background.

Alan walked into the kitchen with a strange look on his face. He was holding a Christmas card. Oh, my God! I had forgotten.

"What's this?" Alan asked.

"Well," I stammered, "my mother's a little crazy." I said anxiously, "Since Dad died she hasn't been able to accept it, and she always signs her cards 'Love Mom and Dad.' " My insides were screaming at me *Stop lying! Tell him the truth! This is your chance!*

Alan just stood there looking at me. "You're all fucked up, aren't you?" he asked quietly.

I couldn't look at him. I stared at the floor. I felt so ashamed. "Yes," I finally said, still looking down. "I'm all fucked up. My dad isn't dead. I don't have any money to speak of." I still couldn't look at him, but relief flowed through my bones. "My dad is a roaring, belligerent, violent alcoholic." I looked into Alan's eyes. I told him everything. The shame, the humiliation, how I left home and wanted to start a new life. When I met him I was so overwhelmed I didn't feel good enough for him, so I made up someone who would be good enough for him. I told him how awful I'd felt being so dishonest these years, but I was in so far I didn't know how to get out. I was sobbing now. I told him my entire story. We talked until early morning. I told him I hoped he could forgive me because the most honest feeling of my life was my love for him.

When it was over, he held me in his arms for a long time. "I always knew there was something that didn't ring true," Alan whispered. "It's not a terrible thing. It's hurt you a lot more than it's hurt me, and I understand why you did it. I love you, too. Let's just start over with the truth from now on."

"I love you so much," I whispered into his ear. In my heart I thanked God for getting me through this one. I was determined to come to grips with the truth about myself. I wasn't my father. I wasn't the drunk. I had my own life to live; and, maybe, now that life could really include Alan. We fell into a deep, peaceful sleep in front of the fire holding each other.

Bruce and I had a wonderful Christmas morning together. Alan had taken his children to Mexico for the holidays. I had done well at the "Wolves' Den" and was able to get Bruce a record player and some records, which he really wanted. Bruce's dad got him a scooter board. It was one of those things on which you lie on your stomach and steer the front two wheels with your hands. I wasn't too happy about this choice. It seemed like a dangerous toy, but Brucie loved it and was very excited.

Two days after Christmas it was chilly and frosty outside. I put firewood in the fireplace to warm up the house and turned on the Christmas tree lights because it was one of those dark days. I filled the bath with hot water; a good long soak would warm me up.

"Mommy, I want to go outside and play with my scooter board," Brucie said.

"Well, I'm just getting into the bathtub, so you can only play in the driveway till I come outside. Okay? *Nowhere else!*" I said sternly.

"I promise, Mommy."

I dressed him in his navy-blue pea coat, jeans and a warm sock hat and he ran outside. Before I got into the tub, I checked from the upstairs window to be sure Bruce was in the driveway. He was, and I took a wonderful relaxing bath. I was drying off when I heard someone pounding frantically on my front door. My instincts told me something terrible had happened. I ran to the window and there in the middle of the street was Bruce lying face down with blood running down the hill like someone had turned on a faucet. He was all alone. There was a car fifty feet away from him also in the middle of the street with the driver's door wide open. There were people standing at their living-room windows looking out from every house in the cul-de-sac, but no one was running to help my baby. I grabbed my robe and ran barefoot to the front door. To this day, I don't know if it was a man or a woman pounding on my door. I only heard, "Your son's been run over by a car." I ran past the person out to the middle of the street. Oh, my God! Oh, my God!

"It's okay, Brucie. Mommy's here," I kept saying over and over.

I didn't know if Bruce was alive or not. Blood was everywhere.

I put his little head in my lap. Blood was pouring out of his head. It was all over his face.

"Mommy," Bruce said groggily.

Thank God, he's alive, I thought. Then he passed out. I prayed he had just passed out.

"It's okay, baby. It's okay. Mommy's here. Mommy will take care of you. Please, someone, call an ambulance!" I yelled hysterically.

I wrapped the bottom of my robe around his head to stop the bleeding. Tears were streaming down my face.

"I love you, Brucie. It's going to be okay. Mommy's here." I don't know how many times I said that. I rocked back and forth holding him. I don't know how many people were there.

An ambulance arrived. I'm sure it had a siren, but I couldn't hear. I'm sure people around me were talking, but shock removes sound. The ambulance attendant came to put Bruce on a stretcher. I didn't want to let go of him.

"Please don't hurt him," I cried. "Please be careful, his head hurts," I cried.

As they lifted his little body, I saw that his pants and jacket were ripped to shreds and there was no skin left on his little bottom.

"Dear God, make him be okay," I prayed out loud.

I got into the ambulance and held his limp little hand. He was unconscious. They put tubes down his throat. They opened his eyes and looked at his pupils with flashlights.

"Is he going to be all right?" I asked desperately.

"Only the doctor can tell you that," was the attendant's answer. "The child seems to be in shock," he said.

"You're going to be okay, Brucie. Mommy's here. Mommy will take care of you. Everything is okay. I love you, honey. It's going to be okay." I kept repeating this over and over into Brucie's little ear hoping he could hear me, hoping to give him strength and, in turn, hoping to give myself strength. I have never felt so afraid.

Once we arrived at the emergency ward, Bruce was whisked away from me. I wanted to stay with him.

"Please let me be with him. Please," I begged.

"Let us get him cleaned off. Then you can stay with him," the nurse said.

I sat for thirty long minutes waiting, praying.

"You can come in now, Mrs. Somers."

I was in shock at what I saw. Bruce was naked, his head was partially shaved, his scalp was wide open, the bones in his knees were exposed and sticking out, the flesh was gone, his mouth was torn open, he had no flesh at all on his buttocks.

"We've cleaned all the gravel out of his wounds and X rayed him," the doctor said. "We need your permission to stitch his scalp and mouth closed. There is no serious damage there. His knees and bottom are going to be very painful and will take quite a while to heal, but they'll be okay; but the X ray shows internal damage. I'm afraid his kidney and spleen have been crushed. The car must have completely run over him. We're going to have to put him in surgery immediately and see what we can do to save him."

" '*Save him*,' " I said. "What do you mean? Is he going to die?"

"At this point," the doctor said gently, "he has a fifty-fifty chance."

51

I felt so alone, so anguished. The thought of losing my little Brucie was unbearable. I called Alan; he was still in Mexico with his children, but his roommate, Leonard, said he would try to reach him by telex. (There were few phones in Puerto Vallarta at the time.) I called Bruce's father; he wasn't home. I called my parents. I called Jack.

I was sitting all alone in the hospital waiting room, lost in my painful thoughts, when Jack walked in. It wasn't until I saw the look of shock on Jack's face that I realized I was barefoot and my robe, legs, feet and hands were still covered with blood.

"Oh, Jesus," Jack said.

I buried my face in Jack's chest and sobbed. "I'm so glad you're here. I'm so scared," I said.

Jack took me to the ladies' room and helped me wash myself. Here I was again, Jack washing blood off of me. I still didn't know any details about the accident. I would piece that together later. I was so thankful to have my friend Jack to lean on.

"He's going to be all right. He's going to make it," I kept repeating.

Bruce was scheduled for surgery at midnight. He looked so fragile. I was able to peek at him once every hour in intensive care. He was being fed intravenously, glucose and morphine. Computerized machines were all around his bed monitoring every part of his body. The nurse would not let me touch him. His usual pink skin was now colorless; his face was bruised and swollen. He looked lifeless.

I called upon my God again. "I know I've made many mistakes," I prayed, "but I must ask you once again. Please, please don't let my beautiful child die. I know I don't deserve any favors, but my child has his whole life ahead of him, and I want him to live."

My body was quivering uncontrollably with fear. I shouldn't have let him go outside alone, I kept thinking. I felt so guilty. Why did I do it? Why did I do it? If only I could make the decision all over again.

"Go home," I heard Jack saying. "Take my car and go home. Change your clothes. Get some rest. The doctor said he won't be out of surgery for at least five hours. I'll stay here," he said, "and if there is any news, I'll call you."

I didn't want to leave, but I had to get clean clothes and some shoes. "You're a good friend, Jack," I told him.

Jack was joined by his friend Don Gold, and the two of them sat vigil over my son's surgery while I went home to get myself together.

I walked outside the hospital into the damp, dark, foggy night. So much had happened in the last eight hours.

I arrived home, to my house, our house, the home I shared with Brucie. It seemed so empty, so lifeless without him. I threw my robe into the garbage; I never wanted to see it again, and filled the tub with hot water. It would be my second bath of the day. While the water was filling, I walked into Bruce's room. His toys were spread about his bed, a wrinkled mass because he had played "fort" in it earlier in the day. Without realizing it, I pulled his sheets off the bed. I took them downstairs to the washing machine. I got all my cleansers and cleaning rags out of the kitchen and started cleaning Bruce's room like an obsessed person. I moved all the furniture to the center of the room so I could wash and disinfect the baseboards. I took everything out of Bruce's closet, dusted and disinfected and replaced every article lovingly. Everything perfectly in its place. I used Windex on his windows, even though it was dark outside and I couldn't see if I was leaving any streaks. On and on I went. I want his room to be perfectly clean when he comes home, I thought. Neat. Perfect. Wonderful. I dusted his shutters, wiped down the redwood walls with warm, soapy water, polished all the furniture, arranged his records. Gotta wash his bedspread, also. I put his clean sheets back on the bed. Smooth, clean, not a wrinkle. He'll like that, I thought. Three hours later I was finished.

I sat in the middle of his spotless room and cried. Please let him be home with me soon, dear God. Please!

Water was running into Bruce's room. What's that from, I wondered. Oh, my God! I forgot to turn the bath water off. Water had flooded the bathroom and was running down the stairs. Now I was running frantically up and down the stairs with the mop and towels trying to stop the water, like a madwoman. Back and forth, up and down.

Ring! I stopped. I looked at the telephone. I looked at the clock. It was 4 A.M. *Ring!* The phone sounded like the fire alarm at school. Maybe it was just the alarm I felt inside. I picked up the phone.

"He's okay," Jack said. "It's not as bad as they thought. They've saved his kidney. He's going to be okay."

"Thank God," I said. "Thank God." Relief flooded through me. "I'll be right over."

"No. Don't," Jack said. "Don will drive me to your house to get my car. Bruce won't be out of intensive care until tonight or tomorrow. You won't even be able to see him and the doctor has already gone home. Stay home. Get some rest."

I thanked Jack and sat on my bed, my head in my hands. Night was over. Daylight was peeking through the windows.

At 8 A.M. my parents arrived upset and concerned. They both loved Bruce a lot. In fact, I was to learn in the coming months that everyone in the family had an extra special attachment to Bruce. He was the only child in the family to come from a "broken home," and everyone felt sorry for him.

It was comforting to have my parents come to take care of me. I needed some taking care of at this time. When my dad was sober and concerned, he could still be the greatest. I wanted to get to the hospital immediately, even though Bruce was still in intensive care. Maybe they'll just let me peek at him, I thought.

I spent every day at the hospital for the next month. Bruce was a wonderful patient. He was in so much pain but never complained. If they put him on his back, the pain in his bottom was excruciating. If they put him on his stomach, the pain in his knees and surgical scar were unbearable. The scar extended from the top of his chest to below his navel. He had so many stitches in his head, it looked like a road map with a few patches of hair here and there. Visitors came every day.

Danny and Mardi were there constantly. Danny adored Bruce and was so upset when he first saw him he went into the hallway and sobbed. Bruce was such a happy, undemanding child; always smiling and laughing, full of wit and personality. He had a happy effect on everyone he met. I was touched to see how much Danny cared.

Bruce's father came through for him at this time also. Up until now, his visits had been infrequent; but crisis has a way of pulling a family together.

Every time I came to the hospital, Bruce's dad had either just been there or had called to say he'd be there later. The two of them laughed and talked and played games. I saw how important it was for Bruce to be around this male influence. I felt relieved that little Bruce would have his father back in his life.

Bruce didn't like it when I left the hospital at night. He would become frightened, so I would stay until he fell asleep and would try to arrive before he woke up. As his mother, it was so difficult to see him in this condition. I wished the pain could be mine so he wouldn't have to endure it. I thanked God constantly for letting him live. Somehow, I would make it up to Him for letting me have my baby back.

I was finally able to piece together the accident. Bruce had lost control of his scooter board at the precise moment a car was coming over the crest of our hill. Bruce's scooter board shot out into the street, the car ran over Bruce and the bumper caught on his jacket and dragged him all the way down the hill. The lady driving the car never realized what happened until she reached the cul-de-sac. She stopped her car and in shock ran into her house. To this day, I have never talked to her. I went by her house after visiting Bruce in the hospital one evening to tell her he was doing okay; but she wouldn't answer her door. Shortly after that she moved away.

This woman had maximum liability insurance of twenty thousand dollars. My SAG Blue Cross insurance was unusable because I did not make enough money within the quarter to cover me. My ex-husband's insurance paid a small amount. I was going to be stuck with the rest.

The hospital presented me a bill of an additional fifteen thousand dollars and it was still rising. I just stared at it.

"I can't pay this," I said to the clerk.

"Well, your son cannot leave this hospital until you do," she said curtly.

"Then he's going to have to live here permanently," I said flatly. Now what was I going to do?

Money! Money! Money! It has a way of beating you down.

The lady who hit Bruce seemed to have less money than I had. She had lost her job as a stewardess and was living on unemployment.

I signed a promissory note to the hospital, and they let me take Bruce home. I needed to work more than ever, but Bruce needed full-time care.

To add to my problems, I received a letter from my ex-husband. He told me how much he loved little Bruce, but his priority in life was making his second marriage work.

Bruce, Sr., also came from a rigid Catholic background. I imagine he was in great emotional turmoil. His second marriage seemed to be disintegrating. He couldn't let that happen.

My son didn't like his stepmother. Whenever he was invited to their house, he came home sullen and unhappy. Bruce, Sr., was caught in the middle. He didn't know what to do, so he decided to devote his energies to stabilizing his marriage. He would deal with his son later on.

In his letter he told me he no longer would be able to have anything to do with the emotional or physical care of Bruce. I felt so alone.

I stopped by Bruce's school every day to pick up his homework. I didn't want him to have to make up this year. Bruce was an easy patient. He was too weak to want to get out of bed much. I loved taking care of him. I would decorate his meal trays and make all his favorite foods, especially custard. He loved custard!

He looked so cute, so vulnerable. His hair was growing out in patches. His lip had healed with a small scar. His knees and bottom were covered with new, fragile, tender pink skin. The scar on his stomach looked like a zipper running from neck to navel.

I never stopped being thankful for his recovery—even with all the new bills and the harassment I knew would be forthcoming. It was all worth it just to look at his beautiful, trusting little face.

I would rub his back at night until he fell asleep and sit there in the darkness listening to his even breathing. I had not written one word of poetry since Sister Jean had thrown me out of high school for my love poems; but during this time of Bruce's recovery, the poet in me re-emerged.

Sometimes I See My Son

Sometimes I see my son
And remember when I thought I'd failed
Because so many told me
A mother who bore a boy
Should not send away his father.
Sometimes I see my son
And remember the pain of unloved pregnancy
And the resentment I sometimes felt
At raising him alone
When I could not have the freedom I deserved.
There were days I was as much a child as he
When I wanted someone to give me
The love I gave so grudgingly to him.
Days that we learned together about life
And had as many questions.
Sometimes I see my son
And wish his mother had it all together

To give him strength and courage I only
  sometimes have
To listen when my own hurts need hearing
To hold him even though I am alone.
But sometimes I see my son
With trust in his eyes no one else could give
With a smiling, shining face that says there
  was no failure
No monstrous mistakes
Only good things and memories of love and
  caring.
Sometimes I see my son
And he touches me in secret corners
And I know that everything is fine
And will always be.
Sometimes I see my son—and I love him.

52

Alan finally sold his television show. It was called "Mantrap," an answer to the feminist movement with three charming, articulate females verbally attacking a male celebrity guest. Alan served as the host/referee. The females changed from week to week; and once the show was under way, Alan asked me if I would like to be on it. I was thrilled. It was the biggest job I had ever been offered. National TV. This could be my chance to get noticed, a chance to get my career off the ground. Most important, the pay was nine hundred dollars. Alan knew I wouldn't take money from him, so I'm sure this was his way of helping me.

The show was taped in Vancouver, British Columbia. I hated the thought of leaving Bruce. My friend Doris said she would care for Bruce while I was gone. It would only be four days.

"Mommy has to go and make money so we can live," I told Bruce.

He understood but was still feeling so fragile. Bruce had started having nightmares. I would hear him scream in the middle of the night. He'd be soaking wet and trembling and wouldn't stop until I rocked him back and forth in my arms.

When was life ever going to get easy? Alan was in the middle of a messy divorce and all the depression and guilt that goes along with it. His mother told him, "Nice boys don't leave their wife and children." His children couldn't understand why he left their mother.

"Isn't Mummy pretty enough?" his daughter Leslie asked.

Alan didn't know what to say to his children. How could he explain? He hated seeing them so upset. They cried on the telephone to him. "Come back home," they would say. His friends all took the side of his wife. Alan was the unfaithful husband, the bad guy.

His mother was extremely unhappy with him. Alan and his mother have a very close, very strong bond; he felt awful that he had displeased her.

Alan's life was in turmoil. There was no way he could commit to me at this time. When we got together, he just wanted to have a good time; relax, laugh, have fun. He didn't want to talk about the future or commitment and certainly not marriage. When we were together, he wanted to leave his problems behind.

My life was wrapped up in the accident, the nightmares and now a whole new set of bill collectors. Nine hundred dollars from "Mantrap" would allow me to get them off my back—temporarily.

Vancouver was beautiful. It was wonderful to be away from all the trauma. It was always a thrill for me to have time alone with Alan. I got a rush just seeing him.

Alan introduced me as the "beautiful and talented actress, Suzanne Somers." Good thing no one asked me for my acting credits. What would I say? I did *Guys and Dolls* in high school? The other ladies on the show were Margot Kidder and the author Jacqueline Susann. They were both real nice. Margot didn't wear a bra and Jacqueline wore a gold ankh around her neck. Jacqueline had just written and produced the movie, *Valley of the Dolls*.

I was good on the show. Nervous, but Alan said that added to my charm. Alan has a way of seeing the positive in everything. Once I got over being nervous, I just pretended I wasn't on television and was having a conversation with this man. I'd always been a good talker and never had any trouble making conversation with people. So it went well.

We did nine shows with nine different men. I talked with authors, actors and doctors. I loved it. I hoped Alan would ask me to be on the show again.

That night we went out to dinner with Jacqueline Susann. She never mentioned she was dying of cancer. When I admired the gold ankh around her neck, she took it off and put it on me. "It's good luck," she said.

"I couldn't," I said. I couldn't believe someone would give away anything so valuable. She insisted I take it; and to this day, I keep it tucked away with my valued possessions.

In our conversation I mentioned I had been writing poetry, and in fact had brought it with me to pass the time on the airplane. Jacqueline asked if she could read some. I felt embarrassed. I said I didn't think it was good enough; but, again, she insisted.

Four whole days and nights with Alan. I hated for it to end, but I had to get back to Bruce. Alan stayed in Vancouver; he had more shows to do. As I was leaving for the airport, Jacqueline called me.

"These poems are wonderful," she said. "They're raw, they need work, but the feeling is there. You should pursue this area of your talent. You're really very good."

I left Vancouver feeling wonderful. I had a friend in San Francisco who was a published poet. Perhaps he would help me smooth out my words. Perhaps I did have something to say.

53

I arrived home and my landlord was waiting in front of my house. "You are a month behind in your rent, and this month's is due tomorrow."

I handed him my nine-hundred-dollar check. He gave me one hundred back. I was broke again. Back to reality. I had to move. I could no longer afford to stay in this house. Doris told me about a duplex that was going to be available around the corner. The rent was one ninety. I could afford that. I put a hundred-dollar deposit on the duplex and gave notice to my present landlord.

At the end of the month we moved. I got my security deposit back, and it took care of first and last month's rent on the new place. It was a wonderful duplex; two bedrooms, one bath, tiny kitchen and a living room with a deck and a glass wall that overlooked the Sausalito Bay. The deck had a swing on it. I felt like I had finally found a home. Somehow, I could always come up with 190 dollars.

My brother Dan got me some more chocolate-brown carpet and installed it in the living room. It looked great with my old natural linen sofa and chairs. I still had the dining-room set with the black leather seats and my chandelier. I threw my hippie pillows on the sofa and in front of the fireplace. Life is going to get better here, I thought.

Bruce was happy. He was only a few doors away from his best friend, Thomas. They came and went from each other's houses all day long. Bruce was better now. He played hard all day. Nights were different. The nightmares were getting worse. I didn't know what to do. He tossed and turned and screamed and cried. The same old dream; Bruce being run over by a car, night after night. He was terrified to cross the street by himself. When I crossed the street with him, his hands would sweat and shake. Night after night the same thing. Screaming, terror. I didn't know what to do for my child.

I sat in my living room listening to my favorite album at that time, *Tapestry* by Carol King, "When you're down and troubled and you need a helpin' hand, and nothin', no nothin' is goin' right."

You're not kidding, Carol, I thought. Nothin' is goin' right. The bill collectors were on my back more than ever; Bruce couldn't sleep through the night; I wasn't getting any work; I could barely make ends meet financially and I was in love with a guy who was gun-shy about marriage and commitment.

I called my ex-husband to tell him of Bruce's nightmares. He suggested therapy and for this I will always be grateful. It changed our lives.

I couldn't afford private therapy and my ex-husband told me about the Marin Community Mental Health Center.

"What do I have to talk to the doctor about?" Bruce asked. He was nervous.

"Just tell her about your bad dreams, honey. She's going to help you make them go away," I said reassuringly.

Our therapist's name was Mrs. Kilgore. She spent an hour with me and an hour with Bruce.

"I'd like you both to come every week, an hour visit each," she said.

"I understand your wanting to see Bruce, but why me?" I asked.

"In order to understand what is happening to Bruce, you need to be in on his therapy. I need information from you as we go along. We'll be able to get Bruce through this trauma, but it will probably take him about a year. We charge according to your ability to pay," she said.

I told her of my financial condition, and we both agreed I could afford a dollar a visit. It would cost eight dollars a month for the two of us.

54

*B*ruce and I started our "sessions." I had no idea of the impact this would have on my life. I only wanted Bruce to stop having his nightmares. I didn't realize this was my opportunity to unravel a lifetime of confusion. I knew there were lots of things wrong with me, but I had accepted them as unfixable. I had no idea that through therapy I could peel away the layers to clarity.

Things began simply; gathering information on my life since the birth of Bruce. I told her about my marriage; the shame and humiliation of "having" to wed, my unfulfilled dreams of a career, my affair with Mr. Bates and the shame and guilt that accompanied it. I also told her of my divorce and my financial problems. My life sounded pretty bleak. "I am a good mother, though," I said confidently. "Bruce has had a good life even though he's from a broken home. No mother could love her child more," I told her.

Mrs. Kilgore worked with Bruce through dolls. Every doll was given a name: Mommy, Daddy, Bruce, Alan, Mary (his father's wife), Jack, Thomas, Doris, Grandpa and Grammy. Then they would act out the scenes with the dolls. I was not allowed in Bruce's sessions. He looked forward to seeing Mrs. Kilgore. She was his friend and was interested in everything he felt and talked about. He liked talking to her. She was consistent. He saw her on the same day at the same time every week. He liked regularity in his schedule. At home we always had dinner at 5:30, and Bruce's bedtime was 8:30. It made him feel secure.

I felt awkward going to a therapist. In those days anyone who went to a "head doctor" was considered mentally ill. It was something you whispered about. Going to a "shrink" meant you were some kind of freak.

My family didn't understand either. I wasn't crazy, so why go tell some stranger your problems?

I liked Mrs. Kilgore. She was of average height and weight, early forties, with short brown, sensibly cut hair. She wore no makeup and dressed conservatively, usually gray shirtdresses or navy skirts with white blouses. Behind her black horn-rimmed glasses were kind, sensitive, understanding eyes; and it was from here that we connected.

As I grew to know her, I was amazed to have another person so focused on me. She genuinely seemed interested in me and my welfare. She was easy to talk with, which gave me the confidence to probe the layers of my making. I was beginning to feel less frightened of finding out who I really was. Mrs. Kilgore made me feel centered and anchored. We didn't talk about Bruce very much in our sessions. That surprised me; after all, he was my reason for being there. Certainly there was nothing wrong with me. But she seemed to feel it was important to know more about me and what I thought about myself. Soon I was telling her my deepest secrets: my arrest, the abortion. We also talked a lot about Alan.

"Why do you settle for so little from Alan?" she would ask.

"I feel so lucky to have him under any circumstances," I would tell her. "I've never known a man like him, and I never meet anyone who even comes close. I love him."

We talked about my financial problems a lot, including the fifteen thousand dollars' worth of medical bills. I told her that Bank of America sent me a MasterCharge Card, and I immediately used it to improve my wardrobe.

"Suzanne, we have to deal with this compulsive buying problem of yours," Mrs. Kilgore said. "It's unrealistic! On one hand, you tell me you don't have enough money for food, and then you tell me you spent fifteen hundred dollars on clothes," she continued.

"But I need them for my work," I protested.

"But it's unrealistic, Suzanne! You can't afford to buy any clothes. We have to talk about your compulsive behavior.

"How are you going to get out of debt? Have you thought about it? Do you have a plan?" she would ask.

"I'll just have to pay all these bills little by little," I would tell her.

"But you hardly earn enough to keep yourself in food and shelter as it is," she would say. "Have you thought about other ways to earn money?"

Mrs. Kilgore would get me thinking. I'd leave each week with my mind opened up to some new thought. Instinctively I knew the value of peeling away the layers. For the first time in my life I was beginning to face the truth about myself. I had so far to go, but for once I wasn't afraid of it. A little glimmer of self-esteem was poking its head out. Not much—I had been buried by my own worthlessness for so long that recovery would be slow and tedious—but I saw a little light.

Therapists point out your patterns of behavior. Mrs. Kilgore was making me take a good look at the destructive things I did to myself over and over again. My life had become financially and emotionally unmanageable. She was going to try to give me a framework in which to live. I needed a grasp on reality. I needed to recognize my worth as a human being.

For the first time in my life I was starting to feel a little anger toward Alan. Was I just his "good-time girl"? His plaything? He never involved himself in any of my problems. That was my life, and he had his. Why couldn't he give me some hope that sometime in the future we would be together? Something to hang on to.

He hadn't told his children about me. I met his son, Stephen, once when I was still living in San Francisco, but I was introduced as "someone Daddy works with." His son was darling but very badly behaved. While at lunch, Alan and I were talking to one another and suddenly Stephen fell to the ground writhing and holding his stomach in pain. Everyone in the restaurant gathered around.

Alan got on his hands and knees saying over and over, "Stephen, what's wrong? Stephen, are you all right? Someone, please call a doctor!"

All of a sudden Stephen started laughing hysterically. He had just wanted attention. Alan laughed and said, "You little brat." I was enraged. I couldn't believe how terrible this was, and Alan didn't deal with it.

Over the years I had chosen to be blind to all these things. I chose to be blind to the fact that Alan treated Bruce as if he were a stranger. He never showed any interest in him. He didn't want to get involved. He was afraid of the responsibility. I was always terrified to bring up any possibility of our getting married someday. How could I? Alan stated often, "I'm never going to get married again. Ever!" I didn't want to risk losing him, so I kept quiet.

Mrs. Kilgore was forcing me to ask questions of myself. Why? Why not risk losing him? What was he offering me? Was my life to be forever in limbo? Alan knew how I felt, and he was taking advantage of the situation.

Bruce's nightmares were becoming less frequent. Bruce's father was also in therapy and that coincided with more regular visits with his son. He would come over and visit Bruce after school; once, sometimes twice a week. It annoyed me to have my ex-husband in my house, using my bathroom, drinking my juice, since he still refused to pay me any child support; but little Bruce was so happy to be having a relationship with his dad that I couldn't say anything. Bruce needed a father, and Alan certainly wasn't filling the bill.

Jack was always there when we needed him. I wished Jack and I could love each other in a romantic way. He would make a wonderful husband and father, but I just couldn't turn off my feelings for Alan. It was 1972. Alan and I had been together for four years. Instead of dissipating, my feelings of love only got stronger.

Mrs. Kilgore encouraged me to have Bruce's father visit anytime he could. She said Bruce often acted out his desire through the dolls to have his original family back together. She said Bruce would put his mommy and daddy dolls in bed together, and Jack would come over and play with the Bruce doll. He never picked up the Alan doll. He told her Alan was always away. Mrs. Kilgore would separate the mommy and daddy dolls, and Bruce would get upset.

I looked forward to my therapy sessions. I would drive to Mrs. Kilgore's office full of my angry thoughts, and she would help me place them in perspective. She helped me to see that I was the maker of all my doings. If I didn't like the way Alan treated me, it was up to me to change it.

My financial crisis was another situation. I couldn't see it as my doing. I felt victimized. I wanted to be in show business and was going about it the only way I knew how; and I had no skills to do anything else.

"You have such a low sense of self-esteem," she would tell me often.

I didn't understand what she meant. I thought I liked myself.

Surprisingly, in all of our sessions we never went back to the crucial formative years. If we did, I've forgotten or perhaps I lied and told her about the dead doctor father. It is something I've repressed, and no amount of soul searching gives me an answer. I know at that time I did not feel my father had any relevance to my life. I never blamed him for any of my problems and never realized that growing up with an alcoholic parent affected who I was as an adult. My therapist might have been able to piece the puzzle together more easily. Low self-esteem is a classic symptom of an adult child of an alcoholic, as is being unrealistic and compulsive. But awareness of these symptoms has only come about recently. Eighteen years ago members of an alcoholic family were not considered co-addicts or part of the disease. The alcoholic was the only person urged to get help. Once that was accomplished, everything would return to normal.

But what was normal? Crises were normal, low self-worth was normal, isolation and loneliness was normal, lying was normal, escape into one's fantasies was normal. Was this any preparation to co-exist in society?

Because of Bruce's accident I found myself, week after week, month after month, talking with this woman who was helping me unravel the emotional mess of all those years. The miracle was my readiness to participate. I was open and ready to be helped. But it would take time.

"Why are you so unrealistic about money?" Mrs. Kilgore would ask. "Why do you continue to create crises for yourself?" Little by little she was making me realize that I did it to myself, but I seemed to thrive on crisis. My entire life was always filled with crisis. I learned to operate within it. It was almost as if I wasn't happy if I didn't have a crisis going.

Alan booked me on "Mantrap" again. This time the girls were Phyllis Diller, Jacqueline Susann and myself. Thank God, another nine hundred dollars.

Jacqueline asked me about my writing. I told her I had been meeting with my poet friend, Jim, and he was helping me with form and layout. I realized, the more he taught me, the more there was to know.

She asked to read my recent work and told me she felt they were ready to be sold. She said she would be glad to make an appointment for me with her publisher.

Jacqueline was so encouraging and so supportive. Unfortunately, my sense of self-worth would not allow me to feel good enough to follow through. I told her I felt I needed a larger repertoire and was working on that.

That part was true. I had been very involved with my writing since starting therapy. I found writing poems helped me form a clearer picture. I was searching for answers and my writing was helping me to find them.

I owed money to the grocery store, the California Medical Collection Agency, the pharmacy, Bank of America. I was behind in my telephone bill. I was sent a twenty-four-hour disconnect notice, and there was also my rent, gas and car payment. This nine hundred would not go far.

The collection agency was now sending people to my house to harass me. They could no longer reach me by phone.

"I'm not leaving until you give me cash or a check to make some form of payment," the man from the collection agency stated.

"Okay, I'll give you a check," I said wearily.

I had paid my monthly bills. I had enough left over to give him a check for one hundred fifty dollars. A drop in the bucket next to the fifteen thousand. Bank of America would have to wait. Mrs. Kilgore commended me for being responsible with my nine hundred dollars.

55

My casting agent called. "They're looking for a blonde for a movie called *American Graffiti*." She gave me the address and time. "Two thirty P.M. tomorrow."

My agent had the warmth of an Eskimo Pie. No "Hello, how are yous" with her. Just the facts. I wasn't one of the ace clients at the agency. They only made a few hundred dollars a year from me, hardly worth the money spent on phone calls.

My biggest problem was digging up the fifty-cent bridge toll and parking money for the next day. I scrounged a dollar fifty from old purses and coat pockets.

I washed and set my hair and put on my new St. Laurent silk blouse, the one I knew I shouldn't have bought. Why do I keep spending money I don't have, I asked myself. Bank of America was calling and sending me letters twice a week for my MasterCharge bill. At least I was beginning to deal with problems through Mrs. Kilgore.

When I got to the toll booth at Golden Gate Bridge, I told the toll-taker I had forgotten my wallet. I had to save my money for parking.

"You'll have to pull over and go inside," he said.

I had anticipated this. Good thing I left early, I thought. Inside the officer told me I would have to leave something for collateral.

"How about my lipstick?" I asked.

"Fine," he said.

I made a mental note. Always keep old lipsticks in the car as bridge collateral. I chuckled to myself as I walked outside. I had just learned something new.

The interview waiting room was crowded with every blonde in the Bay Area. Every one of them was gorgeous. Oh, God, I thought. This is hopeless. I waited for a half hour. That meant seventy-five cents in parking already. If I leave now, I'll still have seventy-five cents left over. That would buy one piece of fresh petrale sole for our dinner. I walked over to the casting agent, whose name was Gino.

"I'm sorry," I said, "I just can't wait any longer."

"Can you wait just another five minutes? The director was very intrigued by your picture," he said.

"He was?" I was amazed. Next to all these beauties I didn't think I had a chance.

"You can go in now, Suzanne," Gino said a few minutes later.

Sitting behind a big desk was a small man. His name was George Lucas. He smiled and asked me if I knew how to drive. I giggled and said yes. Then he just looked at me for a few minutes. I felt very uncomfortable. I couldn't wait to get out of there.

"Thanks for coming," George Lucas said.

I guess I didn't get the part, I thought. Shit! Now I've used up my petrale-sole money, I thought. "Thank you for seeing me," I told him. Then I left.

I raced home. Bruce would be alone in the house, and I didn't like that. When I walked inside, Bruce said, "Your agent called."

"You got the part," my agent said coolly.

"I did?" I screamed.

Her voice was emotionless. "It's one night's work, SAG scale, which is one thirty-seven twenty-five. You have a wardrobe fitting tomorrow, and they shoot the following night. You will be picked up at your house at eight P.M. It shoots all night." *Click.*

"Thanks," I said to the dial tone.

A movie! I had one speaking line.

Two days later I was picked up promptly at 8 P.M. Another girl was in the car. Her name was Cindy Williams.

"Are you an actress?" she asked.

"Oh, yes," I said assuredly.

"So many of the kids up here aren't really actors," she said.

"Really?" I tried to sound astounded.

We arrived in Petaluma, and I was put into hair, makeup and wardrobe. My hair was styled into a flat pageboy, makeup was very light and wardrobe was a gingham spaghetti-strap dress—the kind my sister used to wear to dances. Someone said, "Wait in that trailer over there."

In the trailer were a bunch of kids. They were all really nice and fun, but they had been working together for a while and had that familiarity. I was like the new kid on the first day of school. Besides, I was very unsure. I kept saying my one line over and over in my head, "I love you. I L-O-V-E you! I love *you*! I-love-you!"

The kids' names were Richard Dreyfuss, Ron Howard, MacKenzie Phillips, Cindy Williams, Candy Clark and Paul LeMat. George Lucas walked in and gave everyone notes. So these are the stars of the movie. What a bunch of losers, I thought. Everyone was so ordinary. George told me that my part was very important to the film. I was the fantasy. The dream. Seeing me was a pivotal point in the film for Richard Dreyfuss. I didn't have to say the words out loud, just mouth *I love you* sensually. Shit! I thought, my first line in a movie and I only get to mouth it. George told me that everyone would remember the beautiful blonde in the white '57 Thunderbird.

The next day was back to reality. "Your check bounced," the man from the collection agency announced. "You have twenty-four hours to get down to our office and make it good, or I'll turn you over to the police department for fraud."

"Please, please don't do that." I felt terror. How could this have happened. I had calculated that I had enough money. I had to beg my agent for an advance on my $137.25 from *American Graffiti*. Jack loaned me the rest.

I felt desperate again. The highs and the lows.

Alan knew I was not well off but thought I made enough to take care of myself. I led him to believe that. It was still part of my sickness. Lies of omission, secrets. I didn't want him to envision me as this poor, pathetic, pitiful, broke soul waiting for him to beckon me. I wanted to appear independent and self-sufficient. I had my pride. I never asked Alan for any money, but I needed money desperately. I had to get out of my financial mess. I had over a hundred pages of poetry. I decided to muster the courage to try to sell them.

I arranged my writings in order and called my book *Touch Me*. It was a good name; the poems were about feelings and emotions; loneliness, sadness, love and joy.

What did I have to lose? I asked my friend Jim, the poet, if he could arrange an appointment for me with his publisher.

Two days later he called back and said, "They'll see you Thursday at twelve o'clock for lunch."

I was thrilled. I thanked him over and over for the opportunity.

"Hey," he said, "I can get you in the door, but you and your talent have got to do the rest."

I thanked him for all his help, and he told me he thought I had a real good chance of getting published.

I called Alan and told him about my meeting.

"Great," Alan said. "I'll pick you up at the airport."

My appointment was with the president of Nash Publishing. We would meet at his office, then have lunch. I wore my good Yves St. Laurent peach silk shirt again and a short, tight black wool skirt with high heels. I wore my hair straight, clean and parted in the middle.

I was shaking inside as I walked into his office, but he was very nice and casual. We talked about Jacqueline Susann and what a tragedy it was that she had just died of cancer two days before. I was stunned by the news. I hadn't known about it until I got on the airplane and read it in the newspaper.

"She was a wonderful, generous woman," I said. I told him how encouraging and supportive she had been of my work.

"Let's go to lunch," the publisher said. Three other men joined us. We walked across Sunset Strip to the Cock 'n' Bull. It was one of those noisy, boozy, dark lunch spots; a lot of clinking glasses and waitresses yelling, "Number four for table seven."

In the midst of all the noise the publisher asked, "So what's your book all about?"

"Well," I said meekly, "it's about feelings and emotions."

"Excuse me," the waitress interrupted, "who was having the scotch/soda?"

"It's about being touched," I continued, "not physically." I could see their eyes staring past me.

"Hm-m-m. Touching!" one of the men said.

"That's a good gimmick with the way she looks and all."

"Listen, give me the manuscript. We'll have our girl give it a looking over, and then we'll talk."

We finished lunch and that was that. I'll never hear from them again, I thought.

"How did you do?" Alan asked. He was waiting out in front for me.

"I don't know. Not very well, I think. It was so noisy, and they hardly asked me any questions."

"Well, if they're smart, they'll buy your book. The poems are great, and you're very promotable."

L.A. talk. I didn't get it. I just hoped to get my book published.

I spent the rest of the weekend with Alan and finally met his daughter. Stephen, eight years old, ignored me; and Leslie, ten years old, stared and circled me like a wary animal. This is not going to be easy, I thought.

They must have mentioned "Mummy" a hundred times that day. "Mummy this, Mummy that, Mummy says . . ." Alan would ask them, "Does Mummy know? Does Mummy let you . . . ?" Mummy! Mummy! Mummy!

We drove to Newport Beach to go sailing. After sailing we went to the go-carts. After the go-carts we went to McDonald's for french fries. After McDonald's we went to Baskin-Robbins. After Baskin-Robbins Stephen said, "I want to go to the Crab-Cooker." So we went. We all ordered clam chowder that we didn't want and were too full to eat. After the Crab-Cooker we went to the Santa Monica Pier for a ride on the carousel. Then we dropped off the children's friends. Then finally we took Alan's kids to "Mummy's house!" Talk about superdad! Talk about guilt! I couldn't wait to get to Mrs. Kilgore to discuss this day.

The car suddenly went quiet. An entire day of screaming, demanding children! God! I couldn't wait to get back to Alan's room and take a bath. I wanted to be alone with him. I was starting to realize the depth of his guilt.

56

I was beginning to feel better about things; so was Bruce. He had been seeing Mrs. Kilgore for a year.

"I really think he is fine now," she said to me. "He's a wonderful little boy. During his therapy I believe he's worked out a lot of confusion, and he seems happy, secure, confident and loved. I think you've been a very good mother to him."

Those words made me feel so good. I wanted to be a good mother to Bruce. I promised him on the day he was born that I would make a good life for him, and I didn't ever want to fail him.

"But I would like *you* to stay in therapy," Mrs. Kilgore continued. "You still need a lot of work. Your self-esteem hasn't improved much, and you still don't seem to have a handle on life. You have a real opportunity for success. I feel you need to be better equipped emotionally."

I wonder how I got this way, I thought.

Mrs. Kilgore had me thinking of other ways to make a living. "What do you enjoy? What are your skills? In what areas do you excel?" she would ask.

"I'm an excellent seamstress and I'm a good cook," I said.

"Think about those things," she would say. "Maybe you could turn your hobbies into profit."

I thought about making and selling desserts to restaurants. I made an excellent chocolate mousse cake decorated with chocolate leaves. I went to every restaurant in Sausalito. No one was interested. I went back a second time with samples. Everyone was impressed with the look and taste. "How much?" I was asked.

"The ingredients cost me eight dollars a cake," I said. I used good Belgian dark chocolate and See's fresh white chocolate, fresh cream, butter, sugar, eggs and Amaretto liqueur. "I could give you the cake for twenty dollars, and it serves eight."

"At three dollars a slice my profit on the whole cake would be four dollars. It's not worth it to me," the owner said.

I was turned down at every restaurant. I decided to try something else. My mother had taught me how to sew and I decided to design and make little girls' dresses. I went out and bought small-print English cotton with tiny pink, blue and lavender flowers. I bought narrow satin ribbons in the same colors and French cotton eyelet for trim. I made a darling little dress, Victorian style with puffed sleeves and an empire waistline. I pulled the satin ribbons through the eyelet and trimmed right under the puff of the sleeve and around the neck. It was adorable. I took it to a store in Mill Valley and the owner took it immediately on consignment. Materials cost me twenty-five dollars, and it took a week and a half to make, so I had to charge fifty dollars.

"Not many people are willing to pay fifty dollars for a child's dress, but we'll see," the owner said.

I went home and started on the second dress. In a short time I had made four dresses. Not one sold.

"Everyone who comes in loves them," the owner said, "but no one wants to pay the price."

I couldn't afford to make any more dresses until one of them sold. I had to put my new business on hold. It was a stupid idea, anyway, I thought.

Two months later I received a letter in the mail. "We would like to publish your book of poems. Please contact us." I was ecstatic. I couldn't believe it—from adulteress to authoress. They offered me a twenty-five-hundred-dollar advance.

I called them and accepted it. Alan told me I was stupid.

"If they offered you twenty-five hundred, it meant they would have gone to at least five thousand. You should have let me negotiate."

But he was happy for me. Twenty-five hundred dollars was a wonderful sum of money.

RING! "We can't wait any longer, Miss Somers. We must have our money by the end of this week or we will start garnishment proceedings."

"Please wait a little longer," I pleaded. "I'm coming into some money soon."

My balloon so quickly burst. Without Mrs. Kilgore and my weekly visits, I might have gone crazy. The pressure to get by was so intense. I felt angry and depressed much of the time. My only hope was my book.

Mrs. Kilgore increased my visitation fees. "Why are you doing this to me?" I asked her. "You know better than anyone how broke I am." I was angry.

"You're bringing in enough money to make expenses and keep your bill collectors appeased," she said. "I know you can find an extra twenty dollars a month to pay me. It's only five dollars a visit."

"But why?" I asked incredulously.

"Because," she said, "I want your therapy to be a priority with you. I want getting better to be the most important thing in your life. You bought a new pair of shoes last week. I'm sure they cost more than twenty dollars. I want therapy to be more important to you than a new pair of shoes. I'm trying to teach you priorities about money. So, from now on, if you don't have five dollars when you see me, there will be no therapy session."

I couldn't believe it. My therapist was now on my back. She was "detaching." I had no choice though. Somehow I would come up with the extra twenty dollars a month. I *had* to continue my therapy.

I was seeing less of Jack. My bill collectors hounded me so relentlessly that I asked Jack to co-sign a five-thousand-dollar consolidation loan for me and now was having trouble paying it back. It was part of my disease—the unrealistic part. How could I have possibly imagined I could pay back five thousand dollars? How could I possibly think that five thousand dollars could help me? I owed over fifteen thousand, and my book advance was twenty-five hundred dollars. It was gone before I got it.

Every time Jack was forced to make a loan payment for me, he got a little more angry. Who could blame him? I had convinced him I'd be making *so-o-o* much money from my book, I'd have *no problem* repaying the loan. Now I had screwed up my relationship with my best friend.

Where money was concerned, I was making no progress. It overwhelmed me. I had been so far in the hole for so long, I didn't know how to get out.

When Alan and I were together, he treated me like the most special person in the world. He told me he loved me countless times during the day. When I awoke in the morning, he would be staring at me.

"You are so beautiful," was usually the first thing he said to me.

When I was with him in Vancouver, I would follow him from his dressing room to the studio and watch him from the sidelines in awe. He was so good on camera. So articulate, so charming. He had the unique ability to turn on women and not turn off men. His qualities were very similar to Johnny Carson's in that respect. He could talk to anyone about anything. He was also very funny.

I learned so much from him. He was very driven during this time. Instead of fighting over what he termed "rabbit shit" in his divorce, he gave everything to his ex-wife.

He was determined to start all over and be a big success. Remarriage or even living with me was the furthest thing from his mind. I had no guarantees, and I lived four hundred miles away from him.

I felt tormented at the possibility of losing him. I had no controls in our relationship. When I visited him in Los Angeles, I couldn't help but notice how beautiful all the women were. I felt so insecure. How can I possibly compete? I didn't have money, so I couldn't dress nicely. Thank God it was the sixties, the era of the flower child. When I was not working I had taken to wearing a Peruvian pancho and blue jeans, long straight blond hair and a fresh daisy over one ear. "Hip" was cheap, and I couldn't afford to look any other way.

How long would I have to wait to finally, *really* have Alan? "He's not going to be ready to marry you for ten years," Mrs. Kilgore said. "If you really want him, you must be prepared to wait that long."

Ten years! The idea of waiting so long was overwhelming. The idea of continuing my day-to-day hopeless existence for ten years made me extremely depressed.

I looked around at the girls I knew. None of them were having the struggle I had. They all had husbands who took care of them. They lived in charming Sausalito homes, had lovely clothes and nice cars. They weren't worrying about food on the table or paying the rent. I never knew when my next job was coming. I was constantly stalling my bill collectors. I was constantly begging my modeling agency for an advance. They treated me like scum. "What do you want now?" they would ask disgustedly. I was the agency joke.

"Do we have a future together?" I would ask Alan.

"It's nice the way it is," he would answer.

"I'm going to start going out with other men," I told him, hoping to upset him.

"That's okay," Alan said. I now know he was bluffing.

I felt so disheartened. Angry! "He treats me like shit," I told Mrs. Kilgore.

"You allow him to treat you that way," she said.

"When we're together, I feel like the most special person in the whole world. As soon as I leave, it all stops." It was all or nothing.

"When you feel that you are worth more, everything will change," she said again.

But Bruce was happy. He didn't know there were any pressures. He loved our duplex and the neighborhood. He played Little League baseball in the schoolyard, and I also signed him up for a free pottery class for children at the Sausalito Arts Center, which was across the street. He came and went from our house. He brought his friend Thomas to swing on our deck, and I would give them both cookies. Bruce got twenty-five cents a week allowance every Wednesday, and he and Thomas would walk to the Big G Supermarket and buy a small can of Fritos Bean Dip and a small bag of chips. That was his big splurge. Bruce was having a good life, and that made me happy.

And I *was* making progress as a human being. I felt more deserving of good things that came my way. This new sense of self was not helping my relationship with Alan. I felt strong enough now to ask him if marriage was in our future. I told him I loved him with all my heart but was not prepared to be his eternal girlfriend.

I had started dating other men. Casual dates. No sex. Just dinner and conversation. I was becoming a better conversationalist. My therapy allowed me to be very open. I was no longer hiding the real me. I figured I am who I am; and if you don't like it, too bad. As always, no one could take Alan's place. He was the love of my life; and I remembered Mrs. Kilgore saying, "You'll have to wait ten years before he's ready." I hoped I could.

My dream was seeming less ridiculous to me. Perhaps it was possible. Perhaps *I* could succeed. Thank God for Mrs. Kilgore. Whenever I started to have doubts, she forced me to see the good about myself.

I landed a small part in a Clint Eastwood movie, *Magnum Force.* "You got the part," my agent said dryly. "I'm sending the script over. It shoots next week in Tiburon."

The script called for me to be a floozy at a gangster party that gets raided, and I end up getting shot to death in the breast. It wasn't until I arrived on the set that I realized the gunshot in my bosom would rip off the top of my dress and my bleeding breasts would be exposed for all the world to see.

"But you'll be dead!" the director said. "It's not like you're doing a nude scene," he exclaimed.

"I guess you're right," I said resignedly.

It was a long day of shooting. A device filled with fake blood was applied to my bosom; and every time we shot the scene, a man behind the camera exploded it by remote control. A small amount of gunpowder went off (it felt like getting hit in the bosom with a BB gun) and the fake blood would trickle down my breast. This was my cue that I had been shot, and I would fall backward into the pool and play dead.

The scene attracted a lot of local attention. Besides the presence of Clint Eastwood, two helicopters, two fire engines and enough pyro-technics to create a small mock war, the onlookers had this blonde having her breasts blown off to look at. I was introduced to Clint Eastwood but was too shy to talk to him.

When the sun went down we could no longer shoot, so I was told I could go home. I was tired and exhausted from falling into the cold swimming pool all day. I also felt stressed. I didn't enjoy all these strangers seeing my breasts. It made me feel cheap.

I walked past all the gawkers and heard them whisper, "Who is she?" "Who is she?" I felt like a star. I realized from their point of view all the action had revolved around me. They thought I was *somebody!* I was asked for my autograph. It was fun.

Then I remembered my car. I had had to park my old Volkswagen up the hill in case it didn't start. The door on the driver's side was tied closed with a rope because the closing mechanism was broken. I crawled in the passenger side and started the engine. Nothing. I tried it again. Dead. I'd have to start it on compression. How humiliating. In front of all those people, *chug-a-lug, chug-a-lug, chug-chug-chug.* Their faces looked disgusted as I sputtered past them. I reminded myself of Andy Warhol's quote, "We all get to be famous for fifteen minutes." Oh, well. I had to get home and cook dinner for Bruce.

I was invited to a private screening of *American Graffiti.* It was held at the Sausalito Theater, only cast and crew invited. It was a good movie.

Everyone cheered, screamed and applauded. My part seemed so insignificant. I remembered what George Lucas had told me: "Everyone will remember the beautiful blonde in the white '57 T-Bird." I wasn't sure he was right. It seemed to me that lots of other things in the movie were more memorable than that.

The book would not be out for a year. I was beginning to realize publishing was a very slow-paying business. I had not received my advance even though it had been three months. I didn't want to bother the publisher by asking. Didn't want to "rock the boat."

"You've got a booking for Mexicana Airlines," my modeling agent, Marsha, told me. "It shoots next week in Puerto Vallarta. It's for their travel brochure. They seem to like seeing blondes sitting on their beaches. The pay is a hundred fifty dollars a day for four days."

"Great," I said. Six hundred dollars and a free trip to Mexico. Rent, gas, telephone, car payment and insurance would be covered for another month. The fifteen-thousand-dollar medical bill overwhelmed me; but even though it was always there, I tried not to think about it.

Puerto Vallarta was stunning, as were our accommodations. The advertising agency had rented a large villa with a staff that cooked and cleaned and catered to our every whim. The food was divine; fresh huevos rancheros every morning with huge platters of sweet, ripe watermelon, mangoes and papayas. Lunch was homemade enchiladas or green chili tamales; and dinner was usually a little more exotic, like chicken molé.

We stopped working every afternoon to sit by the pool and sip salty margaritas with lots of fresh lime. I was having a wonderful time.

For the shoot, the ad agency provided my wardrobe, which consisted mainly of skimpy bikinis and coverups. The photographer and I would leave early each morning right after breakfast to take advantage of the morning light. He had me running along the seashore with billowing blond hair, sipping piña coladas under a coconut tree and scuba diving in the reef. He took all the pictures that would make the folks back in the States want to leave their mundane lives and fly off to paradise.

It was paradise; warm, tropical and sexy. Hibiscus and bougainvillea flowers were in bloom everywhere. Everyone looked bronzed and relaxed.

I wished Alan were with me. I tried to call him, but there was only one phone in Puerto Vallarta and it was very difficult to get a connection.

"I want to go inland tomorrow morning," the photographer said. "There's a beautiful waterfall, and I'd like to shoot you standing at the base of it."

He was right. The waterfall was breathtaking. He handed me a very sheer bodysuit to put on.

"You can see right through this," I said.

"Not the way I'll be shooting," he answered.

I felt uncomfortable.

"Sit on that rock," he shouted. "Lie back! Untie the top of the suit! Let it fall open a bit! You look beautiful!"

I was enjoying myself. We were creating something—the smoothness of the rocks, the smoothness of the waterfall, the smoothness of my skin.

"These are great," he said over and over. "Let's stop for a minute." The photographer walked over to me. "You know, I also shoot for *Playboy*. These pictures are going to be gorgeous. If you let me shoot you nude in this setting, I'm sure you'd be chosen as Playmate of the Month. You could make fifteen thousand dollars."

Fifteen thousand dollars! The magic number. The exact amount to get me out of debt. All I had to do was take my clothes off. No more bill collectors. No more harassment. A chance for a fresh start. Just take my clothes off. What a dilemma. This wouldn't be like *Newsweek*, where I was unrecognizable. Nope. For sure, everyone would know who I was. I was vacillating.

"Tell you what," the photographer said. "Let me take the pictures; and if you decide later on you don't want to go through with it, you don't have to sign a release."

I had options. "Okay," I said. I felt nervous.

Back in Sausalito I told Alan what I had done.

"Well," he said, "at least you have time to think about it. These pictures will be around for the rest of your life."

I could tell he wasn't thrilled. Frankly, I didn't feel good about it either. I didn't want Bruce to have to grow up seeing naked pictures of his mother. I knew my family would be appalled. But fifteen thousand dollars would make my life a lot less hassled.

Alan had hired a girl as a talent booker on "Mantrap." Her name was Bonnie. When the show ended after two seasons, she decided to go into personal management. She was a tough-on-the-outside, soft-on-the-inside, New York kind of girl.

"I'd like to represent you," she said to me out of the side of her mouth. "I think you could be a big star."

No one had ever said that to me before. I didn't really believe her but thought, If she's willing to put in the time, there's nothing to lose. We agreed, and she had me sign a contract.

Bonnie said that with my appearances on "Mantrap," my movie role in *American Graffiti* and the book coming out, she could parlay it into something big.

"Okay," I said enthusiastically.

Bonnie set up interviews with agents and casting agents. I flew to Los Angeles as often as I could and found myself spending rent money on airplane tickets. I was starting to like Los Angeles. I had a boyfriend there, a personal manager and real interviews. Besides, Los Angeles was an escape—no bill collectors, no landlord, no disconnect notices, and I got to be with Alan.

The agents were not too impressed with me. "Let's talk when the movie comes out," they all said. I had no film, no tape to show them, and they knew I would be a "hard sell."

Bonnie and I kept plodding along. Mrs. Kilgore kept working on my self-esteem, and I was starting to believe that maybe I *could* make it. Bonnie set up interviews. I'd never get the job, but everyone really liked me. They thought I was nice, unaffected. They'd "keep me in mind," I was told. That was good enough for me.

We sneaked onto movie lots and ate lunch in the commissaries. "Dress to kill," Bonnie would say. I would try my hardest to pull together classy but sexy outfits. My Yves St. Laurent blouse came in handy. I had found a matching tight peach wool straight skirt. My "commissary outfit," I called it. With my straight long blond hair and my peach outfit, I did get noticed! No work, but noticed.

"It's all right," Bonnie would say. "When you finally do get an interview, they'll think they remember you from somewhere."

At Universal Studios I saw posters of Maria Muldaur, *Midnight at the Oasis*. God, I'd love to be on a poster in a major movie studio, I thought.

The following week Bonnie called me screaming. "You have to fly to Los Angeles tomorrow. You have an audition for a sitcom with Dom DeLuise!"

"You're kidding!" I screamed back.

It was a perfect role for me. I was to play a naïve, shy small-town, sexy girl. Dom DeLuise falls head-over-heels in love with her. I didn't have to do much pretending.

I went over and over my lines while waiting in the producer's outer office. I wanted the part so badly.

"You can go in now, Miss Somers," the receptionist said. I walked into a room filled with nice-looking men.

"Hello, I'm Sam Denoff, and this is my partner, Bill Persky."

They asked me questions about my experience; and I was able to say I had just done two movies. Both *Magnum Force* and *American Graffiti* were huge successes at the box office. Luckily, neither of them had seen either movie, so they weren't aware of my minuscule roles; they were impressed by the credits.

I read the script with Sam. "Very nice," he said. "You play shy and naïve real well. We have a couple more girls to read, so why don't you go have some coffee in the NBC commissary."

Bonnie and I sat in the commissary excitedly discussing all the "what-ifs." What if I get the part? What if they like me so much I become a regular? What if I have to move to Los Angeles?

Suddenly, Johnny Carson and his producer, Fred DeCordova, walked in. "Oh, my God! Don't look now, but guess who just walked in?" I whispered out the side of my mouth to Bonnie. I couldn't believe I was seeing him in person. They sat directly across from us.

Johnny said hi and smiled. I felt my face turn the same color pink as my sweater. On their way to the cafeteria line, Johnny and Fred stopped by our table. "What are you girls doing here?" Fred asked.

"I'm waiting to hear if I got the part on Dom DeLuise's new show," I said.

"Well, good luck," Fred said.

"I hope you get it," Johnny said. Then they left.

I couldn't believe it. "You've got to send them your book! Maybe they'll even put you on 'The Tonight Show,' " Bonnie said.

"Me?" I said unbelieving. "Well, it's certainly worth a try," I said positively.

At 1 P.M. Bonnie and I went back to the "Lotsa Luck" office. "Congratulations! You got the part," the producer said.

"I did?" I screamed and jumped up and kissed him. He laughed. He turned me over to the assistant director for instructions.

I can't wait to tell Alan, I thought. That afternoon I went to a wardrobe fitting, a meeting with the hairdresser and the script assistant. Bonnie arranged to send Johnny Carson, Fred DeCordova and all the secretaries for "The Tonight Show" office a copy of my book.

Alan was delighted for me. "I think you'll be great," he said. We went out for dinner to celebrate, but came home early. I didn't want to be tired. Rehearsal started the following morning.

Rehearsal was very relaxed and fun. Dom was a wonderful guy to work with. I told everyone it was my first time acting on television, and they all helped me as much as they could. Thank God for all my therapy. A year before I never would have had the confidence to walk into that rehearsal hall. I wouldn't have had the confidence to try out. I was feeling capable now. I was inching my way into the big time. I had started at the very bottom, and here I was at NBC in Burbank doing a sitcom.

I met Freddy Prinze in the hallway. We talked for a while. He was real nice. I saw Don Rickles walk by. Dean Martin was doing a special down the hall. Helen Reddy was rehearsing her hit song, "I Am Woman" on the "Tonight Show" stage.

On the third day of rehearsal Bonnie called me. "You're not going to believe this. You're not going to believe it!" she screamed.

"What? What?" I asked excitedly.

" 'The Tonight Show' just called, and they've booked you on the show next Friday night!"

"Oh, my God!" I said. "Oh, my God." How wonderful! How incredible! "They must have *really* liked my poetry." It was beyond my wildest imagination. "The Tonight Show"! "Lotsa Luck"! All in one week! Seven hundred fifty dollars for "Lotsa Luck"; three hundred for "The Tonight Show." Over a thousand dollars for one week's work! Of course, I would have done the shows for free. Bonnie and I were ecstatic. Maybe she was right. Maybe I could become a big star.

I called Bruce. I called my mom. I called Mrs. Kilgore. Alan picked me up after rehearsal and I ran screaming to his car to tell him. We both laughed all the way home.

I flew back to San Francisco right after taping "Lotsa Luck" Friday night. I'd been gone over a week. I had to get home to Bruce. I missed him and wanted to share my excitement with him. I enjoyed working with Dom DeLuise. He gave me a bottle of Christian Dior perfume as a thank-you present. I loved it. I kissed him good-bye and told him it had been the most exciting week of my life.

"Hi, Mommy!" Bruce said enthusiastically as he ran into my arms. I wished I never had to leave him.

"Tell me everything," I said. "I want to know every single thing you did while I was gone."

Bruce started his litany of activities. He was such a happy, good-natured child. He always had a smile on his face and his eyes always had a twinkle. I am a very lucky woman, I thought. Thank you, God, from the bottom of my heart.

I could hardly think during the next week. I was going to be on "The Tonight Show" on Friday! The whole neighborhood was excited.

I had to get a dress. I had nothing appropriate to wear for Johnny Carson. I had not been paid yet from "Lotsa Luck" but knew the union rules demanded payment in fourteen days. I had no money. I needed a dress. I'll write a check, I thought; and by the time it clears, I will have already deposited my paycheck. I knew it was a dangerous thing to do. I knew Mrs. Kilgore would lecture me if she knew. I canceled my appointment with her. That meant I hadn't seen her for two weeks.

I chose a pale, sea-foam aqua knit gown for the show. It was tight and slinky, to the floor, and exposed one shoulder. The only jewelry I owned was a pair of rhinestone earrings.

"You are a knockout," Alan said admiringly.

The dress cost 175 dollars. I knew I couldn't afford it, but rationalized it as an investment.

Alan drove me to NBC and held my sweaty hand as I waited in the "green room" to go on. I was a combination of nerves and excitement. This was "the start of something big."

"We're ready for you now, Suzanne," said Howard Papush, my talent coordinator.

I kissed Alan. "Good luck. I love you. You'll be great," he said. He winked at me. Then I left.

Standing behind the curtain waiting to be introduced on "The Tonight Show" was one of my most frightening experiences. I was afraid I was going to throw up in front of all America. Howard stayed with me and held my hand.

I knew my mother and my father were watching. I thought about my father a lot. In spite of everything, his approval still meant a lot to me; the little girl in me. I told Doris to be sure to wake up Bruce to watch. He had never heard of Johnny Carson.

"And now," I heard Johnny say, "we have a beautiful young actress. She's just written a book of poems called *Touch Me* (and I sure would like to! Ha! Ha! Ha!), but you are all going to know her as" (I wondered what he was going to say) "the beautiful blonde in the '57 white Thunderbird in *American Graffiti*. Would you welcome Suzanne Somers!"

"Woo-oo-oo-oo!" the audience reacted. I got a huge, thunderous, surprising reaction. I couldn't believe it. I sat down in that famous chair feeling stunned.

"Everyone has been wondering who the beautiful blonde in the T-Bird was, and now we've found you," Johnny said.

I remembered George Lucas saying exactly the same thing to me. It was amazing.

Johnny asked me where I was from and how long I'd been in Los Angeles.

"One week," I told him honestly.

"Well, you sure don't waste any time," he said, laughing.

I thought of all the years before this moment, all the pain and despair, all the dreams, all the trauma, and here I was. My dream was coming true.

"How'd you get the part in *American Graffiti?*" Johnny asked.

"Well," I said, "George Lucas asked me if I knew how to drive; and I said yes."

"That's it?" Johnny asked. The audience laughed.

"Yeah! I was surprised, too." The audience laughed again.

I found Johnny real easy to talk to. He listened to me. I listened to him, and our "spot" was filled with audience laughter.

"Well, you're a real charming girl. I'd like to have you on the show again. Will you come back and visit us sometime?" Johnny asked.

"Would I!" I said, amazed. "I'd love to."

"You were fantastic," Alan said. We hugged each other for a long time. "You were so likable and you looked incredible."

After the show aired that night, I called Bruce. "Did you see Mommy?" I asked.

"Yeah, you were good," he said.

Years later Bruce told me that when Doris woke him up to watch, he felt sorry for me. He said he didn't think *anybody* stayed up *that* late and thought no one would see me.

The next day I flew back home. As I walked out of the San Francisco International Airport, a policeman yelled at me, "Hey, Suzie! I saw you on the Carson show last night! You were great!" I broke into a big smile.

Mrs. Kilgore said, "I knew you were in a dangerous frame of mind when you avoided your appointment last week." I couldn't pull anything over on her. She looked me right in the eyes. "When are you going to grow up? When are you going to become realistic and develop priorities about money? Why do you continue to create crises for yourself? It's immature and unrealistic to spend money you don't have. You've already been put in jail for being unrealistic. They won't let you off so easy next time."

She was right. I was trying real hard, but I kept having these slips. "I won't do it again," I heard myself saying sheepishly. I sounded just like all the alcoholics in the family.

"Go home and make out a list of your financial priorities," she said. "Figure out how much it costs you to live, and then don't spend one penny each month until you've taken care of your financial responsibilities. You're doing so well," she said gently. "You have a real chance to have a successful, happy, fulfilled life if *you* choose. But it's up to you. You are responsible for your own life. You can make it anything you want it to be. You've worked hard. Don't blow it."

I thought about what she said all the way home. I've never stopped thinking about it to this day. I felt determined to succeed. I felt determined to grow up and be realistic. I want to be a happy, satisfied, successful woman, I thought. I'm not going to blow it.

I also decided not to go ahead with *Playboy*. I had received a letter from them saying I was accepted as a candidate, and would I please make an appointment to fly to Los Angeles and shoot the official pictures. They said they would provide wardrobe, a professional hairdresser and professional makeup.

It just wasn't what I wanted. I knew I was sitting on an opportunity to get some respect as a poet through my book. I didn't want to invalidate myself. It would have been nice to get the money and get out from under my financial noose, but I'd have to find another way.

Alan was happy with my decision. "I'm glad," he said. "If you had done it, you'd always be known as the Playmate."

Maybe when my book comes out, I thought, it will be a big success and my life will change. It was the only dream to hold on to. I was the only one who was going to change my life. The book was my hope.

In April 1973, my book *Touch Me* came out. It was a very exciting time. A book was so "valid." I could now say I was an "authoress." People were impressed. I was invited to the American Book Association convention to pass out autographed books. People liked it. They'd come up to me the next day and say, "I read your book last night. I identified with so much of it." Others would say, "Well written."

I didn't look like a "poet," so I garnered a lot of attention from the media. I did television interviews and print interviews. It was a joyous time. Alan was very proud of me. I gave away thousands of books. I wished I had kept more for myself.

Life started changing. I was asked to give poetry readings in coffee houses. Department stores set up autograph sessions. Unfortunately, poetry is not a big seller, so all the money I naïvely expected was not forthcoming.

I'm so tired of living like this, I thought. I'm tired of waiting for the phone to ring. San Francisco is not where it's happening if I want to make a living in show business. What am I hanging on to? Why am I staying here? To be near my family? The family was fragmented; everyone was lost in his own personal crisis. We saw less and less of one another. I should take a chance and move to Los Angeles, I thought. Try for the big time. I had some success. If I was there, in the arena where it's happening, I think I could have more successes. I would like to be a celebrity. I would like to be an actress, do comedy. I'd like to sing and dance again. I have so much feeling buried deep inside me, I know I could act; but it isn't going to happen in San Francisco. I'll continue to be broke if I stay here. Bonnie would certainly like me to move to L.A. Would Alan? He had never broached the subject. He liked things just the way they were. This way, he had no responsibilities toward me. He ticked me off. I deserved more from him. After six years of loving him, I deserved some kind of commitment.

This was a new me. Never before had I entertained such thoughts. My low self-esteem had never allowed me to consider being good enough to compete in the big time. My low self-esteem had allowed Alan to continue this commitmentless relationship. I felt a new strength inside me, a positive self-attitude. I *was* good enough. I *was* talented.

Mrs. Kilgore was thrilled to hear me speak this way. "What are you going to do about it?" she asked.

"I'm thinking about making the big move to Los Angeles. It's very emotional for me. I'm going to miss my mother terribly. I feel awful about leaving her behind. I'm going to miss the nephews and the regular contact I have with my brothers and sister, even if our visits are less than satisfying. I feel bad removing Bruce from his neighborhood environment. He's so happy where we are. He'll miss his friend Thomas so much. He loves his room and the arts center and the ball field and the ravine. He has a sense of stability now. I hate to uproot him."

"These are choices you have to make. Think it through carefully. You'll come to the right decision for you," Mrs. Kilgore said.

57

During this same time, the rest of my family was going through their own personal hell. Sunday dinners had come to a halt. Maureen was drinking too much to handle it, and my mother had become a nervous wreck.

One day Bruce and I took a drive to see Grammy. "Are you okay?"

I asked my mother when we got there. She looked terrible, tired and stressed. Her psoriasis was worse than ever.

"Oh, we just had a terrible night last night. Dad was real violent. Michael and I had to sleep in the car. At three A.M. I came into the house to check it out, and Dad was passed out on the floor. He had puked all over the place, so after Michael and I dragged Dad to bed, I spent the next hour cleaning up his vomit. He also threw the food from the refrigerator all over the kitchen."

I just looked at my mother. Nothing had changed. Her expectations were so low. She had no tears left, just resignation to this living hell. Dad was killing my mother. I hated him for that. I wished he would die. It was my deepest, darkest thought. He was never going to change. Alcoholics didn't recover at that time. They just got worse and worse, as did the emotional toll they took on all those around them.

Our cute little white house with the white picket fence wasn't looking so good anymore. The inside was in disarray. It smelled of old beer and stale cigarettes. There was no life in it, no love. The outside was showing neglect, I noticed. Dad must be drinking on weekends now.

There had been some good times in our lives. I thought of all our summer camping trips. I remembered the pride I felt watching Dad coach the baseball team. I remembered the thrill when Mother took me to the theater. The excitement of Mom making me a new dress. That was all gone now. The whole family had become a tragedy.

Maureen was pregnant again and drinking every night. What a world to bring a baby into, I thought. Maureen was terrified she'd be drunk when she delivered. She felt guilty and ashamed, but she couldn't stop drinking.

Father had stopped eating dinner at my mother's house altogether. I guess he could no longer stand to witness the destruction of his daughter's life. He now ate dinner at my sister's house three times a week and was watching *her* get drunk.

My brother Danny was drinking every day, also; but he was a quiet drinker and kept "a lid on" until everyone in the house was asleep. After he'd pass out on the kitchen floor, Mardi would get up and drag him to bed.

My mother and Mardi did *not* know they were "enablers." They didn't know that by constantly cleaning up after their drunk husbands, constantly dragging them to bed and continuing to cover up for them with excuses, they were enabling them to continue drinking. They were doing the best they could, trying to be good wives and good mothers. They didn't want to do anything to add to the problems. They buried their feelings and didn't want to say anything to make the alcoholic angry. They were reacting to life—not living.

Going to a counselor was then considered as humiliating as being an alcoholic, so they continued to live with their secrets.

Danny and Maureen did not know that we were all potential alcoholics. That's the irony of the disease of alcoholism. As much as we all hated seeing our dad drink, we were powerless over the disease ourselves. Without information and awareness we could not help ourselves, and the disease continued.

I didn't realize that being a child of an alcoholic carries with it lifelong low self-esteem unless you get help. A child of an alcoholic has trouble with reality, has trouble getting close to people, has trouble achieving. I didn't realize, until years later, how lucky I was to have almost lost my child, since that incident led me into therapy. For without the therapy, I might have spent the rest of my life feeling inadequate, unlovable, unworthy.

I couldn't see it at this time, but Mrs. Kilgore was in the process of forcing me to see my worth as a human being. Until I did, there would be no progress in my growth as a person; I would continue to feel "I wasn't good enough."

If only we could have seen what alcohol was doing to all of us directly and indirectly. If we only knew how desperate and powerless my dad, Maureen and Danny felt with their drinking. They didn't want to do it. They made countless promises to "never drink again." They were fine people who, through no fault of their own, had a terrible disease that had been passed through the genes. Plenty of people have cocktails, and their lives don't become unmanageable. What was the difference? What triggered this compulsion, this obsession? The disease compromised their values, took away their pride, their sense of responsibility, their honesty. They all started as social drinkers, but the disease quickly moved them through the stages from fun and good times to excuses for drinking (such as a rough day or stress) and finally to powerlessness and unmanageability. It was affecting their physical and emotional health. They were exhausted from hangovers and their nerve endings were raw. They wanted to be loved, but the disease made them unlovable.

Everyone was mad at everyone. Bill was disgusted with Maureen. Mardi was upset and stressed over her husband's progressive disease. My mother's soft pink face was pinched and controlled. No one was laughing anymore. No one was loving anymore. We were all struggling to survive.

It's amazing how everyone in the family accepted the circumstances.

Michael's life was the worst of all the children. He was all alone and had retreated within himself. All the hurts and the humiliation were carried inside him. He now talked to no one. Every once in a while he'd have a "wing-ding." That's what we called it. He would scream and yell, throw things, lock himself in his room, have a tantrum. We all thought he was badly behaved. No one heard his cry, his screams for help. My mother took him to a psychiatrist, but he was able to fool the doctor by saying the right things. He let no one inside.

Because alcoholism was not out in the open yet, not even the doctors knew how to help. Doctors and therapists didn't understand alcoholism and its family ramifications.

Now everyone knows that *without treatment* alcoholism *always* ends in death or insanity; but we didn't know that then. We didn't realize how close everyone was to the edge.

58

*A*lan was in Montreal for the season, producing his new show, "The Sensuous Man." He flew me up to see him often. Montreal was beautiful; probably the most interesting city I'd ever been to. During the day I explored. I took the subway to every nook and cranny. The fashion was fabulous; even better than in New York. Everything was from Paris; all the latest looks. I wished I had money. I saw so many things I would love to have. But no way. I would not spend one penny that I couldn't afford, and I could not afford anything.

At night Alan and I went to wonderful, tiny, romantic, French restaurants. I had never tasted such delicious food. Our favorite place was Le Colibri. It was small (eight tables) and run by a husband, wife and their son. We had warm leeks vinaigrette, fresh pan-roasted quail with shallots, mushrooms and red wine sauce; a vegetable I had never tasted called salsify (delicious) and for dessert café filtre and fresh crème caramel. God, how I loved good food. We shared a bottle of red wine over dinner and stared into one another's eyes. Times like these made me forget my anger at Alan for his lack of commitment.

I loved him. He was exciting. He opened my eyes to new worlds, new people; and he was the *most* wonderful lover. Quite a package. Difficult to give up.

I loved Montreal, I loved being with Alan; but I felt guilty leaving Bruce with Doris babysitting just to go off for my own pleasure. I felt guilty leaving my bills behind. I wanted to get rid of them. Vacationing was not going to help me extricate myself from their burden.

"I'd like you to give me a job," I told Alan. "There's lots I can do on your show. I can be the resident poet! I'll read love poems to the Sensuous Man! When I'm not doing that, I can do makeup or props. I just can't afford to come here and visit you all the time and not make any money."

Alan understood, and the next day I was on the payroll doing *everything* I told him I was capable of doing.

The "Sensuous Man" supposedly lived in a wonderful beach house in Malibu, and I became his tanned blond neighbor who stopped by each day to read my latest poem.

> *Touch me*
> > *In secret places*
> > > *No one has reached before*
> > *In silent places*
> > > *Where words only interfere*
> > *In sad places*
> > > *Where only whispering makes sense.*

It would be great publicity for my book and, as I was now thinking, my future books.

The Sensuous Man talked to the ladies at home about the importance of bathing with your lover, rubbing his back with baby oil, lighting your entire apartment with candles and soaking your feet in lime Jell-O.

It was a camp, sexy, fun show. When I wasn't reading poetry, I did props and applied makeup to the guests. It was a demanding job. For instance, on the day the Sensuous Man decided to light his entire beach-house set with candlelight, I ran all over Montreal trying to buy seven hundred candles. I didn't know where anything was in Montreal, and I didn't speak French. Then I had to get all the ingredients for baked Alaska and make two beautiful baked Alaskas for the show. (The second one was in case the first one melted.) When I finished that, I did Meredith MacRae's makeup. I also got coffee and doughnuts for the male guest whose expertise was sexual aids.

"Isn't it sad," the Sensuous Man said in his heavy French accent, "that people feel the need to have help in something as natural as making love."

The next day the Sensuous Man took a bath in flowers. Then he'd wrap a towel around himself and walk out onto the beach. (That part was taped in Los Angeles.) He'd slowly sing (always with a heavy accent) "When love comes in and takes you for a spin, ooh-la-la, c'est magnifique."

Alan was caught up in writing, directing and producing. Jean-Paul Vignon was the Sensuous Man. Alan loved the idea of creating this guy who thought he was so-o-o sexy. He always took the Sensuous Man to the max. He put as much nudity in the show as he could get away with. The Sensuous Man started every show in his antique brass bed and the camera watched him get out of bed nude (camera above the waist). Then we'd either get dressed with him or take a bath with him. Sometimes there would be a girl in his bed, and we'd get dressed with her, too.

Alan worked me real hard and gave me no attention. It was difficult for me to handle. I didn't mind the hard-work part, but I didn't like the no attention. I didn't like being treated like the prop girl. Professional was professional, but our relationship was professional *and* personal. He had to find a way to work it out. I didn't want to be treated like his underling. I deserved more.

One day I was out all morning shopping (the Sensuous Man was making osso bucco today). I came back to the studio to whip together the osso bucco to find that seven French models needed makeup (the Sensuous Man was having a fashion show at his beach house). The entire set needed to be decorated with gardenias (the Sensuous Man's favorite flower) and I was also appearing on the show to read poetry, so I needed to do my own hair and makeup. Also, the Sensuous Man's best friend, who was also a wine expert, was coming over to have a wine-tasting party with the Sensuous Man and his seven French models. That meant they needed fifteen different types of wine and beautiful wineglasses befitting the Sensuous Man.

I was sautéeing the onions and carrots, braising the veal, adding tomatoes, bay leaves, herbs and the red wine. Then I had to grate the lemons and chop more garlic for the gremolata sauce. I had already done the models' makeup and bought the wine. I still had to wash the new wineglasses.

Every time I looked over, Alan was sitting on the sidelines sipping red wine while the models paraded in front of him.

"Alan, ooh-la-la," they said in heavy French accents, "how do you like this?" They would model the lingerie they were wearing on the show. None of them was wearing any underwear. Nipples were everywhere. I kept grating lemons and chopping garlic.

"Try on the black one," Alan said to Nicole.

"Ooh, you nasty boy. You can see right through that one," she said.

"Ha ha ha ha," Alan laughed. He sipped more wine.

Mr. Bigshot, I thought. I burned my finger while stirring the braising veal.

"Would you like some wine, girls?" I heard Alan ask the models.

I was busy carefully placing fresh gardenias all over the set. Now I had to rewash all the wineglasses for the show, since Alan and the girls had used them all.

When all my work was done, after I had read today's poem to the Sensuous Man, I walked over to Alan and whispered in his ear, "I quit." He looked stunned.

I went back to our hotel room to think. I wanted to be taken more seriously. Not only by Alan but by those in his life; his co-workers, his children, even his roommate. I was grateful for the job Alan had given me, but I didn't like my lack of status. I wanted more, and I was determined to get it. I wasn't going to come to Montreal anymore. I was going home to make decisions about my own career. I had decided to really try. I was no longer content to be at Alan's beck and call. If he wanted me, we would have to live together with the intention that it was a trial for marriage. I wanted life on my terms. I wanted respectability and dignity. I wanted marriage *and* a successful career, and I was going to have it. I hoped I could have these things with Alan; but if not, I now knew I was lovable and desirable. I was determined to parlay my poetry book and my small but memorable role in *American Graffiti* into something else.

I told all of this to Alan when he arrived back at the hotel. He was not one to be pushed into anything. We spent a wordless night. I left the next morning.

59

I hadn't seen my sister for quite a while. We talked on the phone from time to time. I told her how good I was feeling. I told her about my new determination and how wonderful it was to be in therapy. I told her she should consider therapy.

Maureen was a good person, and she was raising four wonderful children. They always had dinner, they always had clean clothes, a nice home, a good life. Except, Maureen was drunk every night. I knew she hated herself for it. I knew she wanted to stop.

Maureen took my advice and went to a therapist, but it didn't work. It was the wrong therapist. He didn't understand alcoholism and the way it affects self-esteem. He just made her feel more guilty, so she didn't want to see him anymore.

Weekends were the worst where drinking was concerned. Maureen and Bill would go out on Saturday nights with their friends, and booze was a big part of it. Maureen went with a firm resolve, "I'm only going to drink wine tonight." She didn't realize that an alcoholic can't drink anything. The evenings always ended the same. Maureen got drunk, Bill got mad. (Bill had stopped drinking by this point.)

Once Bill was sober, it was very apparent what was wrong with Maureen. She had been drinking alcoholically for ten years. She was thirty-five. It had begun at twenty-five for her just as it had with Dad. It didn't take long for Maureen to become emotionally and spiritually dead. Nothing meant anything to her anymore. All she wanted was a drink to forget and escape from herself. The "hates" had started. She hated Mom, Dad, me. She loved her children but couldn't stop drinking even for them, so she hated herself. She could not find happiness anywhere; couldn't get her life together.

After years of hard work, Bill's real-estate business was finally becoming successful. On every block in San Bruno there was at least one or two Gilmartin Realty signs. They now had extra money for life's luxuries. One of their first purchases was a beautiful second home in

Lake Tahoe. It would eventually become a charming cobblestoned English Tudor, surrounded by tall pine trees situated right on the lake; but at the moment it was an old wreck—a fixer-upper.

Maureen and Bill decided to spend Thanksgiving at the new house. Years later Maureen told me what happened that weekend. It was November 25, 1975, which was also Dad's birthday. They invited their friends Jim and Rosemary and, of course, all their children.

Maureen did it right; like she always did. She prepared the turkey, Mother's recipe for dressing with herbs, Brussels sprouts, fresh cranberries and giblet gravy. She served the turkey on a large platter surrounded by baked crabapples. It looked just like *Better Homes and Gardens* magazine.

Everyone sat down at the beautiful table, and after saying grace and compliments to the chef, they began to feast on the cornucopia spread out before them. Maureen never ate. She drank wine, then more wine. When dinner was over, she was still drinking wine.

Her guests retired to the living room to sit in front of the fire, let their food digest and maybe take a little nap. Maureen wanted to party.

"What? Is the party over?" she asked. "I work all day in the kitchen, and all you want to do is sit here and sleep?" She was becoming belligerent. "Well, I'm gonna have another drink," she announced. "I guess you're all too good to have another drink with me."

This continued through the evening. The drunker she got, the more hostile she became. She insulted them individually and as a group. Then she zeroed in on Bill. Maureen felt very threatened by Bill since he had stopped drinking. She had lost her playmate. He was no fun to her sober. She could see the disgust in his eyes when he looked at her. She could see his pain, his helplessness. He wanted to help her, but he didn't know what to do.

Maureen verbally attacked Bill in front of their friends. She said all the ugliest, most hateful things she could think of. The more Bill ignored her, the more hateful she became. Her eyes had completely lost focus now. She had no idea what she was saying to anyone. She continued to lash out at all of them.

When drunks are hostile, it has nothing to do with their targets. Their belligerence is really self-hate. A drunk hates being a drunk. Everything they feel about themselves comes out in the form of foul-mouthed abuse, usually to the people they love the most.

Maureen called Dad. "Happy birthday, asshole," she said. "You'll probably never have another one, and I don't give a shit!" She hung up the phone. She yelled at anyone who would listen. She was now completely out of control. One by one her guests left the room and went to bed.

Bill tried to get Maureen upstairs. She continued to lash out and abuse him. "Get out of my life," she kept screaming. She was hysterical, abusive.

"You're just like your father," Bill yelled at her.

"I'd never be like that asshole," she yelled back. "He's a drunk! I hate what he's doing to Mother," she screamed.

"Well, look at you," Bill said. "Look at what you're doing to yourself *and* your mother *and* to us!"

"Oh, leave me alone," she slurred. "I don't need you! I don't need anyone! I want to be around people who drink!"

Maureen awoke the next morning to complete silence. She knew the house was filled with people, but there wasn't a sound. The memories of the previous night came flooding into her head—the shame, the guilt, the humiliation.

Maybe she wasn't as bad as she thought, she hoped. Maybe they won't remember. Maybe they'll forgive me, she prayed. She sat on the edge of her bed, her head throbbing, her stomach queasy, and realized the depth of her problem. She was alone. Alone and sick with a terrible disease.

How can I undo it? she thought. I'll tell them that if I ever act that way again, Bill should leave me and take the children. I'll promise them to be good. I'll never drink again, she thought. Maureen was terrified. She knew she had "gone over the line"; she was frightened that she would lose her husband and children.

I can't let that happen, she thought. They are my life. Without them I'll be alone. Alone and drunk and sick. The thought was so potent, so ugly, so horrifying. She had become everything she had always hated. She had become Dad.

Maureen suddenly realized that it was *her* responsibility to take charge of *her* life. She realized it was manipulative to put Bill in the position to "leave her if she ever acted that way again." It's not *his* responsibility to leave me and take the children. *I'm* not giving *me* another chance. I'm going to change my life. I'm going to be *sober!* she said to herself.

Maureen had grown up. Refusal to grow up is the common denominator of all alcoholics. She had gone to the bottom the night before and she didn't like it. She didn't like confronting the realities of her behavior.

Maureen spent a wordless day with her family and friends. The silence was deafening. What could she say? What could anyone say? It was just like all the days following Dad's belligerence when we were children. Everyone trying to find a way to live with the discomfort of their memories. There was no eraser.

The next night Danny and Mardi arrived. Danny got roaring drunk. Maureen lay in her bed listening to Danny downstairs ranting and raving, using all the foul language that Dad had used.

"You cocksucker, asshole, son of a bitch!" Just like Dad.

Maureen couldn't believe it. Danny's voice came from the back of his throat just like Dad's, his tone was the same, his inflections were the same, the obscenities were the same. Mardi was yelling at him just like Mom did, trying to drag him to bed, trying to get him to be quiet.

We've all become our worst nightmare, she thought. Bill was right. She did grow up to be just like our dad; she could tell by listening to Danny.

Maureen wished she could talk to Bill to tell him she was beginning to understand, but Bill had detached. He talked to her only when he had to, and then it was as if they were perfect strangers. She was all alone. She was afraid. She hoped it wasn't too late.

At dinner the following night Maureen announced, "I'm going to AA." There were no cheers, no hallelujahs. Everyone felt uncomfortable.

It was a courageous step for Maureen to take. She was really alone with this decision.

"Why do you want to go *there?*" Mardi asked.

"Just don't drink so much," Rosemary said.

No one in the family had ever gone this far. AA was for the bums of skid row. No one wanted Maureen hanging out with bums and drunks.

I've always admired Maureen's courage in taking this brave step. She had realized her deep loss—not only the detachment of her husband and children, but the loss of herself. All the shame, guilt and low self-esteem was looking right at her, and she didn't like it. Maureen was determined to get better. She was going to get her family back together, to regain their respect; but most of all, she was going to get *her* self-respect, her dignity. She was going to take responsibility for her own life.

60

Maureen started taking life "one day at a time." She attended AA meetings every day at first and was garnering great strength through the support of the group. But it was rough. All the painful memories came flooding back. She had spent ten years pushing her feelings away, anesthetizing her pain with booze. Now she had no choice but to remember and feel. Her self-esteem suffered terribly. "I had to get all dressed up to go to my meetings so I could feel better about myself," she told me. "It was demoralizing. Here I was in AA sitting next to all the old drunks I used to see in San Bruno. The sad part was I had always felt 'above' these people." Maureen never planned to drink like them. She drank to have fun, to be glamorous; and now here she was sitting next to the "lowlife."

"For the first five months all I could think about was wanting a drink. I wondered if I could ever fit into this life again," she said. "I went to two meetings a week. I wanted to go more often, but my family didn't like my being there. It frightened them. They didn't want to think I was that bad. I took long walks along the ocean. I read books—simple books like Robert Schiller's *Self-Love*. It was all I could handle, but these activities distracted me from my craving to drink again. One drink could take the pain away and erase the ugliness I was being forced to confront.

"Finally, after five months of meetings," Maureen continued, "I was able to admit everything and realized there was no one to blame but myself. I surrendered to the God that I understood and turned my life over to a higher power. I stopped fighting and accepted the fact of my alcoholism. I was powerless over alcohol. My life had become unmanageable, as they said at AA. I realized it was all right to feel the hurts and the pain, so I would never want to be sick again. I never wanted to go back to the way it was."

Maureen was amazed to realize the hold alcohol had on her. She had always thought booze was the answer to her problems. Booze had given her a false sense of confidence. It made her feel pretty and glamorous.

With a couple of drinks she was funny and glib. Now she learned that instead of booze being an answer, it was *the problem*. All her feelings had been fake. Sober she was regaining her confidence. She looked better and was socially acceptable. People flocked *to* her rather than turning away. Booze had made her vulgar; sober she was thoughtful and kind, sensitive and humble. Her God-given wit returned. She truly was funny and glib naturally.

She worked hard. Her life depended upon absorbing self-acceptance into her whole being. She was feeling relieved. Finally she was understanding what had happened to her and accepted it as a *disease*. There were no apologies necessary. She couldn't apologize for something that wasn't her fault.

She was finding happiness. Her beautiful blue eyes were clear again, her skin was losing the puffiness and she was feeling good about herself. AA taught her that alcoholism is an insidious disease. One drink leads to the next. Without treatment all alcoholics end in death or insanity. But we knew that. We were watching it happen at our parents' house.

Through Maureen's AA meetings she found the truck driver had just as much to say as the psychiatrist. It didn't matter who anyone was or what he did for a living. They were getting sober, and that is what she wanted. Sobriety was her priority.

Maureen encouraged Mother to go to Alanon. Alanon attendance was a stigma at that time; an admission that things were out of control in your private life. Maureen's involvement in AA made it easier for my mother to accept that she had a problem. Mother *had* to do something. Her life was in shambles.

Besides Dad's drinking, Michael, now fifteen years old, was using drugs and drinking. His behavior was irrational and erratic. He got into trouble with the police. I was afraid my mother would die from all the stress.

She was ready for help. Maureen's recovery coincided perfectly with my mother's readiness to make a change. Mother saw Maureen's AA meetings make a drastic change in her daughter's life. Mother realized there was an answer; maybe she, too, could get help.

With little urging, Mom went to her first Alanon meeting. She sat quietly in the back of the room listening. To her surprise, she realized for the first time she was not alone with her problems. All these other people had lived or were living the same life of horrors as herself; but they seemed relaxed and happy. They learned and were learning to take care of themselves. *They* were the important ones; not the alcoholic.

How can the alcoholic get better when the co-alcoholic is not better? She learned that once she got better, she would be strong enough to make the necessary choices about her life. For the first time Mom asked God to help *her*.

After a few Alanon meetings my mother stopped dragging Dad to bed. She had learned the first rule: Do not be an enabler. Do not enable the drinker to drink. Do not cover up for him or make up excuses for him. If he vomits, let him lie in it. Let the alcoholic become responsible for his own disease. This way, he might come to the conclusion that he wants to help himself. He also might choose to die. It was called "tough love." It was also survival.

"I was tired of feeling responsible for everyone else's problems," Mom told me. "I decided it was time to concentrate on me. I always felt guilty, I did nothing to change my life. The effects of the Alanon program were making a difference. It was a series of little miracles. Each day lifted another burden because I was changing my way of thinking of it. I took it 'one day at a time,' getting through each minute, each hour, each day. I was letting go and letting God take care of the future. Before Alanon I lived in the past or projected the woes to the future. Taking care of myself 'one day at a time' made my life so much easier. I had hope. Lurking in my subconscious was the feeling, 'There'll come a day . . .' I was beginning to understand acceptance of my power-lessness to change the alcoholic. But I could change my life and myself. *Self* is the only person anyone is capable of changing. I had had ex-pectations. I expected my husband to fill all my emotional needs, but I was fooling myself. Why did I get so hurt every time he got drunk? To protect myself, I built an impenetrable wall around my emotions. Therefore, it became very difficult to experience *any* emotions, except I could cry easily at being hurt. It was very difficult to talk of my emotions at first; but I saw the irreparable harm I had done to myself and others and vowed to spend the rest of my life trying to break down this wall. All my life I had been praying for courage and guidance, but I was never ready to act on that guidance. I had to open my mind to receive it and then have the confidence to use it.

"I no longer wanted to feel sorry for myself. I realized it only weakened my character and took away my dignity. Years of self-control were ready to explode. All that pent-up emotion—anger, love, hurt, shame, martyr-dom. It had been destructive. It paralyzed me. I had not been *living*, I had been *reacting* to my alcoholic husband. I was the sufferer and Dad was the punisher. Finally, I saw it for what it really was—masochism, not virtue."

This was a "new" mom. She was learning to let go and relax. "Why do women spend their whole lives trying to make drunks stop drinking?" she asked me one day. She was right. Why had she made it her problem?

It was part of the disease; assuming responsibility. The drunk in all our lives had made us feel we were only as good as his attitude toward us. Because he thought so little of himself, he projected this onto us; and we accepted it. If he was no good, we were no good.

But each of us were making tremendous emotional leaps. The whole family was sick with a terrible disease, and little by little we were recovering. Little by little we were understanding what had been wrong with us all these years. Even a glimpse brought great relief. To know we had been affected, then eventually infected, helped to nurse our collective ailing self-esteem. To get better was to feel better about ourselves.

Mardi was not doing well. She was depressed, angry and upset all the time. She didn't know what to do. She loved Danny so much but couldn't stand her life anymore. Mardi started asking Mother about Alanon. Mom was not the pushy type but suggested to Mardi she could get help for herself.

Maureen, Mom, Mardi, Auntie Helen and I had all been celebrating one another's birthdays for years. We went out to lunch and the birthday girl was treated by the rest of the group. We looked forward to these lunches. It was a time to connect; a time to discuss that which was on our minds. We trusted and loved one another.

We celebrated Maureen's fortieth birthday at Trader Vic's in San Francisco. She had a lot to celebrate. We all did. Maureen was getting better, Mom was getting better and so was I. As we clinked glasses, Mardi began to cry. We asked what was wrong, but we all knew the answer.

"I'm so jealous of you," Mardi said to Maureen. "I'm jealous 'cause you have a sober life and mine is falling apart." She told us she felt "hopeless." She knew she couldn't control Danny or the alcoholism. She told us she knew she had turned into an angry woman, but she couldn't help herself. She was mad all the time. Danny had changed, she said. He was becoming violent and belligerent when he was at home. It was so unlike him. He shadowboxed in his boxer shorts down the hall just like Dad used to, waking up the kids. He'd sit up all night drinking and talking to his dog.

"You become what you grow up with," Mother said quietly. She knew better than anyone that Danny was playing out a scene he had witnessed over and over as a child. Mother started to cry.

"Come with me to Alanon," she said to Mardi. "Everyone there is hurting the same way. It helps to share your feelings. I know I'm able to feel better about myself since I've gone."

Mardi was desperate and had to do something. They decided they would attend her first meeting that evening.

Mardi sat and listened that night; and when it was her turn to talk, she felt angry.

"I want to talk about him," she said. "There's nothing wrong with me! I want to know how to get that son of a bitch sober and now!"

She felt angry with the group. She felt they were focused on the wrong person. She was there to get her husband sober. She hadn't realized his disease had become her disease. She was on a merry-go-round.

"If you wouldn't drink so much, I wouldn't yell," she'd scream at Danny.

"Well if you wouldn't yell so much, I wouldn't drink," he'd holler back.

Round and round they went. Who was the sickest?

"This is a program for *you* and not the alcoholic," she was told. "One of you has to get better, and you have no control over him, so you'd better work on yourself. You will have to detach with love to get better. You have choices. As you get stronger, you will realize that you can stay or leave him. Whatever you can live with. It is your right to be happy. You don't have to be sick along with him."

Danny hated Mardi going to Alanon. "You go there and hang out all our dirty laundry," he'd say.

But something was changing. Mardi wasn't yelling back. She wasn't fighting anymore. She got off the merry-go-round.

Mom and Mardi depended upon each other during this time. They went to as many meetings as were needed each week. They were getting better together. They needed each other for strength. Each of their husbands were getting worse.

61

"You don't need to come to therapy anymore," Mrs. Kilgore said to me. "It's time to be on your own. You can handle it now. Your self-esteem has improved tremendously. Your priorities are in order. You're looking at life realistically. You seem to understand your crisis cycle."

I protested vehemently. "I still have so many questions. There are still areas of confusion." I felt like my mother was pushing me out of the nest.

"You'll never really grow up if you don't let go," she said. "I'll be here. If things go wrong or you need help, you can always call me."

I still hadn't connected growing up with an alcoholic parent to my problems as an adult. It would be many years before I would piece that ✳ togehter. But for the time being, Mrs. Kilgore had me in good shape. I understood my patterns and didn't want to repeat them. I wanted to be well and productive.

Yet I felt sad. It was the end of something; but it also the beginning. I didn't have the words to tell her the positive influence she had been on my life. She had helped *me* save *my* life. I knew in my heart I was ready to make my life work. I was ready to "go for it." I also knew I *had* to do it on my own.

I felt tears well up in my eyes. Impulsively I hugged Mrs. Kilgore. "Thank you for everything," I whispered. "I'm going to be just fine," I said.

"I know you will," she answered.

Once released I felt great. Free to begin my new life. I knew how far I had come. I felt strong. Ready to explode. I was going to demand a lot of the rest of my life. I wanted to make the most of it.

This new strength, this new surge of self-esteem was what those around me noticed.

Mom, Maureen, Mardi and I became closer than ever before during this time. We had a new language. We were celebrating a new chance at life, an opportunity to find true inner peace and happiness.

We knew we each had a long way to go, but now we were all learning that *we* were in control of our own lives. That *we* could make it whatever *we* wanted it to be.

I had made the difficult and frightening decision to move to L.A. I told Alan, and I let him know that if he didn't want to live with Bruce and me, it would be over between us. It was time, and I would accept it no other way.

He said, "I'm not ready. Too soon."

I said, "Then you'll never be ready. You either know or you don't."

I knew he loved me. I knew I loved him, but I didn't want it to continue the way it was. We had a lot to work out. In all these years we had virtually excluded one another's children from our relationship. I was ready to know and love his children.

There would have to be a lot of patience and understanding, but it was time to be realistic. We both had children. If we were to have a future together, it included them. We could all get along and learn to love one another if we tried real hard. I was willing, ready. I wanted Alan to be willing and ready also.

Alan backed off from me. "Fine," I said. "I'll make it on my own. I've been on my own for a long time, and I'm determined to make a success with my life. I'd like to do it with you because I love you, but you have to listen to your heart and do what's right for you."

It would take time for me to move. I needed money. I had to keep paying my bills and I needed enough money to rent a U-Haul truck for my things. I also needed money for first and last month's rent on my new place (wherever that would be).

I was booked on "The Tonight Show" about every six weeks. It amazed me. Johnny really liked talking to me. I would read poetry and make him laugh. He told me I was "refreshing." We did touching demos, playing on the title of my book. We touched everything you could legally touch on television. I became know as the "touching lady."

This new notoriety got me an interview at KGO-TV. If I got the job, I would be the hostess on the San Francisco morning show. This interview represented a dilemma to me. If I got it, I would not be able to turn down a steady salary and such an opportunity. But I had already made my decision to move to Los Angeles. I'll go on the interview and see what happens, I thought.

Alan didn't believe I would end our relationship. It was hard being strong during this time. He had moved out of his friend Leonard's house and into his own apartment in Beverly Hills. There was room enough for Bruce and me, yet Alan still would not commit to me. I hadn't heard from him for a while and was resigned to the fact that our relationship might be over. Everything in my apartment reminded me of Alan. An ashtray from the Persian Room, the Chinese trunk he had given me for Christmas, the caftans we bought together on vacation, an Eskimo carving from Vancouver, matchbooks from Le Colibri and Mamounia in Montreal. It had been a glorious love affair. It was going to be difficult without him. I would miss all the wonderful times we had cooking for each other. I would miss the laughing. We laughed so much when we were together.

Alan always made me forget my troubles, but I knew in my heart what I needed from him. If after all this time (seven years) he still was not ready to commit to me, our laughter would soon turn to anger. We would become opposing forces rather than a united front. If it had to end, I'd rather it end with love and respect. I had learned to truly love through Alan. I had learned to know what I wanted from a man through Alan. I was grateful for our time together.

I continued to pack my things; Bruce's pottery pieces from the arts center, our photo albums, the Peruvian rug that hung over the fireplace, my hippie pillows, Bruce's Cub Scout hat.

Karen Carpenter was singing on the radio, "We've only just begun." That's true, I thought. "A kiss for luck and we're on our way," Karen continued. The phone rang.

"Hi," Alan said.

"Hi," I said warmly. I wondered if I would always love him.

"I love you," he said. "I miss you, and I want you to come live with me. I haven't been able to resolve my guilt about living with your son and not living with my children, but I don't want to be apart from you anymore. I want to try and make it together."

I felt a flood of emotion. "We'll make it work," I said, "and when the time is right, your children can live with us. Until that time, we can share custody."

Life had taken the most positive turn. Alan was the love of my life, and now we were going to give ourselves a chance to spend our lives together.

In June 1974, Bruce and I piled all our worldly belongings into our rented U-Haul truck. My brother Michael and my friend Doris helped me. Doris said she would come to L.A. with me for a few days to help me settle in. Bruce and Thomas kept hugging each other and saying good-bye. Theirs had been an important friendship. They were both extremely sad to know that they were going to be separated by six hundred miles. They knew their friendship wouldn't be the same.

The phone rang. "Hello," I said.

"You got the job as hostess for the A.M. show," my agent said.

The information stopped me. I looked around. My life was in motion. Boxes were going out the front door, the couch was being lifted into the truck and Alan had committed his love to me.

"Tell them," I answered, "tell them that I *really* appreciate the offer, but something else has come up that I just can't refuse."

I looked around our little apartment. I had loved this place. It had been our home for the last five years. The final box went out to the truck. The apartment was now an empty shell, ready for the next family to bring life into it. I closed the door and walked to my car.

"Want me to drive?" Doris asked.

"Yes, I think you better," I said.

Michael would be behind us driving the U-Haul truck. Doris started the ignition. I turned on the radio to kill the silence that had filled our little car. Karen Carpenter started singing again,

> *Sharing horizons that are new to us,*
> *Watching the sun along the way,*
> *Talkin' it over, just the two of us,*
> *Workin' together day by day.*
>   *Together*
> *We've only just begun.*

As we crossed the Golden Gate Bridge, I looked in the backseat. Bruce looked sad and frightened.

"Come up here, honey. Sit on Mommy's lap."

Bruce climbed over the seat; he was getting big now—eight years old. He put his arms around my neck. I looked behind us. Marin County was getting smaller and smaller.

Good-bye Sausalito, I thought. Good-bye San Francisco. Good-bye to all the pain and trauma, and good-bye to all the good things.

I had grown up a lot in the last few years. It had been an important time for me. Now I was leaving for a whole new life. The man I loved was waiting, and the opportunity to pursue my career lay ahead of me.

I placed my lips on the side of Bruce's head. His face was buried in my neck, and I could feel the wetness of his tears. Karen Carpenter was still singing, "A kiss for luck and we're on our way." I hugged Bruce real tight.

"Don't worry, sweetheart," I whispered. "It's going to be great. We're going to love Los Angeles."

Epilogue

Here I am today in 1987 looking back over the last thirteen years with amazement and gratitude. Miraculous changes have taken place in my life and in the lives of those I love.

Everyone in my family is now recovering. Maureen was first, then my mother found peace through Alanon. My dad followed, then Danny and finally Michael.

I married Alan and my career took off beyond my wildest dreams. I was the star of the number-one television show in America, which gave me the visibility for a diverse, multifaceted career, including headlining in Las Vegas with my nightclub act.

Recently, while I was still working on this book, the American Lung Association gave its annual charity dinner-dance and asked if I would entertain. Coincidentally, my sister was involved in organizing this evening. The dinner was being held in the Grand Ballroom of the Marriott Hotel near San Francisco. It was a unique opportunity to go back home in the way I had always dreamed.

On the evening of the big event, I peeked from behind the curtain to look at the sold-out audience. I saw a sea of familiar faces; and there in front of me was my entire family. My mother looked so proud, so beautiful in her emerald-green silk gown. My dad was seated next to my mother, dressed in his tuxedo. His entire table was laughing hysterically and I knew he had been entertaining them.

I looked around me. I had brought a thirty-six-piece orchestra, eight dancers, and had ten costume changes. The lights were trucked in from Los Angeles along with enough sound equipment to fill a stadium. The energy in the room could have created an earthquake. Everyone was excited. I was "one of theirs," and I wanted this to be the best show I had ever given.

The overture started. I could feel the adrenaline boiling in my toes. Soon it would shoot through my body and try to explode out my skull. I was excited and more nervous than for any performance I had ever given in Las Vegas. The lights dimmed, a hush came over the audience, my backup singers started a cappella . . .

> *I'm feeling good from my head to my shoes,*
> *Know where I'm goin', and I know what to do,*
> *I've tidied up my point of view,*

Then I sang offstage . . .

> *I've got a new attitude.*

The drums began. *Boom! Boom! Boom! Boom!* The orchestra came in full blast while Alan announced excitedly, "Ladies and gentlemen, Suzanne Somers!"

I walked on stage to thunderous applause and cheering. I looked at my mom, my dad, Maureen, Danny, Michael and Bruce. I could feel them. They were touching me and I was touching them. I began to sing.

> *I'm wearing a new dress, new hat*
> *Brand-new ideals, as a matter of fact,*
> *I've changed for good!*

I *had* changed for good, and I couldn't help but think how far we had all come. In 1975, shortly after I moved to Los Angeles, my grandfather died. I cried like a baby when my sister told me. I had loved Father so. Hours before his death, Father took my mother in his arms and told her how much he loved her. Then he said, "Your husband is a good man. He just doesn't know what he wants out of life." Father was forgiving Dad—an important lesson to all of us; for without forgiveness, none of us could ever really get better. I wish Father could have lived a while longer to see the changes that were about to take place in our family. He had been so burdened watching the family disintegration. Nothing in the world would have brought him more happiness than to see what happened next.

> *Somehow the wires uncrossed*
> *The tables were turned*
> *Never knew I had such a lesson to learn.*

I looked at Maureen; beautiful and blond in her red sequined gown and silver-fox full-length coat. Her skin looked so smooth and clear, her blue eyes so bright I could see their sparkle from the stage.

Maureen was the first one in the family to stand up and say she was powerless over alcohol. She was the first one to realize she had a very serious disease. She was the first one to go for help. Maureen is our hero. She led Mom to Alanon; and as Mom was recovering, Mardi followed. Her sobriety was an example to Dad and eventually to Danny.

My sister has been sober for twelve years. As I continued to sing, I could see Bill put his arm around Maureen. He was so proud of her. She is one of the most admired and respected women in her community, devoting much of her time and energies to countless charitable activities. She quietly helps other alcoholics to recover.

A lot of people are sober today because of Maureen. She says alcoholism has given her life worth. Now it has meaning. She is a catalyst, an instrument. She takes no credit. "I'm happy to have been used and will continue to be."

Her home is the core of the family, the gathering place. She loves to entertain, she loves music and laughter and dancing. She dances with such freedom and abandon, you would think she'd have to have a couple of drinks to get so loose. But she's on a natural high; high on life, grateful for her recovery, grateful for the support and love of her family. Her marriage is strong; her children look up to her and ask her advice. She really loves Bill and is proud of him and his achievements. He is one of the most successful real-estate investors in the Bay Area. "I was never going to be drunk much longer in front of him," she says. "I would do anything to make Bill proud of me. Once he stopped drinking, it was so apparent to me what was wrong. If I hadn't stopped, I probably wouldn't be alive today. It's a killer disease. It kills the spirit and then takes the body."

'Cause I've got love like I never, never knew.

Maureen was so keyed up from the music, she could hardly sit still. I admired her strength, her character, her determination to get the most out of life. She was a winner, adored by her husband, her children and four grandchildren. I felt so proud of her; my sister, my teacher, my friend.

Ooh, ooh, ooh, ooh, oooh, I've got a new attitude.

I saw my mother's hands clapping along enthusiastically. This shy, demure, unassuming, *gallant* woman. She kept the family together. She hung in there "in sickness and in health." She made good on her commitment; now, finally after all these years, she has the life she always wanted. "All my dreams have come true," she told me. "I'm so proud of my children; Dad and I have fun together again; I feel peaceful and happy. Each day is wonderful."

Had she never gone to Alanon, none of this could have been possible. She decided to get better no matter what Dad chose to do. As she recovered, she found her original zest for life, her strength, her determination. I never realized how strong my mother was. No matter how sick we all became, none of us wanted to disappoint her. She never stopped believing in us, and this belief gave us our strength to get better.

Alanon changed her life. In looking over her diary, I found this piece written on December 21, 1976. It says . . . "I am basking in serenity because of sobriety. My mind is filled with gratitude to my higher power and the people in Alanon who are responsible for bringing this about. I do not question. I do not expect too much; but everything is happening to bring about this peace. I have prayed and made novenas and had just about given up but decided to try Alanon as a last-ditch stand. I had been looking at condominiums and apartments with the idea of moving out, and then this happened. Because of my nature I know I should be worrying about things, but this inner peace surrounds me. Maybe I have earned it."

> *I'm in control*
> *My troubles are few,*
> *'Cause I've got love like I never never knew!*

I was so proud of my mother. Gathered around her table were her children and grandchildren. She was beaming. They all adored her. No longer did Mom stoop in shame. Now she held her head high, her body erect.

In my mind I could hear her saying to me as a little girl, "Stand up straight, Suzanne, stomach in, chest out."

I thought of all the musicals Mom and I used to attend. I thought of her playing the piano and encouraging me to sing along. I thought of all the beautiful clothes she made for me. I thought of her values, her sense of decency, her faith. She has been such a good mother; so supportive, so caring. Everyone in the family adores her. She has a rich life and she deserves it. She still belongs to her bridge club and now looks forward to having the ladies at her house. She takes china painting classes, tap-dance lessons and teaches Catechism at St. Robert's Catholic School. She works part time at the hospital and recently went back to school to get her certificate as a medical transcriber.

She always thought her children could do anything. Because she never squelched my dreams, because she never put any limitations on my abilities, I was able to take my life on a course that has brought me complete satisfaction and contentment. Mother always said, "Good things come to those who wait." I now realize she was right. She had to wait a long time, but what a prize. She struggled through a difficult disease and never gave up. She is again the woman she was; happy, enthusiastic, proud. The sadness is gone from her eyes, her face is soft and pink again. She looks radiant and is very happy. She keeps working on herself, knowing that healing is a lifetime process. She accepts alcoholism as a disease over which all of us were powerless; and she thanks God for answering her prayers.

I've tidied up my point of view,
I've got a new attitude.

I looked at my dad. It was hard to believe he was the same man I grew up with. He's such a wonderful person now. He stopped drinking in 1976. He wasn't given any ultimatums. There were no verbal threats of divorce. My mother just stopped "rescuing" him. She learned to "detach with love" through Alanon. This seeming indifference was powerful enough for my dad to realize he was no longer going to be the focal point of the family. Through my mother's detachment, Dad was free to be as drunk as he wanted, as belligerent as he wanted, as obnoxious as he wanted.

"Go ahead, kill yourself with your booze," was the unspoken statement. Mother learned that she was free to live *her* life on *her* own terms. The disease belonged to Dad. She no longer had to be sick along with him.

For the first time, Mother *seriously* considered divorce. She never had to say anything to Dad; he could sense it. He sensed her sadness at his disease, her love for him, her new ability to detach and her unwillingness to continue living this way.

The healthier Mom became, the worse Dad became. He sat in a stupor for days watching television and drinking. His only friend in the world was his dog Alice. We had all given up on him. The dog went everywhere with him. She listened to his unintelligible ramblings. He would take her to his favorite bar, coincidentally called the Dog House, and Alice would walk home with him. She didn't care that he stumbled and fell. She sat patiently by his side until he picked himself up and continued on.

Maureen told Mom about a recovery house called Duffy's in Calistoga, California. Duffy himself was a recovering alcoholic who has devoted his life to sobriety and helping other alcoholics to recover.

Mom knew through Alanon that she couldn't make Dad do anything, but she knew he needed help or he would die.

In Dad's stupor he said to his dog Alice, "Maybe I should go to one of these places on TV." He had been watching the Raleigh Hills commercials (a place for alcoholics to recover).

Mom seized the opportunity and told him she'd be happy to drive him to Duffy's. Even though he was drunk, she had brought up the subject.

"Sure, I'll go," Dad slurred. He probably thought it was a bar.

The next morning when Dad was sober, Mom told him what he had said.

Dad must have been thinking about it for some time, and he was ready. He told her that, indeed, he would go and that he would like to go right away. Dad packed up a small bag, grabbed a six-pack of beer, his dog Alice and got in the car. By the time they arrived at Duffy's, Dad was so drunk, he fell off the porch.

"I'm here to get sober," he announced drunkenly.

He picked himself up, said good-bye to Mom and Alice and walked inside.

Duffy attacked my dad's pride. "You're a hell of an example for an Irishman," he said. "You look like a slob."

It was a great place to start with my dad. He had always been a proud man, proud of being Irish, proud of his accomplishments, proud of his family.

"You've got too much class to be a drunk," Duffy said. "If you hang around with fourth-class people and in fourth-class places, you become a fourth-class person. If you hang around first-class people and in first-class places, you become a first-class person. How do you want to go through life? First-class or fourth?"

In the weeks that followed, Duffy gave my dad a desire to clean up his life. "Life isn't the easiest trip in the world. You have to have a desire to *live*. Grab the gusto. You only live once, so you gotta get every bit out of it; and you can't get it if you're drunk."

Duffy gave my dad the twelve steps as an alcoholic's code of conduct.

A guide for living. He asked my dad, "Would you like to know someone who adheres to these principles? The twelve steps are a code for becoming a decent human being. When you become a decent human being, you become attractive and people like you. Just *trying* makes you better. It doesn't take education or brains; *anybody* can be nice."

Duffy's program was all about a new way of life. How to be a decent good person. When you begin to love yourself in a nonegotistical way, you become satisfied with being the very best person you can be. Once this happens, there is no need to be drunk or stoned. Once you accept yourself, you can say, this is what I am and I accept and love me.

It didn't take long. Within a few weeks of this program, Dad put aside thirty-five years of alcoholism and chose sobriety. It was a miraculous recovery. The only one who wasn't thrilled with Dad's new sobriety was his dog Alice. She knew and loved the drunk Dad. She was used to being the total object of his slobbering attention. She had loved it.

Now, he didn't stay up with her all night. They didn't walk to the bar together anymore. Dad's attentions were focused on himself, his wife, his family. He worked on getting better. It was his priority. It was the most important thing in his life. Alice went through terrible depression and withdrawal.

When Dad came out of Duffy's, they told him, "Keep going to meetings." Maureen had been in AA for one year; and in order to truly get better, it was now time for her to tell her story for the first time.

Her meeting that night coincided with Dad's first meeting. It was the most difficult day of her life. She lay on the floor of her bathroom that afternoon hyperventilating. She could not get her breath because she was so frightened.

That night she stood up in front of a group of people at AA, including Dad, and said, "My name is Maureen, and I'm an alcoholic.

"I'm going to tell you what happened, what it was like and what it's like now," Maureen continued with emotion. She told the group that she came from an alcoholic family, that three out of four children were alcoholics. "My dad's sister died of alcoholism. Another brother died making bathtub gin, and another brother had been lying in a hospital for years because he fell off the stairway in a drunken stupor and landed on his head." There were more alcoholics in the family, she told them.

She told the group she never planned to be an alcoholic. She drank to have fun, to be the "life of the party." She thought she could drink and not be like Dad. She had grown up with drinking and she hated it. She never thought her drinking was as bad as Dad's. She didn't plan to be the awful, hostile drunk that he was; and, yet, that was what she became.

Maureen continued her talk, telling the group the specifics of her behavior, baring her soul, nakedly exposing her emotions. With tears in her eyes, she looked right at Dad and talked to him.

"For the first time in my life, Dad, I realize that my alcoholism is a *disease* and so is yours. We had no choice. Once it started, there was no way to stop it. I've been mad at you all these years, and now I realize we have the same disease. If I'm asking everyone to understand me, I realize I can't get better until I understand you. You couldn't help it, and I forgive you. I hope you can forgive me."

Maureen and Dad had tears running down their faces. So did everyone in the room.

Maureen then told the group that she is now a grateful alcoholic, that she had become her own person because of her disease. She told them she was a better, stronger person. She had to get to know herself on her own; and because of it, her life was now whole and complete. She told the group that she had all the choices back then that she has now but that she had to go through all of this to get where she is today.

I'm in control, my troubles are few.

Dad has been sober now for ten years. He is loving, kind, thoughtful, witty and charming. He is the center of attention again, the "life of the party," but for all the right reasons.

Once again, Dad's house is the cutest, sweetest house on the whole block; maybe in the whole town. It's an Irish green color with white trim and white shutters. Lavender bougainvillea follows the windows and banisters. Pots of pink geraniums line the upper porch. It's not the same house in which we were raised. Mom and Dad moved a few blocks away to a new home; "a step up." Now they have three bedrooms, two baths and a two-car garage. Dad is real proud of his vegetable garden and grows the most delicious cherry tomatoes I've ever tasted. He keeps busy taking care of the gardens, running errands and socializing with his friends.

He has lots of friends and is always ready with a joke to make them laugh. He acts out his stories with the energy and timing natural to an entertainer. One block from Mom and Dad's home is the Senior Citizens' Center where Dad hangs out in the afternoons. There is usually a game of pool, cards or even dancing to occupy him; and he still has the ability to dazzle an entire room with his humor and antics.

My mom and dad are having a wonderful life together. Dad loves my mother and tells anyone and everyone who will listen. Mom blushes characteristically when he does this, but I know she likes it. She loves him, too. They need and take care of each other. Dad likes to pamper Mom. He brings her coffee in bed along with the *San Francisco Chronicle.*

They go out dancing and show up all the "youngsters" at family weddings and get-togethers. There are lots of parties again, usually at my sister's house. All the grandchildren and great-grandchildren gather around Dad and ask him to tell jokes and stories about the old days in Butcher Town.

I have wonderful talks with Dad once or twice a week by telephone. I've finally gotten to know him, and what a pleasure. The qualities that kept all of us loving him through the "terrible years" have emerged. He is special. He makes me laugh; he sends little cards in the mail telling me how much he loves me.

Dad cries easily these days; watching a movie, seeing one of his children accomplish something starts the tears flowing. His voice still trembles when he talks about the day Alice died. He has a lot of emotion, a lot of feeling and cares about his family more than anything in the world.

I never thought it could be possible. Through this experience I learned not to lose hope, ever, no matter how dismal the outlook.

Dad takes his disease "one day at a time," knowing it doesn't go away. An alcoholic remains an alcoholic forever. The disease is always ready to reappear.

Dad is one of the lucky ones; he's recovering and is grateful. He doesn't remember much about "the drunk years," except he lost an entire block of his life, a thirty-five-year blackout. He is sad about that but lives in the present, letting the past rest, and he enjoys each day as it comes.

> *I'm feelin' good from my head to my shoes,*
> *Know where I'm goin' and I know what to do.*

Sitting to the left of Dad was Danny. The combination of his blond good looks, his clear blue eyes, his great physical shape, and his brand-new tuxedo was a pretty devastating package. His smile was infectious, and he smiled all the time. It was hard to imagine that life had been anything but roses for him.

"When I drank," he said laughing, "I felt I could talk to anyone. I was sure I could give the president good advice on running the country, and he'd listen. When I was sober, I had nothing to say. I didn't feel as good as anyone."

Not only was Danny an alcoholic, but he was also the adult child of an alcoholic. While battling his addiction, he also suffered all the classic symptoms of the child of the addict; low self-esteem, insecurity, nervousness, crises, inability to get close to people. It took Danny a long time to get better.

In 1980 Dad and Maureen had been sober for four and five years respectively. Danny was not. In fact, he was drinking more than ever. Danny had been sick for four days from drinking an entire half gallon of vodka. He was coughing up blood. It was a bad sign.

Mardi called Maureen and told her, "I'm not coming to Easter dinner. I can no longer play the charade. Everyone loves Danny so much and acts like everything is okay. Everything is *not* okay, and I *cannot* pretend anymore."

"Well, if anyone is not coming, it should be Danny," Maureen said. "We've got to help him."

"What can we do?" Mardi asked desperately. She knew through Alanon she couldn't force Danny to get better.

"Well, we can't just sit here and watch him die," Maureen said. "Let's try an intervention. Maybe he's ready. It's worth the chance. We've got nothing to lose. He can't get any worse."

That morning Mardi, her children Sean and Erin, Maureen, her children Billy, Tim and Joey, and Mom and Dad walked into Danny's house. He was sober because he was sick. He knew by the look on their faces something was up. His eyes darted.

"What's this?" he asked as he backed up into the living room. He continued to back up through the dining room and into the kitchen. He settled into a chair next to the garage door, giving himself an "out" if he wanted to run. His eyes registered fear, like those of a trapped rabbit.

"Dan, we're here to help you. We've all come because we love you, and we know you don't want to be this way," Maureen said.

"What does that mean?" Danny asked.

"We want to take you someplace to get better."

"Where to?" Danny asked.

"Duffy's."

"Why?" Danny asked again.

"Because people are calling us and asking us why we don't do something to help. We are all afraid something will happen to you. We're afraid you'll kill yourself if you don't get better. We're begging you to ask for help. You're not alone. We're with you, and we love you."

Mardi and her children were too overcome with grief to talk.

"Do you know what you've been doing?" Maureen continued. "Do you know when you stay up all night drinking that you call people on the phone? Do you know what you've been saying to them? Do you know your daughter Erin watched you *crawl* up the walkway the other night because you were too drunk to walk? Do you know she watched the police pick you up and bring you down to the station for drunk driving?"

Dad had not said a word yet. "Dan, you're gonna miss the boat," Dad said, his voice trembling. "You've gotta get well now, before you're forty, or your whole life will be gone."

Danny looked at Dad and started to cry. It was an emotional moment for all of them. No one wanted to hurt Danny, but they loved him too much not to try to help.

In his sadness Danny still resisted. "But what about my business?" he asked.

"What difference does it make? You're never there anymore. Mardi's never there. She's always in Lodi at her mother's house trying to get away from you. We'll all help out. We'll work at your store. We'll keep it going until you're better," Maureen said.

They all stood there in silence. Finally, Danny looked up. "Let's go right now," he said quietly.

The timing had been right. Danny was willing to be helped.

It was humiliating for Danny to realize that everyone in the family "knew" he was an alcoholic. He thought it was his secret and his alone. He never wanted Mom to know. He wanted her to be proud of him. He hadn't made the connection between his floundering business and his alcoholism. He hadn't realized how adversely it affected his wife and children. He didn't realize the pain and shame they were experiencing by being an alcoholic family. It was the last thing he ever would have done to his family. He loved them. He knew how alcoholism had affected his childhood, and now his alcoholism had brought unhappiness to his family.

Everyone walked out of Danny's house and got into their cars. A procession of family took Danny to Calistoga. Danny looked in his rearview mirror and saw Maureen with a big smile on her face. She was so happy knowing that Danny was willing and now had the opportunity to get help.

After lunch in St. Helena they all drove over to Duffy's. Mardi went inside to help Danny register. They didn't know which one was the patient. Mardi looked so bad, so stressed. She had not slept for days. Duffy's thought Danny was checking Mardi in to recover. They were able to laugh about that. They also laughed when Danny realized he had packed nothing but socks.

Already things were feeling better. Relief flooded through Mardi. She kissed her husband good-bye and told him she loved him. Then she left.

Dan has now been sober for six years. His business has flourished, his marriage is successful and his children are happy and doing well. He says Mardi is his "best friend." She makes him laugh, he can talk to her. "I think she gets more beautiful all the time, and that comes from the inside." Mardi isn't angry anymore; her face is relaxed.

Best of all, Dan is content, satisfied, happy with himself and his life. He quietly helps other alcoholics to recover, showing through his example how much fun life can be without booze. He has lots of friends, he plays golf two and three times a week. He loves to laugh, he loves to dance, he loves to have fun. Dan is involved with many community projects and charities and is known by everyone as "the nicest guy you would ever hope to meet."

> *Ooh, ooh, ooh, ooh, oo-oo-ooh!*
> *I've got a new attitude.*

Michael was sitting on the edge of his seat keeping time to the music. In a way, Michael had come the furthest. He had endured Dad's disease in the final years, the sickest part. He had been psychologically battered, and it would take a long time for the scars to go away. Dad felt so guilty over Michael. He devoted himself to taking care of him. Dad knew Michael had suffered the worst of his alcoholism, and Michael had come out of it with very low self-esteem. He thought he was dumb, a loser.

He handled his insecurities by using drugs and drinking. No one ever saw him drunk or stoned, but the evidence was all around; drunk driving, jail, inability to keep a job. His girlfriend became pregnant, which added additional pressures.

Dad got on Michael's back. "Shape up," he'd say. "Don't do your job half-assed. Lay off the booze."

Dad gave Michael money, had his teeth fixed and invited Michael, the new wife and baby to live with them. Dad did all these things out of love and guilt, but it enabled Michael to continue drinking and using. It went on for years.

Finally, through the information Mom and Dad had from AA and Alanon, they set Michael free; told him he was on his own.

Michael became a heavy cocaine user coupled with drinking. He was on a self-destructive path. His marriage ended in divorce, and now he had the additional burden of alimony and child support for his two children.

A year later his new girlfriend had a baby, then another baby. She also had three children from her previous marriage. Michael couldn't keep a job. His ex-wife wouldn't allow him to see his children unless he paid child support, but he had no money. He used more drugs.

Cocaine made him feel crazy. All his repressed feelings came out in the form of tantrums.

"I hate Dad," he screamed at his girlfriend. "I don't care if he dies. I hope he does."

So much unresolved anger. When he *was* sober, he didn't feel "good enough." He didn't have the confidence to try for a decent job. He isolated himself from the family. He knew if he came around, he would stick out too much.

Everyone was getting better, putting their lives back together. National attention was being focused on the family because of my success on "Three's Company." It was overwhelming for Michael. He retreated further and further into himself and his disease.

His girlfriend, Terry, tried to help. They talked about his past. She let him rant and rave.

"Get it out," she would say. Finally, Michael had someone listening to him.

In 1982 Michael's youngest child, Jamie, was rushed to the hospital. He had a serious heart condition and was not given much hope for living. It was this trauma that snapped Michael into reality. He had not been able to see his first two children for over three years because of nonpayment, and now he faced losing another child. Michael knew if Jamie lived, he would need lots of care and support. Michael vowed to himself to "clean up his act." He would stop drugs and drinking. He didn't want to lose any more time out of his life. Luckily, Jamie survived the operation.

Michael has been sober now for three years. He has pulled himself out of his pool of booze and narcotics with the help and support of his parents and girlfriend. His relationship with Dad has flourished. They have a particular love and affection for each other. Dad said he can now "rest easy, relax a little." It was the end of the war for Dad and for all of us when Michael recovered. The end, the new beginning.

Michael leads a good life, living in the Sierra foothills of northern California. He enjoys his work, loves his seven children and has a caring, supportive, loving relationship with Terry.

I've got a new attitude!

The audience cheered. They wanted more, and I was going to give it to them.

"Thank you, thank you," I said. "This is a very special evening for me. All the people I love most in the whole world are in this room tonight, and I want you to meet them."

I walked into the audience. I worked my way through the chairs and tables. The spotlight followed me. I saw Auntie Helen and kissed her. I saw all my nephews—Bill, Tim, Joe and Sean. Bill and Tim were married now. Erin had blossomed into a beautiful young woman. I chuckled out loud and said, "I've changed diapers on everyone sitting at this table." The audience laughed. I saw some old schoolmates and neighbors; the man who used to work at Albert's grocery store, the San Francisco chief of police.

I reached my parents' table. "This is my feisty little dad." The audience clapped warmly. Dad stood up, waved to the people and kissed me. "I love you, Dad," I said.

"And I love you too, Sue." He was bursting with pride.

"And this is my beautiful, sweet mother." More applause. Mom was shaking. It made her nervous to be the focal point, but she glowed. She stood tall; stomach in, chest out.

"I love you, darling," she said.

"And I love you, Mom," I said as I hugged her.

"Hello, Bill," I said to my brother-in-law. He gave me a big hug. I had always really liked Bill. I moved on. "In case you're wondering, ladies and gentlemen, this is not Robert Redford. This is my brother Dan." Danny had tears in his eyes. He put his arms around me and held me tight. "I've always thought you were the greatest," I said to him, "and I've always had the maddest crush on you." Danny laughed, so did the audience. He was so choked up he could hardly talk. "If you couldn't marry me," I continued, "I'm glad you married Mardi." I kissed Mardi.

"Yeah, your brother likes brunettes," she said laughingly. She looked gorgeous all in silver and white.

Michael looked as though he'd like to disappear into the floor, and yet I knew he wanted me to acknowledge him. He is much like Mother in that he is so shy. I put my arms around him. "I love you, Mike," I said.

"I love you, too, Sue," he answered.

We had been through a lot together. We were the babies of the family, and our arrival coincided with the worst of Dad's drinking. Michael blushed, but the triumph in his eyes was unmistakable. He was making it.

I was still holding Michael's hand as I asked, "Where is my sister?"

"Right here, right here!" I heard her familiar voice behind me. "I'm so proud of you tonight," Maureen said as she stood. Her voice was trembling, tears were running down her face. "The feeling in this room is magical, and it's because of you. You make us feel so good and so special."

Now I was starting to cry. The audience was hanging on every word. They were enjoying being a part of this intimacy.

"We can't stand here and cry," I said to my sister. "I've got a show to do. I'm real proud of you, too, and glad you're my sister," I said. We hugged. We kissed. I wiped my eyes. I had to move on.

"Would you like to meet my son?" I asked the audience. They clapped eagerly. Bruce stood up. He towered over me. He was six feet tall and twenty years old. "He's eleven now," I joked with the audience, "just a little tall for his age."

I was so proud of Bruce. His eyes sparkled, his skin was shining, his smile lit up his entire face.

"You've always been such a good boy," I told him. I sounded just like my mother. Bruce blushed.

"You're doing a great job, Mom," he said.

"Thank you, honey, but you're the best job I've ever done."

I walked back to the stage and saw Alan standing in the wings, as usual, making sure everything was under control. "Come on out here, Alan," I said to him playfully.

Alan likes to stay in the background, always saying, "There can only be one star in the family." I walked to the wings and gently tugged at his arm.

"I'd like you to meet my husband," I said to the audience. "He is my life." Alan put his arms around me. "I love you, Alan," I said. "You look good without your beard."

"Thanks," he said. "You look good without yours."

The audience laughed and applauded. Alan always knows a good exit line.

It took thirteen years to get to this night. So much had happened during those years. As my self-esteem improved, the pieces of my life and my career fell into place. As job opportunities presented themselves, I seized them with confidence. The old me would have created a crisis.

In April 1977, one year after arriving in Los Angeles, I was called to audition for a new show called "Three's Company." The rest is history. The show aired and became the number-one situation comedy for the next six years. Alan was the star of "The Alan Hamel Show," the number-one talk show in Canada. It was an incredibly exciting time for both of us. Suddenly I was on magazine covers and talk shows. "60 Minutes" came to my home to interview me. *Newsweek* magazine featured me on its cover. I had movie offers and commercial offers. That same year Alan and I were married.

Now I had just about everything; a happy marriage, a successful career. My mom and dad, Maureen and Danny were recovering and happy. Michael's recovery a few years later would complete the picture. Bruce and his stepbrother and stepsister were learning to adjust to this new life. It took a lot of understanding on the part of all of us. Putting families together is a long and difficult process, but Alan and I became a united front. We were devoted to making our lives together a complete success.

As "Three's Company" rose in the ratings, *Playboy* seized the opportunity and published my nude test photos without my release, which caused a nationwide scandal. It was headline material for the news and the gossip magazines.

My lucrative commercial contract as spokeswoman for Ace Hardware was canceled for reasons of "image."

After a lifetime of crises and my subsequent therapy, I was equipped to handle this newest event. I personally went to UPI and openly gave them my side of the story. I told them my son had been run over by a car, I was left with fifteen thousand dollars' worth of doctor bills and saw these pictures as a chance to get out of debt. After shooting the pictures, I had a change of heart and declined to sign a release.

The public rallied to my side. They empathized. Ace Hardware reinstated me. The negative publicity turned into a positive.

Alan and I have been happily married for ten years. Alan is everything I ever wanted in a husband. We have a good relationship. I now realize it was necessary to wait so many years before getting married. It never would have worked while I was still sick. It would have been impossible to have the equal footing we have now. It's not a dependent relationship, but a nurturing one, filled with respect and generosity. I'm so grateful for the opportunity to have Alan as my partner, my lover and my best friend. He is also my manager and producer.

I wanted to get a nightclub career going and Alan convinced the MGM Grand in Las Vegas that I was the one television star who could successfully cross over into the personal-appearance business. This was before I even had an act.

Alan is a devoted father and stepfather and tremendously supportive of my career. We share our lives between the ocean and the desert, careful to keep a balance between work and play. Our hobbies are cooking and fixing up houses.

Our children are a source of joy to us and to one another.

It took a while for Bruce to adjust to Los Angeles. Everything was new and strange. Suddenly he shared me with Alan and his visiting children.

Life in Los Angeles is vastly different from the cozy small-community life of Sausalito. Bruce was a small-town kid in a big city. But a new school brought new friends; and before long the phone and the doorbell were ringing with children looking for Bruce.

Bruce is now attending the University of California, studying film directing and screenwriting. He'd also like to pursue an acting career. He's extremely funny and has the ability to charm an entire room when he wants to. Everyone loves to be around Bruce. The girls love him, the family loves him. He is kind, gentle, funny and smart. I see a lot of my dad's good qualities in him. But most of all, I love his soul. He is very intelligent and his grasp of the human condition astounds me. I love our conversations and am always learning from him.

Leslie, my stepdaughter, graduated from fashion design school and is now designing costumes for various stars, one of whom is me. I adore Leslie. I learn so much from her about fashion and what's happening. We have a lot of fun working together. She designs all the clothes for my Vegas act. She is bright and smart. She is funny and a great friend.

My stepson, Stephen, is a wonderful photographer. He has an artist's eye, inherited from his mother, coupled with a year of art school in Paris. He studied photography at Parsons and now makes his living as a fashion photographer. He is extremely handsome and a lot of fun. He takes the best pictures of me and is always my first choice as a photographer. He produced the cover photo of this book. I feel most relaxed with him; and because he knows me so well, he finds my most flattering angles. Stephen is very creative, never doing anything to conform. He likes to do it his way, his style—very much like his dad. We encourage all our children to develop their own uniqueness.

I am a very lucky woman. My marriage is fantastic, my kids are happy and healthy and I have a successful professional career in a business I love. I never fall asleep at night without thanking God for helping me to help myself. My dreams have come true because somebody cared enough to reach out and help me. I am deeply grateful to Mrs. Kilgore.

> *Somehow the wires uncrossed*
> *The tables were turned*
> *Never knew I had such a lesson to learn.*
> *I'm feelin' good from my head to my shoes,*
> *Know where I'm goin' and I know what to do*
> *I've tidied up my point of view,*
> *I've got a new attitude.*

When the show was over that night, everyone came backstage to my dressing area. Suddenly the room was buzzing with energy and enthusiasm.

"You were great," Danny said.

"Wonderful," my mom whispered.

"You were damn good." Dad's voice was trembling. I remembered that was exactly what he had said to me long ago, after *Guys and Dolls*.

I finally had his approval. I didn't need it anymore. I was no longer a little girl, but nonetheless I enjoyed it. What did matter was the joy and pride we all felt as a family. This night was not "my" night. It was "our" night. We were winners. We made it and we earned it.

I changed out of my costume and packed my bag. I had a plane to catch. Time to move on to the next city. I was opening at the Desert Inn in Las Vegas the next evening.

We all kissed and hugged good-bye. I didn't want to leave, and they wished I didn't have to go either, but they were used to my schedule. They didn't need me to have a good time. Each one of them was a whole, complete, satisfied and happy person.

"Good-bye, everyone. I'll see you soon," I yelled over the noise.

"Good-bye," they answered back.

As Alan and I walked out the door, I spotted Bruce in the corner of the room telling jokes. Everyone was laughing hysterically. He looked at me with his twinkly eyes.

"I love you, Mom," he shouted.

I threw him a kiss. "I love you too, Bruce."

* * *

I never planned to write this book. I've always kept my secret story tucked away deep inside. But ever since that morning in Santa Fe when I awoke from a deep sleep and started to write, I knew I couldn't keep the secret anymore. I had to tell this story. I had to get it out of me. I knew I would never be better or completely whole if I didn't.

I realized I had something to say. I could reach out to other children of alcoholics to help.

The disease I had was so difficult to recognize. It was only when I started writing this book that I was to finally able to put the pieces together.

Mrs. Kilgore didn't solve my problems; she only opened the door for *me* to help *me*.

I could have gone through life continuing the same patterns of crises, lies, secrets and low self-esteem. This disease is hard to identify. Only now, after all these years, can I understand alcoholism and the devastating effect it has on the members of the family. I realize now that I was starving for clarification, and why I was such a mess from childhood into adulthood.

It is estimated that there are ten to thirteen million alcoholics in the United States. If each one of those alcoholics has an average family of four, that brings the number of adult children of alcoholics to somewhere around forty to fifty-two million. One out of every four children in every classroom is a child of an alcoholic. Most of them have never turned themselves in to be statistics.

I know that until now I've never mentioned it nor have my brothers or my sister. Most people keep it to themselves. That is why adult children of alcoholics are numbered at only twenty-eight million. All these untreated people are walking around with the disease and don't know it. They aren't actively alcoholics; so like me, they think they are "okay"; but they carry the disease, and it ruins lives.

I wrote this book for all of us who fell asleep in class, who hid in our closets, who couldn't form friendships, who silently hated ouselves.

I wrote this book for all of us who were violent when violence was something we hated; all of us who lied, who kept secrets, who blamed ourselves, who made excuses, covered up, created crises and told stories to protect the terrible reality we lived with.

We didn't know how to cope as children; therefore, we couldn't cope as adults. We continued the same patterns; we thrived on crises, we lied, we had difficulty forming relationships. We kept secrets.

The odds are against an entire family recovering from this disease. For our family, it was a long and painful journey. We all paid a huge emotional price, but we each came out of it stronger and better human beings.

Recently I told my dad I was sorry that he had his disease for thirty-five years but that I wouldn't change one minute of my life if I had it to do over again. All my greatest lessons came out of his disease. I owe my success to it.

As a family we've never been closer or more connected. We get together as often as possible and revel in the joy of our recovery. We all understand how close we came to the edge. We all appreciate the miracle of our success.

Life is not how you start but how you finish. Each one of us prevailed and finished a winner. Ours is a success story. We have wiped out the disease in this generation. But what about the next generation? Alcoholism is a very patient disease. There are sixteen grandchildren in our family. As I look around, I see the seeds of the disease. It can't be avoided. There is a genetic link. It's like diabetes. You have to be aware and vigilant. I can only hope the children recognize it or listen to us and the information we have to give to them.

But . . . who knows?

I started out writing this book for me. For so long I'd look back over my life and cringe at the girl I used to be. I'd wonder why I did the things I did—so many mistakes, so many bad choices. Writing this book helped me to understand my past. Once I understood, I was able to forgive myself. Because now I understood the reasons. There are no mistakes, only lessons. It wasn't my fault. I came out of it the best I could. I did my best. Understanding that, I didn't have to be so hard on myself. I didn't have to feel ashamed or fearful of being discovered. I didn't have to feel guilty. I could accept who I was and not apologize for who I am.

Soon I realized I was writing this book for you as well. I wondered how many of you, like me, have looked back over your life and cringed at your actions and imperfections. Perhaps you've been too hard on yourself also. Maybe you were merely a victim of your circumstances. You came out of it the best you could. You did your best. Understanding this brings change.

I feel an overwhelming need to speak to as many people as possible so this horrible, insidious desease can be better understood.

It was painful to relive it, but understanding brought relief and clarification. I found sunshine at the end of the road. So can you. Even if the rest of your family doesn't get better, you can. I did.